WALKING THROUGH THE BIBLE

With

H M S Richards

Assignments for reading the Bible chronologically in one year with daily inspirational thoughts selected from the sermons and writings of Harold Marshall Sylvester Richards, founder of the *Voice of Prophecy* radio broadcast.

Kenneth W. Wilson, compiler-editor

WALKING THROUGH THE BIBLE

With

H. M. S. RICHARDS

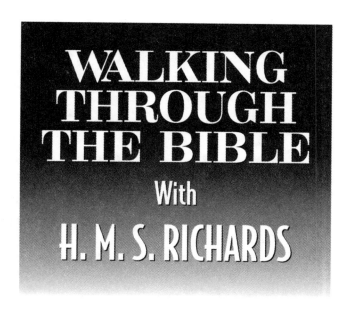

Daily readings that take you through the Bible in a year with comments by H.M.S. Richards, Sr.

Pacific Press® Publishing Association
Nampa, Idaho
Oshawa, Ontario, Canada
www.pacificpress.com

Designed by Dennis Ferree
Cover photo by Photonica

Additional copies of this book may be purchased at
http://www.adventistbookcenter.com

Library of Congress Cataloging-in-Publication Data

Richards, H. M. S. (Harold Marshall Sylvester), 1894-1985.
Walking through the Bible with H. M. S. Richards : daily readings that take you through the Bible in a year / with comments by H. M. S. Richards, Sr.
p.cm.
ISBN: 0-8163-0530-7
1. Devotional calendars. I. Title
BV4811 .R5352 2003
220'.071—dc21 2002029321

04 05 06 • 5 4 3 2

About This Book

You are about to enter into a daily encounter with God's Word that will open up new insights into relationships between various parts of the Bible.

When you have finished reading the 365 daily assignments, you will have made a discovery trip through the entire Bible. If you use the King James Version, you will have read all 66 books with their 1,189 chapters and 23,214 verses and every one of the 773,692 words it contains.

The idea of reading the whole Bible is not new; neither is a plan of daily devotional selections. The difference in this book lies in its special Bible-reading plan. Generally, when people decide to read the Bible through, they begin with Genesis and continue perseveringly until they reach Revelation. However, in this book, we will take you through the Bible as you would follow the narrative in a story; that is, in the order in which things happened. For example, when you read the experience of David, you will read the psalms he composed in that setting; you will read the prophet's message to a ruling monarch at the same time you read about the reign of that king; the letters of Paul to the various churches will parallel the record of his journeys.

One departure from this plan involves the scattering of some appropriate psalms throughout the year to accompany certain events.

The last two assignments in this book—Day/364 and Day/365—were intended for Thanksgiving Day and the day before. Since this book does not have the days dated and since Thanksgiving Day comes on different dates from year to year, it was impossible to insert those two assignments so that they came at Thanksgiving time. If you remember to turn to Day/364 on the day before Thanksgiving, you will have the blessing of enhancing that special season. If you do not make this adjustment, the psalms will make a fitting conclusion to a year of blessing.

Combined with the Bible-reading plan is a daily devotional thought, usually by H. M. S. Richards, founder of the *Voice of Prophecy* radiobroadcast. H. M. S. Richards was a man of the Word. He made it a loving habit to read his Bible through, from cover to cover, at least once a year. For many years he followed a plan of reading the entire Bible, once in the month of January, then again at what he described as a leisurely pace, the rest of the year. When asked how many times he had read the Bible through, he would confess that he had lost count, but his associates can vouch that the number was well over one hundred. In some places it was impossible to find a pertinent selection in any of Pastor Richards's writings. There you will find thoughts from the writings of Ellen G. White, as indicated by the credit line for such quotations.

The chronology of the readings, the explanations of certain words and phrases, and the historical notes are based on information from the seven-volume *Seventh-day Adventist Bible Commentary.*

May God richly bless you as you follow *Walking Through the Bible With H. M. S. Richards.* We sincerely hope that this reading plan will help you discover the Bible as a new and exciting book and make you acquainted with its loving Author, our heavenly Father.
—*Kenneth W. Wilson.*

The Man Who Made the "Voice"

H. M. S. Richards, founder of the international *Voice of Prophecy* radio broadcast, was an inveterate reader and lover of books. His family, friends, and work associates rarely discussed a topic with which he was not acquainted. During his lifetime, his personal library grew to more than 8,000 volumes.

A tireless reader and scholar, Richards was known as a diligent student of the Bible and was rarely found without one in his pocket. He constantly searched for useful information in many fields of knowledge and used what he found in his always fresh and vibrant messages to reach the hearts of men and women.

His biographer, Bob Edwards, recalls: "His reading habit started at an early age. The first book he is reported to have read was his mother's Bible. For that he received a dollar from his father, with the promise that it would be doubled each time thereafter. Of course, Dad had to repent of that promise, for by the time his young son had finished reading the Bible twenty-one times (and in his lifetime he more than tripled that), Dad would have been forced to fork over $1,048,576.00 for that twenty-first reading!

"The next books the boy read were *Conquests of Grenada* by Washington Irving and *Pilgrim's Progress* by John Bunyan. Those books launched an avid reading career that impelled his mother to hold him back from school until he was eight years old. She was afraid he would read himself into an early grave." (*H.M.S. Richards,* pp. 252, 253).

Richards read widely all his life. His interest was not limited to works directly about the Bible—theology, archaeology, and Bible commentaries—but ranged through history, biography, literature, poetry, science, and art. Sometimes he relaxed with a well-crafted story.

But always first and foremost in his reading was the Bible, especially the King James Version. Many times he began on New Year's Day to read from Genesis to Revelation very quickly, to get a fresh overview of the entire message of Scripture, then carefully studied the sixty-six individual books throughout the rest of the year. Often he read through the New Testament every month of the year.

Richards preached almost exclusively from the King James Version, but relied on dozens of other translations and versions for mental and spiritual enrichment. He was keenly aware that recent discoveries of ancient Scripture manuscripts contributed new insights into the meaning of the Bible.

He not only immersed himself in reading the Bible, but also memorized huge portions. In public meetings, those seated behind him as he spoke sometimes noted he was holding his Bible upside down, quoting the text from memory, though the audience assumed he was reading it.

In an interview with Dr. Wilbur Alexander, Richards said, "The Bible is a vast and infinite source of sermons. If you become a Bible preacher, you are never out of sermon material. If you are merely a topical preacher, you will run out of something to say and will have to move on and start again. But when you start preaching the Bible, you'll find it to be an exhaustless mine. As you keep probing into it, you'll get to be a better preacher, and people will want to hear you. Get on fire with the Bible, and people will come to see you burn!

"As you read your Bible, sermons will jump out at you, saying, 'Preach me! Preach me! Preach me!' As I read my Bible, when I come to such a text, I write the letters 'SER' in the margin of my Bible. I won't begin to live long enough to preach all the sermons that are waiting to be preached." (*H.M.S. Richards,* pp. 255, 256).

Richards had a preaching ancestry. His father, Halbert M. J. Richards, was a pastor and evangelist. His grandfather, William Jenkin Richards, was converted by Salvation Army founder, General William Booth, and became first a lay preacher in Cornwall, England, then a Methodist Episcopal circuit preacher in America. An even earlier progenitor was a lay preacher and traveling companion of John Wesley.

The "H. M. S." of Richard's name were initials for Harold Marshall Sylvester, continuing the English heritage of giving children three names besides the family surname. But even as a little boy, when asked if H. M. S. meant "His Majesty's Ship," Richards would answer that it stood for "His Majesty's Servant."

The day he was born in Davis City, Iowa (August 28, 1894) his father held him in his arms and said, "We'll have prayer, and I'll put my hands on his head, and he shall be the Lord's baby boy." When Richards nearly died at the age of two, after indulging in a number of green apples, his mother prayed for his healing, promising to dedicate him to God's service if he survived.

As a youngster, Harold thought he might like to become a lawyer, but knowing that he "belonged to the Lord," he never swerved from his destiny as a preacher. During his father's preaching services, young Richards often imitated his dad and on one occasion was spanked three times to make him realize that "the preaching was going on up front and not where I was." At home during preschool years, the boy would set chairs in a circle and persuade younger brother Kenneth to sit and listen to him "preach." A favorite topic was the story of Lazarus. Four-year-old Harold would declare, "Jesus came and found Lavruth in a deep hole with a big rock over him, so He shouted with a loud voice, 'Lavruth, come forth,' and Lavruth, he comed."

Harold was seventeen when his father asked him to take a Sabbath afternoon preaching assignment. He spoke on the topic of angels and was greatly encouraged a few days later when an elderly woman told him, "You don't know what that sermon meant to me. I live over beyond the tracks all alone and have just a few chickens. I have been afraid someone would kill me there. When you preached on the subject of angels, I thought, 'Surely the angels are guarding me,' and I want you to know I don't have any more fear."

After graduating from Campion Academy in Colorado, H. M. S. Richards attended Washington Missionary College (now Columbia Union College) in Takoma Park, Maryland, from which he graduated in 1919. His first official ministerial assignment was a pastorate in Ottawa, Canada, where he met a young schoolteacher, Mabel Annabel Eastman. After a brief courtship, they were married in 1920.

It was also in 1920 that H. M. S. Richards first conceived the idea of broadcasting the Christian gospel over the airwaves, though his dream was not realized until nine years later. Meanwhile, the young evangelist's ministry was successful, his presentation of Bible themes often drawing large audiences.

In 1926 Pastor and Mrs. Richards were called to California where they conducted successful evangelistic meetings in Fresno, Bakersfield, Lodi, Los Angeles, Long Beach, San Diego, and other cities.

Pastor Richards experimented with radio announcements in connection with his evangelistic meetings in central California in the late 1920s, but his regular broadcasts began in 1929 when KNX and other stations in Los Angeles aired without charge, his (and other ministers') "Family Worship" programs. A few years later, during an evangelistic series in Huntington Park, Richards's daily live broadcasts of *The Tabernacle of the Air* went out over KGER in Long Beach.

In January 1937, the program expanded to a network of several stations and was renamed *The Voice of Prophecy.* Dr. Richards often said that perhaps the greatest thrill of his entire ministry was his first coast-to-coast broadcast over eighty-nine stations of the Mutual Broadcasting System on January 4, 1942.

Inspired by the example of Richards, dozens of Seventh-day Adventist ministers around the world began *Voice of Prophecy* (or *Voice of Hope*) broadcasts in many languages.

Refusing fame for himself, Richards sought only to make Christ known to millions around the world. His dedicated ministry was recognized by fellow broadcasters who presented him the Honor Citation of the National Religious Broadcasters organization in both 1967 and 1970. Andrews University conferred an honorary doctorate on him in 1960.

Because of his spirit-filled preaching, he was much in demand as a speaker at camp meetings and other large gatherings throughout the world. His audiences always left with a deep feeling that they had sensed the presence of Jesus. He became a role model of Christ-centered preaching to ministers around the world.

In addition to hundreds of radio sermons printed in booklet form by *The Voice of Prophecy,* Dr. Richards authored several full-length books including *The Indispensable Man; Promises of God; What Jesus Said; Feed My Sheep; Look to the Stars; Why I Am a Seventh-day Adventist; One World; Revival Sermons;* and *Day After Tomorrow.* He also wrote more than 1,500 verses of his poem, "Have Faith in God," presenting one verse a week on *The Voice of Prophecy* radio broadcast.

A visit to Pastor Richards's home library revealed a book lover's paradise. The walls were lined with books from floor to ceiling, with a double stack through the middle of the room. From his lifetime of reading and immersion in Scripture came *Walking Through the Bible With H. M. S. Richards.*

Have faith in God—
See truth—do not delay;
Have faith in God—
The Scriptures search today;
Have faith in God—
His Holy Word obey.
Have faith, dear friend, in God.

DAY / 1

Read Genesis 1 and 2; Psalms 8; 19; 29; and 33.

Today's reading covers the story of Creation and some poetic passages inspired by contemplating God's creative power.

Memory gem: "By the word of the Lord were the heavens made; and all the host of them by the breath of his mouth" (Psalm 33:6).

Thought for today:

Some seem to feel they have solved the riddle of Creation by pushing it back a billion or a hundred billion years into the past—it doesn't matter which, because nobody has any idea of how much a billion is anyway. They just push it back a few billion years and leave the impression that anything that started that long ago just started itself! But this sort of thinking solves nothing. Whether six billion or six million or six thousand years ago, nothing can originate nothing. Existence cannot come from nonexistence. Every effect must have an adequate cause. In other words, creation must have had a Creator.

"In the beginning God" (Genesis 1:1) are the sublime words with which the book of Genesis begins, and no philosophy can ever go back of those words, "In the beginning God." All reality begins with God. The universe exists—and by this one inconceivable miracle writes the word *Creator* on the wall of the laboratory, across the face of the skies, and in the heart of man.

What we learn about the Creator from His book of nature is confirmed by His other Book, the Bible. These two books agree, because they have the same Author, and they both declare, "In the beginning God."

Difficult or obscure words:

Genesis 1:28. **"Replenish"**—This word simply means **"fill."** It does not connote replacing something that previously existed.

Genesis 2:4. **"Generations"**—Here this word means **"the history or account of their production,"** or that which God **"generated" or "produced."**

Genesis 2:11-13. Geographical names have no significance for identifying present-day locations. The great Flood of chapters 7 and 8 obliterated all landmarks that existed before the Flood.

DAY / 2

Read Psalms 93 through 101; 103; and 104.

Today's reading contemplates, through the writings of the Hebrew poets, the wonders of God's creation. We marvel with the ancient psalmists at the glory and majesty of our Creator.

Memory gem: "O come, let us worship and bow down: let us kneel before the Lord our maker" (Psalm 95:6).

Thought for today:

It was this Word of God, made flesh for the salvation of men, that "in the beginning" (Genesis 1:1) not only made the worlds of our planetary system but all the marching constellations, for the heavens are the works of His hands.

And so it is that he who looks upward may see the hand of Christ in the sky—His works of power, wisdom, and beauty.

The hand of Christ, the Master Workman, had been seen in the vast dome of stars long ages before that anonymous technician ground his first lenses or Galileo put them in his first telescope. As men began to peer out into the boundless voids with stronger and stronger eyes—the mighty glasses of great astronomical observatories—they were struck with silent wonder at the awesome vastness of the universe. Now we know that the human mind can have no conception of the endless and gigantic creation about us.

The creation testifies of its Creator as the eternal, infinite God. "All thy works shall praise thee, O Lord" (Psalm 145:10), said David with the tongue of inspiration. He must have been gazing out into the blue-black sky as there on the verdant meadows of heaven began to bloom, one by one, the lovely stars, "the forget-me-nots of the angels."—Longfellow.

We rejoice in the human Christ, a humble Galilean carpenter; but we must know, too, that He was, and is, the Son of God Most High—that the very heavens are the work of His hands. Indeed, His works praise Him when His worshipers are silent.

Difficult or obscure words:

Psalm 93:3. **"Floods"**—rivers.

Psalm 94:8. **"Brutish"**—rude, uncultivated, dull of perception.

Psalm 95:8. **"Temptation"**—trial or testing.

Psalm 101:4. **"Froward"**—crooked, perverted.

Psalm 104:8. **"Up by the mountains . . . down by the valleys"**—better: "mountains rise; valleys sink."

DAY / 3

Read Genesis 3 through 6.

Today's reading: Four short chapters bridge the whole 1500 years from the Garden of Eden to Noah's ark. They trace the tragic account of ruin caused by the entrance of sin into God's perfect world.

Memory gem: "By faith Abel offered unto God a more excellent sacrifice than Cain, by which he obtained witness that he was righteous, God testifying of his gifts: and by it he being dead yet speaketh" (Hebrews 11:4).

Thought for today:

The religion of Cain is very strong in the world today. It does not deny the existence of God in words, but merely in deeds. It does not deny the need of divine worship and liturgy. In fact, this may be exalted to a very high and aesthetic plane. The "way of Cain" (Jude 11) is a religion of the flesh, a self-willed worship, a self-satisfied justification by works, an insubordinate self-redemption. This religion relies on itself and denies and rejects substitution, while idealizing one's own power and culture. This was the theology of the first murderer.

The way of Abel was different. It was a humble acknowledgment that sin demands death, and a total reliance of the sinner upon the mercy and grace of God revealed in Christ's sacrifice. This sacrifice was God-appointed in expectation of the final triumph of divine redemption through the woman's Seed. And the end will be like the beginning in reverse, for the line of the murdered Abel will attain eternal life (see Hebrews 11:40), while the way of Cain will perish.

The faith of Abel still speaks to our hearts today. Which shall it be—the religion of Cain? or the religion of Abel? We may say that we are neutral, that we shall take neither. The fact is, that if we are not of Abel, we are of Cain. It is only through faith in the Redeemer, faith such as Abel had, that we can find peace of heart. The religion of Cain never brings peace. The millions who are under its sway are forever seeking peace, but never finding it.

So, friend, whoever you are, wherever you are, come today. Accept the religion of Abel. We may have peace in our hearts if we believe on Jesus. "Being justified by faith, we have peace with God through our Lord Jesus Christ" (Romans 5:1).

DAY / 4

Read Genesis 7 through 10.

Today's reading records the story of the great universal deluge that transformed the beautiful antediluvian earth into the largely uninhabitable globe we now occupy.

Memory gem: "By faith Noah, being warned of God of things not seen as yet, moved with fear, prepared an ark to the saving of his house; by the which he condemned the world, and became heir of the righteousness which is by faith" (Hebrews 11:7).

Thought for today:

The covenant of the rainbow is really a promise of God's grace to sinners everywhere—to us today. Think of the hope that this token of the rainbow shining in the clouds must have brought to Noah and his family. Even with the world devastated by the Flood, the evidence of the effect of sin, they could see in the sky the token of God's promise of forgiveness. It was really a message of grace, the unmerited favor of God to us sinners here below.

With this assurance given to Noah is linked one of God's most precious promises of His grace, which we read in Isaiah 54:9, 10: "As I have sworn that the waters of Noah should no more go over the earth; so have I sworn that I would not be wroth with thee, nor rebuke thee. For the mountains shall depart, and the hills be removed; but my kindness shall not depart from thee, neither shall the covenant of my peace be removed, saith the Lord that hath mercy on thee."

Here on this earth we see only half of the rainbow in the clouds. This is no doubt a type of the imperfectness of our present experience. The children of God are still here, subject to sorrow, sickness, and death. But someday, by God's grace and to His glory and praise, we shall see encircling the throne, the complete bow and rejoice in the immortal land. So the rainbow here on earth is the symbol of our eternal deliverance.

My friend—whoever you are, and whatever your troubles in life may have been—remember God's rainbow promise; it's for you. The rainbow is seen only when there is a storm. But there is also sunshine. In the darkest experiences of life, there is hope in God. It shines as the light transfigures the darkness.

DAY / 5

Read Genesis 11 through 15.

Today's reading introduces to us one of the outstanding Bible characters—Abraham, illustrious ancestor of the Israelites and outstanding man of faith.

Memory gem: "By faith Abraham, when he was called to go out into a place which he should after receive for an inheritance, obeyed; and he went out, not knowing whither he went" (Hebrews 11:8).

Thought for today:

"Now to Abraham and his seed were the promises made. He saith not, And to seeds, as of many; but as of one, And to thy seed, which is Christ" (Galatians 3:16).

The promise to Abraham concerning the seed which would inherit all things really was a promise of the coming of Christ, the true Messiah. Now let us read Galatians, chapter 4, verse 29: "And if ye be Christ's, then are ye Abraham's seed, and heirs according to the promise."

The promise was made to the seed of Abraham, and the seed of Abraham is Christ. Therefore all who become true followers of Christ share in the promise. What was the promise to Abraham? That in his seed the whole world would be blessed—that is, all the nations, not merely one nation, but all of them—and that Abraham and his seed would inherit the land.

What land? Let us turn to the book of Romans, chapter 4, verse 13: "For the promise, that he should be the heir of the world, was not to Abraham, or to his seed, through the law, but through the righteousness of faith."

Notice that Abraham was to be heir of the world, not merely Palestine, for the entire earth renewed and brought back to its Edenic condition will be the eternal inheritance of the seed of Abraham. It will come through Christ to all who belong to Him.

Really, friend, it's wonderful to be a Christian. By surrendering our hearts to God and having faith in the Lord Jesus Christ as our sin-pardoning Saviour who died for us upon the cross, we too may "walk in the steps of that faith of our father Abraham" (Romans 4:12). He is our spiritual father.

Note: See **Difficult or obscure words** on next page.

DAY / 6

Read Genesis 16 through 19.

Today's reading recounts, among a number of other occurrences during Abraham's life, the escape of Lot and his two daughters—not his wife—from the destruction of Sodom.

Memory gem: "Remember Lot's wife" (Luke 17:32).

Thought for today:

While Lot's wife was out of Sodom, Sodom was not out of her. Her heart was back in the city, which was soon to be consumed. She fled but desired to look back. And the Scriptures say, "She became a pillar of salt" (Genesis 19:26). She was like a woman who, saved from a burning house, rushes back to find some treasured possession and is burned with her possessions. Lot's wife had been saved from destruction by angels, but she had nothing in common with angels.

Possibly if Lot himself had not lingered, had not argued with the angels, had not hesitated, his wife might have been saved. In that respect, his influence on her was not good.

Just to look may seem like a little sin, but, as Matthew Henry puts it in his quaint way, "There is no little sin, because there is no little God to sin against."

There are too many halfway Christians in the world today, people who are outwardly church members, servants of the Lord, professors of the faith, but whose hearts are still in Sodom, still in the world. That is what Jesus was talking about when He said: "Except a man be born again, he cannot see the kingdom of God" (John 3:3).

Difficult or obscure words for Day/5:

Genesis 11:2. **"From the east"**—better: eastward.

Genesis 11:3. **"Slime"**—better: asphalt or bitumen.

Genesis 12:9. **"South"**—Negeb. That portion of Palestine south and west of the highlands, with Beersheba as its chief town.

Genesis 14:18. **"Melchizedek"**—No one is certain of the ethnic identity of this "priest of the most high God."

Genesis 15:13. **"Four hundred years"**—This period, which is mentioned in Acts 7:6, can be harmonized with the 430 years of Exodus 12:20 and Galatians 3:16, 17 by taking a different starting date. The 430 years begin with Abraham's call to leave Haran. The 400 years begin 30 years later when Ishmael started to "afflict" Isaac. See comment on Exodus 12:40 (Day/31).

DAY / 7

Read Genesis 20 through 23.

Today's reading includes one of the most dramatic short stories in all literature: Abraham's obedience to the divine command to offer his beloved son as a sacrifice.

Memory gem: "And Abraham said, My son, God will provide himself a lamb for a burnt offering" (Genesis 22:8).

Thought for today:

The ram offered in Isaac's place represented Christ, who was to be sacrificed in our stead. When man was doomed to death because of his transgression of God's law, the heavenly Father, looking upon His Son, our Lord Jesus Christ, said to the sinner, "Live! I have found a ransom."

While Isaac was not actually burned as a sacrifice, he was offered up in the heart of Abraham. Abraham had actually sacrificed Isaac to God, as we read in Hebrews 11:17, although he had not killed him. The external completion of the act was suddenly prevented by God Himself. It is not external performance that makes a sacrifice, but the intention of the heart. Not death, but life, is the final goal of all sacrifice. In figure, Abraham received Isaac as resurrected from the dead.

The blood of the sacrificial ram on Mount Moriah pointed forward to the blood of Christ shed to atone for the sins of men. Abraham's sacrifice and those offered in the temple of Solomon built on the same spot all pointed forward to the death of the Saviour who was to come. The Christian ordinances, celebrated in our day—the broken bread and the poured wine—point backward to the same sacrifice of Christ and the same salvation. "For God so loved the world, that he gave his only begotten Son, that whosoever believeth in him should not perish, but have everlasting life" (John 3:16).

Difficult or obscure words:

Genesis 22:2. **"Moriah"**—The site of Solomon's temple is mentioned here and in 2 Chronicles 3:1.

DAY / 8

Read Genesis 24 and 25.

Today's reading tells an old love story. A beautiful and gracious young woman agrees to leave her home and become the bride of a man she has never seen!

Memory gem: "And Isaac brought her into his mother Sarah's tent, and took Rebekah, and she became his wife; and he loved her" (Genesis 24:67).

Thought for today:

This is an old love story—yes, and "love at first sight" too! Even more than that, love at first mention!

In Genesis 24:58 we read the answer that women have been making for thousands of years, "I will go." And how that answer, first made by Rebekah, has been echoing from the lips of millions of her sisters down through the ages!

The question comes, "Will you go?" and back comes the answer, "I will go"—earth's sweetest music to those who are in love. "I will go," and she is gone, although it means separation from family, from friends. It may mean loneliness, sickness, childbearing, grief, disappointments, sorrow, sometimes tragedy, but still she says, "I will go." And the world keeps on going because men ask, "Will you go?" and women still answer in the same old way, with shining eyes and trembling voice, "I will go!"

Rebekah, going to Canaan, found a husband, her true life, and a permanent home. So the soul that comes to Christ enters into true fellowship, rejoices even now in eternal life by faith, and knows that in God's good time there will be the Canaan land in the new earth to come, and eternal rest for the people of God.

So the Holy Spirit has gone forth to win a bride for Christ. Are you willing, friend, to enter into this glorious spiritual relationship with your Redeemer, to belong to Him, to rejoice in Him, and to "live happily ever after"? That is the privilege of all God's children. So today, as the Spirit pleads with our hearts, let us each one say, "I will go."

DAY / 9

Read Genesis 26 through 28.

Today's reading begins with a famine, tells of trouble over a lie, recounts an episode of daring deception, and ends with a vision of angels given to a frightened fugitive.

Memory gem: "Surely the Lord is in this place; and I knew it not" (Genesis 28:16).

Thought for today:

The Bible is full of angel ministry—story after story—binding earth to heaven; space visitors, keeping our little fallen world in touch with the kingdom of the stars. Angels appeared to a forsaken maiden by the hidden well in the desert; under the oaks of Mamre; and in the palatial home of Lot, to save that backslidden believer from a fiery death. They appeared in the mount of the law to Moses. On Mount Moriah an angel held back the hand of Abraham from the slaughter of his son. On the plain of Bethel they appeared to Jacob, ascending and descending a mystical ladder connecting earth with heaven.

These mighty beings who can appear and disappear at will, who excel in strength, who do God's commandments, "hearkening unto the voice of his word" (Psalm 103:20)—what teachers they will be in that land of eternal wisdom! What knowledge they will share with us who find a home there by the shining river of life! How wonderful it will be to meet our guardian angel and have him recount to us the mercies which God has extended to us as we traveled the path of His providence.

This is such a wonderful future, such a blessed experience, and such a holy companionship, that we invite you into the service of Christ.

DAY / 10

Read Genesis 29 and 30.

Today's reading: Another love story! In this one a man chooses a lovely bride, is deceived by his scheming father-in-law, and then signs up for another term of service to get the girl he wants.

Memory gem: "And Jacob served seven years for Rachel; and they seemed unto him but a few days, for the love he had to her" (Genesis 29:20).

Thought for today:

In 1 John 4:8 it is written, "God is love." And the command of Jesus is that "ye love one another" (John 15:12). In 1 Corinthians 13:13, we read that of all the virtues of life, the greatest is love. Love of God in the heart of man, love for our follow beings, and especially the love which leads to marriage are all in God's plan and originated in the mind and heart of God. Of Jacob's love for Rachel we read in Genesis 29:20: "And Jacob served seven years for Rachel; and they seemed unto him but a few days, for the love he had to her."

This is the sort of true love that God wants us to have in courtship and marriage, a love that even the years cannot kill, love that is stronger than time. That's the sort of love we are talking about today, love that "beareth all things, believeth all things, hopeth all things, endureth all things" (1 Corinthians 13:7), a love that never fails.

DAY / 11

Read Genesis 31 and 33.

Today's reading includes the remarkable experience of a man who wrestled with a divine being—and emerged victorious!

Memory gem: "The Lord watch between me and thee, when we are absent one from another" (Genesis 31:49).

Thought for today:

What is your name? A man's name sets him apart from all others and establishes his personal identity. Each of us has a name. Each is different from the other.

My name means "lost sinner," so what can I do? Is there any hope for such a one as I? Yes, indeed, there is hope for you! A man who had a name like yours had a terrible contest at midnight with an angel, and they wrestled until break of day. His thigh was put out of joint at the touch of his divine antagonist, and all he could do was to cling helplessly. He could struggle no more, but in faith he cried out, "I will not let thee go, except thou bless me." And then the angel asked, "What is thy name?"

Ah, that was the worst question of all! Hanging his head, as we may well believe, for the shame that was in his heart, he answered, "Jacob." What did it mean? Why, Jacob meant "supplanter," and every time his name was spoken, his acts and character were made known. He was the man who had lied to his father and had cheated his brother out of his birthright. He had stolen the blessing that belonged to another and had tried to supplant him in the affection of his father. So now, in the darkness by the Jabbok River, alone with One whom he now knows to be more than man, he faces the ultimate question, "What is thy name?" He answers truthfully and with sadness, "Jacob"—the supplanter!

But friend of mine, listen to the enfolding mercy of God which brings him forgiveness for all the past because of present victory: "Thy name shall be called no more Jacob, but Israel: for as a prince hast thou power with God and with men, and hast prevailed" (Genesis 32:28).

How glad we can be today for the men whose names have been changed by the forgiving mercy of God! Old things have passed away and all things have become new to those who are in Christ (see 2 Corinthians 5:17). Like wrestling Jacob, we must find our strength in surrender to Christ.

DAY / 12

Read Genesis 34 through 36.

Today's reading has some unlovely episodes and an account of Jacob's deep sorrow at the death of his beloved Rachel. But through it all shines the promise of God's loving care.

Memory gem: "I will make there an altar unto God, who answered me in the day of my distress, and was with me in the way which I went" (Genesis 35:3).

Thought for today:

Often God's protecting hand is over us when we do not know it. One time, in the Colorado Rockies, a hunter with his young grandson stood in the deep snow and looked at a giant pine that had been killed by lightning. The wind was blowing and the tree swayed in the stormy gusts. After a few moments' rest they started on, when without warning the mighty pine crashed to the ground and covered the tracks they had made in the snow only a few seconds before. There was but a step between them and death. They bowed their heads right there and thanked God for His protecting mercy. This experience made a profound impression on that boy—I know, for I was that boy.

Here is another point: The troubles and sorrows that come upon us can be the means in God's providence of drawing us back to Himself. No religion except the religion of Christ brings to those in trouble the mighty truth that even our sorrows may be a manifestation of God's mercy rather than of His wrath. In Hebrews 12:6, 7 we read: "For whom the Lord loveth he chasteneth, and scourgeth every son whom he receiveth. If ye endure chastening, God dealeth with you as with sons; for what son is he whom the father chasteneth not?"

DAY / 13

Read Genesis 37 through 41.

Today's reading is the first installment of one of the greatest stories of all time—the story of Joseph and his brothers—written by one of the greatest writers of all time—Moses.

Memory gem: "How then can I do this great wickedness, and sin against God?" (Genesis 39:9).

Thought for today:

There are special ways in which the story of Joseph foreshadows the life of Jesus.

First of all, we consider Joseph and his father. Joseph was the beloved son of his aged father.

Second, as with Joseph and his brethren, Jesus "came unto his own, and his own received him not" (John 1:11).

Third, Jesus was sold for money, just as Joseph was. He was betrayed and sold by his brethren for twenty pieces of silver.

The fourth great fact is Joseph's humiliation. He was tempted and yet sinned not. He was alone in the dungeon through no fault of his own. He was the means of blessing to the butler, and a messenger of judgment to the baker.

Jesus took upon Himself the form of a servant (see Philippians 2:7). He was tempted in all points like as we are, yet without sin (see Hebrews 4:15). He was alone, forsaken by God and man. Christ was the means of blessing to the penitent thief on the cross, but He was the occasion of judgment upon the impenitent thief.

Difficult or obscure words:

Genesis 37:25-36. **"Ishmaelites"** and **"Midianites"**—Two possible explanations are offered: (1) The caravan included men of both groups. (2) The two names were used interchangeably in common parlance. In either case only one caravan was involved.

DAY / 14

Read Genesis 41 and 42.

Today's reading continues the story of Joseph—his exaltation from a forsaken prisoner to the position of prime minister of Egypt.

Memory gem: "And Pharaoh said unto his servants, Can we find such a one as this is, a man in whom the Spirit of God is?" (Genesis 41:38).

Thought for today:

Now we take another step in the story of Joseph. We see him before Pharaoh, where he was exalted as a ruler of Egypt. First, his exaltation revealed God's purpose for Egypt. Second, it manifested God's righteousness in bringing Joseph out of prison. Third, it established his position—next to Pharaoh.

Last of all, we notice Joseph's office. Why was he exalted? What was the purpose of it? It was not for his own sake, but that he might be a channel of blessing to the world. So with our Saviour. He was exalted that He might be a Prince and a Saviour (see Acts 5:31). Joseph was exalted that he might provide food in time of famine, and all who came to him received what they needed. Some authorities say that his Egyptian name, ZaphnathPaaneah, may be interpreted "the bread of life." Our Lord was the Bread of Life (see John 6:35). He said, "I am come that they might have life" (John 10:10).

There is quite a difference here, however, between Joseph and Jesus. The people who came to Joseph had to bring money to buy bread, but we may receive the Bread of Life "without money and without price" (Isaiah 55:1).

There was one sole condition of blessing during the years of famine in Egypt—just one—and that was unconditional submission to Joseph.

Friend, in things spiritual, this is the one and only requirement—unconditional, unquestioning, unwavering surrender, submission, and trust in Christ. When we come to Him in this way, all our spiritual needs are provided for and our hopes at last realized.

Difficult or obscure words:

Genesis 41:49. **"Corn"**—an old English expression for any kind of grain. This word in the Bible never means what Americans call "corn," the New World Indian corn.

DAY / 15

Read Genesis 43 through 45.

Today's reading concludes the dramatic encounter of Joseph with his brothers. We notice particularly Judah's touching appeal for Benjamin's release.

Memory gem: "Now therefore, I pray thee, let thy servant abide instead of the lad a bondman to my lord; and let the lad go up with his brethren" (Genesis 44:33).

Thought for today:

The brothers had to go down into Egypt to find Joseph. It was a long, hard journey through a land blasted by drought and famine. But you need not go through any weary desert, nor must you travel to some far-off foreign land to find Christ. You can reach Him at once with the hand of faith.

So, my friend, if you feel a hunger in your heart, if the famine has begun, find your way to Christ at once. Turn to Him by faith. Come to Jesus now in simple prayer. Bow before Him. He is your brother, as Joseph was the brother of his brothers. Christ became a man, yet He is the divine Son of God. He understands our feelings and our need—and He loves us.

Like Joseph's brothers, who rejected him, we may have rejected Jesus, but He has never rejected us. He loves us. He has redeemed us. He longs for our repentance and our love. If we would come to Him in faith, He will not turn us away. This is His blessed invitation: "Come unto me, all ye that labour and are heavy laden, and I will give you rest. Take my yoke upon you, and learn of me; . . . and ye shall find rest unto your souls" (Matthew 11:28, 29).

What better day than today in which to respond to Him!

Difficult or obscure words:

Genesis 44:5. **"Divineth"**—The mention of this practice does not prove that Joseph had taken up this superstitious practice. He was willing to have his brothers believe that he could read their thoughts in order to unnerve them and lead them to abandon pretense.

DAY / 16

Read Genesis 46 through 48.

Today's reading tells of Jacob's incredulous reception of the news about Joseph, followed by the move of Jacob's clan to Egypt, and ends with the unusual circumstances in Jacob's blessing Joseph's two sons.

Memory gem: "So teach us to number our days, that we may apply our hearts unto wisdom" (Psalm 90:12).

Thought for today:

Let's go back to old Egypt, to that day when Joseph brought Jacob, his father, before Pharaoh. As the king looked upon the noble face of the patriarch, he said, "How old art thou?" And Jacob replied in those wonderful words that we find in Genesis 47:9: "The days of the years of my pilgrimage are an hundred and thirty years: few and evil have the days of the years of my life been, and have not attained unto the days of the years of the life of my fathers in the days of their pilgrimage."

In this beautiful oriental expression he humbled himself, and yet he was the greatest man there, because the next verse tells us that "Jacob blessed Pharaoh." And the Holy Bible assures us that the lesser is blessed of the greater. Can't you see the royal head of Pharaoh bowed as the hands of the aged shepherd were laid upon him in blessing! You see, age was more imperial than authority—the old shepherd greater than a mighty king.

As you grow older, there are two words that you will say more and more. They are these: "I remember." The experiences of your youth will mean more and more to you as you get older. You will live again in the school days, the happy days of vacation, the days at home with father and mother, brothers and sisters, and friends. Those days will glow with a golden hue as time goes on, and you will say, "I remember."

DAY / 17

Read Genesis 49 and 50; I Chronicles 1.

Today's reading brings us to the end of Genesis and the conclusion of Joseph's remarkable life. The story ends on a note of optimistic faith in God's providential dealings.

Memory gem: "As for you, ye thought evil against me: but God meant it unto good" (Genesis 50:20).

Thought for today:

Have you ever seen an old-fashioned blacksmith hold a heavy piece of iron on the anvil and lightly touch it here and there with a small hammer to show the spots that needed pounding, while some great giant of a fellow strikes it with a heavy sledge? I have often watched this on my grandfather's forge, while the sparks flew about my ears.

Someone has said that God often permits us to be pounded about in trials and tests, but He means it for our good. He may permit the devil to help pound the saints into shape, but He guides the blows. And here is a word from the apostle Paul about trials—and he ought to know about them, he had so many. He says, "There hath no temptation taken you but such as is common to man: but God is faithful, who will not suffer you to be tempted above that ye are able; but will with the temptation also make a way of escape, that ye may be able to bear it" (1 Corinthians 10:13).

Men may bring us into trouble, and our whole life seem to be ruined, *but God!* Don't forget those words, friends; *but God* will bring you good. He will see you through at last. Give your heart to Him, and when you are God's child His promises are yours, for "the Spirit itself beareth witness with our spirit, that we are the children of God: and if children, then heirs; heirs of God, and joint-heirs with Christ; if so be that we suffer with him, that we may be also glorified together. For I reckon that the sufferings of this present time are not worthy to be compared with the glory which shall be revealed in us" (Romans 8:16-18).

DAY / 18

Read Job 1 through 5.

Today's reading: Nobody can be absolutely sure when Job lived, but various kinds of evidence indicate a period between Jacob and Moses. The story opens with the beginning of Job's troubles.

Memory gem: "In all this Job sinned not, nor charged God foolishly" (Job 1:22).

Thought for today:

Sooner or later trouble comes to us all, for it's the common lot of human beings. Many of us remember this childhood jingle: "Never trouble trouble, till trouble troubles you." That is, never look for it. But we don't have to; it comes, unsought, and all too soon and too often. "Man is born unto trouble, as the sparks fly upward," the book of Job tells us (Job 5:7); and it is certainly an authority. Yes, trouble comes to both good and bad—to saint and sinner—to all men everywhere.

Back in the old days many people had the idea that trouble was a sure sign of God's anger and that the person suffering must be bad. In other words, they thought that trouble was God's finger pointing out the sinner. But we know that was a wrong idea. While it is true that evil does come back upon the doer, it is not always apparent in this world.

And you will remember that Job had a lot of trouble. He lost everything he had—his property was destroyed or stolen; his children were killed—and in his loss and grief he himself was struck down with a terrible sickness. Even his wife advised him to renounce God and die (see Job 2:9). But it is clear that all these troubles did not come to Job because he was a bad man. He did not understand why he should suffer so much, and sometimes he said so in forceful language; but he never "charged God foolishly" (Job 1:22) nor gave up his faith in Him.

Difficult or obscure words:

Job 1:1. **"Uz"**—This area cannot be located positively. Evidence seems to indicate a region southwest of Damascus.

DAY / 19

Read Job 6 through 10.

Today's reading: Poetic language recounts the lengthy debate between Job and his three would-be comforters. The friends try to blame Job for his troubles, and the sufferer steadfastly maintains his innocence.

Memory gem: "Oh that my grief were throughly weighed, and my calamity laid in the balances together!" (Job 6:2).

Thought for today:

The so-called friends of Job had the idea that there was just one reason for his affliction, for his terrible physical condition, and that was his sin. It was the general belief of the people in those days that God's divine government rests upon an exact and uniform correlation between sin and punishment. In other words, that afflictions always come as divine punishment for something that the sinner involved has done, that he is punished unless he repents and submits to God's chastisement. In turn, these punishments lead to the correction and amendment of life when the sufferer repents and turns to God. This is often true. But the fact of suffering was, according to their view, proof of the commission of some special sin, and they tried to apply that principle to the case of Job.

Well, Job answered their arguments one by one. We must remember, of course, that the direct object of this trial that had come to Job was to ascertain whether or not he would deny or forsake God. But we know that this great question had really been settled insofar as God was concerned, for He Himself had said that Job was a good and upright man. For Him that question was really settled.

Job denied the theory of these men that punishment always follows guilt and so proved the commission of wrong. He admitted that God is just. So there was only one thing for him to do, and that was to pray and plead with God to give him an open trial so that all might see that he had been faithful and had not committed any sin calling for these terrible punishments. He thought that if he could die, he would be delivered from his sorrow and trouble. So he prayed to be hidden in the grave until the day when God would try his cause and show him to be upright.

DAY / 20

Read Job 11 through 16.

Today's reading follows the pompous arguments of Job's friends until the poor sufferer exclaims, "Miserable comforters are ye all!"

Memory gem: "Man that is born of woman is of few days, and full of trouble" (Job 14:1).

Thought for today:

Why does trouble come to Christians? The apostle Peter was put to death for his faith, and it is maintained by some that all of the apostles except John died a martyr's death, and he was exiled to the Isle of Patmos. The disciples of Jesus were persecuted by the emperors of Rome, and in every age right down to the present, many of His followers in some part of the world have suffered for their faith—and it will continue to be so.

John Bunyan spent twelve years in Bedford Jail. The Pilgrim Fathers left their homeland to find religious liberty. David Livingstone endured loneliness, wearisome journeys, tropical fever, and finally died on his knees at Ujiji. John G. Patton gave up civilized society and spent his life among cannibals. Baptist missionaries were cruelly slain in the Philippines.

Yes, Christians have trouble—all men do, whether Christians or not. Someone has said that the only way to avoid trouble is to avoid being born.

So much of the trouble in this world is unnecessary trouble, but it is no less trouble. The only way to live through it without ruin is to learn how to trust God, for "he is a shield unto them that put their trust in him" (Proverbs 30:5). Trusting in God is trusting in Jesus, for He came to make the heavenly Father known to men.

DAY / 21

Read Job 17 through 21.

Today's reading finds Job still in the depth of despair because of his afflictions, but even in this extremity he does not lose his hope in eventual redemption.

Memory gem: "I know that my redeemer liveth, and that he shall stand at the latter day upon the earth" (Job 19:25).

Thought for today:

"The Man Who Looked Like a Shadow." This may seem like a strange description, but we find the text for it in Job 17:7: "Mine eye also is dim by reason of sorrow, and all my members are as a shadow."

Sometimes, when we see a person who has been very sick and has become exceedingly emaciated, we say, "He looks like a shadow—the wind might blow him away." So here we find this great man of God saying that all his members had become as a shadow. Physically he was a shadow of his former self. He had gone through so much trouble, so much worry, and so much suffering that he just seemed like a shadow.

But no matter what the world outlook is, the up-look is always good. If trouble leads us to trust in Jesus, it has been a blessing in disguise. Trust in trouble is the greatest lesson we can learn in life. We learn that "God is . . . a very present help in trouble" (Psalm 46:10), and with David we can say, "What time I am afraid, I will trust in thee" (Psalm 56:3).

Note: Verse 26 of Job 19 poses several problems for translators. The KJV inserts three words: "though," "worms," and "body" in an attempt to make it readable. A more literal rendering of the Hebrew would be "And after my skin hath been destroyed, this shall be, even from my flesh shall I see God" (RV, margin). The word rendered "in" (KJV) or "from" (RV) also has a variety of meanings. In any case the verse indicates a belief in a bodily resurrection.

DAY / 22

Read Job 22 through 27.

Today's reading probes still deeper into the problem of human suffering. How will the true child of God relate to trials and difficulties?

Memory gem: "He knoweth the way that I take: when he hath tried me, I shall come forth as gold" (Job 23:10).

Thought for today:

One purpose for trouble coming to a Christian is to draw him nearer to God. It was not until Job had lost everything he had and was worn out with sickness and trouble that he wanted to know God better. It was when he was afflicted with boils that he cried out, "Oh that I knew where I might find him! that I might come even to his seat! . . . But he knoweth the way that I take: when he hath tried me, I shall come forth as gold" (Job 23:3-10).

Trouble can make us depend upon God and not man. Trouble can make us trust. It was when the Flood came that Noah went into the ark. David said that when he walked in the valley of the shadow, he knew God was with him (see Psalm 23:4). And it is written of our Saviour that He learned obedience through the things that He suffered (see Hebrews 5:8).

When you hear a man pray, you can usually tell whether he has ever had any trouble. His prayer is not just a form of beautiful words—he is in earnest. By faith he takes hold of the mighty arm of God. He is humble, for he knows his weakness. He trusts God as he never could have trusted Him before he knew what trouble was. One great preacher has said that the reason why women so often pray better than men is that they have had more trouble.

Many of the psalms of David are prayers. They are among the mightiest prayers ever offered in this world. And why do they still have such power? Why do they so often express our own heart longings in better words than we can manage? Well, for one thing, they are the prayers of a man who was acquainted with trouble. He learned how to trust God in trouble, how to depend upon God. And in Psalm 37:40 David says, "He shall. . . save them, because they trust in him."

DAY / 23

Read Job 28 through 31.

Today's reading: Job delivers a lengthy defense of his innocence. He recites in detail the kind of life he had lived before his afflictions struck him down.

Memory gem: "No mention shall be made of coral, or of pearls: for the price of wisdom is above rubies" (Job 28:18).

Thought for today:

"God has placed you in a world of suffering to prove you, to see if you will be found worthy of the gift of eternal life. There are those all around you who have woes, who need words of sympathy, love, and tenderness, and our humble, pitying prayers. Some are suffering under the iron hand of poverty, some with disease, and others with heartaches, despondency, and gloom. Like Job, you should be eyes to the blind and feet to the lame, and you should inquire into the cause which you know not and search it out with the object in view to relieve their necessities and help just where they most need help." —*Testimonies,* vol. 3, p. 530.

"The merciful are 'partakers of the divine nature,' and in them the compassionate love of God finds expression. All whose hearts are in sympathy with the heart of Infinite Love will seek to reclaim and not to condemn. Christ dwelling in the soul is a spring that never runs dry. Where He abides, there will be an overflowing of beneficence.

"To the appeal of the erring, the tempted, the wretched victims of want and sin, the Christian does not ask, Are they worthy? but, How can I benefit them? In the most wretched, the most debased, he sees souls whom Christ died to save and for whom God has given to His children the ministry of reconciliation."—*Thoughts From the Mount of Blessing, p. 22.*

DAY / 24

Read Job 32 through 35.

Today's reading introduces a fifth speaker, a younger friend who apparently had listened silently to the arguments of the older men, awaiting a chance to express his opinions.

Memory gem: "Search me, O God, and know my heart: try me, and know my thoughts: and see if there be any wicked way in me, and lead me in the way everlasting" (Psalm 139:23, 24).

Thought for today:

At last, after a lengthy observation of the discussion between these men, a fourth friend, a young man named Elihu, arose and expressed his opinion to Job. He showed Job that, instead of being a punishment for some special sin, afflictions are sometimes sent as a means of strengthening and purifying the children of God. They are not the expression of an angry God, but the chastening of a loving Father.

So we see that Elihu was a man whom God could use to help Job and to make things clear in the minds of his three friends. Job accepted that view. And then the Lord Himself, speaking from the whirlwind, reproved Job for his murmurings and showed him that mortal man knows far too little to try to understand the mysteries of God's rule.

David Livingstone, the great explorer and missionary, had a secret sorrow. His son, Robert, had never followed the right path, and he was unable to reach him. The lad went to Boston, joined the Union Army in the Civil War, and at the age of nineteen died in battle on the field of Gettysburg. Before his father knew of his death, he wrote to a friend about the great sorrow of heart caused by this son. He spoke of this sorrow as the " secret ballast" which is often applied by God's hand when outsiders think we are sailing gloriously with the wind. God holds us steady by this secret ballast of sorrow.

DAY / 25

Read Job 36 through 39.

Today's reading: God answers the wordy arguments of these five men: Job, his three friends, and the young man Elihu. God shows how slight is man's wisdom compared to the mighty Creator's power.

Memory gem: "Where wast thou when I laid the foundations of the earth? declare, if thou hast understanding" (Job 38:4).

Thought for today:

Three thousand years ago we find God asking Job if he could do what God is doing every day. He asked Job if he knew what God was doing to "bind the sweet influences of Pleiades" (Job 38:31), or "the cluster of the Pleiades" (RV), so holding them together as a unit. This was an astronomical fact, but no one on earth knew it at that time, unless it was revealed to him by God.

What does science say today? While most of the constellations are gradually drifting through space in different directions, and even changing their shape because of motions of which we know little, this is not true of the Pleiades. Photographs now reveal at least 250 blazing suns in this cluster, all traveling together in a common direction, all sharing in a common motion and drifting through space together.

So, when you look up at the Pleiades tonight, just remember that they are preaching a mighty sermon. They are pointing to the Creator of the universe, who is able to "bind the sweet influences of Pleiades" and keep them together through unimaginable ages as they sweep on in silence toward some common goal, or around some great center.

Difficult or obscure words:

Job 39:9. **"Unicorn"**—wild ox, not a horse with one horn.

Job 39:13. **"Peacock"**—probably ostrich.

DAY / 26

Read Job 40 through 42; Psalms 111 and 112.

Today's reading concludes the story of Job and includes two psalms of praise. These two psalms provide a fitting climax to Job's experience.

Memory gem: "The Lord turned the captivity of Job, when he prayed for his friends" (Job 42:10).

Thought for today:

Job found his friends to be miserable comforters, but he found God a great comforter. And his trust became so deep that he could endure all things and lay his burden upon the Lord. What an example this is for us!

Many modern cities in our land are linked together by a chain of homes for the refuge of those who have been unfortunate and have fallen. A while back the man whose generous gifts made these homes possible died in California, and his body was shipped by train across the country to New York for burial. In every large city where it stopped large groups of women and girls, with tears in their eyes and flowers in their hands, met the train. What was back of his great gifts and wonderful deeds? It is said that he had an only daughter who was the joy of his heart. Her laughter was the music of his soul, but the laughter ceased, and the music was gone. There at her grave, the heartbroken father consecrated his life to Christ and gave his all—his wealth, his time, his influence, his strength—to a ministry of compassion to the homeless and unfortunate. And so, out of his great loss came blessing to his own self and to the world.

Have you had disappointments? Have you experienced eclipses of the sun of joy? Have you had difficulties, heartbreak? Let all these things lead you to Christ and His salvation. Then as you pray for others, blessings will come to you and to them, and your latter days will be "the best of life, for which the first was made" (Robert Browning), as it was with Job.

Difficult or obscure words:

Job 41:1. **"Leviathan"**—possibly crocodile, certainly not whale, perhaps some monster now extinct.

Job 41:3. **"Double bridle"**—meaning obscure; possibly a reference to double rows of teeth.

Job 41:18. **"Neesings"**—sneezings.

DAY / 27

Read 1 Chronicles 2; Exodus 1 and 2.

Today's reading takes up the history of Israel after the death of Joseph. A new king, who did not know or who did not care to acknowledge Joseph, enslaves the numerous descendants of Jacob. We read of Moses' birth, adoption, and eventual flight from Egypt.

Memory gem: "By faith Moses, when he was born, was hid three months of his parents, because they saw he was a proper child; and they were not afraid of the king's commandment" (Hebrews 11:23).

Thought for today:

The greatest man of the Old Testament was doubtless Moses. Think of Moses' mother. She defied the bloody decree of Pharaoh to save her baby's life—hid him three months from the executioners sent out to destroy every boy baby of the Israelites. When she no longer could hide him at home, she placed him in a little basketboat and hid him among the flags on the river's brink.

The Egyptian princess, divinely guided to the spot, discovered the baby. Her heart was melted. She determined to save him by adopting him as her son. And his quick-witted sister, Miriam, as an interested bystander, said: "Shall I go and call to thee a nurse of the Hebrew women, that she may nurse the child for thee?" And then she brought his own mother! "Take this child away," commanded the princess, "and nurse it for me, and I will give thee thy wages" (Exodus 2:9).

"The lessons [Moses] learned at his mother's side could not be forgotten. They were a shield from the pride, the infidelity, and the vice that flourished amid the splendor of the court.

"How far-reaching in its results was the influence of that one Hebrew woman, and she an exile and a slave! The whole future life of Moses, the great mission which he fulfilled as the leader of Israel, testifies to the importance of the work of the Christian mother." —*Patriarchs and Prophets,* p. 244.

Difficult or obscure words:

Exodus 1:9. **"More and mightier"**—obviously an exaggeration by Pharaoh in order to justify extreme measures—not a factual statement.

DAY / 28

Read Exodus 3 through 5.

Today's reading recounts the experience of Moses in encountering the great I AM in a burning bush. Forty years earlier he had tried to free Israel in his own strength. Now he goes reluctantly in God's strength to confront cruel Pharaoh.

Memory gem: "Now therefore go, and I will be with thy mouth, and teach thee what thou shalt say" (Exodus 4:12).

Thought for today:

The Lord asked Moses, "What is that in thine hand?" (Exodus 4:2). Of course God knew what was in his hand; He was merely drawing attention to it. It was the staff or rod, the pastoral crook, which a shepherd always carried.

Now he is told to throw it down upon the ground. He did so, and what happened? It became a serpent, and Moses fled before it. I do not blame him, do you? Moses had been living in the wilderness for forty years, and he knew serpents.

Then came the command of God: "Put forth thine hand, and take it by the tail" (Exodus 4:4).

It would take considerable faith to unquestioningly obey the word of God, and to do it instantly. To pick up an active, dangerous serpent by the tail is more easily said than done, more easily tried than accomplished. The way to catch serpents, especially poisonous ones, is certainly not by the tail with a bare hand. In the case of the large cobra, it would be sure suicide. The serpent would turn on him like a flash. Before he could even touch it, he would be fatally bitten.

God was testing Moses. He was not playing with him. He was testing him for leadership and also to reveal to Moses himself whether he had the requisites that God was looking for then and is still looking for in those who are to be spiritual leaders.

What had seemed a threat to the very life of Moses, when he acted in obedience to God, became a help, an instrument of deliverance and of victory as he faced the mightiest king in the world. Whatever our opposition, however fierce and threatening the foe may be, by God's grace, may we also take it by the tail. In other words, may God help us to meet the issue by faith, obedience, and courage, in Christ's holy name.

Note: See **Difficult or obscure words** on next page.

DAY / 29

Read Exodus 6 through 8.

Today's reading: The preliminary success of Egyptian magicians in counterfeiting the signs Moses and Aaron performed encouraged Pharoah to resist. Soon, however, the magicians were forced to admit their inability to cope with God's power.

Memory gem: "The Lord God of the Hebrews hath sent me unto thee, saying, Let my people go, that they may serve me in the wilderness" (Exodus 7:16).

Thought for today:

There have been times in history when even doubters and opponents of God have had to admit something beyond their own knowledge. When Egypt was smitten by an ancient plague, the scientific brain trust of that time explained it all away until they finally came to a place where they could go no further. Facts were too much for them. No longer could they explain them away as magic. "Then the magicians said unto Pharaoh, This is the finger of God" (Exodus 8:19).

One can think of a dozen places in history where the whole world would have been different had men acted differently. When asked by a news correspondent why the Italians were unsuccessful in landing on the Isle of Malta, Lt. Gen. Sir William Dobbie replied, "I believe it was God."

Why did Hitler not cross the English Channel when the way was open? Why did Napoleon lose the Battle of Waterloo? And so we could continue to ask, on and on. It is, as the poet declared:

Behind the dim unknown
Standeth God within the shadow,
Keeping watch above His own.
—James Russell Lowell

Difficult or obscure words for Day/28:

Exodus 3:22. **"Borrow"**—better: ask. God did not direct the Israelites to deceive the Egyptians.

Exodus 4:21 (and subsequent references). **"Harden"**—God was saying that the signs and wonders would simply make Pharaoh more stubbornly set in his own chosen opposition. Just as many statements say that Pharaoh hardened his own heart. See Exodus 7:13, 14, 22; 8:15, 19, 32; 9:7, 34, 35; 13:15.

DAY / 30

Read Exodus 9 through 11.

Today's reading: The persistent refusal of Pharaoh to free Israel results in increasing intensity of the plagues on the unhappy land.

Memory gem: "How long wilt thou refuse to humble thyself before me? let my people go, that they may serve me" (Exodus 10:3).

Thought for today:

Though the Egyptians had so long rejected the knowledge of God, the Lord still gave them opportunity for repentance. In the days of Joseph, Egypt had been an asylum for Israel; God had been honored in the kindness shown His people. Now the longsuffering One, slow to anger, and full of compassion, gave each judgment time to do its work. The Egyptians, cursed through the very objects they had worshiped, had evidence of the power of Jehovah, and all who would, might submit to God and escape His judgments. The bigotry and stubbornness of the king resulted in spreading the knowledge of God and prompted many of the Egyptians to give themselves to His service.

When the miracles were wrought before the king, Satan was on the ground to counteract their influence and to prevent Pharaoh from acknowledging the supremacy of God and obeying His mandate. Satan wrought to the utmost of his power to counterfeit the work of God and resist His will. The only result was to prepare the way for greater exhibitions of the divine power and glory and to make more apparent, both to the Israelites and to all Egypt, the existence and sovereignty of the true and living God. God delivered Israel with the mighty manifestations of His power and with judgments upon all the gods of Egypt.

Difficult or obscure words:

Exodus 10:19. **"I will see thy face again no more"**—not a promise or a threat, rather, a polite oriental expression meaning, I will not ask for another interview." Chapter 11 indicates (but does not specifically state) that Moses did see Pharaoh once more to deliver God's final warning message.

DAY / 31

Read Exodus 12 and 13.

Today's reading reaches the climax of Israel's conflict with Pharaoh—the solemn Passover and the triumphant Exodus.

Memory gem: "When I see the blood, I will pass over you" (Exodus 12:13).

Thought for today:

That dark night, the destroying angel entered every house in the land of Egypt that had no blood sprinkled over the door. The firstborn of Pharaoh on the throne and the firstborn of the captive in the dungeon perished together. One thing alone guided the angel of death in the dark and dreadful night, and that was the blood. Where there was no blood, there was no salvation. "When I see the blood, I will pass over you."

Some say that it doesn't make any difference whether we believe in the atonement or not, but look at the Israelites and the Egyptians. It made a difference with them that Passover night. Yes, the shed blood made a difference. Christ is our Passover, the apostle says, "sacrificed for us" (1 Corinthians 5:7). Are we sheltered and shielded by the precious blood of the Lamb of God? God says, "When I see the blood, I will pass over you."

How can I know that I am redeemed in Him? Listen to the words of the apostle in Romans 8:1: "There is therefore now no condemnation to them which are in Christ Jesus."

Difficult or obscure words:

Exodus 12:40. **"Four hundred and thirty years"**—This period (see Galatians 3:16, 17) includes 215 years between Abraham's call to leave Haran and Jacob's leaving Canaan to enter Egypt proper, plus 215 years between Jacob's migration and the Exodus. No violence is done to the text in this calculation, because Canaan was a part of the Egyptian Empire during all that time. Also the "fourth generation" (see Genesis 15:16) that would leave Egypt could not extend farther than 215 years. Moses was in the fourth generation of Levi's branch of Israelites. See Exodus 6:16-20.

Exodus 13:18. **"Harnessed"**—probably better: organized; certainly not equipped for battle. Marginal reading: By five in a rank.

DAY / 32

Read Exodus 14 through 16.

Today's reading: The host of Israelites (and large numbers of followers in the camp of Israel—the "mixed multitude") flee from Egyptian bondage, cross the Red Sea, and enter the wilderness.

Memory gem: "Moses said unto the people, Fear ye not, stand still, and see the salvation of the Lord" (Exodus 14:13).

Thought for today:

We had traveled two long days from Cairo, Egypt, across the Suez Canal and along the shore of the Red Sea. We camped there by the sea, not far from where Israel had camped, at a place called Abu Zenima. The next morning we plunged into the real wilderness. The Bible speaks of it as a "waste howling wilderness" (Deuteronomy 32:10), and no description could be more accurate. Several times we started up dead-end canyons before we finally got into the main canyon of the Wadi Feiran. We were crossing the very wilderness in which the Israelites had wandered. No wonder they needed a pillar of cloud to guide them and to shelter them from the burning heat of day, and the pillar of fire by night. No wonder they needed water from the rock, miraculously provided by God. No wonder they needed manna every morning. There certainly would be no food or water for that great convoy of men, women, and children, except as provided by God.

We finally passed the beautiful oasis of Feiran. There are the ruins of an ancient Christian city, now inhabited by a few Arabs who gather dates from the palm trees near the springs. We pushed on up through the sand and stone, often damaging the car. In fact, we had to stop for repairs almost every mile of our way through the desert.

Nightfall came, and it was about ten o'clock and very dark when we finally pulled up to the foot of Mount Sinai, beside the gigantic stone walls of St. Catherine's Monastery. This ancient edifice was built by the Roman emperor Justinian I about 1,450 years ago. It was a mighty fortress, and for over 1,200 years had no gateway or door. All the people who wished to enter, and all food and supplies, had to be lifted up by a windlass to the top of the wall. This was to protect the men inside from attack by the desert tribes.

DAY / 33

Read Exodus 17 through 20.

Today's reading covers various adventures encountered by the wandering Israelites. When they arrive at Mount Sinai, the Lord appears in awful majesty to speak to His people.

Memory gem: "I am the Lord thy God, which have brought thee out of the land of Egypt, out of the house of bondage" (Exodus 20:2).

Thought for today:

God's law was not put into written form until the days of Moses, but that holy law was for all men not only from Adam to Moses, but from Moses to Christ, and throughout the gospel dispensation.

Jesus was faithfully and perfectly obedient to all His Father's commandments, for He said: "If ye keep my commandments, ye shall abide in my love; even as I have kept my Father's commandments, and abide in his love" (John 15:10).

And then notice these words of the apostle John: "He that saith, I know him, and keepeth not his commandments is a liar, and the truth is not in him" (1 John 2:4).

God's law is for God's remnant people in the last days, and they will keep it under great difficulties, even under the attacks of Satan.

"And the dragon was wroth with the woman, and went to make war with the remnant of her seed, which keep the commandments of God, and have the testimony of Jesus Christ" (Revelation 12:17).

They will keep the law of God and have the faith of Jesus. This proves that they are Christians and are living by faith.

Sometimes it is said that no man can keep the law; however, this is but a half-truth. The full truth is that no man in his own strength can keep the law and satisfy God's holy demands. Our righteousness is not of ourselves, but of Him, not of our works, but His.

"For it is God which worketh in you both to will and to do of his good pleasure" (Philippians 2:13).

And so, friend, will you not by God's grace be one of those who follow the path that leads to the city of God—one of those who "keep the commandments of God, and have the testimony of Jesus"?

DAY / 34

Read Exodus 31:18 through chapter 33.

Today's reading, in order to put the sequence of events in order, skips several chapters. We read today about the disgraceful worship of the golden calf and related events.

Memory gem: "Moses stood in the gate of the camp, and said, Who is on the Lord's side? let him come unto me" (Exodus 32:26).

Thought for today:

This great apostasy at Mount Sinai, this worship of the golden calf, has a message for every soul today. Whatever comes between us and obedience to God is an idol. It can be some affair of the daily life. It can be something in reference to our direct worship of God, as it was in this case. It could be a person, plans, property, or money. What is first in my life? Who is first in my life? Who is my god? What is my god? Am I an idolater? These are the big questions.

Robert Browning used to please the children and amuse them by displaying a strange microscopic ability of one of his eyes. He could inscribe the Lord's Prayer inside a small circle, then cover it up completely with a shilling. The Lord's Prayer can be covered up with a coin. We can cover up the words of the Lord's Prayer, "Thy kingdom come, thy will be done in earth, as it is in heaven," with a pile of money; or a few bills may cover them up in our hearts.

This worship of the golden calf is very popular today. We need some plain teaching on this subject. The subject of money is a ticklish one. Talk about heaven; talk about hell; talk about things long ago and far away—but don't talk about my checkbook, my bank account, my property, or what I do with my money. But why not? These things represent life. In a sense money is congealed life. How do we use it? How do we consecrate it? In the secret temple of our hearts many of us still worship the golden calf.

Are you a dedicated man or woman, boy or girl? God loves you. He proved that in Christ. The Saviour died for you upon the cross. Let us all bring our hearts, our lives, as gifts to God. How about it, friend? Will you not make your life a golden gift to Him?

DAY / 35

Read Exodus 34; 24 and 25.

Today's reading takes up the instructions for building the sanctuary, or tabernacle—the center for worship.

Memory gem: "Let them make me a sanctuary; that I may dwell among them" (Exodus 25:8).

Thought for today:

When God's chosen people came out of the land of Egypt under the leadership of Moses, they were instructed by the Lord to make a sanctuary, or movable church, as the center of their worship.

The sanctuary is a dramatized parable of God's dealings with men. In fact, it is the pictured history of the universe in the age of eternity which we call time. It was moreover "the gospel in substance, salvation in epitome," as Robert Thurber says. It was a figure, but more than a form. As we study it, we will find shadows, but not darkness; in fact, the shadows turn into reflections of the very light of heaven. As we study the sanctuary, we think God's thoughts after Him.

It was to be the house of God on earth. During the famous Exodus of the tribes of the Hebrew people from slavery in Egypt, they stopped in their wanderings toward the land of their adoption and camped for nearly a year at the foot of Mount Sinai. There, in obedience to the instructions of the divine Architect, they built the tabernacle or sanctuary of God. It was in tent form so it could be put up and taken down as they moved from place to place in the desert for forty years before entering the Land of Promise.

Every detail of its construction was ordered and described by God Himself. Skilled workmanship was employed. The skins of animals, beautiful woods, fine linen, precious metals and stones—all were blended in the artistry of the great Designer, working through human hands.

Difficult or obscure words:

Exodus 25:5. **"Badgers' skins"**—better: seal skins, probably the hides of the dugong, common in the Red Sea.

Exodus 25:5. **"Shittim wood"**—acacia wood.

Exodus 25:31. **"Candlestick"**—lampstand possessing the shape of the traditional Jewish menorah.

DAY / 36

Read Exodus 26 through 28.

Today's reading has more of the detailed instructions for making the various items for the tabernacle.

Memory gem: "Thou shalt make a plate of pure gold, and grave upon it, like the engravings of a signet, HOLINESS TO THE LORD" (Exodus 28:36).

Thought for today:

What a perfect picture this is of Christ and His work of redemption! No wonder we read in Psalm 77:13: "Thy way, O God, is in the sanctuary."

The central feature of the Christian religion is the mediatorial work of Jesus Christ as our High Priest in the heavenly sanctuary. His sinless life might have been lived. His sacrifice might have been made. He might have risen triumphantly from the tomb. But if it were not for His mediatorial work in the heavenly sanctuary—the sanctuary "which the Lord pitched, and not man" (Hebrews 8:2), which was the original after which the earthly sanctuary was copied—we would not share in the benefits of that redemptive work. It is as a priest that Christ ministers salvation and grace to us. His ability to save to the uttermost is based on the fact that "he ever liveth to make intercession" for us (Hebrews 7:25).

So we see that this tabernacle in the desert carried with it the form of the cross and the teaching of the cross. There were sacrificed the bleeding lambs which pointed to Jesus, the Lamb of God. These animals were brought to the altar of sacrifice, and those who had sinned laid their hands upon them, confessing their sins. They did this to show their faith in the innocent Lamb of God who would someday come to this earth and die for them. By faith they, as we, could say:

Christ has for sin atonement made
What a wonderful Saviour!
We are redeemed! the price is paid! . . .
What a wonderful Saviour is Jesus, my Lord!
—Elisha A. Hoffman.

DAY / 37

Read Exodus 29 through 31:17.

Today's reading, among other things, introduces two men with heaven-imparted abilities. The work of preparing God's house demanded careful and skillful workers.

Memory gem: "I will dwell among the children of Israel, and will be their God" (Exodus 29:45).

Thought for today:

What about God's plan for our lives? Have we tried to find out what it is? Have we been willing to follow it as He has led us step by step? Remember, we are responsible for all the talents the Lord has loaned to us. The Holy Spirit, knowing every heart, divides spiritual gifts "to every man severally as he will" (1 Corinthians 12:8-11).

What would happen today if every professing Christian were ready to do every good work?

God is willing to reveal His plan for us, but there are two requirements if we would know what it is. First, there must be the sympathy of trust; and second, the faithfulness of obedience. There must be sympathetic trust, or we shall never have spiritual insight. God reveals Himself to the trustful, loving heart, and He makes His ways clear to those who obey Him.

Each of us, then, has his work; and how important are those individual peculiarities which God has given to each of us for the accomplishment of that task! How reverently we should guard the diversities that are really revelations of God's will concerning our work! Our service to Him is not a by-product of life; it is life itself. So, working and watching, happy will be the servant whom the Lord shall find so doing—that is, doing the work that is God's plan for him. He is not merely idly looking for Christ, but doing His will here and now, knowing that every man's life is a plan of God.

DAY / 38

Read Exodus 35 through 37.

Today's reading describes more of the beautiful furnishings for the tabernacle. One interesting sidelight mentions the time when people brought too many gifts to church!

Memory gem: "They spake unto Moses, saying, The people bring much more than enough for the service of the work" (Exodus 36:5).

Thought for today:

As we study this great tabernacle in the desert, we pass within the veil to the sacred stillness of the most holy place. Here rests the ark of the covenant, within which are the Ten Commandments written by the finger of God on tables of stone. The ark is surmounted by two golden angels with their wings outstretched over the mercy seat, which is between them. This represents the throne of God in heaven, the very center of the universe. The mercy seat resting over the tables of God's law helps us to understand that "righteousness and judgment are the establishment of his throne" (Psalm 97:2, margin).

Here on the mercy seat, the holy presence of God shone forth in blinding light. No one but the high priest could sprinkle the blood of the sin offering for all the people before the mercy seat, and he could do that only once, at the end of the yearly services. In like manner, Christ appears in the very presence of God for us as our High Priest, our "advocate with the Father, Jesus Christ the righteous" (1 John 2:1).

Friend, will you not send your sins on beforehand to judgment in Christ? Will you not accept Him as your Mediator, the Man Christ Jesus? He is the One who is touched with all the feelings of our infirmities (see Hebrews 4:15). He understands what it is to live in this world, He knows what it is to be a man, for as the Son of man He has carried our humanity with Him to the very throne of God. Does your hope enter into that within the heavenly veil, whither our Forerunner, the Lord Jesus Christ, has entered there in heaven above to appear in the presence of God for us? (see Hebrews 6:19, 20).

Difficult or obscure words for Day/39:

Exodus 38:8. **"Lookingglasses"**—better: mirrors. They were highly polished bronze plates.

DAY / 39

Read Exodus 38 through 40.

Today's reading: Work on the beautiful tent of worship was completed, and it was erected in the wilderness. The Lord approved the project by a special manifestation of His glory.

Memory gem: "Then a cloud covered the tent of the congregation, and the glory of the Lord filled the tabernacle" (Exodus 40:34).

Thought for today:

In the holy tabernacle made by Moses at the command of God and carried by Israel through the desert wanderings, we have a perfect picture of the cross. Notice the arrangement of the altar of sacrifice, the laver, the golden altar of incense, and the ark of the covenant in a straight line from east to west. Then the table of shewbread, the altar of incense, and the golden candlestick, running at right angles to this in another straight line from north to south, formed the arms of the cross. This made a perfect cross, which was displayed wherever the sanctuary was set up.

And the teachings of the sanctuary with its sacrifices of slain lambs and ascending incense pictured, beforehand, the redemptive work of Christ our Sacrifice, offered before God for us.

If we have exalted views of Christ's atoning work, we must study the New Testament and have some knowledge of its deep bloodstained foundation in the Old Testament gospels of Moses and the prophets. In every sacrifice Christ's death was shown.

A visitor said to a wounded soldier of World War II, who lay dying in a hospital, "What church are you of?"

"I'm of Christ's church," he replied.

"I mean, of what persuasion are you?"

"Persuasion?" said the poor dying boy, as he looked heavenward beaming with the love of His Saviour, "I am persuaded, that neither death, nor life, nor angels, nor principalities, nor powers, nor things present, nor things to come, nor height, nor depth, nor any other creature, shall be able to separate us from the love of God, which is in Christ Jesus our Lord" (Romans 8:38, 39).

Is that your persuasion, friend? Do you believe it?

Note: See **Difficult or obscure words** on previous page.

DAY / 40

Read Numbers 1 and 2.

Today's reading: A census was taken at Sinai and the encampment was organized with precise detail.

Memory Gem: "Let all things be done decently and in order" (1 Corinthians 14:40).

Thought for today:

"The Hebrew camp was arranged in exact order. It was separated into three great divisions, each having its appointed position in the encampment. In the center was the tabernacle, the abiding place of the invisible King. Around it were stationed the priests and Levites. Beyond these were encamped all the other tribes. . . .

"The position of each tribe also was specified. Each was to march and to encamp beside its own standard. . . .

"Scrupulous cleanliness as well as strict order throughout the encampment and its environs was enjoined. Thorough sanitary regulations were enforced. Every person who was unclean from any cause was forbidden to enter the camp. These measures were indispensable to the preservation of health among so vast a multitude; and it was necessary also that perfect order and purity be maintained, that Israel might enjoy the presence of a holy God. Thus He declared: 'The Lord thy God walketh in the midst of thy camp, to deliver thee, and to give up thine enemies before thee; therefore shall thy camp be holy.' "—*Patriarchs and Prophets,* pp. 374, 375.

DAY / 41

Read Numbers 3 and 4.

Today's reading concerns largely the duties of the Levites—the tribe set apart to carry on the religious services for Israel. These people were born with a special mission in life.

Memory gem: "I beseech you therefore, brethren, by the mercies of God, that ye present your bodies a living sacrifice, holy, acceptable unto God, which is your reasonable service" (Romans 12:1).

Thought for today:

We meet people constantly who do not know what to do with their lives. They seem to be wandering about in a daze. Many are disappointed at the way things have turned out. Their plans have not worked. They have not found in life what they expected. They know there is something better, and they are reaching for it, staggering along through a fog of misapprehension.

If you want to find life in its highest reaches, give your life to some great cause, some good, though unpopular truth. Then sacrifice, work, and spend your life for it, and you will be happy all the way along.

Remember this: God's Word is the greatest truth; His cause is the greatest and the most unpopular to the natural heart of man; and Jesus Christ Himself is the greatest personality. Avow your allegiance to Him, His message, and His Holy Word. Give your life, all that you have and are, to God's service, and your complete loyalty to Him as revealed in Jesus Christ. Then you will have something to live for; life will have a meaning; and you will have joy, even in the midst of sorrow. There will be no disappointment that is not His appointment.

You will find that there is no sin which He will not forgive. There is no loss which He cannot turn into an eternal gain. You will discover that there is nothing too difficult for God and that His love blots out the darkness of the past and opens the door to the only future worth striving for. Why not try it?

DAY / 42

Read Numbers 5 and 6.

Today's reading takes up various rites and regulations under the ceremonial law. It ends with the beautiful Aaronic blessing.

Memory gem: "The Lord bless thee, and keep thee: the Lord make his face shine upon thee, and be gracious unto thee: the Lord lift up his countenance upon thee, and give thee peace" (Numbers 6:24-26).

Thought for today:

Why should people in our so-called Christian dispensation not be as fully honest as men were to be under the Mosaic law? We may go to church, sing hymns, make donations to missions, give our children a Christian education, and still our prayers will not be heard by God—in fact, they will be an abomination to Him—unless we are completely straightforward in our daily life and our business dealings.

I think it was Charles G. Finney, the great evangelist, who said that one reason for the requirement the apostle penned in Romans 12:2, "Be not conformed to this world," is the tremendous instantaneous influence it would have if everybody would do business on the principles of the gospel. In fact, Finney maintained that if Christians would do business for just one year on gospel principles, it would shake the world. I believe he is right.

You see, Bible righteousness is very practical.

DAY / 43

Read Numbers 7.

Today's reading describes in detail the initiation of services in the newly completed and dedicated tabernacle.

Memory gem: "Thy way, O God, is in the sanctuary: who is so great a God as our God?" (Psalm 77:13).

Thought for today:

In the ancient sanctuary services the believer looked forward to the Redeemer who was to come. We look back to the Redeemer who actually has come and is now in heaven pleading our cause before the heavenly Father. He is our High Priest in the heavenly temple, there appearing before the justice and love of God for us.

In the plan of God, He was "the Lamb slain from the foundation of the world" (Revelation 13:8). God's plan of redemption is revealed in the Man of redemption, even the Lord Jesus Christ, who was both the Lamb of God who died, and the High Priest who offered the sacrifice. So the ancient tabernacle was a type of the way and fellowship of salvation.

Let us look for a moment at some of the wonderful pictures flashed before us from the temple and its services, the type of Christ and His salvation. By faith we are justified from the guilt and power of sin—so teaches the altar of burnt offerings. We are to be sanctified by the washing of His Word (see Ephesians 5:26). There at the tabernacle was the laver of purification. We are to shine as light-bearers, a testimony of the Lord's goodness—the lampstand (see Revelation 1:12). We are to pray. Our prayers are symbolized in the ancient sanctuary by the golden altar of incense which stood in the holy place. Here, the mingling of incense with the ascending prayers typified Christ's merits and intercession, which alone makes man's worship acceptable to God (see Revelation 8:3). We are strengthened by the Bread of Life (see John 6:48), pictured by the shewbread. And we are to look forward, hastening to appear before the very throne of God Himself, as portrayed in the earthly sanctuary by the ark of the covenant.

Our hope is certain; God's promise is sure. My friend, all this wonderful teaching of the sanctuary is for you. Do you not see in Christ, the Lamb of God, the One who has died for you—your hope and your blessing and your salvation? Have you responded to His love?

DAY / 44

Read Numbers 8 through 10:28.

Today's reading returns to a recital of Israel's worship of God in the sanctuary service.

Memory gem: "By his own blood he [Christ] entered in once into the holy place, having obtained eternal redemption for us" (Hebrews 9:12).

Thought for today:

In this day of growing modernism the Bible doctrine of blood-bought salvation grows less and less popular. Look at some of the new church hymnals and try to find the old songs about the blood of Jesus Christ and His sufferings on Calvary. You may be surprised to find many of those old songs omitted.

Not long ago in one of the large denominations it was suggested that all songs referring to the blood or to salvation through the shed blood of Jesus Christ, be eliminated in the revised hymnbook as being too gruesome for our fastidious modern ears!

In spite of this so-called modern attitude toward the shed blood of Christ (this modernism is really as ancient as Cain), it is still true that, according to Holy Scripture, no man ever lived who had his sins remitted without the shedding of blood. We read in Hebrews 9:22: "Without shedding of blood is no remission."

"All have sinned" (Romans 3:23, emphasis supplied). *All* are lost. Therefore, *all* need salvation. *All* can find salvation. It is provided for *all,* because Christ died for *all* (see 2 Corinthians 5:14, 15 and Romans 5:6). But all who are lost must come to God by way of the spilled blood of Christ. There is no other way to climb up to heaven—no other avenue to redemption—no other door—no other gate. "No man cometh unto the Father, but by me" (John 14:6), are the words of Christ.

No human being can be cleansed without the shedding of blood.

DAY / 45

Read Leviticus 1 through 4.

Today's reading begins a section on the many specific regulations about the ceremonial services. Try to find revelations of Christ's ministry in all of this.

Memory Gem: "How much more shall the blood of Christ . . . purge your conscience from dead works to serve the living God?" (Hebrews 9:14)

Thought for today:

When I was a little boy, my father offered to give me a dollar if I would read the Bible through from the beginning to end and do my best to pronounce every word. It took me a long, long time, but finally I finished it. I shall never forget what a hard journey it was, getting through those long chapters of Leviticus, Numbers, and Deuteronomy. What was the meaning of all those sacrifices and offerings of various kinds, those feast days, those yearly sabbaths, the ritual of the priesthood? What was it all about? I couldn't seem to make sense of it. And no wonder. No one who leaves Jesus out of it can make sense of it, for He is in every part of it.

One day a certain father was reading his Sunday paper, hoping that he would not be disturbed by his little girl. So he cut up a map of the world which he happened to have handy and gave it to her to put together. After a short time she returned to him with all in perfect order—every piece in its place. The father was greatly surprised. "Why," he said, "how did you do it, darling? You don't know anything about geography."

The innocent little one replied, "There was a picture of Jesus on the other side, and I knew that when I had Jesus in the right place, the whole world would be all right." And so it is. When you put Jesus in the right place, you will understand all these uninteresting things in the Old Testament, and also everything in your own life will be right.

DAY / 46

Read Leviticus 5 through 7.

Today's reading continues the regulations governing ceremonies in the sanctuary service.

Memory gem: "The priest shall make an atonement for him . . . , and it shall be forgiven him" (Leviticus 5:13).

Thought for today:

There is a great deal of truth for us to study in the temple ceremonies, as they wonderfully depict the gospel and salvation in Jesus Christ. Certainly the temple of the Israelites, in both its movable and its permanent form, had ordinances of divine service that foreshadowed the sacrifice of Jesus and also His work as our High Priest in the heavenly temple. The definite proof of this is the statement made by the apostle in Hebrews 8:1-3, where he says: "We have such an high priest, who is set on the right hand of the throne of the Majesty in the heavens; a minister of the sanctuary and of the true tabernacle, which the Lord pitched, and not man. For every high priest is ordained to offer gifts and sacrifices: wherefore it is of necessity that this man have somewhat also to offer."

"This man," of course, is Jesus. He is our High Priest now in the heavenly sanctuary. There He represents us before God.

The atoning sacrifice that He finished upon Calvary's cross is the offering that He presents for all repentant sinners before the throne of God. What a glorious gospel these temple ceremonies of old picture for us!

DAY / 47

Read Leviticus 8 and 9.

Today's reading: This section on ceremonial rules duplicates what we found in Exodus 40 about the dedication of the tabernacle for worship.

Memory gem: "Aaron and his sons did all things which the Lord commanded by the hand of Moses" (Leviticus 8:36).

Thought for today:

We can see how important it was for the people in those days to take part in daily worship and to turn their minds toward God and the just One who was to come and die for them.

What is the matter with church life today? Largely a lack of prayer. What is the matter with Christian homes today? Largely a lack of prayer. If the family altar were erected in every professedly Christian home this week, there would be a spiritual revolution in the world. Juvenile delinquency would practically disappear, crime would decrease, confidence would take the place of fear, and peace would rule in the hearts of men as well as in the councils of the diplomats.

Do you have family prayer at the golden altar every morning and night? Do you lift up your eyes by faith to our Lord as He ministers in the holy temple above? I realize that many families are divided. In that case, you can have your own private devotions, your own secret prayer. And your petitions will arise, accepted by God, because of the sacrifice of our Redeemer. They will ascend with the merits of our Lord Jesus, like the morning and evening incense from the golden altar of old.

And as we pray, we learn to pray. We do not merely kneel before God and begin to beg for things. We learn to talk to Him and with Him, and we listen to Him speaking through His Word or directly through the impressions of the Holy Spirit upon our hearts.

It has often been said that the family that prays together, stays together. And it certainly is true that the more we have in common, the less likely we are to drift apart. The father and mother who unite in prayer before God and lead their children to Him will be led to settle their little difficulties before they become big ones and alienate their hearts.

DAY / 48

Read Exodus 21 through 23.

Today's reading covers a section of civil laws designed to preserve "domestic tranquility" in a crowded desert camp—as well as later in a new homeland.

Memory gem: "Thou shalt neither vex a stranger, nor oppress him: for ye were strangers in the land of Egypt" (Exodus 22:21).

Thought for today:

These were the laws that God laid down for His people in ancient times, and I believe the principle on which they were based is just as binding today as it was then. If we have wrongfully taken anything from any person or in any way defrauded anyone, let us not only confess it, but do all we can to make restitution. If we have misrepresented anybody, if we have started slander or some false report about someone, we should do all in our part to undo the wrong.

Hugh Latimer, the great reformer, said: "If ye make no restitution of goods detained, ye shall cough in hell; the devil shall laugh at you." This is pretty strong language. Latimer believed it was true.

Let me say this, friend, repentance demands restitution, which is evidence of true repentance. True repentance always brings forth fruit. If we have done wrong to someone, we should ask God to help us make things right, to make restitution. If I have done any man a great injustice and can make it good, I need not ask God to forgive me until I am willing to make matters right and undo the hurt I have caused. Suppose I have taken something that does not belong to me; I cannot expect forgiveness until I make restitution as far as possible.

Difficult or obscure words:

Exodus 22:28. **"Gods"**—more properly: judges.

DAY / 49

Read Numbers 10:29 through chapter 13.

Today's reading: Israel breaks camp at Mount Sinai, and the people start in the direction of the Promised Land. One episode concerns Aaron and Miriam's jealousy of Moses.

Memory gem: "Return, O Lord, unto the many thousands of Israel" (Numbers 10:36).

Thought for today:

A snare so prevalent in this modern age is covetousness. In the Ten Commandments it says: "Thou shalt not covet thy neighbour's house, thou shalt not covet thy neighbour's wife, nor his manservant, nor his maidservant, nor his ox, nor his ass, nor any thing that is thy neighbour's" (Exodus 20:17).

God certainly knew what He was doing when He put that in His law. Jesus said, "Take heed, and beware of covetousness: for a man's life consisteth not in the abundance of the things which he possesseth" (Luke 12:15).

Men covet not only money, but power and esteem, position and praise. Nations have been plunged into war, millions of lives have been blotted out, billions of dollars in property have been destroyed to feed the ambition of a few men in power. Covetousness leads to stealing and dishonesty and marital difficulties. It affects Christians as well as those who are not. It is difficult to realize that "a man's life consisteth not in the abundance of the things which he possesseth" (Luke 12:15), when we see in these modern days the mad race for riches and power and glory and security.

God hates sin with a deadly hatred, but He loves the sinner with an all-encompassing love. Christ can save you from these snares of Satan right now if you will have it so. Right now ask God to forgive your sins in Jesus' name, and you will find real peace and a better life.

Difficult or obscure words:

Numbers 12:1. **"Ethiopian"**—literally "Cushite." Zipporah was a Midianite, descendant of Abraham. Her complexion may have been somewhat darker than that of Miriam, who used the epithet "Ethiopian" in a contemptuous manner.

Numbers 13:16. **"Jehoshua"**—usually given in its abbreviated form, Joshua.

DAY / 50

Read Numbers 14; Leviticus 10 and 11.

Today's reading records Israel's tragic failure on the very border of the Promised Land; it tells a painful story of swift punishment for a grievous sin. It also lists the clean and unclean animals.

Memory gem: "Pardon, I beseech thee, the iniquity of this people according unto the greatness of thy mercy" (Numbers 14:19).

Thought for today:

"At the hour of worship, as the prayers and praise of the people were ascending to God, two of the sons of Aaron took each his censer, and burned fragrant incense thereon, to rise as a sweet odor before the Lord. But they transgressed his command by the use of 'strange fire.' For burning the incense they took common instead of the sacred fire which God Himself had kindled, and which He had commanded to be used for this purpose. For this sin, a fire went out from the Lord and devoured them in the sight of the people.

"Next to Moses and Aaron, Nadab and Abihu had stood highest in Israel. They had been especially honored by the Lord, having been permitted with the seventy elders to behold his glory in the mount. But their transgression was not therefore to be excused or lightly regarded. All this rendered their sin more grievous. Because men have received great light, because they have, like the princes of Israel, ascended to the mount, and been privileged to have communion with God, and to dwell in the light of His glory, let them not flatter themselves that they can afterward sin with impunity; that because they have been thus honored, God will not be strict to punish their iniquity. This is a fatal deception. The great light and privileges bestowed require returns of virtue and holiness corresponding to the light given. Anything short of this, God cannot accept. Great blessings or privileges should never lull to security or carelessness. They should never give license to sin or cause the recipients to feel that God will not be exact with them. All the advantages which God has given are His means to throw ardor into the spirit, zeal into effort, and vigor into the carrying out of His holy will."—*Patriarchs and Prophets,* pp. 359, 360.

Note: See **Difficult or obscure words** on next page.

DAY / 51

Read Leviticus 12 and 13.

Today's reading looks at some of the regulations for preserving the health of God's people.

Memory gem: "Beloved, I wish above all things that thou mayest prosper and be in health, even as thy soul prospereth" (3 John 2).

Thought for today:

The laws given through Moses concerning sanitation, hygiene, diet, and the control of communicable diseases are astounding in their scope and exactness. Medical science today is just beginning to catch up with what was common knowledge to the ancient Israelites in the fifteenth century B.C. Public health played a prominent part in the deliverance of Israel from Egyptian bondage. It certainly helps to account for the fact that God's blessing was upon His people, and that "there was not one feeble person among their tribes" (Psalm 105:37).

Afflictions will come to many of us in spite of the greatest care in obeying health rules. We are living in a degenerate age. We are a long way from the Garden of Eden, but obedience to God's instruction in all these things will bring us blessing and help, no matter what our condition may be. And let us remember the wonderful statement in Exodus 15:26: "I am the Lord that healeth thee."

May the God of Abraham, Isaac, and Jacob, the God and Father of our Lord Jesus Christ, the Creator of the world and the Redeemer of the human race, bless you and yours, physically, mentally, and spiritually—and may He prepare you for a place in that glorious new world which is to be yours and mine through His grace revealed in Jesus Christ.

Difficult or obscure words for Day/50:

Numbers 14:34. **"Breach of promise"**—better: "your hindering or frustration of My promise." Israel's rebellious opposition prevented the fulfillment of God's promise.

Leviticus 11. Some of the creatures mentioned here do not correspond to those modern ones with the same names. The general principles remain the same, however.

DAY / 52

Read Leviticus 14 and 15.

Today's reading has more of the sanitary laws, giving particular attention to the ceremonies for cleansing any defilement.

Memory gem: "Purge me with hyssop, and I shall be clean: wash me, and I shall be whiter than snow" (Psalm 51:7).

Thought for today:

"Now," says Dr. F. B. Meyer, "I contend that Jesus . . . is all through the Book, the Book of God. He is in every chapter and every verse, from the beginning to the end. In fact, every incident and subject in the Bible is either about Jesus or somehow makes a road to Him."

That is especially true of the so-called ceremonial law of the Old Testament. It is just full of types and ceremonies, sacrifices and priests, which are really a picture and prophecy of Jesus. And, in view of what our Saviour accomplished on Calvary's cross, it seems clear to me that we should make a distinction between the Ten Commandments, or moral law, and what is called the ceremonial law. The Ten Commandments, sometimes called the Decalogue, constitute in principle God's holy law which is unchangeable. It is the very foundation of His holy throne. It is the righteous expression of His character. And since that is so, we believe it is as eternal as the everlasting God Himself.

While the moral law of God is eternal in character, it would not be true to say that the rites and ceremonies which He gave to Israel as a nation are eternal. Many of the offerings, the feast days, even the priesthood itself were typical of the redemptive work of Christ; and they all met their glorious fulfillment in the offering of our Saviour on Calvary's cross. This is what was meant by the apostle Paul when he wrote that Christ "abolished in his flesh the enmity, even the law of commandments contained in ordinances" (Ephesians 2:15).

What did Jesus do with this law of ordinances? We read in Colossians 2:14: "Blotting out the handwriting of ordinances that was against us, which was contrary to us, and took it out of the way, nailing it to his cross."

Every sacrificed lamb of the ancient Israelite ritual pointed forward to Jesus. He was the reality that the rites foreshadowed.

DAY / 53

Read Leviticus 16 through 18.

Today's reading describes, among other things, one of the most important aspects of the sanctuary service—the yearly Day of Atonement.

Memory gem: "If we confess our sins, he is faithful and just to forgive us our sins, and to cleanse us from all unrighteousness" (1 John 1:9).

Thought for today:

In Israel of old, when the holy temple was cleansed at the end of the year, each offender had a chance to show that he was still repentant, that he still wanted forgiveness. If that was true, the record of his sin was blotted out when the sanctuary was cleansed. When that day of remembrance was made again of sins, as the writer of Hebrews puts it in Hebrews 10:3, every true Israelite renewed his consecration to God and confirmed his repentance.

"On that day shall the priest make an atonement for you, to cleanse you, that ye may be clean from all your sins before the Lord" (Leviticus 16:30).

How happy they must have been when that day had passed and they were clean from their sins! Friends, we may have that same experience. We read in 1 John 1:9: "If we confess our sins, he is faithful and just to forgive us our sins, and to cleanse us from all unrighteousness."

Notice, we are not only forgiven, but cleansed from all unrighteousness, from all our sins. Then we can sing:

Blessed assurance, Jesus is mine!
O, what a foretaste of glory divine!
Heir of salvation, purchase of God,
Born of His Spirit, washed in His blood.
—Fanny J. Crosby

Difficult or obscure words:

Leviticus 16:8. **"Scapegoat"**—Azazel, a superhuman, wicked spirit. One goat was "for the Lord" and the other was "for Azazel." The blood of this goat was not shed as a sacrifice for the sins of men; its death was in no way substitutionary.

DAY / 54

Read Leviticus 19 through 21.

Today's reading: Among other solemn instructions, God issues a warning against dabbling with the occult.

Memory gem: "Ye shall be holy: for I the Lord your God am holy" (Leviticus 19:2).

Thought for today:

Through human mediums, and even through the priesthood of certain pagan religions, demon powers have made contact with men, in order to take the very place of God in the lives of fallen humanity.

All contact with these unseen demon spirits was forbidden in ancient Israel. Later on, in his desperation when God had forsaken him, King Saul sought contact with the dead Samuel through the intervention of such spirits.

But Saul was punished for his sin, as we read in 1 Chronicles 10:13: "So Saul died for his transgression which he committed against the Lord, even against the word of the Lord, which he kept not, and also for asking counsel of one that had a familiar spirit, to enquire of it."

The "familiar spirit" attempted to palm itself off as the spirit of the prophet Samuel. To this very day these spirits often imitate the dead friends of those who seek their advice. Sometimes they claim to be the spirits or souls of eminent people of past ages. The prophet Isaiah warns against consulting with such familiar spirits claiming to be the spirits of the dead: "When they shall say unto you, Seek unto them that have familiar spirits, and unto wizards that peep, and that mutter: should not a people seek unto their God?" (Isaiah 8:19).

DAY / 55

Read Leviticus 22 and 23.

Today's reading: After prescribing the kinds of sacrifices for different situations the Lord gives instructions for the three great yearly festivals.

Memory gem: "Christ our Passover is sacrificed for us: therefore let us keep the feast, . . . with the unleavened bread of sincerity and truth" (1 Corinthians 5:7, 8).

Thought for today:

We might put it this way: The law of ceremonial sacrifices was the preaching of the gospel, revealing the promised Saviour, who would come and die for the sins of the world. The blood shed in those services pointed forward to Jesus, whose blood was shed for man's sin. In every sacrifice His righteousness was revealed as much as in every Communion service today.

As one travels through India he realizes that the people of the vast land are very religious, and have been for centuries. The altars, the temples, the sacrifices, the multitudes of priests and devotees prove it. Some time ago a Calcutta newspaper reported that a young Brahman, a recognized leader of religion and Hinduism, came to the house of a missionary for an interview. In the course of the conversation he said, "Many things which Christianity contains I find in Hunduism, but there is one thing which Christianity has that Hinduism has not."

"And what is that?" the missionary asked.

The young man's reply was striking—"A Saviour."

And that is just what the sacrifices and ceremonies of the Old Testament promised—a Saviour. That is one reason why we should study the Old Testament as well as the New. The Old Testament promised a Saviour, in prophecy and ceremony, in feast and sacrifice. The New Testament reveals a Saviour who had come and fulfilled the Old Testament promises.

Difficult or obscure words:

Leviticus 23:7, 8. **"Holy convocation"**—that is, a holy or sacred gathering, called a "sabbath" in verse 15. The first and last day of each of the week-long feasts was a "sabbath," regardless of the day of the week on which they fell. These were not the same as the seventh-day Sabbaths of verse 3.

DAY / 56

Read Leviticus 24 and 25.

Today's reading tells of a time in ancient Israel when everything was to be made right, a time for freeing slaves and restoring property—a year of jubilee.

Memory gem: "Ye shall not therefore oppress one another; but thou shalt fear thy God" (Leviticus 25:17).

Thought for today:

It was for liberty of conscience that God brought the Israelites out of Egyptian bondage, where Pharaoh himself had said, "Who is the Lord? . . . I know not the Lord, neither will I let Israel go" (Exodus 5:2).

It was from a godless tyranny that a nation of slaves was delivered "through a mighty hand and by a stretched out arm" (Deuteronomy 5:15). No wonder God instructed their leader, Moses that when they reached the Promised Land, they must continually revive the knowledge and the fact of freedom. At least once every fifty years there was to be a national rejoicing because of these great principles, and a rededication to them.

It is significant that the famous Liberty Bell—which rang for the inauguration of American civil and religious liberty, but was cast in Britain years before—has inscribed upon it the command given to Israel over 3000 years ago: "Proclaim liberty throughout all the land unto all the inhabitants thereof" (Leviticus 25:10).

Certainly every Christian should proclaim liberty, religious liberty. So should every ruler of the people all over the earth.

Some people are ready to proclaim liberty for themselves, but not for others. Dr. Harry Emerson Fosdick reminds us that there was once a famous actress, Charlotte Cushman,who used to greet her friends at her Newport villa by saying: "This is Liberty Hall. Everyone does as I please."

There were some people who came to America when it was a wilderness to seek religious liberty for themselves, but not for others. Someone has facetiously said that when they landed on the shores of Massachusetts, they first fell on their knees and then fell on the aborigines. They found freedom for themselves in the wilderness, but when Quakers, Baptists, and others came to preach and practice the truth as they saw it, they were persecuted. True religious liberty is a religious liberty for all.

DAY / 57

Read Leviticus 26 and 27.

Today's reading brings us to the end of Leviticus with its many ceremonial regulations. Perhaps it is significant that the last instruction concerns tithing.

Memory gem: "And all the tithe of the land, whether of the seed of the land, or of the fruit of the tree, is the Lord's: it is holy unto the Lord" (Leviticus 27:30).

Thought for today:

"God, as the Giver of all our benefits, has a claim upon them all; that His claim should be our first consideration; and that a special blessing will attend all who honor this claim.

"Herein is set forth a principle that is seen in all God's dealings with men. The Lord placed our first parents in the Garden of Eden. He surrounded them with everything that could minister to their happiness, and He bade them acknowledge Him as the possesor of all things. In the garden He caused to grow every tree that was pleasant to the eye or good for food; but among them He made one reserve. Of all else, Adam and Eve might freely eat; but of this one tree God said, 'Thou shalt not eat of it.' Here was the test of their gratitude and loyalty to God.

"So the Lord has imparted to us heaven's richest treasure in giving us Jesus. With Him He has given us all things richly to enjoy. The productions of the earth, the bountiful harvest, the treasures of gold and silver, are His gifts. Houses and lands, food and clothing, He has placed in the possession of men. He asks us to acknowledge Him as the Giver of all things; and for this reason He says, Of all your possessions I reserve a tenth for Myself. . . . This is the provision God has made for carrying forward the work of the gospel."

"The . . . system of tithing was founded upon a principle which is as enduring as the law of God. This system of tithing was a blessing to the Jews, else God would not have given it them. So also will it be a blessing to those who carry it out to the end of time. Our heavenly Father did not originate the plan . . . to enrich Himself, but to be a great blesing to man. He saw that this system . . . was just what man needed."—*Counsels on Stewardship,* pp. 65, 67, 68.

DAY / 58

Read Numbers 15 and 16.

Today's reading recounts the tragic results of haboring a spirit of envy. In this case envy ripened into open revolt, and only divine intervention prevented a coup.

Memory gem: "He [Aaron] stood between the dead and the living; and the plague was stayed" (Numbers 16:48).

Thought for today:

One snare that the evil one uses is found in Galatians 5:19-21: "Now the works of the flesh are manifest, which are these; . . . Envyings, murders, drunkenness, revelings, and such like: of the which I tell you before, as I have also told you in time past, that they which do such things shall not inherit the kingdom of God."

Envy has been the downfall and the defeat of many individuals, saints included. The brothers of Joseph envied him so much that they sold him into bondage (see Genesis 37).

It was because Korah, Dathan, and Abiram "envied Moses also in the camp" (Psalm 106:16-18) that they were swallowed up as the earth opened, and a fire was kindled in their company.

It was because "the Jews which believed not [were] moved with envy" (Acts 17:85) that they tried to kill Paul. It is often because of envy that mankind gets into trouble. James tells us: "Where envying and strife is, there is confusion and every evil work" (James 3:16).

No man is safe from this sin until he has learned to rejoice in the success of others. The musician who cannot bear to hear or see another musician praised is of small caliber. The scientist who is unliberal in his estimate of the accomplishments of other scientists is unworthy of the name. The preacher who is jealous of the success of other preachers and fails to give them due credit had better watch his own Christianity.

In *Canterbury Tales* envy is represented as of two species: "Sorrow at other men's weal [happiness] and joy at other men's harm."

DAY / 59

Read Numbers 17 through 19.

Today's reading points up the importance of following God's will in every detail. The influence we exert may lead another person to decide for or against the right.

Memory gem: "With my whole heart have I sought thee: O let me not wander from thy commandments" (Psalm 119:10).

Thought for today:

At a large evangelistic meeting, a well-known preacher made an earnest appeal for men and women and young people to surrender to Christ. A number came, and among them a girl of fourteen or fifteen years. But as she came, she kept looking back to someone still in the audience.

When the group arrived at the front seats, the minister asked them to remain standing a moment while he made a last appeal for still others to come forward. While waiting there, this young girl kept locking back, so pitifully—and suddenly she could wait no longer. She turned and went back up the aisle and sat down by the side of a man who, the minister later learned, was her father. The minister waited, not knowing what it meant. She put her arms about her father's neck, and one sitting just behind heard her say, "Papa, you and I promised we would meet her in the better world, when she left us last year, and I want to keep that promise. I went forward that they might pray for me—I thought you would come. We have stayed together since Mother died, and I could not stay down there without you. I want to surrender to Christ tonight, but I cannot go without you. Won't you go with me there where the others are—and, with me, surrender to Christ?"

And this big, strong man trembled. He was one of the judges of one of the high courts of the state, and he said, "Little girl, Papa will go with you. You are right."

And together they came and knelt down. And when the prayer was over, the minister said, "Who has given his heart to Christ?" And the judge stretched out his hand and said, "I have." And the girl said, "So have I, Papa!" And she kissed him again and again.

What if he had not come? Oh, friend, wait not for somebody else, because somebody else may be waiting for you! Your influence on the wrong side might mean eternal loss to someone.

DAY / 60

Read Numbers 20 through 22.

Today's reading has several poignant stories: the sin of Moses in striking the rock, Aaron's death, the fiery serpents, and Balaam's talking donkey, among others.

Memory gem: "As Moses lifted up the serpent in the wilderness, even so must the Son of man be lifted up" (John 3:14).

Thought for today:

People today want something deeper than the divine, something more profound than the infinite, something more liberal than free grace. Then it isn't long before evil lust, pride, and sin begin to do their work. The world's fashions and modes of thought lead on to the world's vices and crimes. Homes are broken up, lives are ruined, and thousands go on their way to eternal loss.

Here is an important point: Those ancient people in the wilderness were in trouble; they needed something, and they needed it badly. They must have help. They actually had been bitten by serpents. So the Lord told Moses to make a fiery serpent of brass and put it on a pole, and if those who had been bitten would look upon it, they would live. This was not a matter of curiosity, but a matter of life or death; and only those who had been stung by the fiery serpents derived any benefit from looking at the brazen serpent.

Thousands are going to Christless graves, fatally bitten. There is no new sin in the world—there are just new names for it. Sin is a terrible disease which affects people everywhere—the old as well as the young. And so many neglect God's cure. They will not look at His antidote for the death sting of sin. The Bible says: "The wages of sin is death." But that is not all. It goes right on and finishes the sentence: "But the gift of God is eternal life through Jesus Christ our Lord" (Romans 6:23).

So I say to you today, Look to Jesus upon the cross for your salvation. You will see that sin is slain and hung up, as was the brazen serpent. Death was put to death, for we read in 2 Timothy 1:10: "Christ . . . hath abolished death, and hath brought life and immortality to light through the gospel."

DAY / 61

Read Numbers 23 through 25.

Today's reading continues the remarkable story of a man who professed to be a prophet of God while he stubbornly tried to work against God's will. Such a course could lead only to a tragic end.

Memory gem: "He hath not beheld iniquity in Jacob, neither hath he seen perverseness in Israel: the Lord his God is with him, and the shout of a king is among them" (Numbers 23: 21).

Thought for today:

Think of Balaam, the compromising prophet. He prophesied for God and the people who worshiped Him, but he was not ready to become an out-and-out supporter either of the man who hired him or of the Lord who warned him. He tried to combine the ways of the heathen with the ways of the Lord. He was a fence walker, a balancer. He wanted the best part of both—the good and the evil.

Balaam symbolizes the so-called broad-minded—yes, the very broad-minded. Philosophically he was a syncretist. He tried to mix everything up together and make it look good. But such a thing would have meant the end of the faith of Israel, and it will mean the end of Christianity today. As someone has said, "The modern follower of Balaam has an air of urbanity." He looks very modern, very sophisticated. He is the cosmopolitan who becomes spiritually a jellyfish. In it all "he betrays the integrity of his own soul and the integrity of " the Christian "religion."—*Interpreter's Bible,* vol. 12, p. 386.

What multitudes of people need to hear today is the call of Joshua, who said to the people of his time: "Choose you this day whom ye will serve; . . . but as for me and my house, we will serve the Lord" (Joshua 24:15).

DAY / 62

Read Numbers 26 and 27.

Today's reading includes the appointment of a new leader for God's people. He was a man who had proved his worth and received the reward for faithful service.

Memory gem: "He that is faithful in that which is least is faithful also in much" (Luke 16:10).

Thought for today:

One day while Napoleon Bonaparte was riding before his troops in grand review, his horse suddenly reared, pitched, and charged. He was about to lose control of his steed when a burly private leaped out from the lines, ran up, grabbed the horse's reins near his mouth, and stopped him in his mad dash.

The emperor showed hearty appreciation of this heroism by saluting and saying, "Thank you, captain!"

The private was quick in response. He returned the salute and inquired simply, "Of what company, sir?"

The emperor, highly pleased with this full faith and sincerity, resaluted and said, "Of my bodyguard."

The newly made captain walked over in the uniform of a private to the officers of the bodyguard and said as he saluted, "Your captain!"

The officer in charge returned the salute and asked, "By whose authority?"

Pointing to the emperor, the young captain answered, "By his—he said it."

The event was then closed. The whole transaction hinged upon faith in a man's word, and see what a change resulted. But, friends, it was not nearly so great a change as that which comes to our lives when we simply, sweetly trust our Prince, our Captain, our General, our divine Leader, the Lord Jesus Christ. It is not how we feel, but what He says.

DAY / 63

Read Numbers 28 through 30.

Todays reading returns to the theme of prescribed sacrifices in the ceremonial services. Let us remember that all this shed blood symbolized and pointed forward to that of Jesus as the Lamb of God.

Memory gem: "This is my blood of the new testament, which is shed for many for the remission of sins" (Matthew 26:28).

Thought for today:

Christ is our High Priest now in the presence of God for us, not in "the holy places made with hands, . . . but into heaven itself" (Hebrews 9:24), where He still pleads His blood in our behalf. Some people do not like to hear about the blood of Christ. They resent it. They do not want anyone to die for them. They want to work their own way to heaven; they want to make themselves good enough to be there; they want to make themselves moral enough to be saved. But here is the word of God in Hebrews 9:12: "Neither by the blood of goats and calves, but by his own blood he entered in once into the holy place, having obtained eternal redemption for us."

Jesus is our High Priest of good things to come. My friend, do you not wish to share these good things—cleansing from your sins, the blotting out of your sins, a part in the full atoning sacrifice of the cross, peace which passeth understanding, the guidance and leading of the Holy Spirit, the resurrection from the dead, a place with Christ forever? The apostolic writer tells us that if the blood of the animal sacrifice in the temple of old sanctified to the purifying of the flesh in the symbolic service, "how much more shall the blood of Christ, who through the eternal Spirit offered himself without spot to God, purge your conscience from dead works to serve the living God?" (Hebrews 9:14).

Will you today accept this blood-bought salvation?

DAY / 64

Read Numbers 31 and 32.

Today's reading demonstrates the sad results of the persisting in an evil course. Another episode shows how easy it is to misjudge motives.

Memory gem: "As the Lord hath said unto thy servants, so will we do" (Numbers 32:31).

Thought for today:

"God had sent judgments upon Israel for yielding to the enticements of the Midianites; but the tempters were not to escape the wrath of divine justice. The Amalekites, who had attacked Israel at Rephidim, falling upon those who were faint and weary behind the host, were not punished till long after; but the Midianites who seduced them into sin were speedily made to feel God's judgments, as being the more dangerous enemies. 'Avenge the children of Israel of the Midianites' (Numbers 31:2), was the command of God to Moses; 'afterward shalt thou be gathered unto thy people.' This mandate was immediately obeyed. One thousand men were chosen from each of the tribes and sent out under the leadership of Phinehas. 'And they warred against the Midianites, as the Lord commanded Moses. . . . And they slew the kings of Midian, beside the rest of them that were slain; . . . five kings of Midian: Balaam also the son of Beor they slew with the sword.' Verses 7, 8. The women also, who had been made captives by the attacking army, were put to death at the command of Moses, as the most guilty and most dangerous of the foes of Israel.

"Such was the end of them that devised mischief against God's people. Says the psalmist: 'The heathen are sunk down in the pit that they made: in the net which they hid is their own foot taken.' Psalm 9:15. 'For the Lord will not cast off his people, neither will he forsake his inheritance. But judgment shall return unto righteousness.' When men 'gather themselves together against the soul of the righteous,' the Lord 'shall bring upon them their own iniquity, and shall cut them off in their own wickedness.' Psalm 94:14, 15, 21, 23." —*Patriarchs and Prophets,* p. 456.

DAY / 65

Read Numbers 33 and 34.

Today's reading gives a stage-by-stage account of the Irsaelite campsites during their wanderings. Unfortunately, most of the locations cannot now be identified..

Memory gem: "We, according to his promise, look for new heavens and a new earth, wherein dwelleth righteousness" (2 Peter 3:13).

Thought for today:

As we go on our pilgrimage in this earth just as God's children of old, we know that someday it will belong to His people. Someday they will enjoy it; someday it will be purified and redeemed; someday it will be restored to its Edenic beauty. We are told in plain words of Scripture that this earth, renewed by the hand of God, will be pure and holy. We are told that He Himself will be their God. We also read that "God shall wipe away all tears from their eyes; and there shall be no more death, neither sorrow, nor crying, neither shall there be any more pain; for the former things are passed away" (Revelation 21:4).

This is something to look forward to, isn't it? This is the end of our pilgrimage, the land where dreams come true. And the Holy City, the New Jerusalem which comes down from God out of heaven, will be the capital of the redeemed world—the real, actual, deathless, sinless, immortal world!

Friend, soon the present weary land will be past, our desert wanderings will be over, and all the pilgrims of earth will be home, safe at last.

DAY / 66

Read Numbers 35 and 36.

Today's reading gives instruction for providing forty-eight cities for the Levites, six of them cities of refuge. We also read the conclusion to the interesting story about five unmarried girls and their father's inheritance.

Memory gem: "The Lord is my rock, and my fortress, and my deliverer; . . . he is my . . . refuge, my saviour; thou savest me from violence" (2 Samuel 22:3).

Thought for today:

We read the story of the cities of refuge in three chapters of the Bible—Numbers 35, Deuteronomy 19, and Joshua 20. These cities were necessary because of the ancient custom of private vengeance, by which the nearest relative of a slain person took the responsibility of punishing the murderer. The original law, found in Genesis 9:6, decreed that "whoso sheddeth man's blood, by man shall his blood be shed"; and it was considered in ancient times in the East, and in some places even to this day, that the nearest of kin should avenge the deceased. As many rash executions of this law might take place in the heat of anger, and because a careful distinction between intentional and unintentional killing was not always made, these cities of refuge were instituted to provide for the proper administration of justice.

The cities of refuge were so located as to be within half a day's journey from every part of the land. That is, no one lived more than a half-day's journey from at least one of them. There were six cities of refuge—three on the east side of the Jordan River and three on the west side. Open roads leading to them were always kept in repair and were posted with signs bearing in plain, bold letters the one word "REFUGE" so that a man fleeing for his life would not miss the way nor be delayed for even a moment.

Brother man, flee now to Jesus, the City of Refuge; for the avenger of blood seeks your soul. Don't walk—run, flee, seek refuge now. As the old spiritual puts it, "You better run, you better run to the city of refuge."

DAY / 67

Read Deuteronomy 1 and 2.

Today's reading: The book of Deuteronomy records Moses' farewell to his people. Imagine the old leader—twice as old as the "elders" of the people (except two, Joshua and Caleb)—as he pours out his heart to them. He wants them to remember the lessons of the past.

Memory gem: "The Lord thy God hath blessed thee in all the works of thy hand: he knoweth thy walking through this great wilderness: these forty years the Lord thy God hath been with thee; thou hast lacked nothing" (Deuteronomy 2:7).

Thought for today:

As a leader appointed by God, Moses had led the host of Israel "out of the land of Egypt, out of the house of bondage" (Exodus 20:2). To deliver more than two million slaves from the oppression of the strongest military power on earth was a deed to be remembered as long as time should last. It took courage, intelligence, wisdom, humility, and, above all, faith—faith in the living God. Moses had all these virtues and more. He was a prophet of God and wrote the first five books of the Bible as he was moved by the Holy Ghost (see 2 Peter 1:21). Through him mighty miracles of divine power were performed. The Ten Commandments, written on two tables of stone by the finger of God Himself, were handed to Moses on Mount Sinai. He was God's appointed leader of God's appointed people, at God's appointed time.

Note: **The Four Orations of Deuteronomy**

I. Chapters 1:6 to 4:43.
III. Chapters 5 through 26.
IV. Chapters 27 and 28.
V. Chapters 29 and 30.

(The last four chapters of Deuteronomy concern the transfer of leadership from Moses to Joshua, Moses' song of victory, his words of farewell, and an epilogue, probably written by Joshua.)

DAY / 68

Read Deuteronomy 3 and 4.

Today's reading gives us an insight into the close relationship between Moses and the Lord. Tucked in between military records and solemn warnings is a pathetic prayer and the Lord's response.

Memory gem: "I pray thee, let me go over, and see the good land that is beyond Jordan, that goodly mountain, and Lebanon" (Deuteronomy 3:25).

Thought for today:

Poor Moses! He was human. Like so many of us, he spoke "unadvisedly with his lips" (Psalm 106:33). Someone says, "Well, Moses had enough to provoke him." Yes, he did indeed—more than enough—but that was no excuse for sin. "Ye rebels," he said. Well, they were rebels; but it was God's authority, not his, to say it. Even truth is not to be spoken in passion and impatience.

"Must *we* fetch you water out of this rock?" Moses asked. Numbers 20:10. Here he failed to give glory to God, who alone could give water in the wilderness; and, by smiting the rock the second time, Moses took away the force of the lesson which the Lord designed to teach His people. Christ is the true Rock. And the rock, being a symbol of Christ, had been smitten once, just as Christ was to be offered only once. The second time it was necessary only to speak to the rock, as we too have only to ask for blessings in the name of Jesus. So you see, by smiting the rock twice, Moses marred the symbolism representing Christ.

Sin is sin, and God does not play favorites. He is "no respecter of persons" (Acts 10:34). In his life and death, Moses teaches us that no transgression escapes its appropriate punishment. "The wages of sin is death" (Romans 6:23). The loftiest saint who disobeys does not escape the law of retribution.

Friend, let us learn from this story of Moses that sin is sin; that God's law is immutable; but that, through Christ's atoning blood shed for us upon the cross, God's grace is greater than all our sin; that we may find forgiveness and eternal salvation in Him.

DAY / 69

Today's reading includes a repetition of the Ten Commandments and gives some good advice to parents.

Memory gem: "Know therefore that the Lord thy God, he is God, the faithful God, which keepeth covenant and mercy with them that love him and keep his commandments to a thousand generations" (Deuteronomy 7:9).

Thought for today:

In 1 John 3:4 we read that "sin is the transgression of the law." But Jesus came to save us from our sins—in other words, our transgression of the law. This shows His relationship to God's law, or the Ten Commandments. If Christ did not consider the law of God to be the very character of God Himself, He would not have come to this world to die for the sins of men. It is good for us to remember that the cross of Jesus is the absolute proof of the eternal validity of the Ten Commandments.

In Christ's time there were people who hated the Ten Commandments, just as there are today. One modern writer and would-be political aspirant in the United States said some time ago: "There is no law save the law of man's own being; no check upon his will save that which he himself imposes. True pleasure is the end of being."

On the other hand, it is written in the Scriptures: "It is time for thee, Lord, to work: for they have made void thy law" (Psalm 119:126).

One of the latest of these godless theories comes from the realm of science. A professor of an institute of scientific learning diagnoses the whole thing this way: "Crime is simply the result of too much pyruvic acid in one's thalamus cells; or it may be from no cocarboxylase operating in the thalamus and not enough acetylchlorine being delivered to the midbrain." But the apostle said: "Sin is the transgression of the law," not a physical defect.

The Lord never says "must not" about anything that is harmless or good. But He has put up some warning signs which are like lighthouses. These signs say: "This is a bad place—keep out. Danger—you will wreck your ship." The Ten Commandments are God's lighthouse. They help us to sail our bark past places that would wreck our lives.

DAY / 70

Read Deuteronomy 8 through 10.

Today's reading: Moses recalls the worship of the golden calf and the breaking of the stone tablets at Sinai almost forty years earlier.

Memory gem: "The Lord your God is God of gods, and Lord of lords, a great God, a mighty, and a terrible, which regardeth not persons, nor taketh reward" (Deuteronomy 10:17).

Thought for today:

After the people had gone through their purification, and the sacrifices had been offered in their behalf for the sin of worshiping the golden calf, what did the Lord tell Moses to do? He instructed Moses to make two new tables of stone. God had made the first tables, but Moses made the second tables.

Moses cut out of stone two tables, just like the first, and took them up to God on the mountain. There God wrote on them the words that were on the first tables.

Friend, did you ever stop to think what Moses had to do? He had to hew out two tables like the first. Suppose you had been in Moses' place, with broken and crushed pieces of stone lying at your feet, and God should say: "Now, you must cut out two tables of stone just like the first." What would you have to do first of all? You would have to get down on your knees and pick up those pieces, wouldn't you? You would have to pick up all the pieces and put them together in order to get the proper and exact dimensions—the length, width, thickness, and shape. Oh, I imagine Moses spent a good deal of time down there on his knees, bending over, poking around, picking up those broken pieces, and fitting them together. It was a big task. It was a humble work, humiliating work, back-breaking work; it was knee work. But he finally got the pieces together and the measurements taken. Then he had to find some stone, like the stone of the first tables, and go to work with a chisel and hammer and cut it out from the ledge, smooth it off, and prepare it. I often think what a job that was, carrying those heavy tables of stone to the top of Mount Sinai. It wasn't a notebook job; it was a great burden to be carried up that mountain. And there in the cloud and fire and glory, God wrote the words again.

DAY / 71

Read Deuteronomy 11 through 13.

Today's reading: Moses repeats warnings against various kinds of false religion.

Memory gem: "Ye shall walk after the Lord your God, and fear him, and keep his commandments, and obey his voice" (Deuteronomy 13:4).

Thought for today:

The Voice of Prophecy, we believe, is a part of the great world-wide proclamation calling men away from modern idols to the worship of the God who created all things. And just now, as the universe itself is seen to be greater than men ever dreamed, so our God is greater than men have ever known. The God who marshals the electrons in their ceaseless vibrations finds nothing too little in our lives to draw His interest, and the God who guides the constellations in their ceaseless march amid the uncounted universes revealed by modern astronomy is great enough to look after all of our affairs. Let us worship Him.

Where are the modern idols placed—these idols that usurp the place of the living God? In Ezekiel 14:3 we read the secret of their power: "Son of man, these men have set up their idols in their heart."

Modern men do not believe in the lesser gods of antiquity—the graven images, the sacred trees, the fetishes—but in spite of this fact, millions are polytheists. They no longer think of Mars as a person, of Saturn as a sacred deity; but men today worship the things for which these ancient pagan idols stood with the same devotion as was shown in the long ago. No longer do men bow at the shrine of Venus, the goddess of immorality; but the things for which Venus stood, still enslave and defile millions. Men today never dream of worshiping Bacchus, the god of wine and revelry, but he has never been shown greater honor nor had more willing worshipers, though they know it not.

This challenge comes to us today: "Fear God, and give glory to him; for the hour of his judgment is come: and worship him that made heaven, and earth" (Revelation 14:7).

Let us turn from these modern idols of the heart—turn to the living and true God as revealed in His Son, Jesus Christ.

DAY / 72

Read Deuteronomy 14 through 16.

Today's reading covers a number of the rules and regulations governing the Hebrew economy. Among other things it lists again the clean and unclean meats.

Memory gem: "Thou art an holy people unto the Lord thy God, and the Lord hath chosen thee to be a peculiar people unto himself" (Deuteronomy 14:2).

Thought for today:

The health laws written down by Moses forbade the use of unclean animal foods and particularly the flesh of swine (see Leviticus 11 and Deuteronomy 14). Dr. David Macht, a noted authority on drug and animal poisons, squeezed out the juices of more than seventy different species of fish and injected them into mice, and also used them in tests on seedling plants. Tissue extracts from unclean fish killed some of the mice and retarded the growth of the seedlings. Extracts from the edible fish were seen to have no injurious effects on either mice or plants.

It was not until 1847 that Joseph Leidy discovered in pork the parasitic worm *Trichinella spiralis.* If this is why the use of swine's flesh as food was forbidden by God in the law of Moses, we are not told; but certainly modern science has at least one good reason to be wary of it. Who wants to be infected by trichina worms? But the fact is that millions are and wonder what is wrong with them. Unless pork products are thoroughly cooked, there is always a dangerous possibility of trichina infection.

If any reader wishes to encourage himself to avoid the danger of eating such infected meat, I suggest that he write to the United States Department of Agriculture and request the bulletin on trichinosis.

One of the greatest prophets of the Bible wrote about certain ones who continually provoked the Lord to His face. You can read it for yourself in Isaiah 65, verses 3 and 4.

Difficult or obscure words:

Deuteronomy 14:2. **"Peculiar people"**—better: private or treasured, the real meaning of "peculiar."

DAY / 73

Read Deuteronomy 17 through 20.

Today's reading mentions again the cities of refuge that were to be established in the land.

Memory gem: "God is our refuge and strength, a very present help in trouble" (Psalm 46:1).

Thought for today:

Now let us look for a moment at the beautiful and pure gospel that is taught by the cities of refuge. The apostle seems to refer to them in Hebrews 6:18, when he says that "we might have a strong consolation, who have fled for refuge to lay hold upon the hope set before us." And in Philippians 3:9, he speaks of believers as being found in Christ. By the shedding of His own blood, our merciful Saviour has provided a sure retreat for the repentant transgressors of God's law. The refuge of Christ provides pardon for the repentant sinner, and here no power on earth can destroy him. Says the apostle Paul: "There is therefore now no condemnation to them which are in Christ Jesus, who walk not after the flesh, but after the Spirit" (Romans 8:1).

He who fled to the city of refuge could not delay. He had to leave his family, his house, his property, his job—everything! He had no time to say good-bye. His life was at stake, so he couldn't wait, or delay, or neglect, or procrastinate. He had to forsake everything and make one supreme effort to reach the city of refuge before the avenger of blood found him. He did not walk—he fled, he ran.

And so it is with those who are sinners, without Christ. Let me say just now: Do not wait—do not delay—"now is the accepted time" (2 Corinthians 6:2).

DAY / 74

Read Deuteronomy 21 through 23.

Today's reading gives us another look at the civil laws governing many aspects of community living in the ancient Israelite commonwealth.

Memory gem: "Husbands, love your wives, even as Christ also loved the church, and gave himself for it" (Ephesians 5:25).

Thought for today:

We are talking today about the victims of divorce. There are at least three, and others to a minor extent—the husband, the wife, and especially the children. Many a divorce could be avoided if the wronged party were willing to forgive and forget.

When a child is deprived of a father or mother, he is cheated out of half his home. Remarriage often occasions jealousy, so the child suffers mentally, spiritually, and often physically. He becomes baffled, ashamed, embittered. When he tries to hide the situation from his friends, maladjustments follow which affect his entire life as well as the lives of others with whom he comes in contact. Children desire to belong to somebody and to be somebody.

These children are "orphans of divorce." Without a doubt, a great deal of our modern juvenile delinquency comes from broken homes, and these orphans of divorce are more likely to acquire dishonest habits, lax morals, and perverted personalities than are children who have the security of a normal home.

Homelife is the foundation of civilization. It is the foundation of every solid nation. The breakup of the home, of which divorce is the outward evidence, is the great danger facing every civilized government on earth, directly or indirectly. The victims of divorce are not only the heartbroken husband and wife, embittered, skeptical, dissatisfied; the children uprooted and denied the association of a father or mother; but society itself, the world itself.

Difficult or obscure words:

Deuteronomy 22:19. **"Amerce"**—fine.

Deuteronomy 23:18. **"Dog"**—not a canine animal, but the "sodomite" of verse 17.

DAY / 75

Read Deuteronomy 24 through 26; Psalm 90.

Today's reading has instructions about being fair to the poor, to widows, and to servants. Tucked in among other civil laws we find a warning to deal justly in business. Also we read a psalm, apparently composed by Moses near the end of his earthly life.

Memory gem: "O satisfy us early with thy mercy; that we may rejoice and be glad all our days" (Psalm 90:14).

Thought for today:

"An honest man, according to Christ's measurement, is one who will manifest unbending integrity. Deceitful weights and false balances, with which many seek to advance their interests in the world, are abomination in the sight of God. Yet many who profess to keep the commandments of God are dealing with false weights and false balances. When a man is indeed connected with God and is keeping His law in truth, his life will reveal the fact; for all his actions will be in harmony with the teachings of Christ. He will not sell his honor for gain. His principles are built upon the sure foundation, and his conduct in worldly matters is a transcript of his principles. Firm integrity shines forth as gold amid the dross and rubbish of the world. Deceit, falsehood, and unfaithfulness may be glossed over and hidden from the eyes of man, but not from the eyes of God. The angels of God, who watch the development of character and weigh moral worth, record in the books of heaven these minor transactions which reveal character. If a workman in the daily vocations of life is unfaithful and slights his work, the world will not judge incorrectly if they estimate his standard in religion according to his standard in business. . . .

"It is not the magnitude of the matter that makes it fair or unfair. As a man deals with his fellowmen, so will he deal with God. . . . The children of God should not fail to remember that in all their business transactions they are being proved, weighed in the balances of the sanctuary."—*Testimonies,* vol. 4, pp. 310, 311.

DAY / 76

Read Deuteronomy 27 and 28.

Today's reading: Moses gives explicit instructions, including the words of blessing and of cursing that were to be used for the solemn service on Mount Ebal and Mount Gerazim when the Israelites entered the Promised Land.

Memory gem: "Blessed shalt thou be when thou comest in, and blessed shalt thou be when thou goest out" (Deuteronomy 28:6).

Thought for today:

In the Rocky Mountains of western Canada one comes to the Great Divide. In fact, you see a sign by the road, "The Great Divide"; but there is no great mountain. You are not climbing up a ragged cliff and looking thousands of feet on either side. You are not on top of a gigantic ridge. The change is so gradual you don't notice it. A little spring comes forth and trickles along and strikes a rock. Each drop of water seems to hesitate—one goes to the right side of this little stone, one to the left. That which goes to the left goes down to those great rivers which flow into the Arctic Ocean—into the frozen zone of ice and snow and cold, the long winter midnight. The other drop that hesitates finally turns to the right and goes down to the Fraser River into the Pacific Ocean and washes the shores of Hawaii and islands of the tropics.

There might be a Great Divide for you, just now. You may not know it, you may not feel it, and you may not even see it. You may be trembling on the great decision, the width of a hair, as it were, in your own heart. You might be a church member; but still some decision, which here and now at this moment may seem little, but could change your whole life for all eternity, for all ages to come.

Make that decision now. May the good Lord speak to your heart through His Holy Spirit. I only wish I could speak to you with the love and kindness and blessing and power of Jesus. May our dear heavenly Father help you to put Christ above all and at last be with Him forever.

DAY / 77

Read Deuteronomy 29 through 31.

Today's reading: Moses foretells the conditions that would come as a result of obedience or of disobedience.

Memory gem: "See, I have set before thee this day life and good, and death and evil" (Deuteronomy 30:15).

Thought for today:

Are there things in the Bible hard to understand? That is the way it ought to be. If the Bible were a common book, we would read it through once and understand everything in it. In Deuteronomy 29:29 we read: "The secret things belong unto the Lord our God: but those things which are revealed belong unto us and to our children for ever."

Sometimes young people go through a stage in which they feel confident of success in attacking any problem. They have an idea that things are different now from what they have ever been before. Of course, this is really a good thing, or they wouldn't have the faith and courage to tackle many great problems, to bring fresh viewpoints and energy to the task before them. This doesn't mean, however, that they are always wise and can settle every question. There is a great mysterious world around us which can be known only by revelation, and that from God. So it is good in youth to accept the Word of God and to find in it the answers to all life's problems.

Oh, friend, open up the Book of God and go deeper down for the truth and the light. From the dark unknown comes the light. In the beginning God caused the light to shine out of darkness (see Genesis 1:3). So in this great Book you will find where man came from—God created him. You will find where he is going—to heaven or hell. You will find how he should live—in the way of God's commandments. You will find how he may be saved—"by grace . . . through faith; and that not of yourselves: it is the gift of God" (Ephesians 2:8).

DAY / 78

Read Deuteronomy 32 through 34.

Today's reading brings us the song of Moses, his last blessing on Israel, and a sequel probably written by Joshua (chapter 34).

Memory gem: "There arose not a prophet since in Israel like unto Moses, whom the Lord knew face to face" (Deuteronomy 34:10).

Thought for today:

Moses climbed the mountain, from the top of which he could look across the Jordan into the Promised Land. He saw the land, but could not enter it. After this wonderful vision, he died there alone, with God Himself. "Moses the servant of the Lord died there. . . . And he [the Lord] buried him in a valley in the land of Moab, over against Bethpeor: but no man knoweth of his sepulchre unto this day" (Deuteronomy 34:5, 6).

What a story! No man was with Moses when he died. No man dug his grave. Satan knew his grave. Satan, the enemy of God and man, who had led Moses to commit the one sin that kept him out of the Land of Promise, contended for his body, as it is written: "Yet Michael the archangel, when contending with the devil he disputed about the body of Moses, durst not bring against him a railing accusation, but said, The Lord rebuke thee" (Jude 9).

Moses, the man of God, did arrive at last in the Land of Canaan. He was resurrected from the dead. How do we know this? The answer is, he appeared with Elijah (who never died and was taken to heaven by translation) on the mount of transfiguration, to speak with Jesus Christ, our Lord, as recorded in Luke 9.

Just think of it. Moses, who was not permitted to enter the Promised Land because of his sin at the waters of strife, was by the grace of God raised from the dead and permitted to appear on the mount of transfiguration in the Land of Canaan. He encouraged Jesus as He faced His death on the cross. Moses, a man raised from the dead, could speak with Jesus and encourage Him.

Difficult or obscure words:

Deuteronomy 32:4. **"Rock"**—the first of thirty Old Testament uses of this word in reference to the Lord. The Bible specifically states that the Rock was Christ. See 1 Corinthians 10:4.

Deuteronomy 32:15. **"Jeshurun"**—a poetical name for Israel.

Deuteronomy 32:44. **"Hoshea"**—Joshua.

DAY / 79

Read Psalm 119:1-88.

Today's reading takes another departure from the strictly historical narrative. We have finished the books of Moses; it is appropriate that we consider the psalmist's evaluation of God's Word—His recorded communication with humanity.

Memory gem: "Open thou mine eyes, that I may behold wondrous things out of thy law" (Psalm 119:18).

Thought for today:

A colporteur selling Bible portions was held up at the point of a revolver in a Sicilian forest in the dead of night and ordered to light a bonfire and burn his books. Having made the fire, he asked if he might read a brief selection from each book before consigning it to the flames. From one he read the twenty-third psalm, from another the parable of the Good Samaritan, from another the Sermon on the Mount, from another Paul's hymn to love, and so on.

After the reading of each extract the brigand who had held him up exclaimed: "That's a good book. We won't burn that one. Give it to me." In the end, not a book was burned but passed, one by one, into the brigand's hands. He then went off, books and all, into the darkness.

Years later this same man happened to meet the colporteur, but this time as an ordained Christian minister. Telling his story, he said, "It was the reading of your books that did it."

Yes, the Bible is a book that changes things—it changes people. Victor Hugo once said, "England has two books—one which she made, and the other which made her—Shakespeare and the Bible."

Wherever the Bible has gone it has changed civilization by changing people. Why is this? If you want to start life over, if you want a new birth, then read the Bible, believe the Bible, obey the Bible. It is the living Word of God. Faith will grow in your heart. You will see that the Bible reveals a man—the Man, Christ Jesus—from Genesis to Revelation. If you will accept Him, the living Word of God, as your atoning sacrifice, as your Saviour and Lord, you will find salvation here and now. You will have joy here, and the certainty of everlasting life in the world to come. So, read the Bible!

DAY / 80

Read Psalm 119:89-176.

Today's reading: We read the last half of this longest chapter in the Bible—a poetic tribute to the value of God's Word.

Memory gem: "Thy word is a lamp unto my feet, and a light unto my path" (Psalm 119:105).

Thought for today:

The Bible changes things. When the crew of the *Bounty* mutinied and landed on lonely Pitcairn Island, they burned the ship to hide all trace of their existence. There were nine white sailors and seventeen Polynesians—six men and eleven women. One of the sailors discovered a method of making alcohol, and the island was soon debauched with drunkenness, vice, and bloodshed. Finally only one of the sailors survived, Alexander Smith, surrounded by the women and children. In one of the chests taken from the *Bounty,* he found a Bible and began to teach its principles to the people on the island, with the result that his own life was changed, and at last the life of the whole colony.

In 1808, nearly twenty years after the mutineers with their followers had landed on Pitcairn Island, the S.S. *Topaz* put a boat ashore there and found a prosperous community without drunkenness, without crime, without a jail, and with no insanity. The Bible had changed the life of that island, and it has remained a monument of God's grace to this day.

So it is in every age—the Holy Scriptures make things safe. They change things, they illuminate the dark places of the earth, as it is written in Psalm 119:130: "The entrance of thy words giveth light."

Difficult or obscure words:

Psalm 119:147, 148. **"Prevent"**—an old English word meaning precede; come or go before.

Note: In the Hebrew this psalm is an acrostic poem. Each of the eight verses in each section begins with the same letter. The twenty-four sections represent the twenty-four letters in the Hebrew alphabet.

DAY / 81

Read Joshua 1 through 4.

Today's reading includes Joshua's initiation as the new leader, the episode of the two spies in Jericho, and the dramatic crossing of Jordan.

Memory gem: "Be strong and of a good courage; be not afraid, neither be thou dismayed: for the Lord thy God is with thee whithersoever thou goest" (Joshua 1:9).

Thought for today:

In a real Christian home the children have the right to hear the voice of prayer, to hear Father and Mother pray for them, and to be taught to pray. When Robert Burns wrote his famous poem, "The Cotter's Saturday Night," in which he describes the scene of family worship in a humble cottage of Scotland, family prayers were commonplace. Read that wonderful poem again for yourself, and if you can do it with dry eyes, I'll be surprised. A real home should have family worship. It holds Father and Mother together, it makes every home a house of prayer.

When the people of Israel came into the Holy Land, they were instructed to destroy the military fortress of Jericho. Only one family was saved, a family that lived in a house on the city wall. Here are the instructions to the head of that house. They are found in Joshua 2:18: "Behold, when we come into the land, thou shalt bind this line of scarlet thread in the window which thou didst let us down by: and thou shalt bring thy father, and thy mother, and thy brethren, and all thy father's household, home unto thee."

Let us notice this one point: The folks who came to that home and shut the doors about them in wicked old Jericho were safe when the scarlet thread was in the window. And so every true home is a place of safety when the scarlet thread of Christ's blood is in the window, and where those in charge of the home are Christians whose hope is in the sacrifice of Jesus upon Calvary. When the home is protected by this scarlet thread, there is safety within. Gather the children in, fathers and mothers, grandfathers and grandmothers, and protect them with the scarlet thread of faith in Christ as our Redeemer. That is the only hope of a lost and ruined world, but it is a gloriously sufficient hope.

DAY / 82

Read Joshua 5 through 7.

Today's reading recounts the dramatic fall of Jericho and the results of Achan's tragic sin.

Memory gem: "Take heed, and beware of covetousness: a man's life consisteth not in the abundance of the things which he possesseth" (Luke 12:15).

Thought for today:

Covetousness is a "respectable" sin. It is a sin we are afraid to mention. It is like pride. Even church members can be guilty of it and not know it. No doubt many who are covetous do not realize that they are. That is why they never confess their sin of covetousness. It is deceitful and prevalent.

Covetousness dries up the resources of the church, holds back the gospel, paralyzes foreign missions. Covetousness deadens the soul to the influence of the Holy Spirit, dries up the milk of human kindness. Covetousness, being a form of idolatry, sets up another god in the heart (see Colossians 3:5). This is why it is such a great sin—it takes the place of the true God and Jesus Christ, our Lord. Covetousness caused the fall of Lucifer and made the cross necessary. Covetousness has ruined churches and homes and nations. It has blighted millions. Covetousness, the original sin of Lucifer in heaven and of Eve in Eden, is the fundamental rebellion against God.

God gave heaven's greatest gift for our salvation. Jesus Christ, our Lord, gave Himself for our redemption. The cure for covetousness is true regeneration and conversion by the power of the Spirit of God. Then, those who are born as the sons of God may walk in the Spirit of the Lord Jesus Christ, who, though He was rich, became poor that we through His poverty might become rich (see 2 Corinthians 8:9).

Let us seek God for victory over selfishness and the sin we are afraid to mention.

Difficult or obscure words:

Joshua 6:9. **"Rereward"**—an obsolete English word meaning rear guard.

DAY / 83

Read Joshua 8 and 9.

Today's reading tells of a quick plunge from the flush of victory (under the Lord's direction) to the chagrin of falling into a clever deception (without consulting the Lord).

Memory gem: "Trust in the Lord with all thine heart; and lean not unto thine own understanding" (Proverbs 3:5).

Thought for today:

"The Gibeonites had pledged themselves to renounce idolatry, and accept the worship of Jehovah; and the preservation of their lives was not a violation of God's command to destroy the idolatrous Canaanites. Hence the Hebrews had not by their oath pledged themselves to commit sin. And though the oath had been secured by deception, it was not to be disregarded. The obligation to which one's word is pledged—if it do not bind him to perform a wrong act—should be held sacred. No consideration of gain, of revenge, or of self-interest can in any way affect the inviolability of an oath or pledge. 'Lying lips are abomination to the Lord.' Proverbs 12:22. He that 'shall ascend into the hill of the Lord,' and 'stand in his holy place,' is 'he that sweareth to his own hurt, and changeth not.' Psalms 24:3; 15:4.

"The Gibeonites were permitted to live, but were attached as bondmen to the sanctuary, to perform all menial services. 'Joshua made them that day hewers of wood and drawers of water for the congregation, and for the altar of the Lord' [Joshua 9:27]. These conditions they gratefully accepted, conscious that they had been at fault, and glad to purchase life on any terms. 'Behold, we are in thine hand,' they said to Joshua; 'as it seemeth good and right unto thee to do unto us, do' [Joshua 9:25]. For centuries their descendants were connected with the service of the sanctuary. . . .

"They had adapted the garb of poverty for the purpose of deception, and it was fastened upon them as a badge of perpetual servitude. Thus through all their generations their servile condition would testify to God's hatred of falsehood."—*Patriarchs and Prophets,* pp. 506, 507.

DAY / 84

Read Joshua 10 through 12.

Today's reading condenses into three chapters the account of Joshua's campaigns to conquer the whole of Canaan. It includes the famous episode of the long day.

Memory gem: "There was no day like that before it or after it, that the Lord hearkened unto the voice of a man: for the Lord fought for Israel" (Joshua 10:14).

Thought for today:

We owe our present calendar to the Romans, as is clearly shown by the Latin names given to the twelve months. Although several different systems of calendation have been and still are used in the world, yet the continuity of the cycle of the seven-day week has been preserved without disruption, and in perfect synchronization by nations around the world.

In Bible times the Jews had a sacred or ecclesiastical year which began in the month Abib, about our April, and a civil year which began six months later in the fall. New Year's Day might fall on any day of the week, just as our January 1 may come on Sunday, Monday, or any other day of the week. The seven-day cycle of days has come down to us unaltered from the very beginning of history. It has been unaffected by the many changes that have otherwise taken place in the calendar.

Dates may change; new calendars, new calendar arrangements come and go, but they have not broken the weekly cycle. Yesterday, today, and tomorrow are established in their natural order: Sunday, Monday, Tuesday, Wednesday, Thursday, Friday, Saturday go on their way, unmovably and fixedly. As the seventh-day Sabbath is in this changeless weekly cycle, men have never lost track of it.

Note: Nothing in the record of the long day indicates any disruption of the weekly cycle. The day is measured by the complete period between one sunset and the next. The extension of daylight several extra hours simply delayed the beginning of the next day; therefore, the order of the days of the week was not altered.

DAY / 85

Read Joshua 13 through 15:19.

Today's reading, concerned as it is with dividing the Land of Canaan among the tribes, contains a heartwarming story about faithful old Caleb and his family.

Memory gem: "Well done, good and faithful servant; thou hast been faithful over a few things, I will make thee ruler over many things: enter thou into the joy of thy lord" (Matthew 25:23).

Thought for today:

"Before the distribution of the land had been entered upon, Caleb, accompanied by the heads of his tribe, came forward with a special claim. Except Joshua, Caleb was now the oldest man in Israel. Caleb and Joshua were the only ones among the spies who had brought a good report of the Land of Promise, encouraging the people to go up and possess it in the name of the Lord. Caleb now reminded Joshua of the promise then made, as the reward of his faithfulness. . . . He therefore presented a request that Hebron be given him for a possession. Here had been for many years the home of Abraham, Isaac, and Jacob; and here, in the cave of Machpelah, they were buried. Hebron was the seat of the dreaded Anakim, whose formidable appearance had so terrified the spies, and through them destroyed the courage of all Israel. This, above all others, was the place which Caleb, trusting in the strength of God, chose for his inheritance. . . .

"His claim was immediately granted. To none could the conquest of this giant stronghold be more solely entrusted.

"Caleb's faith now was just what it was when his testimony had contradicted the evil report of the spies. . . . Caleb did not ask for himself a land already conquered, but the place which above all others the spies had thought it impossible to subdue. By the help of God he would wrest this stronghold from the very giants whose power had staggered the faith of Israel. It was no desire for honor or aggrandizement that prompted Caleb's request. The brave old warrior was desirous of giving to the people an example that would honor God, and encourage the tribes fully to subdue the land which their fathers had deemed unconquerable."—*Patriarchs and Prophets,* pp. 511–513.

DAY / 86

Read Joshua 15:20 through chapter 18.

Today's reading continues the description of tribal boundaries. In the midst of this territorial business we find a brief mention of setting up the tabernacle in a permanent location.

Memory gem: "The whole congregation of the children of Israel assembled together at Shiloh, and set up the tabernacle of the congregation there" (Joshua 18:1).

Thought for today:

"Heretofore Gilgal had been the headquarters of the nation and the seat of the tabernacle. But now the tabernacle was to be removed to the place chosen for its permanent location. This was Shiloh, a little town in the lot of Ephraim. It was near the center of the land, and was easy of access to all the tribes. Here a portion of country had been thoroughly subdued, so that the worshipers would not be molested. 'And the whole congregation of the children of Israel assembled together at Shiloh, and set up the tabernacle of the congregation there.' The tribes that were still encamped when the tabernacle was removed from Gilgal followed it, and pitched near Shiloh. Here these tribes remained until they dispersed to their possessions.

"The ark remained at Shiloh for three hundred years, until, because of the sins of Eli's house, it fell into the hands of the Philistines, and Shiloh was ruined. The ark was never returned to the tabernacle here, the sanctuary service was finally transferred to the temple at Jerusalem, and Shiloh fell into insignificance. There are only ruins to mark the spot where it once stood. Long afterward its fate was made use of as a warning to Jerusalem. 'Go ye now unto my place which was in Shiloh,' the Lord declared by the prophet Jeremiah, 'where I set my name at the first, and see what I did to it for the wickedness of my people Israel. . . . Therefore will I do unto this house, which is called by my name, wherein ye trust, and unto the place which I gave to you and to your fathers as I have done to Shiloh.' Jeremiah 7:12-14."—*Patriarchs and Prophets,* pp. 514, 515.

DAY / 87

Read Joshua 19 through 21.

Today's reading completes the dividing of the Land of Canaan, and then names the six cities of refuge and the other cities given to the Levites throughout the land.

Memory gem: "In the fear of the Lord is strong confidence: and his children shall have a place of refuge" (Proverbs 14:26).

Thought for today:

The safety afforded by the city of refuge did not depend upon its wall, gates, or guards, but solely upon the divine appointment. So it is the word of God that gives us all safety in Christ, "for him hath God the Father sealed" (John 6:27).

All who flee to Christ will be received. All races, all classes, all kinds of people are invited—yes, urged to come. The Saviour says, "All that the Father giveth me shall come to me; and him that cometh to me I will in no wise cast out" (John 6:37).

As it was the death of the high priest which made the prisoner in the city of refuge free, so the death of our Lord Jesus Christ upon the cross was for us, and it sets the believer free from condemnation. God cannot overlook sin, the transgression of His commandments (see 1 John 3:4). Divine justice must be done, and the righteous sentence must be pronounced; but Christ Himself pays the debt and the sinner is set free.

My friend, are you in God's city of refuge? It is the only safe place in the world today. Has Psalm 142:4 been your experience? "I looked on my right hand, and beheld, but there was no man that would know me: refuge failed me; no man cared for my soul."

Has human refuge failed you? Have there been times when it seemed that no man cared for your soul? Well, there is a refuge—there is one Friend who cares. Just read the next verse: "I cried unto thee, O Lord: I said, thou art my refuge and my portion in the land of the living" (verse 5). There it is: the Lord is our refuge. As we read in another place: "In the fear of the Lord is strong confidence: and his children shall have a place of refuge" (Proverbs 14:26).

That's what a man needs when he is in trouble—"strong confidence" and a "place of refuge." And that's what you will find in Christ. I have found it so, and thousands—yes, millions—testify to the same blessed truth.

DAY / 88

Read Joshua 22 through 24.

Today's reading: We come to the end of another dedicated man's life. Joshua's farewell address sounds a challenge down through the ages to our own time.

Memory gem: "Choose you this day whom ye will serve; . . . but as for me and my house, we will serve the Lord" (Joshua 24:15).

Thought for today:

What multitudes of people need to hear today is the call of Joshua, who said to the people of his time: "Choose you this day whom ye will serve; . . . but as for me and my house, we will serve the Lord" (Joshua 24:15).

It was a compromise with the state and with pagan practices that brought the church into the great apostasy of the Dark Ages. It was compromise that brought ecclesiasticism into the church and destroyed the life of faith. Apostate Christianity and the ancient pagan Roman state were united in adulterous union. The emperors claimed to be Christians and by force compelled acceptance of religious doctrines. Christianity was poured into the grooves of pagan thought, rites, images, idols, and ceremonies.

Let me put the question directly to you, friend: Are you willing to be separated to God, to Christ? Are you willing to be His child? It is not always easy from a human standpoint. It means something to be a Christian. It means a change of life. It means a turning away from sinful practices. It often means being different. But here is the word of Christ, the warning of Christ, "Repent; or else I will come unto thee quickly" (Revelation 2:5).

Difficult or obscure words:

Joshua 24:2, 14, 15. **"Flood"**—Hebrew word used here in reference to the Euphrates River—not to Noah's Flood.

DAY / 89

Today's reading reviews, by three poetic passages, God's dealings with Israel from the Exodus to the days of the judges.

Memory gem: "Thou calledst in trouble, and I delivered thee; I answered thee in the secret place of thunder: I proved thee at the waters of Meribah" (Psalm 81:7).

Thought for today:

When you are in trouble, remember the Bible record of God's care for His people Israel. Read again the story of their deliverance from bondage in Egypt—the escape at the Red Sea—the bitter waters turned sweet—the guidance of the cloudy pillar—the miracle of the manna diet and water out of the rock. This is just a part of the story, but it's encouraging to keep in mind that these deliverances took place in the wilderness—in a desert land—a lonesome, gloomy, dangerous, desolate wasteland—a place where no human help was possible. Read it all over again, and you will find comfort in God's dealings with wandering Israel. When the waters are bitter to you and the thunders of trouble seem to roll about your head, you can turn to the secret place and find help in time of need.

Israel called when in trouble, and God answered "in the secret place of thunder." They cried to Him in their bitter bondage as slaves, and He answered in thunder and lightning in the plagues of Egypt.

Difficult or obscure words:

Psalm 105:22. **"Bind"**—better: instruct.

Psalm 105:22. **"Senators"**—literally: elders.

DAY / 90

Read Judges 1 through 3.

Today's reading: From the account of Israel's victorious conquest of Canaan we turn to one of the darkest portions of Holy Writ—the history of the judges. How soon after their settlement in the land the Israelites forgot God and turned to heathen practices!

Memory gem: "Then they cried unto the Lord in their trouble, and he delivered them out of their distresses" (Psalm 107:6).

Thought for today:

The Bible depicts men just as they are. It does not try to cover up the faults of good men, God's men, as a merely human book would do. It records Adam's fall, Noah's drunkenness, Abraham's lie, Moses' anger, David's impurity, Peter's denial. The Book tells the truth to make the record clear, but that's not the way man would do it. A famous portrait of Alexander the Great was painted with his head resting on his hand as if he were in deep thought, but really it was to hide an ugly scar on his cheek. Wilhelm, emperor of Germany, was photographed and painted in such a position that his withered arm would not show.

So it is with men, but the Bible paints men just as they are. It tells the truth. With its marvelous prophecies proved true by history, its fearless depiction of human character, its unbreakable unity, the Bible is the miracle Book of the ages, the Inspired Book of God's word to men. John Randolph said that it would have been as easy for a mole to write Sir Isaac Newton's treatise on optics as for uninspired men to write the Bible.

DAY / 91

Read Judges 17 through 19.

Today's reading: The two episodes recorded in Judges 17 through 21 occurred at some unknown time earlier in the period of the judges, probably even before Othniel became the first judge.

Memory gem: "Turn ye not unto idols, nor make to yourselves molten gods: I am the Lord" (Leviticus 19:4).

Thought for today:

It is easy for us to study the history of days gone by and to forget that the problem of idolatry is one that confronts us in this modern age. I have seen various kinds of paganism in different countries of the world. I have seen idolatry in its rankest forms. But, friends, let me say this: Idolatry is found in *every* country, not only in so-called uncivilized portions of the world.

We may not worship at a shrine in some pagan temple filled with graven images, but there may be false gods in the temple of our souls—yes, idols of the heart.

The worship of false gods in Bible times was repugnant to God. Just so, in the days in which we live, there are modern gods worshiped in the temple of man's heart, which are just as repulsive to God.

We sometimes forget that there are many kinds of idols and many forms of idolatry. Whatever or whoever we love and serve more than the Creator God is an idol. This is worshiping the "creature more than the Creator" (Romans 1:25).

Self-love always leads to self-worship and on to other sins. Self is the creature that is worshiped above all others, and this leads to the exaltation of other false deities. Many worship at the shrine of pleasure. This is a very dominant sin of the last days and is another species of idolatry.

We could go on with a long list of modern gods that are receiving obeisance from their followers. We must admit that the gods of self, appetite, pleasure, fashion—even the god of the cash register—are evident in this modern age in which we live.

Let us abolish the idols and images in our hearts and worship the true and living God, our Creator.

Note: See **Difficult or obscure words** on next page.

DAY / 92

Read Judges 20 and 21.

Today's reading: The sad chronicle of Israel's "ups and downs" under the judges ends on a "down," with the repeated alibi that "every man did that which was right in his own eyes."

Memory gem: "There is a way which seemeth right unto a man, but the end thereof are the ways of death" (Proverbs 14:12).

Thought for today:

The night was very dark. The road was unfamiliar. In fact, it was a wild, lonely road which became rougher and rougher as we proceeded. We were in the far, wild, mountainous interior of New Mexico. We had left the main highway, making a detour of forty or fifty miles, to enjoy some very fine scenery and interesting wonders of nature, intending to get back onto the main highway farther west. But we were disappointed. The road wound around hills and forests and lava flows for many weary miles—in some places deep in mud; in others, rugged with stones.

Now it was late at night, and suddenly, as we approached a dry arroyo, the road simply ended. A flash flood had washed out the bridge and cut a deep canyon, which yawned in front of us not twenty feet beyond the car in which we were riding. This was the end of our journey for that day. Here we had to spend the night and pick our way out of trouble the next morning in the light of day. The highway, though longer, would have been better. It was safer, faster, more certain. The obvious lesson of this experience is, If you want to arrive at your destination, keep on the highway.

Every one of us is a traveler. We are all going somewhere, fast. Every human being is on the highway traveling from yesterday toward tomorrow. Unfortunately, many are not on God's highway. Millions are wandering on byways, twisting and turning through the darkness toward Destination Unknown.

Let us open the Holy Scriptures and read a highway text found in Proverbs 16:17: "The highway of the upright is to depart from evil: he that keepeth his way preserveth his soul."

Difficult or obscure words for Day/91:

Judges 18:30. **"Manasseh"**—Strong evidence exists that this name should be "Moses"; in Hebrew the only difference in the two is the letter "n" in the longer name. It has been suggested that the letter may have been added by copyists in order to remove from Moses the stigma of admitting that his grandson was a renegade priest.

DAY / 93

Read Judges 4 through 6.

Today's reading: A dynamic woman encourages a timid soldier to lead his people into battle; then they sing a song of victory. Later, an angel enlists a reluctant soldier into the Lord's service.

Memory gem: "Oh that men would praise the Lord for his goodness, and for his wonderful works to the children of men!" (Psalm 107:8).

Thought for today:

Friends, before we can do any great work for the Lord, we must overthrow the idols in our lives and be ready to worship God in sincerity. Gideon had to declare war upon idolatry before going out to battle with the enemies of his people.

What followed after this is what will always follow when one obeys God in this way.

First, it made trouble. The men of the city changed their attitude toward him. They were ready to kill him.

Second, he received a changed name. His name was changed from Gideon to Jerubbaal, Baal's antagonist. You know, it is a blessed thing to be called a hater of false gods, an enemy of ignorance and superstition.

Third, Gideon was encouraged. The Scripture says, "The Spirit of the Lord came upon Gideon, and he blew a trumpet" (Judges 6:34). His fitness for the service of God was found only in the Spirit of God.

Convincing proof that the Spirit of God, and not the blind workings of chance, was leading Gideon, is found in the three miracles that were performed in connection with his call from God. First, the miracle of fire: When he brought the covenant angel an offering and placed it upon a stone, the angel touched it and fire broke forth from the stone and consumed the sacrifice. Then, the two miracles of the fleece: In answer to Gideon's prayer, the fleece which he had put out overnight was wet with dew, while the earth around was dry. Then the next night the fleece was dry, while the earth was wet with dew.

Every servant of God may have this threefold witness. The fire of God will burn. He will see the evidence of God's power working in hearts about him. Then, in his own heart, in his own life, he will see a twofold witness—God's Spirit within, and the special tokens of God's workings without.

DAY / 94

Read Judges 7 and 8.

Today's reading: We follow Gideon through a marvelous victory to an unexplainable lapse into idolatry. He failed to keep the light shining.

Memory gem: "O send out thy light and thy truth: let them lead me; let them bring me unto thy holy hill, and to thy tabernacles" (Psalm 43:3).

Thought for today:

Friends, what we need today is the glittering blade of God's divine truth, which is mightier than all the powers of darkness. And what a victorious and blessed day it will be for God's people when everywhere that unmistakable cry is given: "The sword of the Lord, and of His church!"

Gideon and his men blew the trumpets; they broke the pitchers; they held the lamps; and they shouted—those four things. Every man had a trumpet, a pitcher, and a lamp. Every man's faith was in the sword of the Lord. Every man sounded his trumpet as his own individual testimony, yet they all worked together. It was a united cry. The great battle was quickly won, and not one of the 300 struck a blow.

Oh, friends, lips telling the gospel of Christ in clear trumpet tones; the light and knowledge of God shining forth from broken hearts; Christ, the Word of God, uplifted—that's what will stir the world.

What was the source of Gideon's great triumph? The men were united. They had not only unity, but unison. They were obedient, and they were faithful. Every man stood in his place. But it was God who gave them the victory.

The world needs light. It has always needed light, but the need is greater now than ever before. The Word of God is light. "Thy word is a lamp unto my feet, and a light unto my path," we read in Psalm 119:105. And so every Christian should be a lamplighter, a lamp holder.

As in the case of Gideon, it is the responsibility of all God's people to turn on the light. The apostle Paul says in Philippians 2:15, 16: "That ye may be blameless and harmless, the sons of God, without rebuke, in the midst of a crooked and perverse nation, among whom ye shine as lights in the world; holding forth the word of life."

DAY / 95

Read Judges 9 and 10.

Today's reading: Shakespeare has Mark Antony say of Julius Caesar, "The evil that men do lives after them." This was certainly true of Gideon. The evil he introduced into Israel bore fruit in the foul deeds of Abimelech and the men of Shechem.

Memory gem: "Evildoers shall be cut off: but those that wait upon the Lord, they shall inherit the earth" (Psalm 37:9).

Thought for today:

If we reject, ignore, or forget the divine law, we must receive the consequences. As men sow, they shall reap—always. It is the law of life.

An old but true story is told about the influence a teacher has over a child. One day a Sunday School meeting was in progress. A ragged man was noticed sitting in a pew in the rear. Finally, at the testimony meeting, he rose and said:

"Look at me; I am a lost man. If the officers of the law knew where I was, they would be after me. I was one of five boys who attended Sunday School here, and our teacher, to make it more interesting for us in Sunday School, taught us to play cards. After a while, with us, it was more cards and less Bible, and finally, all cards and no Bible; and soon we had a system of our own, and went to gambling. We went from that to worse and at last committed crimes to make money. Two of the boys are in prison now, one was executed, and two of us are fugitives from justice. The police would be here for me if they knew I was here!"

He paused a moment, overcome by deep emotion, and added: "My father was the minister in this church, and our family sat in this very pew."

He left the church and was gone. As he left the building, a tall woman dressed in black arose in the front row and cried, "I was that boy's teacher!" And she fell to the floor unconscious. What an influence a sheep has on the lambs!

DAY / 96

Read the book of Ruth.

Today's reading gives us a charming story of old-fashioned love. These ancient loyalties and customs have solid value for our sophisticated society. The exact date for this story is unknown, but it probably occurred about halfway through the time of the judges.

Memory gem: "Whoso findeth a wife findeth a good thing, and obtaineth favour of the Lord" (Proverbs 18:22).

Thought for today:

Young people should have an ideal, and it should be a high ideal. An ideal concerning the man whom she would like to have as her husband or sweetheart should be set up in the heart of every young woman. Boys, in your mind's eye, you should have an ideal of the girl who is to be the woman of your choice, who is to have your supreme affection, and who, someday, is to carry your name. And you should see that that ideal is kept before you.

You say: "I want to meet that true ideal." She may not be in your school or in your life right now, but if you will be faithful, just as surely as God is love, He will certainly bring it to pass.

But, you say: "I have made my decision, but sometimes I wonder if I made the right choice for my ideal?" Well listen, friend, here is a great and comforting thing: God can give you a new heart and can give the one you have chosen a new heart. God can make a previous union ideal—by His creative power.

There are six marks of love, and you can surely know whether you have found your true love or not. It is sometimes very difficult to distinguish, but here are some sure marks:

First—an intense longing to do something for the one loved, and to give something without thought of return.

Second—love is utterly forgetful of self.

Third—a willingness to sacrifice without any return—real sacrifice. (This is the highest stage of the second.)

Fourth—love plays the part of the surgeon. Real love will take the knife and cut in deep to help the one it loves.

Fifth—real love longs for fellowship—spiritual as well as physical—with the object of its love.

Sixth—true love makes us want to be near the one loved. And this love will not vary with circumstances—not if God is in it.

Difficult or obscure words:

Ruth 2:2. **"Corn"**—grain, in this case, barley.

Ruth 2:8. **"Daughter"**—a respectful term used by an older person for a young woman—not necessarily a literal daughter.

Ruth 2:14. **"Left"**—that is, she had some left over after she had eaten.

Ruth 3:7. **"Merry"**—better: had a happy sense of well-being. There is no inference of intoxication.

Ruth 3:8. **"Afraid"**—startled.

Ruth 3:9. The Jewish Talmud explains Ruth's action as a proper proposal for marriage, a custom retained by some Arab tribes until modern times.

Ruth 4:3. **"Brother"**—better: kinsman.

Ruth 4:8. **"Drew off his shoe"**—The other kinsman took off his own shoe and handed it to Boaz as a legal release of all right to Elimelech's property—including Ruth.

TELL HER SO!

Once we make this mortal journey
Daybreak on to sunset glow;
By your side a comrade travels—
If you love her, tell her so!

When the road is bright and cheery,
Health and fortune you may know;
No one like a wife to share it—
If you love her, tell her so!

Though the way be dark and stormy,
And the tears of heartbreak flow;
She has shared your loss and sorrow—
If you love her, tell her so!

Say the words! She waits to hear them,
As you said them long ago;
Faithful then, and on forever—
If you love her, tell her so!

—H.M.S.R.

DAY / 97

Read Judges 11 through 13.

Today's reading: The exploits of Jephthah are recounted, as well as the results of his rash vow; then, after brief mention of three other judges, we come to the birth of one of the most remarkable of all—Samson.

Memory gem: "Teach us what we shall do unto the child that shall be born" (Judges 13:8).

Thought for today:

Let us go back, back to that day when a child was born in a land under terrible foreign oppression. It is the land of Israel. The oppressors are the Philistines. An angel appears to the childless wife of Manoah, who is a worshiper of the true God. The angel brings a message that a child is to be born who will begin to deliver Israel. In view of this, instruction is given as to the treatment of this child: "Now therefore beware, I pray thee, and drink not wine nor strong drink, and eat not any unclean thing" (Judges 13:4).

This same prohibition was imposed upon the child, with the addition that his hair should not be cut, for from his birth he was to be consecrated to God as a Nazarite. And, by the way, if more mothers were careful regarding their physical and spiritual habits, more children would be strong and healthy, wise and true. A mother cannot be uncontrolled and intemperate and expect the children to whom she gives birth to be any different. And fathers, as well as mothers, are involved in this responsibility.

The instructions given to these parents so long ago show the importance of home influence. Lessons of temperance, self-denial, and self-control should be taught children even from babyhood. The angel's prohibition included not merely strong drink, but every unclean thing. Right sanitary principles were involved. "True temperance teaches us to dispense entirely with everything hurtful, and to use judiciously that which is healthful."—*Temperance,* p. 138.

Difficult or obscure words:

Judges 11:2. **"Gilead"**—In this verse the term is the name of a man, Jephthah's father. Everywhere else in the story, Gilead is the name of the region east of Jordan in the territory of the tribe of Manasseh.

DAY / 98

Read Judges 14 through 16.

Today's reading: The story of Samson continues—his remarkable feats of strength, his utter failure to subdue his own sinful nature, and his inglorious death.

Memory gem: "Ye are bought with a price: therefore glorify God in your body, and in your spirit, which are God's" (1 Corinthians 6:20).

Thought for today:

There is an important lesson for us in Samson's death. No matter how you have failed God, no matter how you have broken your vows, no matter how far you have drifted from Him, no matter how low you have descended into sin, God, the Almighty One, through the merits of the Lord Jesus can lift you into victory and triumph, regardless of your past failures.

If anyone reading this has lived a life of defeat, God wants you to feel around for the pillars. Even now in your blindness when you can see no light, take hold of the pillars upon which evil men are standing and trusting for their strength, and God will give you supernatural power to bring those pillars down in your own life and in that of others.

When your life is fully surrendered to God and empowered by Him, you can do more for Him in the few remaining years or months or days than you did in your whole life before. God wants us to reach out and seize our opportunities to work for Him. So I want to encourage every one of you. You may have felt that there is nothing more that you can do, that you have failed God, that there is no hope for you. Go on praying, go on reaching out.

Remember Samson! Ask God to forgive you. Lay hold on His strength and power by faith, and He will turn your defeat into victory. If you will turn to Him, God will take the remnant of a lost life, which seems so small to you, and make it powerful in His service. Remember Samson, and feel for the pillars!

Difficult or obscure words:

Judges 15:8. **"Hip and thigh"**—a figure of speech of unknown origin meaning " completely " or " entirely. "

Judges 15:19. **"Hollow place . . . in the jaw"**—rather, "in Lehi," as in the last part of the verse. The name of the place, "Lehi," means "jawbone," and the same Hebrew word occurs in both parts of the verse.

DAY / 99

Read 1 Samuel 1 through 3.

Today's reading introduces us to one of the remarkable mothers of the Bible and her dedicated son—Hannah and Samuel.

Memory gem: "The child Samuel grew on, and was in favour both with the Lord, and also with men" (1 Samuel 2:26).

Thought for today:

Samuel's mother so impressed him with the thought that he was God's child that he grew up from a beautiful boyhood to be a holy prophet and an upright ruler. Each year the mother took him a "little coat"—surely it was simple and modest. She had too much sense to treat her boy like a doll or a plaything.

But the mother does more than clothe the body of her child. She forms his habits—clothes the soul for glory and immortality, or for degradation and death.

The coat of character is never worn out. She forms it, like Samuel's, thread by thread, stitch by stitch.

But, Mother, a stream can rise no higher than its source, and the *source* of life is in the mother—just as truly spiritually as physically. *What you are* trains and influences your child far more than what you command. What you are is largely what *he* will be.

Mother, give yourself to Christ. Then you can lead your child to Him. It is never too late to start. Even yet much can be done. He who knows a mother's desire to train her child aright says: "A new heart also will I give you, and a new spirit will I put within you: and I will take away the stony heart out of your flesh, and . . . will give you an heart of flesh. And I will put my spirit within you, and cause you to walk in my statutes, and ye shall keep my judgments, and do them" (Ezekiel 36:26, 27).

Here is a power within the reach of every mother—and it may be had *only* by asking—and believing—that "he is faithful that promised" (Hebrews 10:23).

Boys and girls (we are all boys and girls in our own hearts), we are fortunate, we are blessed, if we have a praying mother. If your mother is living, tell her you love her and prove it to her by your life. If she is far away, write her, not only on Mother's Day, but often! Every day is Mother's Day. Her love and prayers are worth everything to you and me!

DAY / 100

Read I Samuel 4 through 7.

Today's reading: The ark of God, irreverently taken out to battle as a sort of good-luck token, is captured by the enemy. God's judgments on the captors cause them to return it by unusual means.

Memory gem: "The Lord is a great God, and a great King above all gods" (Psalm 95:3).

Thought for today:

The people of Beth-shemesh were glad when the ark of God returned. They stopped their harvest work and offered a sacrifice. But they did something else—they looked into the ark, against the plain teachings of the Word of God. Even the heathen Philistines had not dared to remove its coverings. The irreverent daring of the people of Beth-shemesh was speedily punished, and many were smitten with sudden death.

The survivors, however, were not led by this judgment to repent of their sin, but only to regard the ark with superstitious fear. They wanted to be rid of its presence. So they sent a message to the inhabitants of Kirjath-jearim and asked the people to come and take the ark away. It remained there in the house of Abinadab about seventy years.

The ark was the symbol of the presence of God. Is God in your home today? Is your home blessed with the presence of the ark of God? Is it like the home of Obed-edom, with all the children gathered around the Word of God for morning and evening worship? Do they love Jesus? Is Christ the head of your house? Is He your best friend, loved by all?

If you wish your home to be a place where angels love to dwell, a little sanctuary, a harbor in the storm of life, then believe in Christ. By God's grace your home will be a place blessed with the presence of God.

Difficult or obscure words:

1 Samuel 6:19. **"Fifty thousand and threescore and ten men"**—The Hebrew of this verse is difficult to translate. Literally, "seventy men, fifty thousand men;" or perhaps, "seventy men, fifty families." Beth-shemesh was a small town, with a total population probably of not much more than fifty families. Some Hebrew manuscripts omit the words "fifty thousand." Most commentators believe that only seventy men died.

DAY / 101

Read I Samuel 8 through 11.

Today's reading: Weary of foreign oppression and convinced that a monarch would solve their dilemmas, the Israelites demand a king. Samuel reluctantly yields, but he solemnly warns of the consequences.

Memory gem: "The king shall joy in thy strength, O Lord; and in thy salvation how greatly shall he rejoice!" (Psalm 21:1).

Thought for today:

During the reign of Queen Victoria a Zulu king came to London to visit the "Great White Mother," as the Africans affectionately called her. The queen took him through London and showed him the great city and the treasures of the empire. When, toward evening, they returned to the throne room in the palace, this giant king stood before the queen with his hand upon his spear, and through his interpreters asked her for the secret of the greatness of her kingdom. He said: "White Mother, when I return to Africa and go back to my people and tell them of the things that I have seen here, they will not believe me. I would not have believed them myself had I not seen them. I would have said that they were impossible. You are just a woman, and your people are just men and women as my people are. We have taller, stronger, and perhaps even braver men than you have. We have more land; we are a large people. But tell me, What is the secret of your greatness, of your power?"

Taking her Bible from a small table beside her, Queen Victoria arose and, holding the Book out toward the Zulu chief, said: "This Book, O king, contains in its pages the foundation, the secret, the key to all the greatness and wealth and power of my empire. Take it as my gift to you."

And, friends, this Book which presents to us religious liberty in Christ, this holy Book of God, makes men great and nations great when they honor it. Yes, the price of heaven is Jesus. The price of soul freedom is the Saviour. Accept Him, the Son of God and Redeemer of mankind, who gives peace and liberty of soul. That is the message of this hour, the message that the poor, tired world needs.

DAY / 102

Today's reading: Israel's first king, Saul, soon brings trouble upon himself by his headstrong impatience. First he acts as priest when Samuel does not appear as scheduled; then he almost executes his own son because of a rash vow.

Memory gem: "God forbid that I should sin against the Lord in ceasing to pray for you: but I will teach you the good and the right way" (1 Samuel 12:23).

Thought for today:

Do you know, Christian friends, that we are actually sinning against God if we do not pray for one another?

How often wandering boys are held back from ruin by mothers' prayers. Dr. James McCosh, president of Princeton, had the custom of praying with members of the senior class before he bade them good-bye when they went out into the world. But a certain young graduate said to him, "I don't believe in God or prayer." The president was surprised and hurt, but he shook hands with the young man and wished him success.

Some years later, when Dr. McCosh was delivering a series of lectures in Cincinnati, a man came to him and said, "What is this I hear, Dr. McCosh, about your turning out infidels at Princeton?" Dr. McCosh was surprised and asked what he meant. The man gave the history of this student who had refused to pray with the doctor, saying that he had advanced to an important post in the schools of Cincinnati and was sowing the seeds of unbelief and infidelity everywhere. "But," the man added, "he has a godly, praying mother, and I believe that in the end she will win."

A year or two later Dr. McCosh was in his study in Princeton one day when a young man and his wife came to see him. The man said: "You don't remember me, but I am the student who refused to pray with you. I thought I was an unbeliever, and everywhere I went I spread unbelief. But all the time my mother was praying for me. Her prayers have won at last, and here I am to enter the seminary and prepare for the ministry. Before I go I want you to kneel down with me and my wife and offer that long-postponed prayer." Like thousands of others, he could say, "And though I wandered far away, my mother's prayers have followed me the whole world through."

DAY / 103

Read 1 Samuel 15 and 16; Psalm 23.

Today's reading: Saul's second great sin of open disobedience results in his turning from the Lord. God then indicates His choice of a shepherd boy to be the next king.

Memory gem: "Behold, to obey is better than sacrifice, and to hearken than the fat of rams" (1 Samuel 15:22).

Thought for today:

Consider the story of Saul from 1 Samuel 15—you all know it. God said, "Don't keep anything taken from the wicked Amalekites; none of their cattle, sheep, silver, gold—nothing." Saul goes. He keeps some of the best—he keeps this; he keeps that. He comes back. Samuel, the prophet, asks, "What does this mean, the bleating of the sheep? What did God tell you?"

Saul answers, "But, you see, to help God, I just kept some of the best stuff to offer, to put in the church collection. See? I am going to give it to God. That purifies it, giving it to God!" Not when you disobey God to get it, my friends.

When God eventually departed from Saul, he went—as many thousands have done; as one of my own relatives did—from a spiritualist's seance to a suicide's grave out on those dark hills of Gilboa, where he fell upon his sword when the Philistine archers pressed him in the heat of battle. Yes, my friends, God means what He says. "The way of transgressors is hard" (Proverbs 13:15).

DAY / 104

Read 1 Samuel 17 and 18.

Today's reading: The well-known story of David and Goliath describes the first public action to draw the people's attention to the talented shepherd boy.

Memory gem: "The Lord saveth not with sword and spear: for the battle is the Lord's" (1 Samuel 17:47).

Thought for today:

As David slew Goliath with the sword of Goliath, so Jesus slays Satan with the sword of Satan and delivers His people forever. Let us this day come to Him in faith, believing. Let us look and live. "Is not this the son of David?" (Matthew 12:23). Indeed it is. By faith, His victory is ours.

At last the great controversy between good and evil, the war of the ages, will be over, and the liberation of the world will come when our King returns in His glory. Then all men and angels will bow before Him, David's great Son, our Lord Jesus Christ, who is "God blessed for ever" (Romans 9:5). But are we the King's men now? Are we waiting and watching and preparing the way for Him?

DAY / 105

Read I Samuel 19 and 20; Psalms 58; 59; and 64.

Today's reading: David flees for his life from the insanely jealous Saul, and the darkness of despair engulfs him. Through this gloom shines the sustaining light of true brotherly love.

Memory gem: "I will sing aloud of thy mercy in the morning: for thou hast been my defence and refuge in the day of my trouble" (Psalm 59:16).

Thought for today:

In a southern city, a bright young mother was loving her little girl one afternoon—and that same night the mother was dead A child of six years was left without a mother. The young husband was heartbroken over his loss. The neighbors tried to comfort him and the child. They said, "Joe, you can't stay there tonight." But Joe said, "No, I'm going back to the room where she left me and fight it out tonight."

Soon the father heard the sobbing of his child, and he reached over, patted her in her little bed, and said: "Go to sleep, dear, Daddy is here—he loves you."

The father thought she was asleep, when he heard her little voice, "Oh, Daddy, it's so dark tonight." He tried to calm her; he told her he was with her. Pretty soon he heard that soft voice again, and again he told her to go to sleep—he loved her.

She said, "Daddy, I tried to because you wanted me to. But, Daddy, it is so dark tonight; it's never been so dark as this."

The father took the little child in his big arms and carried her right over to his bed. He tried to comfort her as her mother would have done, and pretty soon she was sound asleep on her father's breast.

Then the father started to talk to the heavenly Father above. Through blinding tears he said, "Oh, Father, it is dark, it's never been so dark before; but You love me, even if it is dark, don't You, Father?" And he felt a great peace in his soul, that was never born on land or sea, a peace that can be found nowhere but in Jesus. He found peace and rest in Jesus, the great Consoler, the Light of the world.

Dear friend, is it dark tonight? Do you want to step over the line and find Jesus before the final sounding of the trumpet? Do you want to say, "Father, it is dark, but You love me"?

DAY / 106 Read 1 Samuel 21; Psalms 34 and 56; 1 Samuel 22; Psalms 27; 52; and 57.

Today's reading: David, in his flight, receives help from the priests at the tabernacle and then goes on to live in a cave. Saul learns of the aid and orders the priests executed.

Memory gem: "I had fainted, unless I had believed to see the goodness of the Lord in the land of the living" (Psalm 27:13).

Thought for today:

A town in England had been bombed one night by the German Luftwaffe. When the workers were clearing away the debris in the days that followed, they found on top of a pile of rubbish a sailor's prayer book opened to Psalm 27. There verse 13 was marked: "I had fainted, unless I had believed to see the goodness of the Lord in the land of the living." This incident was publicized widely in Britain at the time, for it seemed to show the secret of endurance of that nation during the worst days of her trial and affliction.

The victory of life is not won by air fleets and armies. It must be won through faith, through repentance and turning back to God. And so, friend, do not faint. Have faith in God! The Christ who could forgive and love Peter and make him a great tower of strength in the service of the Lord will do the same for you and for me. Oh, be the man who cried out loud! Be the man who sorrows for sin. Be the man who repents with strong crying and tears, and you will be heard. Sincerity, wholeheartedness in forsaking the wrong and turning to God is what the Lord is looking for.

My dear friends, let us come back to hope, back to trust, back to prayer, back to faith, back to the Bible, back to Christ, back to the cross, back to salvation.

Difficult or obscure words:

1 Samuel 22:6. **"Ramah"**—The Hebrew word here is not a place name; rather, it means "height" or "high place." Saul could not be in two towns at the same time; he was in Gibeah (his capital city), sitting under a tree in the high place.

DAY / 107 Read I Samuel 23; Psalms 11; 31; 54; and 63; I Samuel 24; Psalms 142 and 143.

Today's reading: One amazing characteristic of David was his ability to maintain his trust in the Lord despite all the trouble that dogged his steps.

Memory gem: "Be of good courage, and he shall strengthen your heart, all ye that hope in the Lord" (Psalm 31:24).

Thought for today:

"Move forward courageously, assured that the Lord will be with those who love and serve Him. He will work in behalf of His covenant-keeping people. He will not suffer them to become a reproach. He will purify all who yield themselves to Him, and will make them a praise in the earth. Nothing in this world is so dear to God as His church. He will work with mighty power through humble, faithful men. . . .

"Difficulties will arise that will try your faith and patience. Face them bravely. Look on the bright side. If the work is hindered, be sure that it is not your fault, and then go forward, rejoicing in the Lord. Heaven is full of joy. It resounds with the praises of Him who made so wonderful a sacrifice for the redemption of the human race. Should not the church on earth be full of praise? Should not Christians publish throughout the world the joy of serving Christ? Those who in heaven join with the angelic choir in their anthem of praise must learn on earth the song of heaven, the keynote of which is thanksgiving.

"Never let your courage fail. Never talk unbelief because appearances are against you. As you work for the Master you will feel pressure for want of means, but the Lord will hear and answer your petitions for help."—*Testimonies,* vol. 7, pp. 242–244.

DAY / 108 Read 1 Samuel 25; Psalms 120 and 121; 1 Samuel 26; Psalms 16; 42; and 43.

Today's reading: Still David flees from one hideout to another, but he waits for the Lord to work out his deliverance—even when he could have killed his relentless enemy.

Memory gem: "Why art thou cast down, O my soul? and why art thou disquieted in me? hope thou in God: for I shall yet praise him for the help of his countenance" (Psalm 42:5).

Thought for today:

Turn now to the forty-second psalm and read the eighth verse: "Yet the Lord will command his lovingkindness in the daytime, and in the night his song shall be with me, and my prayer unto the God of my life." That's what I call happy living—loving-kindness all day long, God's song in the night, and prayer without ceasing.

Friends, we ought to fill our hearts with the Bible. We ought to memorize large sections of the Word of God so that in times of trouble, or when we are alone at night, these great words will come uncalled into our hearts and we can sing, not our song, but God's song. It will be with us in the darkest night.

Life is made up of tears and gladness, sunshine and shadow. Both have a part in our lives. When we find ourselves in the shadows, in the night, it is good to do what the psalmist did, as we read here in Psalm 77:5, 6: "I have considered the days of old, the years of ancient times. I call to remembrance my song in the night: I commune with mine own heart: and in my spirit made diligent search."

Remember what God has done for you in the past. Think about His great mercies to others, to His own people. That will give you courage and faith for the future. David goes on to say, "I will remember the words of the Lord: surely I will remember thy wonders of old" (verse 11). That's what we need to do. That will give us faith even in the night, so we can sing our song and His song in the darkest place.

DAY / 109

Read 1 Samuel 27 through 30.

Today's reading: David, in desperation, seeks refuge in Philistine territory—and almost finds himself warring against his own people. Saul consults a witch and hears his doom.

Memory gem: "Put on the whole armour of God, that ye may be able to stand against the wiles of the devil" (Ephesians 6:11).

Thought for today:

According to the Bible, who are the spirits of the unseen world? The Holy Scriptures describe spiritual powers of two classes: first, the good, called angels, whom God uses for the protection of believers; and second, evil ones who voluntarily departed from their original loyalty to God and have become rebels.

The Bible is a book of angels. It is filled with the stories of angel guardianship, angel care, angels communicating with the prophets of old in their holy ministry.

If the spirits who contact men in psychic and occult manifestations are not the returned dead, can they be good angels? No. These spirits claim to be the spirits of dead human beings and in doing so they tell a falsehood. They are impostors; therefore they cannot be the good angels of God.

The supernatural manifestations at the present time, as well as of ancient times, have three distinguishing characteristics:

1. They are invisible spirit beings, and only occasionally materialize, even then in an elusive form.

2. They are liars, impostors, for they claim to be the spirits of the dead who, according to the Holy Scriptures, cannot return to this world (see Ecclesiastes 9:5, 6).

3. They are powerful, intelligent, and capable of performing feats impossible for man. Scientific investigations have proved that many occult manifestations are unexplainable within the framework of known natural laws, and should be included among the phenomena called "miracles" in religious language.

The Bible says that Satan and his demonic spirits will act "with all power and signs and lying wonders" (2 Thessalonians 2:9), especially just before the end of this age at the second coming of Christ (see Revelation 13:13, 14).

It is our duty to stand against Satan's wiles, to "put on the whole armour of God," in preparation for the coming of the Lord Jesus Christ, who overcame the evil principalities and powers.

DAY / 110

Read Psalm 78; 1 Chronicles 3 and 4.

Today's reading: These long lists of names can become more readable if we realize the importance Hebrew people attached to names and genealogies. Try to think of the names as people.

Memory gem: "That they might set their hope in God, and not forget the works of God, but keep his commandments" (Psalm 78:7).

Thought for today:

In Bible times, a name really meant something, usually about the person named. It would be interesting to know how our names originated. Our ancestors in many cases were named after their trades; so we have our Smiths and Carpenters and Masons and Taylors and Hoopers, and many others. Some were the sons of distinguished fathers, and so we have the Johnsons, Williamsons, and scores of others. Some took their names from the place where they were born, so we have the Dutch van and the German van prefixed to names, indicating the town or family from which the child came. Indians sometimes named their children after some incident of their own experience or of the child's in its early surroundings. We have such names as Black Hawk, Laughing Water, Crying Thunder, White Eagle, etc., from some incident connected with the day of the child's nativity.

So names were given, and are given, for various reasons; but sooner or later they all come to stand for the personality of the persons bearing them. It is a fine thing when boys and girls really like their names, for a person will bear his name as long as he lives. It will be written on his marriage certificate, on the church register, and in a dozen other important records. It will be engraved on his tombstone, and may it also be written in the Lamb's book of life! (see Revelation 21:27).

DAY / 111

Read 1 Chronicles 5 and 6.

Today's reading: More names! But sprinkled along in these genealogies you will find interesting bits of history also. Look for them.

Memory gem: "To him that overcometh will I give . . . a white stone, and in the stone a new name written, which no man knoweth saving he that receiveth it" (Revelation 2:17).

Thought for today:

Did you ever hear of a man without a name? We sometimes hear of people who have forgotten their names or whose names for some reason are not known, and in such cases efforts are made at once to identify them. When a man's name cannot be found, we give him a name and call him Mr. X or John Doe.

Someone may ask, "But what's in a name, anyway?" And the answer is, "A good deal, usually." A man's name is the thing that sets him apart from all others and establishes his personal identity. The first question asked in any case of identification is, "What is your name?" The name you bear has a history behind it. And when we ask, "How did you get it?" you reply, "My father and mother gave it to me." Perhaps it is in honor of some great man or good friend, and every time it is spoken it memorializes noble deeds.

When we turn to the Bible we find that names, for the most part, were a declaration of the faith of men who feared God and received their children as from His hand and made in their names a dedication to Him. So Hannah names Samuel "God has heard," and Elijah means "Jehovah is my God."

DAY / 112

Read 1 Chronicles 7 through 9.

Today's reading finishes off the family trees. As we see how carefully the Hebrews preserved the names of their ancestors, our faith in the inspired Word should be strengthened.

Memory gem: "A good name is rather to be chosen than great riches, and loving favour rather than silver and gold" (Proverbs 22:1).

Thought for today:

Dr. Charles L. Goodell tells of meeting a mule driver in Palestine whose name was Abuscandra. On asking what it meant, he was told that it meant "the father of Alexander." The doctor thought that was strange, and told the man, "In America we name our children after their fathers, but here you seem to name the fathers after their children." And, you know, there might be something good about such a custom. If every father had to bear the name of his child, men would estimate his worth by the character of the children he had trained up for life. In that case, a good many fathers would probably give a little more time and attention to the most important job any man can ever have.

A good name cannot be taken away from anybody, because it represents character. No matter what enemies may do, the character represented by that name will stand until the judgment day. The one who trusts in God may always rest in the assurance of Job, who said: "Also now, behold, my witness is in heaven, and my record is on high" (Job 16:19).

By God's amazing grace, your name may be made more eternal than the stars of heaven. Are you a Christian? If so, you may be glad for the promise of your Lord Jesus Christ and rejoice that your name is written in heaven, as we read in Luke 10:20. And let us not forget that the power of Christ alone creates and sustains pure personality.

DAY / 113 Read 1 Chronicles 12:1-22; 1 Samuel 31; 1 Chronicles 10; 2 Samuel 1 and 2; Psalm 7.

Today's reading: Saul and all but one of his sons die in battle. Does David rejoice at the death of his enemy? No! Rather, he mourns. The people of Judah make David their king, but the other tribes at first accept Saul's son.

Memory gem: "I will praise the Lord according to his righteousness: and will sing praise to the name of the Lord most high" (Psalm 7:17).

Thought for today:

One of the most touching incidents recorded of the late Duke of Windsor, when he was Prince of Wales, tells of his visit to a small private hospital where thirty-six hopelessly injured and disfigured veterans of World War I were cared for. He stopped at each cot, shook hands with the veteran, and spoke words of encouragement to him. He spent about an hour doing this.

Finally the head nurse led him to the exit; but before leaving he said: "I understand you have thirty-six patients here. I have seen only twenty-nine." He was told that the others were hideously disfigured, and that was the reason he was not taken into their ward. On learning of this consideration for his feelings, he insisted on seeing them. He was led into the room and bent over every cot long enough to thank each soldier for the sacrifice he had made and to assure him that neither he nor England would ever forget it.

When he had finished, he said to the nurse: "I've seen only six men here. Where is the seventh man?" She replied that no one was permitted to see him. He was blind, maimed, hideously disfigured, and was kept alone in a room from which he would never go alive. "Please do not ask to see him, Sir," the nurse pleaded; but the prince insisted.

Reluctantly she led him to the darkened room. As the prince approached the bed, his face was white, his lips drawn. In that dim light he looked down and saw what had once been a man but now seemed only a horror. Tears came to his eyes. Then impulsively he bent down and kissed the cheeks of that poor broken hero. This was his tribute to the British Empire's 900,000 dead and her 2 million wounded men. You see, he did not forget his comrades in arms. He did not desert or betray them.

DAY / 114

Read 2 Samuel 3 through 5; 1 Chronicles 11 and 12:23-40.

Today's reading: David does not immediately become king of the whole nation. More than seven years of strife, intrigue, and heartache intervene before the people accept him.

Memory gem: "Wait on the Lord: be of good courage, and he shall strengthen thine heart: wait, I say, on the Lord" (Psalm 27:14).

Thought for today:

"After the death of Ishbosheth, King Saul's son, there was a general desire among the leading men of Israel that David should become king of all the tribes. Thus through the providence of God the way had been opened for him to come to the throne. He had no personal ambition to gratify, for he had not sought the honor to which he had been brought.

"More than eight thousand of the descendants of Aaron, and of the Levites, waited upon David. The change in the sentiments of the people was marked and decisive. The revolution was quiet and dignified, befitting the great work they were doing. Nearly half a million souls, the former subjects of Saul, thronged Hebron and its environs. . . . The hour for the coronation was appointed; the man who had been expelled from the court of Saul, who had fled to the mountains and hills and to the caves of the earth to preserve his life, was about to receive the highest honor that can be conferred upon man by his fellow man. Priests and elders clothed in the garments of their sacred office, officers and soldiers with glittering spear and helmet, and strangers from long distances, stood to witness the coronation of the chosen king. David was arrayed in the royal robe. The sacred oil was put upon his brow by the high priest; for the anointing by Samuel had been prophetic of what would take place at the inauguration of the king. The time had come, and David, by solemn rite, was consecrated to his office as God's vicegerent. The scepter was placed in his hands. The covenant of his righteous sovereignty was written, and the people gave their pledges of loyalty. The diadem was placed upon his brow, and the coronation ceremony was over. Israel had a king by divine appointment. He who had waited patiently for the Lord, beheld the promise of God fulfilled."—*Patriarchs and Prophets,* pp. 701, 702.

DAY / 115

Read 1 Chronicles 14; 2 Samuel 6; 1 Chronicles 13 and 15.

Today's reading: David decides that the ark of God should be moved to better quarters; a tragic episode interrupts proceedings, but God blesses one man's home while the ark remains there for three months.

Memory gem: "The Lord blessed the house of Obed-edom, and all that he had" (1 Chronicles 13:14).

Thought for today:

When people enter your house, they should know that it is a Christian home, for the presence of God is there. The Bible is on the table, and it is read to the whole family every day. The voice of prayer is heard there too. The children who go out from such a home are armored against the sin and trouble that they are bound to meet in this old world. In the days in which we are living now, there is a great need of a revival of home religion.

It is said that Coleridge, the poet, was once talking with a man who did not believe in giving children religious training. He thought that they should be allowed to grow up without any religious instruction so that they would not be prejudiced in any direction; then, when they come to the years of discretion, each should be permitted to choose for himself. The poet said nothing, but invited the man out to see his garden. There was nothing growing there but weeds—weeds everywhere! The man looked at his host in surprise and said, "Why, this isn't a garden; this is just a weedpatch." Coleridge replied, "Oh, yes, it's a garden. I am giving it a chance to express its own personality."

So, friends, like Obed-edom, we need the ark of God in our households. It would be good if the holy commandments of God were indeed engraved upon our doorposts, if we taught them to our children when we rise up and when we sit down (see Deuteronomy 6:7). Every home ought to be a Christian school. The same hand that punished Uzzah's proud presumption rewarded Obed-edom's humble boldness.

Note: "Nachon's threshingfloor" of 2 Samuel 6:6 is called "the threshingfloor of Chidon" in 1 Chronicles 13:9. This is one of many instances in the Bible of two (or more) names for the same person or place.

DAY / 116

Read 1 Chronicles 16 and 17; 2 Samuel 7; Psalms 24 and 132.

Today's reading: David, secure on his throne and dwelling in a fine palace, wants to build a house of worship for the God he has learned to love. His desire is denied him, and he has to be content with promises of blessing for his descendants.

Memory gem: "I will also clothe her priests with salvation: and her saints shall shout aloud for joy" (Psalm 132:16).

Thought for today:

"It was David's purpose to make Jerusalem the religious center of the nation. He had erected a palace for himself, and he felt that it was not fitting for the ark of God to rest within a tent. He determined to build for it a temple of such magnificence as should express Israel's appreciation of the honor granted the nation in the abiding presence of Jehovah their King.

"But . . . the word of the Lord came to Nathan, giving him a message for the king. David was to be deprived of the privilege of building a house for God, but he was granted an assurance of the divine favor to him, to his posterity, and to the kingdom of Israel. . . .

"David knew that it would be an honor to his name, and would bring glory to his government, to perform the work that he had purposed in his heart to do; but he was ready to submit his will to the will of God. The grateful resignation thus manifested is rarely seen, even among Christians. How often do those who have passed the strength of manhood, cling to the hope of accomplishing some great work upon which their hearts are set, but which they are unfitted to perform! God's providence may speak to them, as did His prophet to David, declaring that the work which they so much desire is not committed to them. It is theirs to prepare the way for another to accomplish it. But instead of gratefully submitting to the divine direction, many fall back as if slighted and rejected, feeling that if they cannot do the one thing which they desire to do, they will do nothing. Many cling, with desperate energy, to responsibilities which they are incapable of bearing, and vainly endeavor to accomplish a work for which they are insufficient, while that which they might do, lies neglected. And because of this lack of cooperation on their part, the greater work is hindered or frustrated."—*Patriarchs and Prophets,* pp. 711–713.

DAY / 117

Read I Chronicles 18; 2 Samuel 8 and 9; Psalms 60 and 108.

Today's reading: David searches for some remnant of Saul's house. Why? For vengeance? No! He wants to honor that person—a cripple!

Memory gem: "Thy mercy is great above the heavens: and thy truth reacheth unto the clouds" (Psalm 108:4).

Thought for today:

Before Louis XII became king of France, he suffered terrible cruelties and indignities at the hand of his cousin, Charles VIII. He was slandered, thrown into prison, and was in constant fear of death. However, when he became king himself and his close friends urged him to avenge himself for this shameful abuse, he would not heed any of their suggestions.

His friends were amazed to see him preparing a list of the names of all the men who had been guilty of crimes against him. They noticed that beside each name he placed a red cross. His enemies heard about this list, and they were filled with dread. They thought that the sign of the cross meant that they were sentenced to death on the gallows, so, one after another, they fled the court and even the country.

But when the king learned about it, he called a special session of the court. There he explained that the little red crosses on his list of names did not mean the execution of his enemies. No, indeed. "Be content," he said, "do not fear. The cross which I drew by your name is not a sign of punishment, but the pledge of forgiveness." And it is a seal for the sake of the crucified Saviour, who upon His cross forgave all His enemies, prayed for them, and blotted out the handwriting that was against them (see Colossians 2:14). It is through the blood of the cross that the enemies of God are forgiven.

DAY /118

Read 2 Samuel 10; 1 Chronicles 19 and 20; Psalms 20 and 21.

Today's reading: When David sent messengers to congratulate a new king of Ammon, they received insult and disgrace. The resulting war dramatically converted David's small kingdom into a prestigious empire.

Memory gem: "The Lord hear thee in the day of trouble; the name of the God of Jacob defend thee" (Psalm 20:1).

Thought for today:

The city is called Amman today. It is the capital of the kingdom formerly called Trans-Jordan but now the Hashemite Kingdom of Jordan. The interesting thing about this ancient-modern city is that in Bible times it was called Rabbah, the capital of the Ammonites, one of the nations that opposed the Israelites.

This city of Rabbah is about twenty miles east of the Jordan Valley, on the main highway from the east to Jerusalem. We stopped there overnight on our way to the Holy City. The town is situated at the headwater of the Jabbok River, mentioned in the Bible. At this particular place it flows eastward, makes a circle to the north and finally empties into the Jordan to the north of Jericho. A great spring, the source of the Jabbok, breaks forth right here at Rabbah. The valley of the Jabbok is fertile, and every inch of it is farmed, in contrast to the desert hills about us.

Today Amman is a Moslem city; there are very few Christians here. However, there are some small churches. A good friend of the Voice of Prophecy held Bible studies and won some of the inhabitants—descendants, no doubt, of the ancient Ammonites—to the message of Christ.

This city has been rebuilt and destroyed, rebuilt and destroyed, time and time again in its long history. What does the future hold for it? We do not know, except that all cities and all nations someday will be replaced by the kingdom of Christ when He shall sit, not upon a throne of silver and gold, but upon the throne of God's promised kingdom.

DAY / 119

Read 2 Samuel 11 and 12; Psalms 32 and 51.

Today's reading: David, whom in his youth and innocence God characterized as "a man after mine own heart" (Acts 13:22), falls into grievous sin. He finds forgiveness after heart-searching repentance.

Memory gem: "Hide thy face from my sins, and blot out all mine iniquities" (Psalm 51:9).

Thought for today:

God blots out our sins, the charges that were against us. By the blood of Christ, the terrible record is gone. It is forever obliterated. The debt is paid, and we are free!

It is said that Napoleon once found a man implicated in a plot against the empire. The letter which the man had written was brought to Napoleon, and the death sentence was pronounced upon the man. The condemned man's wife came and pleaded with Napoleon to save her husband.

Napoleon had his secretary bring the letter, and said, "Is that your husband's handwriting?" The wife admitted that it was.

"Is that the only evidence there is against him?" he asked the secretary.

"That is all," was the reply.

Then Napoleon took the letter and before the eyes of the weeping woman and the secretary, he threw the letter into the fire

Turning to the woman, he said, "There is no evidence that your husband is a traitor; go in peace."

So, friends, if we come to Jesus and ask forgiveness in His name, God will destroy all evidence and blot out our sins and remember them no more forever (see Isaiah 43:25).

DAY / 120

Read 2 Samuel 13 and 14.

Today's reading: David, apparently as a result of his own sins, seems to have lost control over his sons. This dark period is brightened by a remarkable example of human concern.

Memory gem: "Neither doth God respect any person: yet doth he devise means, that his banished be not expelled from him" (2 Samuel 14:14).

Thought for today:

Notice the story of the pretended widow of Tekoah. We go first to the royal court of King David in Jerusalem. A woman stands before the throne and says, "Help, O king . . . I am indeed a widow woman, and mine husband is dead." She tells the sad story of the fight between her sons, in which one was killed. She expresses her fear that the other son will be executed and the family name forever destroyed. The king promises to give an order concerning her case.

The woman, having been coached by the king's general, Joab, in a clever attempt to induce David to bring back his own son, Absalom, from voluntary exile, suggests that the king himself was really at fault in not bringing home again his banished. Then she adds, "Neither doth God respect any person: yet doth he devise means, that his banished be not expelled from him."

As the result of this appeal, Prince Absalom did return.

We are reminded by this that God has devised means whereby those who are banished from His presence by rebellion and sin may be brought home again. Think here of the patience of God toward sinners. His law has been broken, but He does not immediately take away the life of those who break it. He does not strike them dead in the act of sin, as He might justly do, but waits to be gracious.

"God has suffered Absalom to live," the woman argued; "then why shouldn't David permit him to return?" And so with our heavenly Father. The unclean leper was banished from the presence of the people and sent away from civilization, but provision was made for his cleansing that he might not be expelled. The state of the sinner is really banishment from God, but atonement has been made for him by sacrifice. Christ's atoning sacrifice is God's means of the wrongdoer's deliverance; so it is the sinner's own fault if he is cast off. God is "not willing that any should perish" (2 Peter 3:9).

DAY / 121

Read 2 Samuel 15 through 17.

Today's reading: David flees for his life from his rebellious son. In his time of distress he finds loyal supporters who provide shelter and food.

Memory gem: "Thou, Lord, wilt bless the righteous; with favour wilt thou compass him as with a shield" (Psalm 5:12).

Thought for today:

When Robert Bruce was fleeing from the English army that had invaded Scotland, he came to a poor Highland woman's cottage and asked for a night's lodging.

"Who are you?" she asked.

"I'm a stranger, a traveler, and need a place to sleep."

"All strangers and travelers are welcome here," she said, "for the sake of one."

"And who is that one?" asked the king.

"Our good King Robert, Robert the Bruce," she replied. "He is hunted with hounds and horns, yet I acknowledge him to be the rightful king of Scotland."

This poor woman could not enthrone him except in her heart, but she would if she could. Even in his rejection, she acknowledged him as her rightful king.

Jesus was certainly a king incognito, as someone has said—a king in disguise. This was because people did not recognize Him as king. They were looking for someone who would come in the glory of military power and all the trappings and robes of royal authority; but Jesus was the King of truth, the King of holiness, the King of love.

When Jesus comes as King of kings, the glory of the Lord will cover the earth as the waters cover the sea (see Isaiah 11:9; Habakkuk 2:14). What is the secret of it all? It is the King, the King of glory crowned with thorns. Do you recognize Him? Is He your king? It means something to receive Him as king now. It often means trial, tribulation, and even danger—sometimes death. It means sacrifice and service, but all springing from the love of God in Christ Jesus.

DAY / 122

Read Psalms 3 through 6; 61; 84.

Today's reading: David wrote these psalms during the dark days and nights when his own son almost succeeded in overthrowing the aging king.

Memory gem: "I will both lay me down in peace, and sleep: for thou, Lord, only makest me dwell in safety" (Psalm 4:8).

Thought for today:

In the night, when there are no distractions, we can commune with God, we can get in touch with the eternal world through faith. Then we think of God's Word and meditate upon it. In the night seasons His Spirit can speak to our hearts.

This is also true of times of trouble. It is then, often, that we are brought nearer to God than at any other time. As in the daytime there are too many distractions for us to see the great truths of God's purpose for us, so when things are going well we are often too busy to see His will in our lives; but when we enter into some deep distress, then we begin to know God's truth.

This was true in the experience of David. Take that wonderful third psalm. Notice what the Hebrew inscription at the beginning of the psalm says—"A psalm [or song] of David, when he fled from Absalom, his son." When he rose that morning he was the king over a great kingdom, with thousands of willing subjects. He had the praise and glory of the world. That night he was sleeping with fugitives there on the desert sand by the Jordan River. Absalom, his spoiled son, had risen up against him, willing to take his father's life, and with a great army was seeking him at that very moment.

Just read the song that David could sing in the night. In spite of this trouble, in spite of his broken heart, with the majority of those whom he had helped and befriended on the side of the enemy, and those he had benefited turned traitor against him, still he could say, "I cried unto the Lord with my voice, and he heard me. . . . I laid me down and slept; I awaked; for the Lord sustained me" (Psalm 3:4, 5).

It is a wonderful thing to be able to sleep in time of trouble. We need an experience like that. This man who could sing in the night gives us a wonderful lesson, a marvelous example.

DAY / 123

Read 2 Samuel 18 and 19.

Today's reading: Absalom's poorly trained host is no match for David's seasoned troops. The young rebel dies a tragic death, and David mourns.

Memory gem: "Be not deceived; God is not mocked for whatsoever a man soweth, that shall he also reap" (Galatians 6:7).

Thought for today:

Many years ago the New England newspapers carried the story of a lighthouse keeper and the tragic loss of his son. The boy was in a whaling expedition, and the father expected him home on a certain night.

Strange to say, on that very night the father fell asleep at his task. While he slept a terrible gale arose and swept up the coast but there was no light in the lighthouse. On that stormy night, of all nights, the father fell asleep on duty.

When he awoke the next morning, he looked toward the shore and saw a vessel which had been wrecked by the storm. He rushed to the beach and was horrified to see the body of his own son washed ashore by the raging waters. He had been waiting for him for months, yet when the boy was in sight of home he was lost, and lost because his father had carelessly permitted his light to go out.

The light of a Christian life shines only in consecration, and consecration comes through submission and surrender to the Holy Spirit. So, let us make sure that our light is shining.

DAY / 124

Read 2 Samuel 20 through 22.

Today's reading: A period of turmoil follows the collapse of Absalom's rebellion as David tries to reinstate himself. One touching episode concerns a mother's undying love.

Memory gem: "God commendeth his love toward us, in that, while we were yet sinners, Christ died for us" (Romans 5:8).

Thought for today:

Norman MacLeod has told a wonderful story of what even human love will do for others. Years and years ago, a Scottish Highland widow was ordered evicted from her home because she was unable to pay the rent. With her only child—a little boy—she started to walk ten miles over the mountains to the home of a relative. Before she could get to the house a terrible snowstorm came down upon the hills. The poor woman did not reach her destination, and the next day a searching party set out. There on the high pass, where the blizzard had been the fiercest, they found her in the snow, dead and almost naked. But in a sheltered nook, they found the child, safe and well, wrapped in his mother's clothes.

Years afterward, the son of the minister who had conducted this woman's funeral went to Glasgow to preach a sermon. It was a stormy night, and the audience was small. The falling snow reminded him of the story he had often heard his father tell, and so he left his prepared sermon and told this story.

A few days later he was called to the bedside of a dying man who was a stranger to him. When he went into the room, the man seized his hand and said: "You don't know me, but I know you, and I knew your father before you. Although I have lived in this city for many years, I have never gone to church. But the other night I happened to pass your door and, hearing the singing, I stepped inside and took a back seat. There I heard the story of the widow and her son." His voice choked up, and then trembling, he continued: "I am that son! Never did I forget my mother's love, but I never saw God's love in giving Himself for me until now. It was God who made you tell that story. My mother's prayer is answered now. She did not die in vain."

Look now to Christ, our Lord, who "while we were yet sinners" loved us and gave Himself for us—dying alone on dark Calvary, for our redemption. He was forsaken, but He did not forsake us. Will you not call upon Him now?

DAY / 125

Read 2 Samuel 23 and 24; 1 Chronicles 21 and 22.

Today's reading: David, in a display of vanity, brings another calamity upon his kingdom; but as a result he acquires the site for the great temple. He begins to assemble material.

Memory gem: "Now set your heart and your soul to seek the Lord your God" (1 Chronicles 22:19).

Thought for today:

We are visiting the place of the temple in Jerusalem. We follow our guide through the massive stone gates into this holy place. Here is a great platform, partly paved with stone, approximately 1,500 feet long and 900 feet wide. It is the top of the ancient Mount Moriah,the place where Abraham offered Isaac.

In the time of David, this hill was the property of the Jebusite named Ornan (or Araunah), who had a threshing floor on its summit. David, through vanity, gave orders for the numbering of the people of Israel, and God punished his vanity by pestilence. One day the king saw in the heavens over this threshing floor the destroying angel with a sword drawn and pointed toward Jerusalem. David repented of his fault, went to Oman, and purchased the hill. There he erected an altar to God, where he offered sacrifice. He promised to build a temple, but he was not allowed to do this because he was a man of blood.

As we enter the present-day building (the Mosque of Omar or Dome of the Rock), we see the irregular surface of the naked rock itself rising about six feet above the floor. It is in strange contrast to the gorgeous decorations of the dome. This was the threshing floor of Ornan (Araunah), the Jebusite.

Under the rock is a grotto which must have served Ornan as a storehouse for his grain.

Note: The totals given for David's census differ in 2 Samuel 24:9 and 1 Chronicles 21:5. Various explanations are offered, the most likely having to do with the inclusion or exclusion of the standing army of 288,000 (see 1 Chronicles 27:1-15). Differences in handling round numbers may account for the rest of the variance.

"Seven years" of 2 Samuel 24:13 is called "three years" in 1 Chronicles 21:12. The Septuagint (Greek translation of the Old Testament) has "three years" in both verses.

DAY / 126

Read I Chronicles 23 through 27.

Today's reading concerns mostly the plans David made for the organization of priests and Levites for service in the temple Solomon would build.

Memory gem: "I had rather be a doorkeeper in the house of my God, than to dwell in the tents of wickedness" (Psalm 84:10).

Thought for today:

"In planning for the administration of the affairs of the kingdom, after David abdicated in favor of Solomon, the aged king and his son and their counselors regarded it as essential that everything be done with regularity, propriety, fidelity, and dispatch. So far as possible, they followed the system of organization given Israel soon after the deliverance from Egypt. The Levites were assigned the work connected with the temple service, including the ministry of song and instrumental music, and the keeping of the treasures. . . .

"The thoroughness and completeness of the organization perfected at the beginning of Solomon's reign; the comprehensiveness of the plans for bringing the largest number possible of all the people into active service; the wide distribution of responsibility, so that the service of God and of the king should not be unduly burdensome to any individual or class,—these are lessons which all may study with profit, and which the leaders of the Christian church should understand and follow.

"This picture of a great and mighty nation living in simplicity and comfort in rural homes, every person rendering willing and unsalaried service to God and the king for a portion of each year, is one from which we may gather many helpful suggestions."—Ellen G. White Comments, *Seventh-day Adventist Bible Commentary,* vol. 3, p. 1128.

DAY / 127

Read 1 Kings 1; 1 Chronicles 28; Psalm 72.

Today's reading: As all mortals do, David became old and approached the end of the road. He personally chose his successor and gave solemn instructions to the young man.

Memory gem: "David said to Solomon his son, Be strong and of good courage, and do it: fear not, nor be dismayed: for the Lord God, even my God, will be with thee" (1 Chronicles 28:20).

Thought for today:

Think about John Wesley and his "unparalleled apostolate," as Augustine Birrell beautifully described it. With eighty-eight years of life behind him and over sixty of ceaseless activity in the cause of Christ, he was not sighing for the good old days of wanting things to be changed for the future. Great as his active years had been, those last hours there in his room on City Road were just as good as any. To him, the best time in the service of God was "right here and now." As the young ministers stood around his bed, he opened his eyes a moment before they closed in his last sleep and said, "The best of all is, God is with us."

And when Dean Stanley put up the tablet to the memory of the Wesleys in Westminster Abbey, he summed up all of Wesley's life in those wonderful words of his, "The best of all is, God is with us."

DAY / 128

Read 1 Chronicles 29; 1 Kings 2; Psalm 89.

Today's reading: David's long and eventful career comes to an end. Before the old king dies, he gives Solomon the task of executing judgment on various offenders.

Memory gem: "Justice and judgment are the habitation of thy throne: mercy and truth shall go before thy face" (Psalm 89:14).

Thought for today:

A young minister was confronted, just as his congregation expected, by the village skeptic, Burt Olney. At the close of the first service, Olney said to him: "You did well, but you know, I don't believe in the infallibility of the Bible."

"It is appointed unto men once to die, but after this the judgment," was the young minister's calm assertion.

"I can prove that there's no such thing as a judgment after death," declared the skeptic.

"But men do die," the young minister said. "For 'it is appointed unto men once to die, but after this the judgment.' "

"That's no argument," the skeptic protested. "Let's get down to business. Let's discuss this matter in regular forum."

The young minister shook his head. "I'm not here to argue. I'm here to preach the Word of God, not to argue over it."

Olney was annoyed and turned away with the remark, "I don't believe you know enough about the Bible to argue about it."

"Perhaps you're right," said the young preacher, "but remember this: 'It is appointed unto men once to die, but after this the judgment.' "

As Olney walked away through the darkness, the very tree toads seemed to be singing that verse. As he crossed a little stream, the frogs seemed to croak, "Judgment, judgment, judgment!"

The next morning he called on the young pastor. "I have come to see you about that verse of scripture you gave me last night," he said. "I have spent a terrible night. Those words just burn in my heart. I can't get rid of them. Tell me what I must do to be saved. How may I meet the judgment?"

When he left the minister, he was a child of God through faith in the finished sacrifice of Christ upon the cross.

DAY / 129

Read Psalms 1; 2; 9; 10; 12 through 15; 18.

Today's reading: We break into the historical sequence to read some of the psalms that cannot be positively related to specific incidents.

Memory gem: "Blessed is the man that walketh not in the counsel of the ungodly, nor standeth in the way of sinners, nor sitteth in the seat of the scornful" (Psalm 1:1).

Thought for today:

One day in Glasgow Green in Scotland a man stood up after hearing a preacher give a gospel message at an open-air meeting, and said: "I don't believe what this man has said. I don't believe in hell or heaven—I don't believe in the judgment or in the devil or in God, because I have never seen one of them."

Just then another member of the crowd stood forth and said: "Friends, you say there is a river running not far away from this place, the River Clyde. There is no such thing. It's not true. It's all a delusion. You tell me there are trees and grass growing near where I stand, and that there are people standing near me—but it can't be true. There are no such things. I have never seen one of them. I was born blind. No one but a blind man can talk as I have." Then, turning toward the unbeliever, he said, "The more you talk, the more you expose your ignorance, because you are spiritually blind and cannot see."

When a man does not love God supremely, he is really saying that God is not supreme. He is giving aid and comfort to the unbeliever, blind to God's works, the evidence of His existence. The breaking of the greatest command by professed followers of the Lord is one of the saddest sights on earth and brings reproach on the cause of Christ among out-and-out unbelievers.

Difficult or obscure words:

Psalm 2:12. **"Kiss the Son"**—do homage to the Son.

Psalm 18:26. **"Froward"**—crooked or perverse.

DAY / 130

Today's reading: The first psalm in this group contains some of the most remarkable of the Messianic predictions.

Memory gem: "Hear, O Lord, and have mercy upon me: Lord, be thou my helper" (Psalm 30:10).

Thought for today:

Psalm 22:16: Remember, this was written a thousand years before our Saviour's crucifixion: *"The assembly of the wicked have inclosed me: they pierced my hands and my feet."*

This chapter is so filled with the very words and expressions that our Saviour used upon the cross that it is called the Psalm of Sobs. And His hands and feet were pierced by nails as we read of the crucifixion in Luke 23:33.

Psalm 22:8: The people ridiculed Him and said: *"He trusted on the Lord that he would deliver him: let him deliver him, seeing he delighted in him."*

We read the fulfillment of this in Matthew 27:41-43.

In Psalm 22:17 we read that the people were astonished: *"I may tell all my bones: they look and stare upon me."*

The crowd stood about and gazed, as upon a great spectacle. Luke 23:35: "The people stood beholding."

Psalm 22:18: His garments were parted and lots were cast. John 19:23, 24 describes this. The four soldier guards divided His garments, but when they came to His seamless robe, they cast lots for it rather than tear it, so what seemed to be antagonistic prophecies were fulfilled literally.

In Psalm 22:1 Christ's cry upon the cross is foretold: *"My God, my God, why hast thou forsaken me?"*

In Matthew 27:46 we have the record of the fulfillment.

Psalm 22:14 declares that Jesus died of a broken heart. Also Psalm 69:20: "Reproach hath broken my heart."

There are many other prophecies about Jesus that were literally fulfilled in His life and ministry on earth, His resurrection and ascension to heaven.

These prophecies with their fulfillment are enough to show that Jesus was the right Man. He was the Son of God; He came at the right time; He did the very things predicted. At least twenty-four prophecies were fulfilled in twenty-four hours on the day of His death.

DAY / 131

Read Psalms 35 through 40.

Today's reading: In this group of familiar psalms we find the trustful reassurances of Psalm 37.

Memory gem: "Commit thy way unto the Lord; trust also in him; and he shall bring it to pass" (Psalm 37:5).

Thought for today:

As boys, my brother and I were taught the Word of God. Our father, a minister, was away from home a great deal in evangelistic work. So in his absence the burden of training us in the things of God fell largely upon our mother. She was very faithful and did all she could to teach us a love for and an understanding of the Word of God.

One thing she consistently did was to train us in memorizing great chapters of the Bible. One of those was the thirty-seventh psalm. I remember how difficult it was to learn, because its verses are all separate statements of truth. They do not seem to be connected one with the other as in most Bible passages; yet each one is a jewel.

I am so glad that she continued her efforts until we actually memorized every verse of that tremendous chapter. The thirty-seventh psalm contains prophecies of the restoration of this planet. As we see the power of wicked men and their influence in the world, we may be tempted to conclude that it never can be broken. The prophet said, "I have seen the wicked in great power, and spreading himself like a green bay tree" (Psalm 37:35).

We, too, can say that we have seen it in our day. Sin seems to march on to victory. We know that the end of it is ruin and death for men and for the world, but still on it goes. However, God has decreed that sin shall cease to exist. He has prophesied that it will, and His prophecy will come true. The time will come when there will be no more sin, and therefore no more death, no more pain, no more war, no more evil in this world. Although a man may seem to prosper in his evil doings, the psalmist-prophet continues: "Yet he passed away, and, lo, he was not: yea, I sought him, but he could not be found" (verse 36).

It is good for us to remember the first verses of this psalm. "Fret not thyself because of evildoers, neither be thou envious against the workers of iniquity. For they shall soon be cut down like the grass, and wither as the green herb."

DAY / 132

Read Psalms 41; 44; 45; 49.

Today's reading: Many of the psalms express the truth that the Lord expects His people to be merciful, even as He is merciful.

Memory gem: "Blessed is he that considereth the poor; the Lord will deliver him in time of trouble" (Psalm 41:1).

Thought for today:

"The merciful are 'partakers of the divine nature,' and in them the compassionate love of God finds expression. All whose hearts are in sympathy with the heart of Infinite Love will seek to reclaim and not to condemn. Christ dwelling in the soul is a spring that never runs dry. Where He abides, there will be an overflowing of beneficence.

"To the appeal of the erring, the tempted, the wretched victims of want and sin, the Christian does not ask, Are they worthy? but, How can I benefit them? In the most wretched, the most debased, he sees souls whom Christ died to save and for whom God has given to His children the ministry of reconciliation.

"The merciful are those who manifest compassion to the poor, the suffering, and the oppressed. . . .

" . . . There is sweet peace for the compassionate spirit, a blessed satisfaction in the life of self-forgetful service for the good of others. The Holy Spirit that abides in the soul and is manifest in the life will soften hard hearts and awaken sympathy and tenderness. You will reap that which you sow. . . .

"He who has given his life to God in ministry to His children is linked with Him who has all the resources of the universe at His command. His life is bound up by the golden chain of the immutable promises with the life of God. The Lord will not fail him in the hour of suffering and need. 'My God shall supply all your need according to His riches in glory by Christ Jesus.' Philippians 4:19. And in the hour of final need the merciful shall find refuge in the mercy of the compassionate Saviour and shall be received into everlasting habitations."—*Thoughts From the Mount of Blessing,* pp. 22–24.

DAY / 133

Read Psalms 50; 53; 55; 62; 69; 70.

Today's reading: One never ceases to be amazed at the universal appeal of the psalms. These poems, written in ancient times, still speak to the modern mind.

Memory gem: "Whoso offereth praise glorifieth me: and to him that ordereth his conversation aright will I shew the salvation of God" (Psalm 50:23).

Thought for today:

Do you know that God speaks to the bad as well as to the good? Certainly He does!

I heard of a boy who played with his sister around their mother's chair. As they grew up, the sister became a Christian, but the brother became wild and wicked. He finally found himself in prison, but his sister never stopped praying for him.

One day, as he was led back to his cell from the courtroom, he was cursing God, cursing the judges, cursing the law, cursing himself and everybody else. While in this desperate mood, the first thing he saw as he walked into his cell was a Bible. It had been there before, but he had not noticed it. He just opened the good old Book, and his attention fell on Psalm 50:16. "Unto the wicked God said . . . " He was surprised. "Well," he said, "does God talk to the wicked? I thought He just talked to the good."

So he read on and came under conviction. Then he fell on his knees and turned back and forth through the Bible and read here and there. The Spirit of God must have guided him, for, before he arose from his knees, he had accepted Jesus Christ as his Saviour. A wonderful peace came into his soul. He began to love the Bible and studied it every day for the eighteen months that he had to remain in prison. As soon as he was freed, he was baptized and became a faithful worker for Christ.

Yes, Christ's love brings a message to the wicked, and if a bad man will listen and respond to it, he will become a good man. God will not *drive* him—He will *draw* him "with cords of a man, with bands of love," as we read in Hosea 11:4.

DAY / 134

Read Psalms 71; 73; 77; 80.

Today's reading: Many of the psalms express the truth that trials often bring the afflicted soul to a new understanding of God's tender care.

Memory gem: "I call to remembrance my song in the night: I commune with mine own heart: and my spirit made diligent search" (Psalm 77:6).

Thought for today:

It has often been said that character is what a man is in the dark. Well, a song in the night is what a Christian is in his heart. It is said that in training the very best songbirds, they are often taken into a dark room and kept there for a long time. There they are permitted to hear only the song of some other good bird. In the darkness they learn to sing the beautiful song they hear. So it often is with us. We learn to sing in the night of trouble.

It is said that Jenny Lind, the great singer, once sang in a public performance where Otto Goldschmidt heard her. As he walked out of the opera house someone asked him how he liked her voice. "Well," he said, "there is something about it that needs changing, needs toning down. If someone would marry her and break her heart and crush her feelings, then she could really sing." Strange to say, he himself married her later on, and he broke her heart too. He crushed her feelings. And then Jenny Lind sang with the sweetest voice ever heard, some say so sweet that the angels wished to stop and hear her sing. It was in the night of suffering and heartbreak that Jenny Lind learned to sweeten her song.

No matter how the darkness may be gathering about you, friend, God will give you a song, and through that song He will bless you and bless others. And someday the morning will come, the eternal morning. Heaven's gates will open, and then, with nights all passed and shadows gone, you will sing in heaven, and there will be no night there.

DAY / 135

Read Psalms 81; 82; 91; 92; 102.

Today's reading: Again we read a number of psalms that breathe a spirit of quiet trust in God despite the troubles that plague our lives.

Memory gem: "I will say of the Lord, He is my refuge and my fortress: my God; in him will I trust" (Psalm 91:2).

Thought for today:

You know, dear friends, the clouds may sometimes hide the sunshine in life. In fact, they often do. But we may always have radiant inward life. And in the far land of trial and tribulation—yes, even in the cave of discouragement—we may hear the voice of God in our hearts. As the prophet Isaiah says: "And thine ears shall hear a word behind thee, saying, This is the way, walk ye in it, when ye turn to the right hand, and when ye turn to the left" (Isaiah 30:21). Faith in Christ as our Saviour will keep us to the end.

Eisleben is just a little German town, but one of the most interesting in the world. At one end of the town, in a house which was then an inn, Martin Luther was born on a November night in 1483. At the other end of the town stands the inn in which he died. It is a strange coincidence that one of the greatest men of the last ten centuries should have been born in an inn and also have died in one.

Luther had returned to Eisleben to reconcile two brothers. He spent the last days of his life working for Christ. On the night of February 18, 1546, he awoke in great pain and cried out: "Lord God, how I suffer! I believe I am going to remain here in Eisleben, where I was born and baptized." Then he sank into a stupor.

Later, a friend aroused him by asking, "Reverend Father, do you stand firm for Christ and the doctrines you have preached?"

He barely whispered, "Yes." Then those impressive eyes, which had opened for the first time sixty-three years before in that same town, closed for the last time, and Luther was at rest. But his faith had sustained him.

DAY / 136

Read Psalms 109; 110; 113 through 116.

Today's reading: These psalms breathe the message: "Have faith, dear friend, in God."

Memory gem: "Ye that fear the Lord, trust in the Lord: he is their help and their shield" (Psalm 115:11).

Thought for today:

One evening in 1919, a mother in the Northwest sat with bowed head as a little white-clad figure knelt at her knee and prayed before she was tucked into bed: "God bless Mamma; and oh, please take care of Daddy—he's awfully far away!"

As the child whispered "Amen," she opened her eyes and looked up into her mother's face and said, "Thank You, God!" The mother stroked her little one's curls and wished for the perfect trust of a child as she murmured a prayer for the safety of her husband.

That night a telegram came saying: "I am safe and sound. More by letter. Daddy."

The mother did not understand until later in the night when the phone rang and a man's voice asked: "Are you alone? No? Well, your husband was killed this evening in a railroad accident."

She answered, "Oh, no! I had a telegram from him a few minutes ago, and he is safe."

The morning paper carried the headline: "Sheep Train Wrecked; All on Board Killed." Then followed the story of how the failure of a brakeman to give the right signal had resulted in the collision of two trains and the death of all on board.

Now, that father was a strong-willed man and could hardly understand his own actions when, on the afternoon before the wreck, he was approached by a stranger whom he had never seen before and never saw again. This man also had sheep on the train, and he suggested that they get off and feed their sheep at a certain stockyard and take a later train for Omaha. Although this meant more expense, the father yielded to the suggestion and thus escaped the wreck.

"O for the faith of a child!" we may say. Well, it may be yours and mine, but it comes by hearing and obeying the Word of God (see Romans 10:17). Let us say, "Thank You, Lord," for what His providence may bring, and so "have faith in God" (Mark 11:22).

DAY / 137

Read Psalms 117; 118; 122; 123.

Today's reading finishes the psalms—except for a few we are saving for special occasions later on. The first one in this group, known as the Passover hallel, is the shortest chapter in the Bible. Let's memorize the whole chapter.

Memory gem: "O praise the Lord, all ye nations: praise him, all ye people. For his merciful kindness is great toward us: and the truth of the Lord endureth for ever. Praise ye the Lord" (Psalm 117).

Thought for today:

"It is a law of nature that our thoughts and feelings are encouraged and strengthened as we give them utterance. While words express thoughts, it is also true that thoughts follow words. If we would give more expression to our faith, rejoice more in the blessings that we know we have,—the great mercy and love of God,—we should have more faith and greater joy. No tongue can express, no finite mind conceive, the blessing that results from appreciating the goodness and love of God. Even on earth we may have joy as a wellspring, never failing, because fed by the streams that flow from the throne of God.

"Then let us educate our hearts and lips to speak the praise of God for His matchless love. Let us educate our souls to be hopeful, and to abide in the light shining from the cross of Calvary. Never should we forget that we are children of the heavenly King, sons and daughters of the Lord of hosts. It is our privilege to maintain a calm repose in God."—*The Ministry of Healing,* pp. 251–253.

DAY / 138

Read 2 Chronicles 1; 1 Kings 3 and 4.

Today's reading: We return to the story of Solomon, Israel's most glorious king. His reign had an auspicious beginning.

Memory gem: "Give therefore thy servant an understanding heart to judge thy people, that I may discern between good and bad" (1 Kings 3:9).

Thought for today:

Solomon was the great king of Israel, noted for his wisdom, his glory, and his riches. We are told that when he went to offer sacrifice to God at the great altar in Gibeon, the Lord appeared to him in a dream by night and said, "Ask what I shall give thee." And Solomon requested wisdom to rule justly and righteously.

In this dream the Lord told Solomon that He was pleased that he had made this request rather than asking for long life or riches or the lives of his enemies, and that his request would be granted. But, when Solomon awoke, it was only a dream. Yet it was a dream given him by God. It was not a dream caused by worry, nervous tension, or wrong diet. It was a divine intervention in the affairs of men. Solomon had dreamed about God because God wanted to bring him a message.

Note: The "high place" referred to in 1 Kings 3:2, 4 and 2 Chronicles 1:3 is simply a place of worship. This should not be confused with other uses of the term to indicate places of idolatrous worship. At this time Solomon still "loved the Lord." The sacrifices offered in "high places" were apparently often done by legitimate priests in good faith (see Judges 6:25, 26 and other references).

Difficult or obscure words:

1 Kings 4:6. **"Tribute"**—better; levy, the conscription of forced laborers for public works.

1 Kings 4:19. **"The only officer"**—meaning unclear. The Septuagint has "one officer in the land of Judah."

1 Kings 4:26. **"Forty thousand stalls"**—given as "four thousand" in 2 Chronicles 9:25. Possibly a copyist's error, since the Hebrew words for "four" and "forty" are very similar. In either case it indicates a large military force, in violation of Deuteronomy 17:16.

DAY / 139

Read the Song of Solomon.

Today's reading: Probably sometime during his early reign Solomon wrote this intricate oriental love poem. Many Bible students believe it represents Christ's love for His church.

Memory gem: "I am the rose of Sharon, and the lily of the valleys" (Song of Solomon 2:1).

Thought for today:

Let us look to Christ, our Intercessor, now while He still pleads His blood for our sins. Dear friend, will you not yield your heart to Him now? Repent and turn to God, whose grace is greater than all our sins.

There is an old story of a royal prince who, under the disguise of a beggar, wooed and won his bride. He brought her to the capital city and right into the audience chamber in the king's palace. There he left her on some pretext or other, and she became fearful and shrinking.

When at last she looked up, she saw there on the throne her lover, her husband, in royal robes. Then all her fear was gone. He was the one she loved, and "perfect love casteth out fear" (1 John 4:18).

So the believer, wooed and won by Christ who took upon Himself the form of a servant, lifts up his eyes at last and sees upon the throne the face he has learned to love. Then all fear is gone; love is made perfect. And he has boldness in the day of judgment and will go to dwell with love forevermore.

So, friend, may God give us all the faith that gains the victory over the world. And may our faith be fixed upon Jesus Christ, the One altogether lovely and the fairest of ten thousand to our souls.

Difficult or obscure words

Song of Solomon 1:5. **"Black"**—better; dark-complexioned.

Song of Solomon 2:5. **"Stay me with flagons"**—rather: sustain me with cakes of dried grapes. Then, as now, raisins were considered desirable for a quick supply of energy.

Song of Solmon 2:12. **"Turtle"**—turtledove.

DAY / 140

Read 1 Kings 5 through 7.

Today's reading: Solomon, secure on Israel's throne, now begins the great task outlined for him by his father—building a magnificent temple on Mount Moriah.

Memory gem: "I will dwell among the children of Israel, and will not forsake my people Israel" (1 Kings 6:13).

Thought for today:

The great temple of Solomon was in Jerusalem. It was built of stone, including marble, and other valuable materials—gold, silver, and cedar wood. This mighty building stood for many hundreds of years as the center of God's worship in the earth.

The temple was composed of two compartments, the holy place and the most holy. In front of the eastern entrance was the altar of sacrifice, where the bleeding lambs and other victims were offered in sacrifice to God. Between this altar and the great central door stood a brass laver, or water container, with facilities for washing, so that the priests might always be clean.

In the first room, the holy place, on the north or right side, was a golden table on which twelve loaves of bread were placed fresh every Sabbath, representing the twelve tribes of Israel and God's care for them. On the left, or south side, stood the golden lampstand or candlestick on which seven lamps burned continually. Immediately ahead, in the center, was a golden altar on which incense was offered every morning and evening.

Behind the incense altar a great and costly veil hung from the ceiling to the floor, dividing the holy place from the most holy. In the most holy place was one article of furniture, and one only: the holy ark, covered with pure gold. On each end stood a golden cherub, or angel, with wings outstretched, each toward the other. Between these cherubim the presence of God often shone forth in blinding glory. The cover of the ark was called the mercy seat. Beneath the mercy seat, and inside the ark, were placed the two stone tables of the Ten Commandments written by the finger of God.

Note: The numbers given for Solomon's officers in 1 Kings 5:16 and 9:23 differ with those in 2 Chronicles 2:18 and 8:10. Kings lists 3,300 plus 500 (3,800). Chronicles gives 3,600 plus 250 (3,850). The difference can be explained as a variation of 300 in the "chief officers" in the two accounts.

DAY / 141

Read 2 Chronicles 2 through 5.

Today's reading: We cover essentially the same subject as yesterday's, with some different details. Try to visualize the beauty of the marvelous building and its furnishings.

Memory gem: "The house which I build is great: for great is our God above all gods" (2 Chronicles 2:5).

Thought for today:

Notice that the arrangement of the articles of furniture in the temple formed a cross, with the foot at the great altar outside, the head at the ark in the most holy place, and the crossbeam reaching from the golden table of shewbread to the golden candlestick. And well this was, for the services of the sanctuary pointed forward to man's salvation through the Redeemer-Messiah who was to come.

Those who had broken God's law—in other words, those who were sinners—brought their sacrifice, usually a lamb, to the great altar. There it was slain, and the blood, which represented its life, was shed. Some of the flesh of the offering was burned upon the altar. Sometimes the blood of the victim was carried inside the holy place and sprinkled before the veil. In other cases the flesh was eaten by the priests.

All through the year the various sacrifices offered daily in the temple pointed forward to a Redeemer who would come and give His life as a sacrifice for men. Each sacrifice was a sort of enacted prophecy of the coming Redeemer.

There was a yearly round of service, closing with the service called the "cleansing of the sanctuary," in which the high priest alone entered the most holy place with the blood of a sacrifice which he sprinkled upon the mercy seat of the very ark of God itself. How appropriate this appears when we read in the Scriptures that the transgression of God's law is sin. These sacrifices, with the shed blood of the victims, pointed forward to the Redeemer, who would come and die for the sins of the world.

DAY / 142

Today's reading: The great temple is finished, and the Israelites gather in Jerusalem for the dedication. Solomon's prayer even now lifts us to heights of devotion to our merciful heavenly Father.

Memory gem: "Then hear thou in heaven thy dwelling place, and forgive, and do, and give to every man according to his ways, whose heart thou knowest" (1 Kings 8:39).

Thought for today:

In the ancient temple of Solomon, only when the lamb was slain was the sacrifice fully accepted. And so every believer believes not only in Christ, but in "Christ crucified." 1 Corinthians 1:23.

The temple of Solomon was more than a building. It was a parable—a great marble book of atoning love. It revealed God to man. As Jesus said (see Mark 11:17), it was a house of prayer for all nations. It is true that many had forgotten its real meaning, but some remembered it.

When at last its true meaning was almost completely forgotten, then it was destroyed, never to be rebuilt. Jesus said that one stone would not be left upon another, that all would be cast down (see Matthew 24:2), and that is the way it is today.

The great platform on top of Mount Moriah, which was smoothed off by King Solomon, is still there. This platform, covering about forty-two acres, is one of the most interesting spots to visit in ancient Jerusalem today. The corners, built up to level by King Solomon and later by King Herod, are still a wonder of mighty masonry. The southwest corner wall to this day is called the Wailing Wall, where many for centuries have gone to weep and to pray that the temple might be rebuilt. But of the temple itself, not one stone remains upon another. The prophecy of Christ was fulfilled completely.

Those who forgot the blood atonement forfeited their prosperity. And it is the same today. Men may uphold Jesus as a great man, a world teacher, a wise philosopher, but that is not enough. He is the Redeemer of the world. He came to die. If we forget the cross, we have really forgotten Him.

DAY / 143

Read 2 Chronicles 6 and 7.

Today's reading: We retrace essentially the same events as the previous reading in 1 Kings. Imagine the awe inspired by the overpowering visible glory of God as He accepted the temple dedicated to Him.

Memory gem: "If my people, which are called by my name shall humble themselves, and pray, . . . and turn from their wicked ways; then will I hear from heaven, and will forgive their sin, and will heal their land" (2 Chronicles 7:14).

Thought for today:

You will remember that in ancient times the place marked by God's special presence was regarded with reverence and awe.

The worshipers in Solomon's temple of old were reverent and walked in the fear of God. As we consider the mighty truths of God, should we not be reverent before Him? When we meet in the assemblies of His people, we should put away every evil thing. We should not be among those people mentioned in the fifteenth chapter of Matthew, of whom the Lord declared: "This people draweth nigh unto me with their mouth, and honoureth me with their lips; but their heart is far from me. But in vain they do worship me" (verses 8, 9).

God "dwelleth not in temples made with hands" (Acts 7:48), yet He honors with His presence the assemblies of His people and by His Holy Spirit He dwells in the hearts of those who truly love and obey Him. Those who worship God must worship Him "in spirit and in truth: for the Father seeketh such to worship him" (John 4:23).

The temple of Solomon is gone. The worship of God is not now confined to any one race or people. It is not necessary to go to Mount Gerizim or to Jerusalem, to Rome, to Moscow, to London or to New York to worship God. He seeks today the temple of the surrendered heart. That is His true sanctuary. Shall we not open our hearts to His presence now, and prayerfully say: "The Lord is in his holy temple: let all the earth keep silence before him" (Habakkuk 2:20)?

DAY / 144

Read Psalms 125; 131; 133; 134; 138 through 141.

Today's reading: These psalms, although probably not written by Solomon, reflect the theme of his prayer—an abiding confidence that God will hear and answer the sincere prayer of a repentant soul.

Memory gem: "Search me, O God, and know my heart: try me, and know my thoughts: and see if there be any wicked way in me, and lead me in the way everlasting" (Psalm 139:23, 24).

Thought for today:

While we know that God cannot be contained in any earthly building, that even the heaven of heavens is the workmanship of His hands, still this temple of Solomon was a place where His presence was especially revealed, and was therefore sacred. At its dedication King Solomon knelt down and prayed, and all the people bowed in reverence.

When we come before God today in a house dedicated to His worship, should we not come with reverence, remembering the words of the psalmist: "The Lord is a great God, and a great King above all gods. . . . O come, let us worship and bow down: let us kneel before the Lord our maker" (Psalm 95:3-6).

Both in public and in private worship, it is our privilege to bow on our knees before God when we offer our petitions to Him. We read of Jesus that He "kneeled down, and prayed" (Luke 22:41). It is also recorded of His disciples that they too "kneeled down, and prayed" (Acts 9:40). And the apostle Paul declared: "I bow my knees unto the Father of our Lord Jesus Christ" (Ephesians 3:14).

The hour and place of prayer are certainly sacred, and we should manifest reverence in attitude and demeanor, remembering that "holy and reverend is his name" (Psalm 111:9). If the angels veil their faces when they speak the name of God, with what reverence should we who are fallen and sinful take His name upon our lips!

Difficult or obscure words:

Psalm 141:5. **"It shall be an excellent oil . . . their calamities"**—The Hebrew cannot be understood. Perhaps the Septuagint translation is better: "Let not the oil of the sinner anoint my head; for yet shall my prayer be in their pleasures."

DAY / 145

Read Proverbs 1 through 4.

Today's reading: We begin a study of Solomon's proverbs. The wise man has a lot to say about "wisdom," "knowledge," and "understanding"—obviously referring to a correct grasp of God's plan for living.

Memory gem: "If thou seekest her as silver, and searchest for her as for hid treasures; then shalt thou understand the fear of the Lord, and find the knowledge of God" (Proverbs 2:4, 5).

Thought for today:

Some years ago there was a big scare in London—the alarm sounded which indicated that the crown jewels of the British Empire had been stolen. These jewels, set in swords, crowns, and scepters, are kept in the Tower of London. The great Star of Africa, one of the world's largest diamonds is there. The great crown with its 6,170 diamonds, emeralds, and sapphires, which King George V wore when he was crowned as Emperor of India, is there. The imperial state crown is there, said to be the most valuable and most beautiful in the world. Almost 3,000 jewels are in that one crown. Think of the responsibility of guarding that treasure! The governor of the ancient Tower has it all in his hands.

Well, London's worst scare in thirty years came when suddenly the alarm system began to sound and a recorded voice boomed out in Scotland Yard, "Intruders have entered the jewel house of the Tower of London." The Scots Guards jumped to their posts at the Tower. Yeoman warders rushed to their emergency stations. A flying squad roared out of Scotland Yard. Radio cars started for the Tower. Police boats came racing down the Thames. City police cordoned off Tower Hill. A sixteen-ton steel cage dropped down over the jewels.

It was a big scare all right, but everything was safe. The governor of the Tower confessed that he himself had set off the alarm to see how well England's crown jewels were being protected. Someone from Scotland Yard asked him, "Why didn't you tell us that it was only a practice?"

The governor replied, "What's the use of having a test, if it is not carried out properly?"

Are you, friends, sure that your soul is safe?

DAY / 146

Read Proverbs 5 through 9.

Today's reading: One recurring theme in Proverbs is the warning against unfaithfulness in love. Modern young people—and older ones too—might do well to heed these warnings.

Memory gem: "Can a man take fire in his bosom, and his clothes not be burned?" (Proverbs 6:27).

Thought for today:

Love should be expressed in words and deeds. During courtship a man usually goes out of his way to show affection and kindness to the lady of his choice. How can he expect to hold her affection and love unless after marriage he continues to show the same affection, interest, and gentleness as he did before?

After his wife's death Carlyle wrote this in his diary: "Oh, if I could see her once more to let her know that I always loved her. She never did know it." Poor Carlyle—and poor wife! He wrote great books, but certainly he could have written greater ones had he been wise enough to express his love to his faithful wife.

Ramsay MacDonald, three times prime minister of Great Britain, paid a beautiful tribute to his wife when he said that to turn to her in stress and storm was like going into a sheltered haven where the waters were at rest. "When I was weary and worn, buffeted and discouraged, thinking only of giving up to thankless strife, . . . my lady would heal and soothe me with her cheery faith and conviction, and send me forth to smite and be smitten."

It is as plain as can be that success in marriage consists not only in finding the right mate, but also in being the right mate. It is important to remember that a marriage license is a license for marriage, not a license for the roving eye and the faithless heart.

On the night that Mr. and Mrs. Henry Ford celebrated their golden wedding anniversary, a reporter asked to what they attributed their fifty years of successful married life. "The formula," said Ford, "is the same formula I have always used in making cars—just stick to one model."

Christ honored marriage when He performed His first miracle in Cana long ago. By His grace many who have found themselves in most uncongenial marriage relationships have been able to bring order out of chaos and hope out of despair. Every effort should be made to preserve marriage. In the confusion of our world today, it is still the blessed refuge of the heart.

DAY / 147

Today's reading: Among these sage remarks we find warnings against various kinds of sin. The wise man tries to show that, in the long run, it pays to do right.

Memory gem: "The blessing of the Lord, it maketh rich, and he addeth no sorrow with it" (Proverbs 10:22).

Thought for today:

Is it safe to keep on sinning? Can a man persist in committing every kind of evil, disregard every moral restraint, continue to be a traitor to God, to his family, to himself, to his country and then die with the assurance that death is the end of it all and that there is no trouble ahead for him?

The story is told of a burglar who entered a servicemen's center in St. Paul, Minnesota, and left with only $23.50. He left a note addressed to Mrs. Margaret Wood, the director, which read: "I am sorry that I did this. There is coming a day when I will pay."

According to the Bible, this thief's statement contained more truth than he realized. A day is coming when he will pay, when all who break God's law will pay.

What does the Bible say about this topic?

"The wages of sin is death" (Romans 6:23). "The fearful, and unbelieving, and the abominable, and murderers, and whoremongers, and sorcerers, and idolaters, and all liars, shall have their part in the lake which burneth with fire" (Revelation 21:8). "There shall in no wise enter into it any thing that defileth, neither whatsoever worketh abomination, or maketh a lie: but they which are written in the Lamb's book of life" (verse 27).

DAY / 148

Read Proverbs 14 through 18.

Today's reading: Many of these proverbs point up the contrast between the wrong way and the right way in daily living. Each of us must choose the way to go.

Memory gem: "There is a way that seemeth right unto a man, but the end thereof are the ways of death" (Proverbs 16:25).

Thought for today

The streamlined body of a high-powered roadster swerved around a sharp corner and stopped beside a young barefoot boy. Beckoning the lad to the side of the car, the driver asked, "How far is it to Washington, Sonny?"

"Going the way you are headed, I think it's about 25,000 miles, Mister," replied the boy.

"What do you mean?" asked the bewildered driver.

"Well, sir," replied the boy, "If you will turn around and go the other way it is only forty miles to Washington. If you continue the way you are headed now, you'll never reach the city."

The man drove on about a quarter of a mile to the nearest filling station and had his car filled up with gasoline. He told the man who was serving him of the conversation he had had with the small boy and in conclusion said, "I thought sure I was on the right road."

"Tain't the way ye believe ye're travelin'," replied the man, "but the way ye actually do travel, Son, that counts in this here life. And if ye aim to git to Washington terday, ye better turn square 'round right here!"

You see, it isn't the way we think we are traveling from day to day, but the way we are really going that counts.

DAY / 149

Today's reading: Another truth that Solomon teaches over and over is the importance of proper parental training.

Memory gem: "Train up a child in the way he should go: and when he is old, he will not depart from it" (Proverbs 22:6).

Thought for today:

William Cady tells about a visit his mother made with her three small children out to the farm of Uncle John and Aunt Sarah. The greatest wonder of the many the little boy saw there was a square bottle containing an apple much larger than the neck of the bottle. He couldn't figure it out, so he took it to Aunt Sarah and asked her about it. She said, "Ask Uncle John; he did it." So he carried the bottle to Uncle John, who looked at it thoughtfully, then into the boy's eyes, and said, "Someday, Willie, you will know!" And all Willie's begging could get no more from him.

The next summer Willie was determined to learn the secret, and he spent hours searching the whole farm. Finally in the orchard he found another bottle fastened to a limb, with a little apple growing in it. He ran and told Uncle John that he had found out his secret. "Yes," he said, "I put it in there when it was little—and it stayed."

The best time to get people into the kingdom of God is when they are young. Professed Christian mother, are you working at this—or are you too busy? With the father, you share the apostolic command concerning the children, to "bring them up in the nurture and admonition of the Lord" (Ephesians 6:4).

Thousands of children are now practically parentless, because so many mothers are working. But we must not neglect the work God has given us as parents. Don't expect the judge to teach your child obedience—you must teach him if he ever learns it. The earliest years are the most important.

Difficult or obscure words:

Proverbs 21:4. **"Plowing"**—better; light, or prosperity.

Proverbs 21:18. **"Ransom"**—not in the sense of payment. Rather, the idea is that the trouble from which the righteous are saved will come upon those who refuse salvation.

DAY / 150

Read Proverbs 23 through 26.

Today's reading: Good advice couched in pithy sayings continues to point out the good life. Over and over the young person is urged to heed the counsel.

Memory gem: "My son, give me thine heart, and let thine eyes observe my ways" (Proverbs 23:26).

Thought for today:

One of America's great preachers grew up as a little boy in Atlantic City. He loved music, and one day he read in the newspaper that the great Italian violinist Giovanni Viotti was coming to give a concert and would play on a $5,000 violin.

This little boy, then twelve or thirteen years of age, saved his nickels. He ran errands, sold newspapers, begged money from his father and mother, until finally he had five dollars saved up. That is what it cost to hear Viotti play.

When the great night came, his mother helped him get all fixed up in his best clothes to go to the concert. The lad sat spellbound as the great violinist came out, put his violin to his chin, and began to play. Wonderful! Every note seemed to melt into every other, and the audience sat enthralled.

Then after a while something seemed to go wrong. Viotti appeared to be in a nervous state, and jerked the strings of his violin. Finally he became violent and angry at the violin; he threw it down and smashed it into splinters. The audience gasped in amazement—a $5,000 violin ruined because of a man's passion!

Finally the artist said: "Sit down, folks; sit down! That was not a $5,000 violin. I found it right here in your own town and bought it for $1.69. You came here to see a $5,000 violin. But I wanted you to come here to hear a man play. I played on a violin that cost less than two dollars, and you sat entranced with my music. I just wanted to show you that it is not the violin; it's the man. Now I will play on the $5,000 violin."

My friends, it may seem to you that your violin, your talent, your life, doesn't amount to much. It may seem to you that you have ruined everything. Listen! If you will put the violin of your life fully into the hands of the heavenly Artist, He will bring from it the very music of the angels, the harmonies of heaven. Give your heart to Him today. And may the great God take you and mold you and refine you and use you!

DAY / 151

Read Proverbs 27 through 30.

Today's reading: Notice again that the good life pays. These chapters have a lot to say about moral values.

Memory gem: "Where there is no vision, the people perish: but he that keepeth the law, happy is he" (Proverbs 29:18).

Thought for today:

The other day I was reading of a church member who worked for an infidel, building boats that required nonrusting copper rivets. These copper rivets were quite expensive, and every day this supposed-to-be Christian would take a few home with him. In time he had a good many. He would say to himself: "My boss has thousands of these rivets—he will never miss the few I take, and anyway, he doesn't pay me enough for my work."

Then he began hearing a certain minister preach. After a few nights he said to him: "Pastor, I am in trouble. I have heard you preach about how we ought to be honest. I want to serve the Lord Jesus. I am a Christian, a church member, and I love the Lord but, you know, I have been taking copper rivets from my employer, and now I want to put them back. But if I do, and that infidel finds out that I have been stealing, he won't come to your meetings. It will ruin my influence with him if he hears that I have been stealing copper rivets from him. If he finds out that I'm just a common thief, he'll lose all faith in Christianity. You see, I've been trying to get him to come to these meetings. I want to be a Christian, but I don't know what to do."

The preacher said, "You had better do right."

A few nights later, this man came to the minister with a glow of happiness on his face, and said, "Well, I went and told my employer what I had been doing, and handed him the money for those rivets. He said, 'Well, Jones, there must be something to this religion after all. I knew all the time that you were taking those copper rivets—that is one reason why I had no use for you Christians. I said to myself, "They are all a bunch of hypocrites." But if it is going to make you an honest man, I think I will go and hear that man preach. There must be something to it.' "

I just wonder if any of us have a few copper rivets to take back or to pay for. Oh, we would have a greater revival than we have had yet if all the copper rivets were taken back to their owners. And don't you think we would be happier?

DAY / 152

Read Proverbs 31; Psalms 127; 128; and 144; Ephesians 5:22 through 6:4.

Today's reading: The book of Proverbs closes with a beautiful eulogy on a happy home. We include three psalms and a passage from the New Testament.

Memory gem: "Charity [love] suffereth long, and is kind; charity [love] envieth not; charity [love] vaunteth not itself, is not puffed up" (1 Corinthians 13:4).

Thought for today:

I shall never forget the motto that hung in our dining room when I was a boy: "Christ is the head of this house, the unseen guest at every meal, the silent listener to every conversation."

You see, friends, a present God—present by His Holy Spirit in this world—is a blessing to His people, but a terrible curse and burden to those who reject Him. We need to live as in the presence of God, remembering the words of Scripture, "Thou God seest me" (Genesis 16:13). Neither the darkness nor the night can hide from Him.

Our God is a living God, a present God. If we will, He will be in our home. Then, when people enter, they will know that it is a Christian home, for the presence of God is there. The Bible is on the table, and it is read to the whole family every day. The voice of prayer is heard there too. The children who go out from such a home are armored against the sin and trouble that they are bound to meet in this old world. In the days in which we are living now, there is a great need of a revival of home religion. Like Obededom, we need the ark in our households. It would be good if the holy commandments of God were indeed engraved upon our doorposts, if we taught them to our children when we rise up and when we sit down (see Deuteronomy 6:7). Every home ought to be a Christian school.

Difficult or obscure words:

Proverbs 31:1. **"Lemuel"**—unknown; maybe Solomon.

Proverbs 31:10. **"Virtuous"**—literally: powerful; probably meaning strong character.

Proverbs 31:22. **"Silk"**—rather: fine white linen.

DAY / 153

Read 1 Kings 9; 2 Chronicles 8.

Today's reading: We resume the record of Solomon's glorious reign. The Lord appeared to Solomon a second time with a solemn warning, but the king became obsessed with riches and worldly glory.

Memory gem: "He that trusteth in his riches shall fall; but the righteous shall flourish as a branch" (Proverbs 11:28).

Thought for today:

Solomon indulged desire and passion; he married for beauty, lust, and political power rather than for love. He preached much but practiced little. He dispensed wisdom and embraced folly.

He acquired wealth. He gathered "silver and gold, and the peculiar treasure of kings and of the provinces" (Ecclesiastes 2:8). His wealth was unrivaled. The ships of his navy returned from each trip with 12 million dollars' worth of the gold of Ophir, as well as silver, ivory, apes, and peacocks, with "great plenty of almug trees, and precious stones" (1 Kings 10:11). It has been said that when the Queen of Sheba visited him, she left three and a half million dollars in gold alone. His annual gold revenue was 18 million dollars. But even this did not satisfy him. Solomon was trying to settle for a fool's bargain.

Today the Lord Jesus invites you and me to decide for Him, to reject the fool's bargain. He says, "Come now, and let us reason together" (Isaiah 1:18).

Being a Christian is a reasonable thing. Following Jesus in all that we know to be truth is a reasonable thing. It is foolish to do otherwise. God wants us to prepare now for eternity. Will you not include Christ in your plans today?

Note: The numbers given in 1 Kings 9:23 need to be harmonized with those in 2 Chronicles 2:18. See note on Day/140.

Difficult or obscure words:

1 Kings 10:28. **"Linen yarn"**—rather: from Kue, an ancient name for Alicia, then under Hittite control.

DAY / 154

Read 2 Chronicles 9; 1 Kings 10 and 11.

Today's reading: Solomon's mad pursuit of worldly pleasure plunged the unhappy king into apostasy and sowed the seeds of ruin for his kingdom.

Memory gem: "Trust not in oppression, and become not vain in robbery: if riches increase, set not your heart upon them" (Psalm 62:10).

Thought for today:

Now just a word about this man Solomon. He had a desire for happiness as all of us have, and he tried to find it. The book of Ecclesiastes, which he wrote late in life and after sincere repentance, brings us the story of his search for happiness. He had opportunities that very few of us have. He had unlimited money, he had great wisdom, he had supreme authority. If any man could find happiness in this world, surely he could.

The whole world today is like a mighty procession marching on, seeking happiness but seldom finding it. At most, the end of the trail is despair and sorrow and disillusion. Like a boy hunting for the pot of gold at the end of the rainbow, most human beings are forever seeking and never finding.

Solomon, the wisest man in his generation—possibly the wisest man who ever lived—set himself to search for happiness. He says: "I gave my heart to seek and search out by wisdom concerning all things that are done under heaven" (Ecclesiastes 1:13).

And did he succeed?

There was no science known in his day that he did not understand. He studied the laws of nations; legends and history became his heritage; the story of the world and the course of mankind were his treasured knowledge. He gathered together the priceless works of literature. He acquired a vast knowledge of nature, the flora and fauna of the world. He knew about botany, from the cedar in Lebanon to the hyssop that grows out of the wall.

But did this wisdom and knowledge bring him happiness? He answers: "For in much wisdom is much grief: and he that increaseth knowledge increaseth sorrow." "Behold, all is vanity and vexation of spirit" (Ecclesiastes 1:18, 14).

Note: See **Difficult or obscure words** on next page.

DAY / 155

Read Ecclesiastes 1 through 5.

Today's reading: Solomon's old age brought repentance and a valiant attempt to warn others against the folly of pursuing pleasure.

Memory gem: "I said in mine heart, God shall judge the righteous and the wicked: for there is a time there for every purpose and for every work" (Ecclesiastes 3:17).

Thought for today:

Solomon sought happiness in riches. He became the world's richest man. His fleet brought him shipments of gold, ivory, and precious stones. It has been said that he erected one building that cost five billion dollars; he was worth millions, at least, in gold But did this wealth bring him happiness?

He lived in a gold-filled palace, the like of which the world had never seen; possessed tapestries and gems and luxury of the East; constructed beautiful buildings, parks, lakes, fountains, zoological and botanical gardens; founded and built museums to preserve his priceless works of art; and erected the great temple which he had built and crowned with gold like a mountain topped with snow, with its golden altar and golden furnishings. Surely Solomon must have found happiness in it all.

But no, he says: "Then I looked on all the works that my hands had wrought, and on the labour that I had laboured to do: and, behold, all was vanity and vexation of spirit, and there was no profit under the sun" (Ecclesiastes 2:11).

Difficult or obscure words for Day/154:

1 Kings 11:5, 7. **"Milcom"**—Molech; also called Malcham (see Zephaniah 1:5); one of the most repulsive aspects of Baal (see Jeremiah 19:5, 6; 32:35). Children were burned alive as offerings to this deity.

1 Kings 11:40. **"Shishak"**—identified as Sheshonk I, a Libyan army commander who established the twenty-second dynasty of Egypt.

DAY / 156

Read Ecclesiastes 6 through 12.

Today's reading: The repentant wise man continues his reminiscences and advice; he ends his appeal with a solemn conclusion.

Memory gem: "Let us hear the conclusion of the whole matter: Fear God, and keep his commandments: for this is the whole duty of man" (Ecclesiastes 12:13).

Thought for today:

Solomon's example is at once a warning and an inspiration; for, though he failed in his efforts to find happiness through the devices of this world, through intellect, pleasure, and labor, he did find true happiness at last.

"He that keepeth the law," wrote Solomon, "happy is he" (Proverbs 29:18).

He found happiness in obedience to God. Here is his advice on the subject: "Let us hear the conclusion of the whole matter: Fear God and keep his commandments: for this is the whole duty of man. For God shall bring every work into judgment, with every secret thing, whether it be good, or whether it be evil" (Ecclesiastes 12:13, 14).

These are almost the same words that we find in Revelation 22:14: "Blessed [happy] are they that do his commandments."

There is one thing certain: Disobedience to God brings unhappiness. Everywhere it appears, it brings confusion, suffering, pain, and finally death. When we break the laws of nature, we suffer for it. When we break the moral laws of God, we suffer for our disobedience. There is an effect for every cause.

It was God's plan that man should be honest, faithful, reasonable; that he should walk in the ways of God and follow a righteous life. If he does not do this, he pays for it in disease of body and disease, restlessness, and dissatisfaction of heart. His conscience troubles him. He is unhappy.

Do you want to have joy? Do you want to be happy? Then believe in God. Give your heart to Christ and be happy forever.

DAY / 157

Read 2 Chronicles 10 through 12; 1 Kings 12.

Today's reading: We begin the sad story of Israel's decline from the glory of Solomon to the ignominy of captivity and dispersion. The trouble starts with a foolish refusal to follow sage advice.

Memory gem: "When he humbled himself, the wrath of the Lord turned from him, that he would not destroy him altogether: and also in Judah things went well" (2 Chronicles 12:12).

Thought for today:

"With the rending of the kingdom early in Rehoboam's reign, the glory of Israel began to depart, never again to be regained in its fullness. At times during the centuries that followed, the throne of David was occupied by men of moral worth and far-seeing judgment, and under the rulership of these sovereigns the blessings resting upon the men of Judah were extended to the surrounding nations. . . . From time to time mighty prophets arose, to strengthen the hands of the rulers, and to encourage the people to continued faithfulness. But the seeds of evil already springing up when Rehoboam ascended the throne, were never able to be wholly uprooted; and at times the once-favored people of God were to fall so low as to become a byword among the heathen.

"Yet notwithstanding the perversity of those who leaned toward idolatrous practices, God . . . would do everything in His power to save the divided kingdom from utter ruin. And as . . . His purpose concerning Israel seemed to be utterly thwarted by the devices of men inspired by satanic agencies, He still manifested His beneficent designs through the captivity and restoration of the chosen nation."
—*Prophets and Kings,* pp. 96, 97.

Note: It will be impossible to keep the narratives in Kings and Chronicles strictly parallel. Another difficulty will be the variant spelling of names in the two records and the fact that some kings of Judah had the same names as some kings of Israel.

Difficult or obscure words:

2 Chronicles 10:11. **"Scorpions"**—probably a figure of speech for whips of thongs armed with metal or bone hooks or points.

2 Chronicles 11:18, 20. **"Daughter"**—probably: granddaughter. The Hebrew word can mean a female descendant, even as "son" can mean a male descendant.

DAY / 158

Read I Kings 13 and 14.

Today's reading: The Lord attempts to turn King Jeroboam I from his apostasy—a sin from which the northern kingdom never recovered.

Memory gem: "He shall give Israel up because of the sins of Jeroboam, who did sin, and who made Israel to sin" (1 Kings 14:16).

Thought for today:

"At the time of the feast at Bethel, the hearts of the Israelites were not fully hardened. Many were susceptible to the influence of the Holy Spirit. The Lord designed that those who were taking rapid steps in apostasy, should be checked in their course before it should be too late. He sent His messenger to interrupt the idolatrous proceedings, and to reveal to king and people what the outworking of this apostasy would be. The rending of the altar was a sign of God's displeasure at the abomination that was being wrought in Israel.

"The Lord seeks to save, not to destroy. He delights in the rescue of sinners. 'As I live, saith the Lord God, I have no pleasure in the death of the wicked.' Ezekiel 33:11. By warnings and entreaties He calls the wayward to cease from their evil-doing, and to turn to Him and live."—*Prophets and Kings,* pp. 102–105.

Note: Rehoboam's son Abidam (Abijah in Chronicles) became the second king of Judah. Jeroboam's son Abidah died before his father did.

Difficult or obscure words:

1 Kings 14:3. **"Cracknels"**—probably hard, brittle cakes.

DAY / 159

Read 2 Chronicles 13 through 15.

Today's reading has at least one bright spot: the reformation under Asa in Judah. Even good King Asa, however, became careless later and lapsed into sin.

Memory gem: "Be ye strong therefore, and let not your hands be weak: for your work shall be rewarded" (2 Chronicles 15:7).

Thought for today:

Do we need a revival of true religion today? There is no question about the answer. But will we have the revival we need? Will it come? Friends, it will never come until we fulfill the laws of revival. God will do His part, but not until we do our part. We will not have a revival until we obey the rules.

For just a moment let us see how the revival came in the days of King Asa. As we read 2 Chronicles 15, it seems that we are looking at a picture of our day. It was a time of trouble. Many had forsaken the worship of God. Religious education was on the decline. This is the case with millions today.

Well, what are the rules? What do we need for a revival?

First: *Courage* (see verse 7). It takes courage to break with evil habits and bad associates.

Second: *Put away all idols* (see verse 8). What about our idols today? Anything that comes between us and God is an idol; and, judged by that standard, this is an idolatrous age. This applies especially to idols of the mind, and they must be put away. Are we willing to give them up?

Next, after courage and putting away idols, we come to the third step toward a revival *renewing the altar of the Lord.* That's what King Asa did (see verse 8), and that is what everyone who has ever had a real revival has done. God's altar must be renewed in our hearts, in our homes, and in our churches. Do you pray, privately and alone? Do you have family worship in your home? Do you take part in public worship? We must pray if we are to have a revival today. It will never come without prayer.

What was the result when King Asa obeyed the laws of revival? The answer is in verse 9. The people responded and came from all directions to help him when they saw the result of his consecration. And we are told that the revival caused the people to dedicate themselves and their possessions to the Lord. Then happiness came to them.

DAY / 160

Read 1 Kings 15; 2 Chronicles 16; 1 Kings 16.

Today's reading: Conditions in the northern kingdom degenerated from bad to worse, each king adding more evil to the existing apostasy.

Memory gem: "The eyes of the Lord run to and fro throughout the whole earth, to shew himself strong in the behalf of them whose heart is perfect toward him" (2 Chronicles 16:9).

Thought for today:

"The apostasy introduced during Jeroboam's reign became more and marked, until finally it resulted in the utter ruin of the kingdom of Israel. Even before the death of Jeroboam, Ahijah, the aged prophet at Shiloh who many years before had predicted the elevation of Jeroboam to the throne, declared: 'The Lord shall smite Israel, as a reed is shaken in the water, and he shall root up Israel out of this good land, which he gave to their fathers, and shall scatter them beyond the river, because they have made their groves, provoking the Lord to anger. And he shall give Israel up because of the sins of Jeroboam, who did sin, and who made Israel to sin.' 1 Kings 14:15, 16.

"Yet the Lord did not give Israel up without first doing all that could be done to lead them back to their allegiance to Him. Through long, dark years when ruler after ruler stood up in bold defiance of Heaven and led Israel deeper and still deeper into idolatry, God sent message after message to His backslidden people. Through His prophets He gave them every opportunity to stay the tide of apostasy, and to return to Him. . . . Even in the darkest hours, some would remain true to their divine Ruler, and in the midst of idolatry would live blameless in the sight of a holy God. These faithful ones were numbered among the goodly remnant through whom the eternal purpose of Jehovah was finally to be fulfilled."—*Prophets and Kings,* pp. 107, 108.

Note: No attempt is made in these brief notes to explain the chronology of various reigns and events. Many factors concerning Hebrew reckoning most be considered in order to understand precisely the order of events. For example, "the six and thirtieth year of Asa" (2 Chronicles 16:1) has to be the thirty-sixth year of Judah as a separate kingdom in order for Baasha to provoke war with Asa.

DAY / 161

Read 1 Kings 17 and 18.

Today's reading: One of the most dramatic stories in the Bible recounts Elijah's mission to convince apostate Ahab and his people of God's supremacy over Baal.

Memory gem: "How long halt ye between two opinions? If the Lord be God, follow him: but if Baal, then follow him" (1 Kings 18:21).

Thought for today:

Poor Elijah! He had been at high tension for days, and his physical exertion had been extreme. He had looked death in the face. For a few hours he had lived in supreme spiritual exultation and had won a mighty victory over the opposition of the idolatrous king, priests, and people. Now came the reaction.

The weary prophet lay down under a desert juniper tree and wanted to die—he even prayed to die. It is good that God does not always give us what we ask. Elijah thought that his work was done and there was nothing more to live for. He wanted to die. But God knew that what he needed was rest, sleep, and food. And there under the juniper tree Elijah found them at an angel's hand. How blessed it is that God does not forsake us when we forsake ourselves—when we are tired, sick, blue, discouraged, sitting under the little juniper tree of our own private wilderness. Instead, he sends His angel of mercy to minister His blessing to us.

Later, in the cave on Horeb, came the word of God, which sustained Elijah through everything. Out of his black discouragement, he came back into the light of faith and obedience when he heard the divine whisper. True, all the visible prospects were against him, but God was for him and God's word had come to him. So he went on to Jezreel and to Jordan and to the chariot of fire. No, he did not die under the juniper tree as he had prayed to do, nor in the cave, nor by the hand of Jezebel or the prophets of Baal. He never died at all. He kept on living; he is living now.

Can you, friend, not draw encouragement from this man of God? God has a place for you; He has a work for you. Are you in that place, and are you doing that work? If not, will you not listen to His Word and look to the Lord Jesus Christ for salvation? Repent and obey His divine Word. Now is the time. This is the hour to start. May God help you to go forward in the way of faith as did Elijah, the man who heard God whisper.

DAY / 162

Read 1 Kings 19 and 20.

Today's reading: Despite the positive evidence Ahab had of the Lord's power, the wicked king seemed unable to realize that all his evil doings were open to God's view.

Memory gem: "All things are naked and opened unto the eyes of him with whom we have to do" (Hebrews 4:13).

Thought for today:

Mr. Westlake, a news reporter, arrived home late one afternoon and found that his wife and children had gone to the zoo. He was just having a little snack as he relaxed in the living room. As he finished his sandwich, he said to himself, "I hope they got there all right." Then he turned on his television set to see if there was anything worth looking at. The first thing he saw was his wife and children at the zoo! He watched until they went off the screen.

Then he said to himself: "I had no idea that there was to be any televising at the zoo. And when I turned the TV on I never dreamed of seeing the zoo; and least of all did I expect to see my wife and children." In fact, they did not know that they had been televised until they returned home.

If such television should become general, many people would be panic-stricken and fear that their every action might be open to others. Yet millions go about their daily pursuits completely oblivious to the fact that God does not miss an act, an attitude, a word, or even a thought.

Note: The Ben-hadad against whom Ahab warred is not the same one Asa encountered (see 1 Kings 15). This is Ben-hadad II. A Ben-hadad III appears later (see 2 Kings 13).

Difficult or obscure words:

1 Kings 20:38. **"Ashes upon his face"**—rather: bandage over his eyes. The bandage served a double purpose: It indicated a battle wound, and it disguised the man's identity (see verse 41).

DAY / 163

Read 1 Kings 21 and 2 Chronicles 17.

Today's reading: A wicked king allows his evil wife to commit a great wrong on an innocent man—all because of covetousness.

Memory gem: "Take heed, and beware of covetousness; for a man's life consisteth not in the abundance of the things which he possesseth" (Luke 12:14).

Thought for today:

We might call this "The Sin of Sins." As a minister, I have had people confess practically every sin and crime possible to man, but I don't remember one single instance that anyone ever confessed this sin to me. Yet it is the sin back of all sin.

What is this sin? It is the sin forbidden in the tenth commandment.

Covetousness is really selfishness. That is why it is the sin of sins. It is back of all sins—self-exaltation, egotism. The man who, by the Holy Spirit, observes this commandment will not desire glory for himself.

Covetousness and love are opposite poles in the human heart. When one comes in, the other goes out.

Life does not consist of things—a fine home, a new car, and so on and so on. These things are nice to have, and it is not wrong to have them if they are rightly obtained, but life does not consist of them. Remember the story that Jesus told about the rich man who pulled down his barns to build greater, that he might take his ease, eat, drink, and be merry.

Covetousnes is a "respectable" sin. It is like pride. Even church members can be guilty of it and not know it. No doubt many who are covetous do not realize that they are. That is why they never confess their sin of covetousness. It is deceitful and prevalent.

God gave Heaven's greatest Gift for our salvation. Jesus Christ, our Lord, gave Himself for our redemption. The cure for covetousness is true regeneration, conversion, the power of the Spirit of God, that those who are born as the sons of God may walk in the Spirit of the Lord Jesus Christ who, though He was rich, became poor that we through His poverty might become rich (see 2 Corinthians 8:9).

Let us seek God for the victory over selfishness and the sin we are afraid to mention.

DAY / 164

Read 1 Kings 22; 2 Chronicles 18.

Today's reading: Good King Jehoshaphat becomes involved in a friendship with wicked King Ahab. Tragic results follow.

Memory gem: "Righteousness exalteth a nation: but sin is a reproach to any people" (Proverbs 14:34).

Thought for today:

In one of the famous battles of the Old Testament, Jehoshaphat, king of Judah, went with Ahab, king of Israel, to fight against the Syrians for the return of Ramoth-gilead. Just before the battle, the king of Syria called his thirty-two captains together and said to them, "Fight neither with small nor great, save only with the king of Israel" (1 Kings 22:31). They knew that when King Ahab was killed, his whole cause would collapse and they would win the victory. And so it turned out. Even though Ahab was disguised, one soldier drew a bow at a venture, and Ahab, who was really responsible for this terrible battle, could not avoid the arrow of retribution. It found him in one of the joints of his armor; it found him in a weak spot, just one weak spot. He went down in defeat and soon was dead, and the battle was over. His army was dissipated, and Syria was victorious.

My friends, this is a picture of human life. Let us make war with neither small nor great, save only our besetting sin, whatever it may be, and under God through Jesus Christ, gain the victory. Then we'll be on the road toward the City of God.

Sin drives us out from friendship. Sin drives us out from holiness. Sin drives us out from peace. Pride, envy, intemperance, avarice, anger, lust, and sloth—the seven deadly sins—drive us out, out, always out! Peter denied his Lord and *went out* and wept bitterly. Judas betrayed his Master, and *went out* into the night and hanged himself. Always *out*—sin always separates.

Repentance brings us back, draws us near. Peter repented and went back to Jesus, and to Pentecost. Ah, friends, repentance brings us back—back to God, back home, back to friendship, back to the church, back to peace.

DAY / 165

Read 2 Kings 1 through 3.

Today's reading: A variety of incidents includes the fiery ascension of Elijah and the beginning of Elisha's ministry.

Memory gem: "The righteous shall be glad in the Lord, and shall trust in him; and all the upright in heart shall glory" (Psalm 64:10).

Thought for today:

What a tremendous spectacle this must have been! Nothing could part Elisha from Elijah on their journey to the schools of the prophets; not even the turbulent Jordan could separate them. But now as they are walking and talking together, a luminous cloud descends upon them. A flaming chariot of fire, drawn by horses of fire, swirls down between them—the only thing that could separate them. Elisha looks heavenward and sees Elijah as he goes up "by a whirlwind into heaven." This was a triumphant and dramatic event for the Prophet of Fire.

God had used Elijah in a remarkable way. Before the time of his ministry, the children of God had strayed from the principles of righteousness that He had given to them. A real reformation was needed, and God had thoroughly fitted Elijah for this work. The great problem of that day was idolatry.

It is easy for us to study the history of days gone by and to forget that the problem of idolatry is one that still confronts us. I have seen various kinds of paganism in various lands. I have seen idolatry in its rankest forms. But, friends, let me say this: Idolatry is found in *every* country, not merely in the non-Christian portions of the world. Whatever or whomever we love and serve more than the Creator God is an idol. This is worshiping the "creature more than the Creator" (Romans 1:25).

When facing the matter squarely, we must admit that there are many modern gods that need to be destroyed by fire as were the idols of Baal.

Let us abolish the idols in our hearts and worship the true and living God, our Creator, the God of the prophet Elijah.

Note: Jehoram, a second son of Ahab, succeeded Ahaziah as king of Israel. He is also called Joram (see 2 Kings 8:16 and elsewhere). Further complicating the identity problem is the fact that his contemporary in Judah, Jehoshaphat's son, is also named Jehoram (see tomorrow's reading).

DAY / 166

Today's reading: We return to Judah under Jehoshaphat. Notice particularly the unusual battle plan Jehoshaphat used.

Memory gem: "Believe in the Lord your God, so shall ye be established; believe his prophets, so shall ye prosper" (2 Chronicles 20:20).

Thought for today:

We should notice especially here that when Israel began to sing and to praise, the Lord began to work. This proves that their faith was real. They believed that the promises of God were as good as the actual accomplishment of the promises. They believed the Lord or, as more literally translated, "they built upon the Lord," and so they were established or built up. They proved the truth of the scripture which says, "This is the victory that overcometh the world, even our faith" (1 John 5:4).

They began to praise God for the victory which they expected.

Now, let us apply this principle to our own lives so that we may live above defeat. Here comes a strong temptation to do wrong. The strength of temptation is in our weakness to overcome, as we have often proved to our sorrow. We have been vanquished and have fallen into sin. Now we turn to God. Our eyes are upon Him, and we begin to pray. What do we say first? Do we begin to talk about the great temptation and our weakness? Do we begin with a mournful statement of the hopeless situation in which we find ourselves? No. If we follow the example of Jehoshaphat, we will begin first with a joyful acknowledgment of God's mighty power. We will remind Him of His promises, and then we will tell Him about our troubles and our weakness. We are not to put our weakness before God's power, but His power before our weakness. The contrast will bring us courage.

Then as we pray, God's promises come to our minds, brought there by the Holy Spirit. We can begin to praise God for the victory that has not yet come, because it is already in His promise. By faith we can see God's hand already bringing us victory.

DAY / 167

Read 2 Kings 4 and 5.

Today's reading: Elisha is sometimes called the "miracle-working prophet." We marvel at the ministry of this man of God among the stiff-necked people of an apostate nation.

Memory gem: "If the prophet had commanded you to do some great thing, would you not have done it? How much rather, then, when he says to you, 'Wash, and be clean'? " (2 Kings 5:13, RSV).

Thought for today:

We raise the question, Is God particular? For one example, take your Bible and turn to the fifth chapter of the second book of Kings. Naaman comes from a far country. He comes in his great chariot with his fine horses and retinue of servants.

He drives up in front of the prophet's house, but Elisha merely sends his servant to the door. If such a man of nobility should come to your door, would you not rush out to greet him yourself? But no, that is not what the prophet of God did. Acting on God's instruction, he sent his servant out with the message, "If Naaman wants to be healed of leprosy, let him go down to Jordan and bathe seven times."

Naaman went away very angry, saying: "Here I am, the captain of the army of Syria, with my fine horses, my chest of great treasures, and all my fine apparel. I thought he would place his hand on the malady and call upon his God to heal me. I am not going to get down in that muddy Jordan. If I need a series of baths, why not Abana and Pharpar, the crystal-clear rivers of Damascus?" And so he went away in a rage.

But, friends, later he thought better of it. On the advice of one of his servants, he finally went down and bathed in old Jordan just as God had instructed him. He dipped beneath the water, but when he came up he was still just the same. Down again; up again—just the same. What difference did it make? Why go down *seven* times, as God had said—water is water! He was just the same after he came up the sixth time.

But when he came up the *seventh* time, a new light was in his eyes—he was healed—his flesh was like a baby's. Ask Naaman, as he comes up dancing with health and vitality, if God is particular. He will say, "Yes, God is particular." Thank God he learned that lesson in time—God is particular!

DAY / 168

Read 2 Kings 6 through 8.

Today's reading: Elisha, as a citizen of Israel, finds himself in peril of capture by an angry Syrian king; but only Elisha's servant is worried.

Memory gem: "The angel of the Lord encampeth round about them that fear him, and delivereth them" (Psalm 34:7).

Thought for today:

We can imagine the excitement and fear of Elisha's servant when he saw the town of Dothan surrounded by the enemy. He asked the prophet, "What shall we do?"

Elisha calmed his fear by saying, "They that be with us are more than they that be with them" (2 Kings 6:16).

Then the prophet prayed that God would open the young man's eyes. He did, and suddenly Elisha's servant saw all the hills surrounding the city covered with the shining hosts of God.

So it is with us today. "They that be with us are more than they that be" against us—more in power, more in wisdom, more in loyal service to the King of kings. Let us be of good courage, remembering that we are no farther away from heaven today than were Abraham, Daniel, the apostles Peter and John. The angels of God are with us now, as they were with God's people of old. They are interested in you; they are interested in me; and they care for us. So let us open and read the book of Holy Scripture, the Holy Bible, the Book of the angels.

Note: The king of Syria mentioned here is Ben-hadad II. Ahaziah, only surviving son of King Jehoram of Judah, had the same name as the sickly successor of Ahab. This king of Judah is also called Jehoahaz (see 2 Chronicles 21:17) and Azariah (see 2 Chronicles 22:6). He was a nephew to King Jehoram (Joram) of Israel through his mother Athaliah.

Difficult or obscure words:

2 Kings 6:25. **"Fourth part of a cab"**—about a cupful.

2 Kings 8:26. **"Daughter of Omri"**—This is the same as the "daughter of Ahab" of verse 18. A common Hebrew practice is to mention the originator of the regnal family rather than the immediate parent. Athaliah was the daughter of Ahab and wicked Queen Jezebel, therefore sister of Jehoram (Joram) of Israel.

DAY / 169

Read 2 Kings 9 and 10; 2 Chronicles 22.

Today's reading: The evil results of Ahab's wicked reign bring tragedy to the unrepentant worshipers of Baal; Jehu destroys one false religion but fails to bring about a true reformation.

Memory gem: "Jehu took no heed to walk in the law of the Lord God of Israel with all his heart: for he departed not from the sins of Jeroboam, which made Israel to sin" (2 Kings 10:31).

Thought for today:

Mrs. Richards and I had the privilege of riding in a taxi from the town of Mosulin Mesopotamia to the ancient mounds which cover the biblical city of Calah, one of the oldest cities in the world. In 1845 Layard found the Black Obelisk of Shalmaneser III there. On that monument, now in the British Museum, was a picture of King Jehu of Israel paying tribute to Shalmaneser. So here we find the name of an Israelite king actually inscribed on an obelisk by the king of Assyria who forced him to pay tribute.

But one of the most interesting finds of Calah consisted of many beautiful carved ivory plaques which archaeologists believe may have covered the walls of Ahab's palace. These plaques had evidently been taken as loot from the destruction of Ahab's "ivory house" in Samaria. When the city was looted by the Assyrians in 722 B.C., many of these plaques were torn from the walls and carried away to Assyria.

So we see that one discovery after another sustains the historical authenticity of Bible statements. They all join together in one voice saying, "The Holy Bible is true."

Why not read this Bible? Why not study it, believe it, accept its teachings, meditate upon its truths, find your life changed for good, and your hope enriched and strengthened?

Difficult or obscure words:

2 Kings 9:1. **"Box"**—rather: flask, or vial.

2 Kings 9:14. **"Joram had kept Ramoth-gilead"**—rather: Joram's forces ("all Israel"). The king himself had left the field to seek healing at Jezreel (see verse 15).

2 Kings 9:21. **"Against Jehu"**—rather: to meet Jehu. They did not suspect danger, or they would have taken a bodyguard.

DAY / 170

Read 2 Kings 11 and 12; 2 Chronicles 23.

Today's reading: The apostasy of the northern kingdom spread into Judah because of Jehoshaphat's unwise friendship with Ahab. Wicked Queen Athaliah shares the same fate as that of her idolatrous mother Jezebel.

Memory gem: "Jehoiada made a covenant between the Lord and the king and the people, that they should be the Lord's people" (2 Kings 11:17).

Thought for today:

"Jehoiada commanded the officers to lay hold of Athaliah and all her followers, and led them out of the temple to a place of execution, where they were to be slain.

"Thus perished the last member of the house of Ahab. The terrible evil that had been wrought through his alliance with Jezebel, continued till the last of his descendants was destroyed. Even in the land of Judah, where the worship of the true God had never been formally set aside, Athaliah had succeeded in seducing many. Immediately after the execution of the impenitent queen, 'all the people of the land went into the house of Baal, and brake it down; his altars and his images brake they in pieces thoroughly, and slew Mattan the priest of Baal before the altars.' 2 Kings 11:18.

"A reformation followed. Those who took part in acclaiming Joash king, had solemnly covenanted 'that they should be the Lord's people.' And now that the evil influence of the daughter of Jezebel had been removed from the kingdom of Judah, and the priests of Baal had been slain and their temple destroyed, 'all the people of the land rejoiced: and the city was quiet.' 2 Chronicles 23:16, 21."—*Prophets and Kings,* p. 216.

Note: Joash (see 2 Kings 11:2) is called Jehoash in verse 21 and elsewhere. Later a king of Jehu's dynasty in Israel was named Jehoash, also sometimes called Joash.

Difficult or obscure words:

2 Kings 11:5. **"Without the ranges"**—between the ranks or under armed escort.

DAY / 171

Read 2 Chronicles 24; 2 Kings 13 and 14.

Today's reading: The succession of evil deeds continues generation after generation, king after king, with only an occasional break in the deadly pattern.

Memory gem: "Yet he [God] sent prophets to them, to bring them again unto the Lord; and they testified against them: but they would not give ear" (2 Chronicles 24:19).

Thought for today:

Some time ago, one of the strangest tragedies in the record of wildlife occurred at Niagara Falls. The wild geese were migrating southward for the winter. Great flocks of them, wearied by the long journey from the north, settled down to rest on the quiet waters of the Niagara River above the falls. At first slowly, then faster, the careless birds were carried toward the brink of the thundering falls. On the very edge of the plunge, each bird trumpeted wildly and, by a supreme effort of wings, lifted itself from the clutching waters; then, wheeling in triumph over the chasm, returned upstream to repeat the performance. Like boys taking turns on a slippery slide, these birds by the hundreds kept up their dangerous sport.

Fog settled down and night came on. Many of the players began to show signs of weariness, but they did not stop. Game wardens tried to frighten the birds away, but a strange fascination seemed to hold them. All night the swish of wings and the trumpeting of triumph or despair continued.

The next morning the lower parts of the Niagara River were strewn with the white bodies of those birds that, in the darkness, had misjudged the precipice or were too tired to lift themselves from the plunging waters. And, strange to say, this experience is repeated every year. In varying numbers, the southbound flocks take up this fight with the falls.

They are only geese; but how like them is our race! One generation after another repeats the dangerous game of sin and crime and war, and plunges on over the falls.

The best way to break away from the deadly cycle of sin is to give your heart to Christ, your Saviour, and consecrate your energies and life to Him and bear your witness wherever you are.

DAY / 172

Read Jonah.

Today's reading: A hot-headed prophet reluctantly goes on a mission for the Lord. He conducts a very successful evangelistic campaign—and then becomes angry at the results!

Memory gem: "When my soul fainted within me I remembered the Lord: and my prayer came in unto thee, into thine holy temple" (Jonah 2:7).

Thought for today:

My friend, if you have been buying tickets to Tarshish, I plead with you, Come back to God. Every drink of liquor is a ticket to Tarshish; every evil word, every impurity is a ticket to Tarshish. When you buy a ticket to Tarshish, away from God, away from the church, away from religion, you start to go down. And often, like Jonah, you may not stop until you get to the bottom.

But, wherever you are on the road to Tarshish, now is the time to call on the Lord. He will hear you. Come back to God, back to duty, back to prayer, back to the Bible, back to purity, back to mother, to wife, to children, to home, and to heaven.

Judas betrayed Christ, and Peter denied Him. As far as we know, one sin was about the same as the other. But Judas went to a suicide's grave, while Peter went to Pentecost. The difference between the two men was that Peter came back.

God can change you and use you in His great work, just where you ought to be! Come back from Tarshish and get on the road to Nineveh, back to family worship, back to the Bible.

May God give us a vision of this hour when the world's statesmen labor hard to bring the boat of civilization to a safe harbor! Arise, Christian, and renew the altar fires of prayer. Pray for your country's leaders, pray for the church, pray for your family—for the wandering boys and girls.

And you, friend, if you are on the road to Tarshish, will you not, deep in your heart, pray this prayer:

I'm tired of sin and straying, Lord
Now I'm coming home;
I'll trust Thy love, believe Thy Word;
Lord, I'm coming home.

—William J. Kirkpatrick

Note: See **Difficult or obscure words** on next page.

DAY / 173

Read 2 Chronicles 25 and 26; 2 Kings 15:1-17.

Today's reading: Two fairly good kings brought better times to Judah. Amaziah served God, "but not with a perfect heart." His son, Uzziah (Azariah), followed the same pattern; but when "his heart was lifted up," personal tragedy brought him low.

Memory gem: "Pride goeth before destruction, and an haughty spirit before a fall" (Proverbs 16:18).

Thought for today:

We can hide nothing from God. With their super X-ray, men can look through heavy layers of solid steel. So God can read the secrets of the hardest heart. As with mysterious radar the operator sees objects through the thickest fog on the darkest night, so, God sees through mist and darkness.

We do not know just how God knows our actions and our thoughts; we do not know the secrets of His radar, if we may call it that. But the Scriptures tell us that He sees and He knows.

Friend, we can never persuade our real selves that wrong is right. A person may wish to do wrong and pretend to others, and even to himself, that he has convinced himself that it is right. Yes, a person may try to rationalize wrong into right; but away in the back of his mind he knows—especially when he awakens at three o'clock in the morning and thinks—that wrong is still wrong and not right. Did you ever notice the words of Isaiah 5:20? "Woe unto them that call evil good, and good evil; that put darkness for light, and light for darkness; that put bitter for sweet, and sweet for bitter!"

If a man puts his standard low enough, he can always make a favorable judgment concerning himself. If all other men were only four feet high, a man of five feet would be a giant. Some seem to think that by making others small they look quite good themselves. But, friend, the judgment which we face now in Christ, or later without Him, is not man's judgment, but God's.

Difficult or obscure words for Day/172:

Jonah 1:17. **"Great fish"**—The Hebrew word is a generic term for fish of any kind. The Greek word here in the Septuagint and in Matthew 12:40 (translated "whale" in the KJV) means "sea monster" of unspecificied kind. Nothing can be determined as to the nature of the "fish" or "monster." In any case, the Lord "prepared" the animal.

DAY / 174

Read Isaiah 1 and 2.

Today's reading: One of the greatest of the Old Testament prophets, Isaiah also had one of the longest careers. Today we begin reading this wonderful book, much of it in beautiful Hebrew poetic form.

Memory gem: "Come now, and let us reason together, saith the Lord: though your sins be as scarlet, they shall be as white as snow; though they be red like crimson, they shall be as wool" (Isaiah 1:18).

Thought for today:

This offer of God is not for tomorrow—it is for today. "Come now," He says. When Augustine came under conviction of sin, he prayed, "O God, cleanse me from all my sins, but *not now.*" A little later he prayed, "Lord, deliver me from all my sins but one." At last, in full surrender, he cried, "O God, deliver me from all my sins *now.*" And that is the only way for anyone to pray, the only way for those who really wish to come to Christ.

"If you see your sinfulness, do not wait to make yourself better. How many there are who think they are not good enough to come to Christ. Do you expect to become better through your own efforts? 'Can the Ethiopian change his skin, or the leopard his spots? then may ye also do good, that are accustomed to do evil.' Jeremiah 13:23. There is help for us only in God. We must not wait for stronger persuasions, for better opportunities, or for holier tempers. We can do nothing of ourselves. We must come to Christ just as we are. . . .

" Beware of procrastination. Do not put off the work of forsaking your sins and seeking purity of heart through Jesus. Here is where thousands have erred to their eternal loss. . . . There is a terrible danger—a danger not sufficiently understood—in delaying to yield to the pleading voice of God's Holy Spirit, in choosing to live in sin; for such this delay really is. Sin, however small it may be esteemed, can be indulged in only at the peril of infinite loss."—*Steps to Christ,* pp. 31–33.

Note: Isaiah's prophetic ministry covered a longer period than that of any other prophet—more than fifty-five years from the closing years of Uzziah's reign (before 740 B.C.) until after the close of Hezekiah's reign (after 686 B.C.).

DAY / 175

Today's reading: Amos, a citizen of Judah, bore a solemn message from the Lord to the northern kingdom, Israel. First he pronounced God's judgments on the surrounding nations as a warning to erring Israel.

Memory gem: "Because I will do this unto thee, prepare to meet thy God, O Israel" (Amos 4:12).

Thought for today:

The first doctrine of the Bible is the doctrine of God. "In the beginning God" (Genesis 1:1). The Holy Scriptures reveal the doctrine of God. On it all other doctrines rest. With full faith in the doctrine of God, the future is full of hope. Without it, life itself is "a narrow vale between the cold and barren peaks of two eternities," in the words of one of America's great skeptics. "God is He without whom one cannot live," was Leo Tolstoy's definition of God.

But what does the Holy Scripture say? We turn to the prophet Amos. "Lo, he that formeth the mountains, and createth the wind, and declareth unto man what is his thought, that maketh the morning darkness, and treadeth upon the high places of the earth, The Lord, The God of hosts, is his name" (Amos 4:13).

The existence of God is proved by the existence of the universe. Every effect must have an adequate cause. There is design in the world, so there must have been a designer. There is a mathematical plan in the universe, so there must have been a great mathematician. All things must have had an origin, a beginning, a creation. Either they created themselves or they came into existence by mere chance or they were made by a creator. Self-creation is a contradiction, for it supposes that a being can act before it exists. Creation by chance is absurd, for to say that a thing is caused with no cause for its production, is to say that a thing is effected when it is effected by nothing. All things, then, that do appear must have been created by some being. That being is God.

Note: The earthquake (Amos 1:1) is undated; but Josephus, the Jewish historian, says that it occurred when Uzziah was struck with leprosy in the temple.

Read Amos 5 through 9.

Today's reading: In the second half of the book of Amos, the prophet tries over and over to impress rebellious Israel with the greatness of God and the folly of forsaking His worship.

Memory gem: "Seek him that maketh the seven stars and Orion, and turneth the shadow of death into morning" (Amos 5:8).

Thought for today:

God has two great books: the book of nature, of which astronomy is one of the brightest chapters; and the Holy Scriptures, God's other book of revelation. Both books reveal Him.

"Lift up your eyes on high, and behold"—this is the study of astronomy. "Behold who hath created these things!" I believe it would do every young man and young woman good to spend at least one night awake under the starry heavens on some desert or high mountaintop where the skies are clear, and watch the rising and setting of the stars, the march of the constellations across the heavens. Looking at such a starry night, one may ask himself, Can anyone really tell us about these things? What is their purpose? Their destiny? How did it all begin? How will it all end? Or did it ever begin, and will it ever end?

The Bible gives us the working hypothesis regarding the origin and destiny of the universe. The study of astronomy in the light of the Bible is therefore the best rational way to study it. By a contemplation of God's Word and His works, we shall rise to a measure of real knowledge. Thus we shall never lose reverence for God or confidence in His Word. Since He is the Originator, the Creator, and the Upholder of the universe, the more we actually know about it, the more respect we shall have for God and the more faith in His wisdom and love in dealing with men. As we look at the shining heavens, we remember the words of Holy Scripture: "The heavens declare the glory of God; and the firmament sheweth his handywork. Day unto day uttereth speech, and night unto night sheweth knowledge" (Psalm 19:1, 2). We bow our heads in humility and wonder before His glory, power, and wisdom; and we whisper, "O Lord, my God, how great Thou art!"

Difficult or obscure words:

Amos 6:7. **"Banquet"**—an idolatrous cult festival.

Amos 9:6. **"Troop"**—a Hebrew word of uncertain meaning; probably "structure" or "vault."

DAY / 177

Today's reading: Another prophet sent to Israel during the reign of Jeroboam II enacted in his own life a tragic object lesson of God's dealings with His unfaithful people.

Memory gem: "I will even betroth thee unto me in faithfulness: and thou shalt know the Lord" (Hosea 2:20).

Thought for today:

Years ago in the deep South, a judge was engaged to marry a beautiful girl, but they quarreled. Pride so ruled her life that she wouldn't consent to a reconciliation.

The judge became reckless in his sorrow, and when a terrible scourge of yellow fever came to that southern town, he volunteered to spend his entire time caring for the sick. At last he succumbed to the dread disease and lay deathly sick for days.

One day when his physician happened to meet the judge's former sweetheart, whom he had known since his childhood, she asked in a careless way, "Well, how is your patient, Doctor?"

He replied, "He's passed the critical point, but he is dying."

"I don't understand that," she said. "If he has passed the crisis, why doesn't he get well?"

The old physician replied, "Don't you know why? He is dying of a broken heart, of hopeless love for you."

Her eyes filled with tears as she said, "Doctor, will you come with me?" She led the way to the florist shop and placed an order for some beautiful flowers. On the card she wrote, "With the love of all my heart," and signed the pet name that the judge had loved to call her. Then she said, "Doctor, will you see that he gets this box of flowers right away?"

When they were brought to the judge, he reached out his trembling hand for the box and drew out the card. He was almost afraid to look at it, for he was hoping against hope that it might be from her. When he saw that name he said, "Doctor, did she really send these flowers?"

The next day he was sitting up in a wheelchair, and on the fifth day there was a quiet wedding.

O friend, the world is desperately sick and millions of people are sick with it, a sickness unto death, eternal death. There is only one hope for it—the love of God in Christ Jesus.

DAY / 178

Read Hosea 5 through 9.

Today's reading: The prophet faithfully delivers his warnings, but almost in agony he pleads with the people to turn from their evil ways.

Memory gem: "Come, and let us return unto the Lord: for he hath torn, and he will heal us; he hath smitten, and he will bind us up" (Hosea 6:1).

Thought for today:

"My people are destroyed for lack of knowledge: because thou hast rejected knowledge, I will also reject thee, that thou shalt be no priest to me: seeing thou hast forgotten the law of thy God, I will also forget thy children" (Hosea 4:6).

People reject the Word of God, do not live for Christ, have no regard for the church; and then they wonder why their children so often drift out into a life of sin. One big reason for the tide of crime on earth today is the lack of religious and moral training in the homes. A true, consistent, Christian life of the parents in the home will do more to hold John and Mary for God than all the preaching they are likely to hear. The power of example is a mighty power; and when Father or Mother, or both, disregard the Ten Commandments in life and word and forget Christ in the homelife, it's a sad day for the children.

In how many homes—I mean Christian homes—is family worship a regular thing? Millions of children have never heard Father or Mother pray. You say you are too busy—you have no time for family prayer, no time for training the young. There is time to feed the body, but no time to feed the soul. No wonder the home is broken down, when God is not honored.

If we reject, ignore, or forget the divine law, we must receive the consequences. As men sow, they shall reap—always.

But when we turn to God in faith, He forgets our sins, but He does not forget us (see 1 John 1:9; Micah 7:18, 19; Isaiah 49:15). In an age of profound skepticism, the greatest need of each one of us is a return to faith in God.

Difficult or obscure words:

Hosea 5:13. **"Jareb"**—probably a descriptive term meaning "great" or "exalted" king, or possibly the king "who contends."

Hosea 6 9. **"By consent"**—better: toward Shechem.

DAY / 179

Read Hosea 10 through 14.

Today's reading: Hosea's prophecy breathes the agony of God's despair in trying to bring Israel to repentance. The Lord yearned for His people's return.

Memory gem: "I will heal their backsliding, I will love them freely; for mine anger is turned away from him" (Hosea 14:4).

Thought for today:

Grant Colfax Tullar, the singer and publisher of Christian songs, was left an orphan when a small boy and was farmed out to a man who treated him with utter cruelty. The man had ropes and a pulley fastened to the ceiling of the barn, and he used to draw the boy up by his thumbs until his toes barely touched the ground. Sometimes he would leave him hanging that way for nine hours at a stretch.

The boy swore with a dreadful oath, "If I ever live to be as big as this man, I will beat him to death with my own fists."

When he was twelve, Grant ran away and went down into the depths of sin. But the love of God found him. He became a follower of Christ, who teaches us to love even our enemies.

Later some friends asked Grant to preach. Well, just as they were singing the last verse of the song before the sermon, he looked down and saw right in front of him the man who had abused him when he was a child. He was a young giant now; and as he looked at the man, and at his wife, who had helped him in his cruelty, suddenly the flood of old resentment overwhelmed him.

Turning to the choir, he said, "Sing another song while I pray." Then he went down on his knees in that old box pulpit where no one but the choir and God could see. And this was his prayer: "Lord, I've promised with an oath to whip that man if I ever lived to be big enough to do it. I believe I could do it today. He needs the whipping; but, Lord, if You will whip him, I will preach to him of Your wondrous love." Then he arose from his knees and began to preach.

Later he made an altar call, and the first to respond were that man and his wife. The young preacher left the pulpit and went down to them. Kneeling between the two, he put an arm around each. There on his knees he led them both to Christ.

Nothing but the love of God could accomplish such a miracle. And that love is drawing you and me and all men today.

DAY / 180

Read 2 Kings 15:8 through chapter 16 and 2 Chronicles 27.

Today's reading: The sad record of six kings of Israel traces the continuing slide toward oblivion. Even the king of Judah "walked in the way of the kings of Israel."

Memory gem: "My people are destroyed for lack of knowledge: because thou hast rejected knowledge, I will also reject thee" (Hosea 4:6).

Thought for today:

"The iniquity in Israel during the last century before the Assyrian captivity, was like that of the days of Noah, and of every other age when men have rejected God and have given themselves wholly to evil-doing. The exaltation of nature above the God of nature, the worship of the creature instead of the Creator, has always resulted in the grossest of evils. Thus when the people of Israel, in their worship of Baal and Ashtoreth, paid supreme homage to the forces of nature, they severed their connection with all that is uplifting and ennobling, and fell an easy prey to temptation. With the defenses of the soul broken down, the misguided worshipers had no barrier against sin, and yielded themselves to the evil passions of the human heart.

"Against the marked oppression, the flagrant injustice, the unwonted luxury and extravagance, the shameless feasting and drunkenness, the gross licentiousness and debauchery, of their age, the prophets lifted their voices; but in vain were their protests, in vain their denunciation of sin. . . .

"The transgressors were given many opportunities to repent. In their hour of deepest apostasy and greatest need, God's message to them was one of forgiveness and hope. 'O Israel,' He declared, 'thou hast destroyed thyself; but in Me is thine help. I will be thy King; where is any other that may save thee?' " Hosea 13:9, 10. . . .

"From generation to generation, the Lord had borne with His wayward children; and even now, in the face of defiant rebellion, He still longed to reveal Himself to them as willing to save. 'O Ephraim' He cried, 'What shall I do unto thee? O Judah, what shall I do unto thee? for your goodness is as a morning cloud, and as the early dew it goeth away.' Hosea 6:4."—*Prophets and Kings,* pp. 281–285.

DAY / 181

Read Micah 1 through 4.

Today's reading: During this period of general apostasy God sent Micah as His messenger. Still the Lord pleaded with His people to repent and return to Him.

Memory gem: "He hath shewed thee, O man, what is good; and what doth the Lord require of thee, but to do justly, and to love mercy, and to walk humbly with thy God" (Micah 6:8).

Thought for today:

"The prophet Micah, who bore his testimony during those troublous times [the reign of King Ahaz], declared that sinners in Zion, while claiming to 'lean upon the Lord,' and blasphemously boasting, 'Is not the Lord among us? none evil can come upon us,' continued to 'build up Zion with blood, and Jerusalem with iniquity,' Micah 3:11, 10. . . .

"Inspiration declares, 'the sacrifice of the wicked is abomination: how much more, when he bringeth it with a wicked mind?' Proverbs 21:27. . . .

". . . It is not because He is unwilling to forgive, that He turns from the transgressor; it is because the sinner refuses to make use of the abundant provison of grace, that God is unable to deliver from sin. . . .

"This was indeed a time of great peril for the chosen nation. Only a few short years, and the ten tribes of the kingdom of Israel were to be scattered among the nations of heathendom. And in the kingdom of Judah also the outlook was dark. The forces for good were rapidly diminishing, the forces for evil multiplying. The prophet Micah, viewing the situation, was constrained to exclaim: 'The good man is perished out of the earth: and there is none upright among men.' Micah 7:2."—*Prophets and Kings,* pp. 322–324.

Note: Micah 4:1-3 is almost identical with Isaiah 2:2-4. These two prohecies have often been misunderstood. They probably belong with many other descriptions of God's plan for Israel—provided Israel would be faithful. Israel failed, as we shall see, therefore, the promise could not be fulfilled. It has also been suggested that the promise not attained by literal Israel may find ultimate fulfillment to spiritual Israel in the final triumph of the gospel.

DAY / 182

Today's reading: Tucked away in the grim judgments God predicted for rebellious Israel is one of the specific prophecies that would identify the Messiah.

Memory gem: "Unto you is born this day in the city of David a Saviour, which is Christ the Lord" (Luke 2:11).

Thought for today:

In Micah 5:2 we read the prophecy of the exact place where Jesus would be born. Remember, this was written about 700 years before Christ. The Messiah (Hebrew)—Christ (Greek)—Anointed (English)—must have a birthplace. Three continents—Europe, Asia, and Africa—were known to the ancient world. Asia is chosen. But Asia had many countries and regions. One of them—little Palestine—is pointed out. In Palestine were three divisions—Galilee, Samaria, and Judea. Judea is named. But in Judea are many villages; and "of the thousands of Judea," Bethlehem is the chosen place for His birth.

But Bethlehem means "the house of bread," and more than one village in a fertile place was so named. The prophet puts his finger on one spot: "Bethlehem Ephratah," in the land of Judah. What wonderful fulfillment!

Now, Christ's virgin mother did not live in Bethlehem of Judea, but at Nazareth in Galilee. And it was not very likely that she would be traveling at that time, by the difficult means of transportation of that day from one place to another. But a decree of imperial Rome compelled all to go to the place from which the family originally came, to be enrolled. So God brought the Blessed Virgin from Nazareth to Bethlehem at the precise time that would fulfill the prophecy of Micah.

DAY / 183

Read 2 Chronicles 28; Isaiah 3 and 4.

Today's reading: A somewhat good king (Jotham) is succeeded by Ahaz, one of the most wicked of all the kings of Judah.

Memory gem: "Sanctify the Lord of hosts himself; and let him be your fear, and let him be your dread. And he shall be for a sanctuary" (Isaiah 8:13, 14).

Thought for today:

"The accession of Ahaz to the throne brought Isaiah and his associates face to face with conditions more appalling than any that had hitherto existed in the realm of Judah. Many who had formerly withstood the seductive influence of idolatrous practices, were now being persuaded to take part in the worship of heathen deities. Princes in Israel were proving untrue to their trust; false prophets were arising with messages to lead astray; even some of the priests were teaching for hire. Yet the leaders in apostasy still kept up the forms of divine worship, and claimed to be numbered among the people of God." —*Prophets and Kings,* p. 322.

"As the apostate king neared the end of his reign, he caused the doors of the temple to be closed. The sacred services were interrupted. No longer were the candlesticks kept burning before the altar. No longer were offerings made for the sins of the people. No longer did sweet incense ascend on high at the time of the morning and the evening sacrifice. Deserting the courts of the house of God, and locking fast its doors, the inhabitants of the godless city boldy set up altars for the worship of heathen deities on the street corners throughout Jerusalem. Heathenism had seemingly triumphed; the powers of darkness had well-nigh prevailed.

"But in Judah there dwelt some who maintained their allegiance to Jehovah, steadfastly refusing to be led into idolatry. It was to these that Isaiah and Micah and their associates looked in hope as they surveyed the ruin wrought during the last years of Ahaz."—*Ibid,* p. 330.

DAY / 184

Today's reading: When wicked King Ahaz refused to ask God for a sign, God still gave him one, as well as a prophecy of the miraculous birth of the Messiah more than seven centuries later.

Memory gem: "Behold a virgin shall conceive, and bear a son, and shall call his name Immanuel" (Isaiah 7:14).

Thought for today:

Jesus Christ entered this world through birth. He had a human mother, yet He was the Son of God. He understands even the "feeling of our infirmities" (Hebrews 4:15). He knows what it is like to be a human being—to be hungry, to be weary, to be thirsty, to be rejected. He knows what it's like when enemies threaten and persecute. He also knows what it's like when friends desert us.

The birth of Christ—by which we mean His entrance into this world, including His miraculous conception—will always be a mystery. It is God's secret. The apostle Paul says: "Without controversy great is the mystery of godliness: God was manifest in the flesh, justified in the Spirit, seen of angels, preached unto the Gentiles, believed on in the world, received up into glory" (1 Timothy 3:16).

We cannot understand this in all its fullness, but we can believe it with all its wonder and blessed deliverance, salvation, and peace. The whole gospel is based upon it. How the Creator—for such Jesus was, with the Father—could become a man, is beyond our comprehension; but He did.

Christ entered this world through what has been called a "biological miracle." But what would we expect? Would we expect to understand the nature of God and all His mighty works? Could we do so, we would be equal to Him. Christ had a human mother, but no human father. Our Saviour Himself said: "I and my Father are one" (John 10:30). They were one in mind, one in nature. Christ was divine in the highest sense.

The purpose of His coming to this world was twofold: first, to reveal God; second, to redeem man. This is one reason why Jesus was sinless. God is sinless. This is why He was holy, for God is holy. No wonder the angel Gabriel said to the Blessed Virgin: "That holy thing which shall be born of thee shall be called the Son of God" (Luke 1:35).

DAY / 185

Today's reading: One of the remarkable prophecies of the coming Messiah is accompanied by beautiful promises for God's faithful people.

Memory gem: "For unto us a child is born, unto us a son is given: and the government shall be upon his shoulder: and his name shall be called Wonderful, Counsellor, The mighty God, The everlasting Father, The Prince of Peace" (Isaiah 9:6).

Thought for today:

It is said that our Lord Jesus Christ has at least sixty-five names in the Bible. Fifty-two of them are in the Old Testament; and five of those are in the wonderful prophecy in Isaiah 9:6.

This passage of prophecy is like a mighty carillon with five great bells. The prophet Isaiah is the bell ringer. Every time he rings a bell, there floats out into the centuries a mighty harmony. Since Isaiah wrote these words down by the inspiration of God 700 years before Christ was born, and since 2,000 years have already passed in the Christian era, the words of this text are at least 2,700 years old. Yet the echoes of these great bells ring as sweetly as ever. Listen to the five tones: "Wonderful, Counsellor, The mighty God, The everlasting Father, The Prince of Peace."

As the prophet Isaiah wrote these words in the future tense, he was looking forward to what was to come, what was to be. He predicted, he prophesied by the inspiration of the Holy Spirit. The New Testament records the fulfillment of this Old Testament prophecy about the holy Son of God. But to me the greatest wonder of all is not that the Good Book testified of Him, not that history stands up and bears witness for Him; but, thank God, that my own heart can testify, "I know whom I have believed" (2 Timothy 1:12). The wonder of all wonders to me is not that Christ was and is all that these other witnesses have claimed Him to be, but that this wonderful Christ is my wonderful Saviour and that through Him my sins have been forgiven. He gives me peace like a river (see Isaiah 48:18). He has planted my feet upon the rock (see Psalm 40:2). He is my Companion and Friend. He gives me access to the Father, for no man cometh to the Father but by Him (see John 14:6).

And because of this, all believers can sing, "What a wonderful Saviour is Jesus, my Lord!"

DAY / 186

Today's reading: Many of Isaiah's prophecies have been fulfilled with striking accuracy. Today's reading contains one of these—Isaiah 13:19, 20. Another well-known passage—Isaiah 14:12-15—describes Lucifer's rebellion against God.

Memory gem: "I will make a man more precious than fine gold; even a man than the golden wedge of Ophir" (Isaiah 13:12).

Thought for today:

The prophet Isaiah says that Babylon, "the glory of kingdoms, the beauty of the Chaldees' excellency, shall be as when God overthrew Sodom and Gomorrah" (Isaiah 13:19). It is a brief statement, a brief prophecy, but it is direct and literal.

There is still more. In Isaiah 13:20 we read: "Neither shall the Arabian pitch tent there." Now, how did Isaiah know that the Arabian would continue to exist even after Babylon had become dust? Twenty-five hundred years ago the Babylonians were the haughty rulers of the world, while a few humble Arabs lived in tents about Babylon. The Babylonians are gone; the Arabs still live in that country. But they do not live in Babylon. They don't pitch their tents there.

This same prophet Isaiah who gave us some of the remarkable prophecies about these nations and cities brings us this wonderful word from God: "Come now, and let us reason together, saith the Lord: though your sins be as scarlet, they shall be as white as snow; though they be red like crimson, they shall be as wool" (Isaiah 1:18).

Will you receive this from the same prophet whose prophecies have come true and are coming true now and will come true to the end of the world, over into the new earth which has been promised to all of God's saints?

Difficult or obscure words:

Isaiah 13:21. **"Owls"**—Hebrew, ostriches.
Isaiah 13:21. **"Satyrs"**—wild goats.
Isaiah 13:22. **"Dragons"**—Hebrew, jackals.
Isaiah 14:4. **"Golden city"**—probably better: terror.
Isaiah 14:29. **"Cockatrice"**—adder, a poisonous snake.
Isaiah 17:10. **"Pleasant plants" and "strange slips"**—representations of the gods and goddesses of fertility often worshiped by idolaters.

DAY / 187

Read Isaiah 16 through 19.

Today's reading: More prophecies of future events in the nations constitute further links in the chain of evidence for the inspiration of the Bible.

Memory gem: "Behold, the Lord rideth upon a swift cloud, and shall come into Egypt: and the idols of Egypt shall be moved at his presence, and the heart of Egypt shall melt in the midst of it" (Isaiah 19:1).

Thought for today:

Fulfilled prophecy is especially adapted to serve as a test, for we are 1,900 years from the writing of the last Bible book, and 3,400 years from the first.

"Miracles performed 2,500 years ago cannot be seen now, so they are often flatly denied," says Earle Rowell. "But a prediction made 2,500 years ago, which was contrary to all analogy at that time and a stumblingblock to the generation which heard it, but which has recently been fulfilled, is evidence even more convincing than a miracle. In fact, such a fulfilled prediction is the greatest of all miracles, and is so admitted by the skeptic Hume." (And there was no greater skeptic than he.)

Other evidence can be falsified or lost; but prophecy relates to history, and history is recorded factual experience.

God calls as His witnesses the great nations and cities of antiquity—Egypt, Syria, Phoenicia, Arabia, Tyre, Sidon, Palestine, Babylon, Assyria, Persia, Nineveh, India, Rome, and many other countries. Before the jury of the twenty-first century, God brings His witnesses; and the testimony of the witnesses grows stronger every year, as new facts are searched out by the historian or dug up by the archaeologist. No counterproof has even been attempted. And every year that rolls by is itself a witness of the fulfillment of many of these prophecies, as the scroll of history unrolls.

Remember this, friend, the Bible stakes everything on its ability to foretell the future. If its claim to make genuine predictions is true, it is a miracle of foresight beyond human ability.

DAY / 188

Read Isaiah 20 through 23.

Today's reading contains more messages of doom to other nations besides rebellious Israel and Judah. But God longed for the people to repent and forsake their evil ways.

Memory gem: "The Lord is . . . not willing that any should perish, but that all should come to repentance" (2 Peter 3:9).

Thought for today:

The inhabitants of Judah were all undeserving, yet God would not give them up. By them His name was to be exalted among the heathen. Many who were wholly unacquainted with His attributes were yet to behold the glory of the divine character. It was for the purpose of making plain His merciful designs that He kept sending His servants the prophets with the message, "Turn ye again now every one from his evil ways."

Have you, reader, chosen your own way? Have you wandered far from God? Have you sought to feast upon the fruits of transgression, only to find them turn to ashes upon your lips? And now, your life-plans thwarted and your hopes dead, do you sit alone and desolate? That voice which has long been speaking to your heart, but to which you would not listen, comes to you distinct and clear, "Arise ye, and depart; for this is not your rest: because it is polluted, it shall destroy you, even with a sore destruction." Return to your Father's house. He invites you, saying, "Return unto me; for I have redeemed thee" (Micah 2:10; Isaiah 44:22).

Do not listen to the enemy's suggestion to stay away from Christ until you have made yourself better, until you are good enough to come to God. If you wait until then, you will never come. When Satan points to your filthy garments, repeat the promise of the Saviour, "Him that cometh to me I will in no wise cast out." Tell the enemy that the blood of Jesus Christ cleanses from all sin. Make the prayer of David your own: "Purge me with hyssop, and I shall be clean: wash me, and I shall be whiter than snow."

Note: It is impossible to locate the seventy years of Isaiah 23:15, 17 in the history of Tyre. Some think that it may be roughly parallel to the seventy years of Jewish captivity.

DAY / 189

Read Isaiah 24 through 28.

Today's reading: The book of Isaiah contains surprises all the way through. In the midst of solemn denunciations of sin and prophecies of doom for wickedness, one finds sublime promises for faithfulness.

Memory gem: "Thou wilt keep him in perfect peace, whose mind is stayed on thee: because he trusteth in thee" (Isaiah 26:3).

Thought for today:

We ask the question, Is death the end of existence? For the answer, we turn to the Holy Scriptures, God's revelation to men, and the answer in a few words is this: There is death, but there is also resurrection. To the man whose hope is in Christ, there is life beyond the tomb—endless life (see Romans 6:23; 1 Thessalonians 4:13-18).

It is said that early Christians inscribed upon their tombs the Latin word *resurgam,* meaning "I shall rise again." There was certainty in their faith. They really believed something. They had no doubts about the future. And that was because they believed in the Bible and its divine prophecies of resurrection.

These prophecies are plain and clear, in the Old Testament as well as in the New. The resurrection prophecies are not surmises, wild guesses, or even hopes—they are revelations from God.

We find a great prophecy of the resurrection in Isaiah 26:19: "Thy dead men shall live, together with my dead body shall they arise. Awake and sing, ye that dwell in dust: for thy dew is as the dew of herbs, and the earth shall cast out the dead."

Just now, accept Christ as your Lord and Saviour. Repent and be converted and obey the gospel, and you will be among the "blessed and holy" who will have part in the first resurrection. "On such the second death hath no power" (Revelation 20:6), for their lives will be "hid with Christ in God. When Christ, who is our life shall appear, then shall ye also appear with him in glory" (Colossians 3:3, 4).

May this be your happy experience—and mine—so that, whether we wake or sleep, we may "live together with him" (1 Thessalonians 5:10).

DAY / 190

Read Isaiah 29 through 31.

Today's reading: Each of these three chapters begins with a pronouncement of woe. But amid the solemn words of judgment we find God's mercy.

Memory gem: "In returning and in rest shall ye be saved; in quietness and in confidence shall be your strength" (Isaiah 30:15).

Thought for today:

When asked how to eliminate psychiatric problems, a prominent specialist in that field answered that there would be much less strain on men and women if they would team up with God as a daily partner. People literally worry themselves into sickness.

You know that Christ has died for your sins; believe also that He will be your partner and guide. You can talk to Him and have His help every day.

Christ foresees the future, so why not let Him bear the burden of it? We do not know what a day will bring forth, but He does. In Matthew 24 Jesus gave an outline of the future, a prophecy of days to come.

He not only takes care of the past, but He takes care of the future too. He promises that those who love Him will be with Him where He is. We need never be separated from Him—neither now in spirit, nor then in actual presence (see John 17:24). He said: "Lo, I am with you alway, even unto the end of the world" (Matthew 28:20).

Why not take a verse from the old gospel song, learn it, believe it, and live it?

Yes, 'tis sweet to trust in Jesus
Just from sin and self to cease;
Just from Jesus simply taking
Life, and rest, and joy, and peace.
—Louisa M. R. Stead

Difficult or obscure words:

Isaiah 29:1. **"Ariel"**—a symbolic name for Jerusalem, perhaps meaning an altar in the last part of verse 2.

Isaiah 29:9. **"Cry ye out, and cry"**—rather: look about, and look.

Isaiah 30:24. **"Ear the ground"**—old English for "till the ground."

DAY / 191

Read Isaiah 32 through 35.

Today's reading: This passage contains one of the favorite descriptions of the new earth (chapter 35). It also has wonderful promises—our memory gem, for example.

Memory gem: "The work of righteousness shall be peace; and the effect of righteousness quietness and assurance for ever" (Isaiah 32:17).

Thought for today:

An interesting title made by combining a word with Jehovah is found in Judges 6:24: "Then Gideon built an altar there unto the Lord, and called it Jehovah-shalam," which means "Jehovah is peace." Parallel to this, in the twenty-third psalm we find the words, "He [the Lord] leadeth me beside the still waters," the waters of quietness. And the apostle Paul writes of Jesus, "He is our peace" (Ephesians 2:14).

In the days of Gideon, Israel had forsaken God and therefore knew no peace. Only occasionally did they turn back to God; and then, we are told, the land had peace.

The wicked never have any peace. "The wicked are like the troubled sea, when it cannot rest, whose waters cast up mire and dirt. There is no peace, saith my God, to the wicked" (Isaiah 57:20, 21).

First comes righteousness, then peace. We read in Isaiah 32:17: "The work of righteousness shall be peace; and the effect of righteousness quietness and assurance for ever."

But the only righteousness that God accepts is the righteousness of the Lord Jesus Christ and of those upon whom it is bestowed by faith in him; for Jesus "made peace through the blood of his cross," we read in Colossians 1:20.

And, friend, if you trust in Him, "the peace of God, which passeth all understanding, shall keep your hearts and minds through Christ Jesus" (Philippians 4:7). And He will lead you every day and every night by the still waters of His love.

Difficult or obscure words:

Isaiah 33:16. **"Munitions"**—strongholds.

Isaiah 34:5. **"Idumea"**—Edom.

Isaiah 34:11. **"Bittern"**—probably hedgehog or porcupine. (See Day/186 for the identity of some of the other creatures mentioned in verses 13-15.)

DAY / 192

Read 2 Kings 17 and 18; 2 Chronicles 29.

Today's reading: Like a clean breeze that sweeps away the chilling fog, King Hezekiah's zeal for God brought revival to Judah after many years of prevailing wickedness. (The northern kingdom fell in 722 B.C.)

Memory gem: "Hezekiah rejoiced, and all the people, that God had prepared the people: for the thing was done suddenly" (2 Chronicles 29:36).

Thought for today:

"Hezekiah proved to be a man of opportunity. No sooner had he ascended the throne than he began to plan and to execute. He first turned his attention to the restoration of the temple services, so long neglected; and in this work he earnestly solicited the cooperation of a band of priests and Levites who had remained true to their sacred calling. Confident of their loyal support, he spoke with them freely concerning his desire to institute immediate and far- reaching reforms. . . .

"In a few well-chosen words the king reviewed the situation they were facing—the closed temple and the cessation of all services within its precincts; the flagrant idolatry practiced in the streets of the city and throughout the kingdom; the apostasy of multitudes who might have remained true to God had the leaders in Judah set before them a right example; and the decline of the kingdom and loss of prestige in the estimation of surrounding nations. The northern kingdom was rapidly crumbling to pieces; many were perishing by the sword; a multitude had already been carried away captive; soon Israel would fall completely into the hands of the Assyrians, and be utterly ruined; and this fate would surely befall Judah as well, unless God should work mightily through chosen representatives. . . .

"It was a time for quick action. The priests began at once. . . . They engaged heartily in the work of cleansing . . . the temple. Because of the years of desecration and neglect, this was attended with many difficulties; but the priests and the Levites labored untiringly, and within a remarkably short time they were able to report their task completed. The temple doors had been repaired and thrown open; the sacred vessels had been assembled and put into place; and all was in readiness for the re-establishment of the sanctuary services." —*Prophets and Kings,* pp. 331–333.

DAY / 193

Read 2 Chronicles 30 and 31.

Today's reading: Good King Hezekiah's all-out efforts to restore true religion in Judah brought his people to a spiritual high by observing the long-neglected Passover.

Memory gem: "There was great joy in Jerusalem: for since the time of Solomon the son of David king of Israel there was not the like in Jerusalem" (2 Chronicles 30:26).

Thought for today:

"The good beginning made at the time of the purification of the temple was followed by a broader movement, in which Israel as well as Judah participated. In his zeal to make the temple services a real blessing to the people, Hezekiah determined to revive the ancient custom of gathering the Israelites together for the celebration of the Passover feast.

"For many years the Passover had not been observed as a national festival. The division of the kingdom after the close of Solomon's reign had made this seem impracticable. But the terrible judgments befalling the ten tribes were awakening in the hearts of some a desire for better things; and the stirring messages of the prophets were having their effect. By royal couriers the invitation to the Passover at Jerusalem was heralded far and wide, 'from city to city through the country of Ephraim and Manasseh even unto Zebulun.' The bearers of the gracious invitation were usually repulsed. The impenitent turned lightly aside; nevertheless some, eager to seek God for a clearer knowledge of His will, 'humbled themselves, and came to Jerusalem.' . . .

"The occasion was one of the greatest profit to the multitudes assembled. The desecrated streets of the city were cleared of the idolatrous shrines placed there during the reign of Ahaz. On the appointed day the Passover was observed; and the week was spent by the people in offering peace offerings, and in learning what God would have them do. Daily the Levites 'taught the good knowledge of the Lord;' and those who had prepared their hearts to seek God, found pardon. A great gladness took possession of the worshiping multitude; . . . all were united in their desire to praise Him who had proved so gracious and merciful."—*Prophets and Kings,* pp. 335–337.

DAY / 194

Read 2 Kings 18:13 through chapter 19.

Today's reading: When a heathen king and his godless henchmen poured contempt on God, a godly king asked the Lord to defend His honor. The result left no doubt.

Memory gem: "O Lord our God, I beseech thee, save thou us out of his hand, that all the kingdoms of the earth may know that thou art the Lord God, even thou only" (2 Kings 19:19).

Thought for today:

A man who played God was Sennacherib, who invaded the Holy Land. Because of the sins of Judah, God permitted this invasion by the Assyrian army, but Sennacherib assumed to himself the character of God and took to himself the glory that belonged to the God of heaven. Referring to his conquest of other nations, he said that none of their gods had been able to deliver them out of his hand. "Where are they?" he cried. Here he put his hand above God's.

Sennacherib sent a letter threatening good King Hezekiah and the people of Jerusalem. Hezekiah took this letter up to the temple of God and spread it out before the Lord and prayed. My friend, that's a good thing to do when men around you try to play God. Take it to the Lord. Talk to Him about it.

And the answer came through the prophet Isaiah. Speaking of His dealings with the Assyrian king, God said: "I will put my hook in thy nose, and my bridle in thy lips, and I will turn thee back by the way which thou camest" (2 Kings 19:28).

Sennacherib returned to Assyria, and, while he was worshiping in his heathen temple, two of his sons killed him with the sword.

My friends, it's dangerous for any man to play God. He is liable to find that he is very human, very mortal after all.

Difficult or obscure words:

2 Kings 18:4. **"Nehushtan"**—probably bronze god, or possibly serpent.

2 Kings 18:17. **"Tartan and Rabsaris and Rab-shakeh"**—titles, not given names. The "Tartan" was chief general, the "Rabsaris" was probably chief eunuch, and "Rab-shakeh" was the chief cup-bearer or personal valet of the king. In this case the Rab-shakeh spoke for the king.

DAY /195

Read Isaiah 36 and 37; 2 Chronicles 32:1-23

Today's reading: In the parallel accounts of the Assyrian siege of Jerusalem, we notice again how God honored the faith of good King Hezekiah.

Memory gem: "Because thy rage against me, and thy tumult, is come up into mine ears, therefore will I put my hook in thy nose, and my bridle in thy lips, and I will turn thee back by the way by which thou camest" (Isaiah 37:29).

Thought for today:

In Isaiah 36 and 37 we read about Sennacherib, king of Assyria, and his invasion of the land of Judah. In spite of his great army, he had failed to take Jerusalem. Something happened to him which he did not record, but the Bible recorded it. Read it for yourself in 2 Kings 19:35 and Isaiah 37:36.

Sennacherib had returned to Nineveh, his capital, and in the official record of his campaign in the west he said concerning King Hezekiah, "As for himself, like a bird in a cage in his royal city Jerusalem, I shut him up."

Sennacherib made as good a story as he could out of the siege and simply said that he shut poor Hezekiah up like a bird in a cage. Actually, Hezekiah was reposing quite safely in his cage. But the Bible says that soon after Sennacherib's return to Nineveh after his failure in Judah, two of his own sons assassinated him (see 2 Kings 19:37).

Another son, who was his successor, tells of this event in the following words from an official inscription: "In the month Nisanu, a favorable day, complying with their exalted command, I made my joyful entrance into the royal palace, the awesome place, wherein abides the fate of kings. A firm determination fell upon my brothers. They forsook the gods and turned to their deeds of violence, plotting evil. . . . To gain a kingship they slew Sennacherib, their father." Again history proves that God spoke the truth. The Bible is literally true in its statements of historical facts.

It is good for us Christians—yes, for all men—to read the Bible over again from cover to cover, and to read it often. We are glad to see that it is literally true; but above all, that it presents to us the Lord Jesus Christ, the only, but all-sufficient, hope of a lost and ruined world.

DAY / 196

Read Psalms 46; 47; 48; 75; 76; 124; 129.

Today's reading: Prayers for deliverance from the arrogant Assyrians gave way to joyful songs of rejoicing. These psalms (although probably not composed at this time) express the deep emotion of God's people.

Memory gem: "Be still, and know that I am God: I will be exalted among the heathen, I will be exalted in the earth" (Psalm 46:10).

Thought for today:

"Hezekiah's pleadings in behalf of Judah and of the honor of their Supreme Ruler were in harmony with the mind of God. Solomon, in his benediction at the dedication of the temple, had prayed the Lord . . . to show favor when, in times of war or of oppression by an army, the chief men of Israel should enter the house of prayer and plead for deliverance [See 1 Kings 8:33, 34] . . .

"The land of Judah had been laid waste by the army of occupation; but God had promised to provide miraculously for the needs of the people. To Hezekiah came the message: 'This shall be a sign unto thee, Ye shall eat this year such things as grow of themselves, and in the second year that which springeth of the same; and in the third year sow ye, and reap, and plant vineyards, and eat the fruits thereof.' 2 Kings 19:29. . . .

"The God of the Hebrews . . . prevailed over the proud Assyrian. The honor of Jehovah was vindicated in the eyes of the surrounding nations. In Jerusalem, the hearts of the people were filled with holy joy. Their earnest entreaties for deliverance had been mingled with confession of sin and with many tears. In their great need they had trusted wholly in the power of God to save, and He had not failed them. Now the temple courts resounded with songs of solemn praise."—*Prophets and Kings,* pp. 359–362.

Note: Psalm 46 has been called Luther's psalm, because it was the inspiration for the great Reformer's hymn, "A Mighty Fortress Is Our God."

Psalm 47, closely related to 46 and 48, is read in Orthodox Jewish synagogues on the Hebrew New Year's Day before sounding the shofar.

DAY / 197

Read 2 Kings 20; 2 Chronicles 32:24-33; Isaiah 38 and 39.

Today's reading: King Hezekiah falls ill, and unusual events accompany his healing.

Memory gem: "The living, the living, he shall praise thee, as I do this day: the father to the children shall make known thy truth" (Isaiah 38:19).

Thought for today:

You will notice in this case the promise of healing came at once, even before the prophet Isaiah had time to get out of the palace, and that the king was instructed by the prophet of God to cooperate in the work of healing by putting a plaster or poultice of figs on the boil which was afflicting him. This showed no lack of faith. It was ordered from the same source that gave the promise of recovery.

Let us continue to study Christ's ministry of healing power. And let us not forget that it is not a denial of our faith to make use of the remedial agencies available—the things that God has provided to alleviate pain and to aid nature in her work of restoration. God could have cured Hezekiah instantly, but specific directions were given regarding natural treatment in his case. On one occasion Jesus anointed a blind man's eyes with clay. The cure was wrought only by the power of Christ, yet He made use of the simple agencies of nature. When we have prayed for the recovery of the sick and have asked God's blessing on the means which He Himself has provided, we can work with all the more hope and energy and thank God for the privilege of cooperating with Him.

After we have prayed, let us have faith in God, whatever the outcome. If bereavement comes, let us remember that the bitter cup is held to our lips by our Father's hand. Should health be restored, let us not forget that the person healed is placed under added obligation to the Lord. He is healed to help; he is saved to serve. His added days of life and health are for a purpose, and that purpose is to glorify God and to do good to others.

Difficult or obscure words:

2 Kings 20:12. **"Berodach-baladan"**—Correctly spelled Merodach-baladan in Isaiah 39:1. He was at this time a king in exile seeking for allies in his lifelong attempt to free Babylon from Assyrian domination.

DAY / 198

Read Isaiah 40 through 42.

Today's reading: These chapters issue challenge after challenge for the false gods to prove their power. Also some of the most beautiful prophecies of the Messiah and the most precious promises are found there.

Memory gem: "Fear thou not; for I am with thee; be not dismayed; for I am thy God; I will strengthen thee; yea, I will help thee; yea, I will uphold thee with the right hand of my righteousness" (Isaiah 41:10).

Thought for today:

I live on the edge of a great city. One reason that I should like to live far away from the city, in the mounains or on the seashore, is this—the great cities rob us of the glory of the stars. There is too much light in cities. It would do us all good, at least once in our lifetime, to be alone beneath the stars, to watch the majestic march of the constellations across the sky from dusk to dawn. It seems to me that no thinking mind could ever, after that, doubt the existence of the Supreme Being.

It is the will of God that we should look at the stars. Every modern astronomical observatory is the fulfillment of a scriptural command. Have you ever read the words of Isaiah 40:26?

"Lift up your eyes on high, and behold who hath created these things, that bringeth out their host by number: he calleth them all by names by the greatness of his might, for that he is strong in power; not one faileth."

Look at the stars. Look upward. Study astronomy. That's the Bible command. Look at the stars and see who hath created them. Look at the midnight sky and see God in His works. As flowers bloom here on earth in summertime, so, as Longfellow has said, "Silently, one by one, in the infinite meadows of heaven [blossom] the lovely stars, the forget-me-nots of the angels."

Note: Isaiah 41 contains the first of several remarkable prophecies of Cyrus the Great, who would conquer Babylon a century and a half later. Chapter 42 predicts the coming Messiah (see Matthew 12:17-21).

DAY / 199

Today's reading: God, through the prophet Isaiah, continues to challenge the false gods for a showdown. God insists over and over that He alone is God.

Memory gem: "Look unto me, and be ye saved, all the ends of the earth: for I am God, and there is none else" (Isaiah 45:22).

Thought for today:

In the apostle Paul's great sermon to the intelligent pagans of Lystra, he declared that God has "left not himself without witness" (Acts 14:17). For God's existence, God's work, God's presence in the world, He has seen to it that there are witnesses—in nature and in history, which is crystallized human experience, as well as in the Sacred Scriptures.

In fact, God challenges the skeptic of all historic times to consider evidence, even coercive evidence. Show us the former things, He challenges. Bring forth the records of the past and bear witness to any failure of divine prophecy. But if history proves the absolute truth and foreknowledge of prophecy, then you become My witness, God says.

Remember this, friends: the Bible stakes everything on its ability to foretell the future. If its claim to make genuine predictions is true, it is a miracle of foresight beyond human ability, and it is absolute proof of supernatural knowledge in the prophet.

God claims to be the *only one* able to foretell the future absolutely, to write history in advance. And remember, many of these Bible prophecies pointed forward for centuries and even millenniums to the time of fulfillment. There could be no collusion between prophet and the fulfiller of it.

God challenges the heathen gods to do the same, to produce real prophecy—which of course they never could, and never did, because they didn't exist except in the minds of their worshipers.

God calls for "strong reasons," in other words, coercive reasons.

Note: In Isaiah 44:28 and 45:1, Cyrus is called by name. Chapter 45 is addressed to this "shepherd," this "anointed" one, who was to accomplish God's purpose more than 150 years later.

DAY / 200

Read Isaiah 47 through 50.

Today's reading: Having presented conclusive evidence of His power as the only true God, the Lord now tries to reason with His people and bring them to repentance.

Memory gem: "O that thou hadst hearkened to my commandments! then had thy peace been as a river, and thy righteousness as the waves of the sea" (Isaiah 48:18).

Thought for today:

Not long ago the public press carried a headline like this: "The Rock of Ages Can't Be Bought." It was followed by a reference to Mark 8:36.

The editorial under this heading referred to a multimillionaire railroad tycoon who had committed suicide in his luxurious twenty-five-room showplace in Palm Beach, Florida. It spoke of his tragic end after attaining what most people consider success.

Winters at Palm Beach, summers at Newport, wealth of untold millions with billions under his control; yet the financial wizard of this era stamped himself a failure in the final analysis. He had everything that money could buy; but there was one thing that all his money could not purchase, and that was the Rock of Ages. Yet he could have had it for the mere asking. He could pyramid a fortune and control one of the world's greatest railroads, he could operate a fabulous hotel as a kind of hobby; but he failed to secure those inner resources which would have carried him through the despondency that finally drove him out of this world.

You cannot carry your burden alone, and God does not want you to. He loves you. You are His child. He can give you the peace which you long for.

How can we stop worrying and grieving? By believing with all our hearts that Jesus will do what He says He will do. The peace you and I need is the peace that only Jesus can give.

Difficult or obscure words:

Isaiah 49:12. **"Sinim"**—popularly, but probably incorrectly, applied to China. More likely Aswan in upper Egypt, or some other location remote from Palestine but within the Fertile Crescent.

Isaiah 49:23. **"Nursing fathers"** and **"Nursing mothers"**—foster parents.

DAY / 201

Today's reading: What beautiful words these chapters contain! And, surrounded by assurances of God's forgiving love, the fifty-third chapter points to the suffering Messiah.

Memory gem: "He was wounded for our transgressions, he was bruised for our iniquities: the chastisement of our peace was upon him; and with his stripes we are healed" (Isaiah 53:5).

Thought for today:

The theologians, who seem to delight in long words, might say that we need justification, regeneration, and sanctification in order to get to heaven. These three needs make clear what the three steps are which we must take with Jesus as we turn to the right and start for the Holy City.

Our first need is to have our sins forgiven. To confess Christ as our Saviour from sin is our first step with Him. This step with Jesus must be taken by everyone because "all have sinned, and come short of the glory of God" (Romans 3:23).

In Isaiah 53:6 it is written that "all we like sheep have gone astray." Notice that word *all.* It is universal. Now read the whole text: "All we like sheep have gone astray; we have turned every one to his own way; and the Lord hath laid on him the iniquity of us all."

Someone has said that salvation starts at the first "all" (all have sinned) and ends at the last "all" (the Lord hath laid on Him— Christ— the iniquity of us *all).* At the beginning of this wonderful verse, acknowledge that you are a sinner; and then at the end of the verse, by faith, lay your sins on Jesus.

I once heard of a young lady who was worried about her spiritual condition, for she couldn't understand how God could forgive her sins. An old minister told her to read this fifty-third chapter of Isaiah, and when she came to the fifth verse, to substitute the first person singular pronoun for the plural form. And so she read it that way: "He was wounded for my transgressions, he was bruised for my iniquities: the chastisement of my peace was upon him." Then she stopped, and a wonderful light came into her eyes as she read, "And with his stripes I am healed."

That's it, my friends! When Jesus died of a broken heart, it was the sins of the world that killed Him. Doesn't the Bible say in 1 John 2:2 that Jesus died "for the sins of the whole world"?

DAY / 202

Read Isaiah 56 through 60.

Today's reading: Among so many familiar and meaningful passages, it is hard to choose which to highlight. Let's notice that the blame for a poor relationship with the Lord lies with the sinner—not with God.

Memory gem: "Behold, the Lord's hand is not shortened, that it cannot save; neither his ear heavy, that it cannot hear: but your iniquities have separated between you and your God, and your sins have hid his face from you, that he will not hear" (Isaiah 59:1, 2).

Thought for today:

Some time ago I visited a man of superior intelligence. He had good looks, a quick mind, and a great deal of knowledge; but he was a failure in life. My interview with him took place in a prison cell. By his own confession he was guilty of more than one crime—many of them.

I said, "Why do you do these things?"

His answer was: "I don't know. It just seems that I must do them."

He told me that when he committed these various crimes he knew they were wrong; he was convinced they were wrong; he was condemned by their wrongness, and still he kept on doing them.

Sin was the great barrier that prevented his spiritual victory. He was like the mouse that was caught in the trap by the tip of its tail, yet went right on nibbling the cheese.

Many people are doing that very thing today. They know that what they are doing is wrong. They know they are guilty. They dread the punishment here and hereafter, but they go right on nibbling at their pet sins.

The reason that blessings are often denied us is because of our sins. It is not that God is unable to help. The words of our memory gem point out the barrier.

Whatever it is, my friend, you know and God knows. So break down the barrier; then God can give you a life of victory.

DAY / 203

Today's reading: Jesus read the first verses of Isaiah 61 to announce His mission, thus approving the use of prophecy to prove His Messiahship. Chapter 65 gives a heartening glimpse of life in the new earth.

Memory gem: "I will greatly rejoice in the Lord, my soul shall be joyful in my God; for he hath clothed me with the garments of salvation, he hath covered me with the robe of righteousness" (Isaiah 61:10).

Thought for today:

The prophet Isaiah proclaimed this wonderful promise for our planet and penned these beautiful words of God Himself:

"Behold, I create new heavens and a new earth: and the former shall not be remembered, nor come into mind. But be ye glad and rejoice for ever in that which I create: for, behold, I create Jerusalem a rejoicing, and her people a joy" (Isaiah 65:17, 18).

The evil of past days in this old earth will not oppress the mind or cause worry and sorrow to the inhabiters of that earth made new. They will see all the events of this world as in the providence of God leading to the salvation of souls. They will recognize God's hand in His providence as they cannot now see it. They will rejoice in their salvation, and gladness will fill the world.

So we today ought to be happy and joyful when we think of the wonderful future of this planet. And we ought also to heed the command of the apostle found in 2 Peter 3:13, 14:

"Nevertheless we, according to his promise, look for new heavens and a new earth, wherein dwelleth righteousness. Wherefore, beloved, seeing that ye look for such things, be diligent that ye may be found of him in peace, without spot, and blameless."

Friends, let us look for these things, and let us indeed be diligent that we may be found of Him in peace at His returning. And let us be, by His redeeming grace, prepared for a home with the holy and the good of all ages and with our blessed Saviour, whom having not seen, we love.

DAY / 204

Read Isaiah 66; 2 Kings 21; 2 Chronicles 33.

Today's reading: We finish the book of Isaiah and return to the sad history of Judah's decline.

Memory gem: "If my people, which are called by my name, will humble themselves, and pray, and seek my face, and turn from their wicked ways; then will I hear from heaven, and will forgive their sin, and will heal their land" (2 Chronicles 7:14).

Thought for today:

Someone might say, "Pastor Richards, I have tried to overcome my evil habits and come back to the Lord, but I am just too great a sinner."

Do you recall the story of that young prince of Judah, Manasseh? He was only twelve years old when he became king upon the death of his father, King Hezekiah, who had been a wonderful example to the nation and had brought in a number of outstanding reforms.

But things quickly changed after Hezekiah's death, and his son Manasseh became one of the most wicked kings that ever ruled. He was a murderer, for he shed much innocent blood. He resisted every attempt on the part of good men to halt the spread of evil. He turned from the God of his fathers and went into idolatry and spirit worship.

Because of his evil life, he was captured by the king of Assyria and taken down to Babylon. Confined in a dungeon, with his hands and feet in chains, he had time to think things over. Finally he came to himself, as we read in 2 Chronicles 33:9-13.

Now, Manasseh had been a sinful man and certainly deserved death, but when he returned to the Lord in earnest, humble confession, the Lord heard him. God was ready to receive him.

I know that sometimes it is difficult for us, as human beings, to realize that God is interested in us. We have disappointed Him so often. We have rejected His invitation to come to Him. We have spurned His call. But if God could forgive that penitent King Manasseh, He certainly will forgive and accept you.

Note: Isaiah may have delivered the warning of 2 Kings 21:10-15, although no identification is possible. According to tradition, Isaiah was among the first victims of Manasseh's cruel persecutions, being placed in a hollow log and sawn in two. No other prophets are known for this period.

DAY / 205

Read the book of Nahum.

Today's reading: Although Nahum's prophecy was directed against Nineveh (Assyria) shortly before that nation's collapse, it has value as warnings against evildoers and assurances for the righteous.

Memory gem: "The Lord is good, a stronghold in the day of trouble; and he knoweth them that trust in him" (Nahum 1:7).

Thought for today:

"The rise and fall of the Assyrian Empire is rich in lessons for the nations of earth today. . . .

" . . . The rulers of Assyria, instead of using their unusual blessings for the benefit of mankind, became the scourge of many lands. Merciless, with no thought of God or their fellow men, they pursued the fixed policy of causing all nations to acknowledge the supremacy of the gods of Nineveh, whom they exalted above the Most High. God had sent Jonah to them with a message of warning, and for a season they humbled themselves before the Lord of hosts, and sought forgiveness. But soon they turned again to idol worship, and to the conquest of the world.

"The prophet Nahum, in his arraignment of the evildoers in Nineveh, exclaimed:

" 'Woe to the bloody city! It is all full of lies and robbery; the prey departeth not. . . . Behold, I am against thee, saith the Lord of hosts.' Nahum 3:1-5.

"With unerring accuracy the Infinite One still keeps account with the nations. While His mercy is tendered, with calls to repentance, this account remains open; but when . . . the account is closed, divine patience ceases. Mercy no longer pleads in their behalf. . . .

" 'The Lord is good, a stronghold in the day of trouble; and he knoweth them that trust in him. But with an overrunning flood he will make an utter end' (Nahum 1:7, 8) of all who endeavor to exalt themselves above the Most High. . . .

" . . . In the day of final awards, when the righteous Judge of all the earth shall 'sift the nations' (Isaiah 30:28), and those that have kept the truth shall be permitted to enter the City of God, heaven's arches will ring with the triumphant songs of the redeemed."—*Prophets and Kings,* pp. 362–366.

DAY / 206

Read 2 Kings 22; 2 Chronicles 34:1-28.

Today's reading: The boy king Josiah came close to turning his nation back to God completely; one powerful factor in effecting the reformation was finding the book of the law.

Memory gem: "Because thine heart was tender, and thou hast humbled thyself before the Lord, . . . I have also heard thee, saith the Lord" (2 Kings 22:19).

Thought for today:

Why was the king so deeply affected by the reading of this book that was found in the house of the Lord? Evidently it was the first five books of Moses—Genesis, Exodus, Leviticus, Numbers, and Deuteronomy. Shaphan must have opened the book to the twenty-eighth, twenty-ninth, and thirtieth chapters of Deuteronomy, in which are recorded the renewal of God's national covenant with the people of Israel and a list of the terrible curses pronounced against all who violated the law, whether prince or people. We can see why the king was filled with grief and terror.

During the wicked reigns of Manasseh and Amon, the temple had been profaned and the ark had actually been removed from its proper place. During these troublous times the book had somehow become lost. Now, as the temple was repaired, it was found and delivered to the high priest. He recognized it for what it was and drew the attention of Shaphan to it.

And notice, Shaphan read it. That is what we all ought to do with the Word of God. Many people honor the Bible as a sort of talisman or charm, but it is nothing of the kind. It is the Word of God to the hearts of men, and it is to be read. Everyone who does not read it suffers a terrible loss.

Friend, have you ever found the Book of God, and has the Book found you? Those who take this Book of God to lands where it has never been known can testify to its power in finding men; and what testimonies these workers can bear! It finds the human heart right where it is, and transforms it.

And this Book will do the same for you and for me, and for everyone who truly finds it. It is a Book that has been lost many, many times and found many, many times; but it will never be destroyed. Its work will go on until Jesus comes, for it is "the word of God, which liveth and abideth for ever" (1 Peter 1:23).

DAY / 207

Today's reading: Habakkuk's short prophecy is undated, but evidence indicates that it belongs roughly to about the time of Amon's wicked reign or early in the reign of Josiah before the finding of the law.

Memory gem: "The Lord is in his holy temple: let all the earth keep silence before him" (Habakkuk 2:20).

Thought for today:

"Confident that . . . the purpose of God for His people would in some way be fulfilled, Habakkuk bowed in submission to the revealed will of Jehovah. 'Art Thou not from everlasting, O Lord my God, mine Holy One?' he exclaimed. And then, his faith reaching out beyond the forbidding prospect of the immediate future, and laying fast hold on the precious promises that reveal God's love for His trusting children, the prophet added, 'We shall not die.' Habakkuk 1:12. With this declaration of faith, he rested his case, and that of every believing Israelite, in the hands of a compassionate God. . . .

"The faith that strengthened Habakkuk and all the holy and the just in those days of deep trial, was the same faith that sustains God's people today. In the darkest hours, under circumstances the most forbidding, the Christian believer may keep his soul stayed upon the source of all light and power. Day by day, through faith in God, his hope and courage may be renewed. 'The just shall live by his faith.' (Habakkuk 2:4.) In the service of God there need be no despondency, no wavering, no fear. The Lord will more than fulfill the highest expectations of those who put their trust in Him. He will give them the wisdom their varied necessities demand."—*Prophets and Kings*, pp. 386, 387.

Difficult or obscure words:

Habakkuk 1:9. **"Sup up"**—a Hebrew word occurring only here in the Scriptures. Its meaning and therefore its translation are uncertain.

Note: With the collapse of the northern kingdom only Judah remained a bastion of truth in a heathen world. But even in this favored nation God's people could not shake off their fascination with the allurements of idolatry.

God did not give up trying to arouse His people to the consequences of their iniquities. We will be reading messages of warning and calls to repentance from six prophets—two of them major. Jeremiah and Ezekiel watched in dismay as the last five kings of Judah allowed the nation to disintegrate. Jeremiah is known as the "weeping prophet" because of the pathos of his writings.

It will be of help to have an outline of the five kings involved, three of them sons and one a grandson of Josiah. (The number before each name indicates the order of the reign, and the figures following the name indicate the B.C. dates.)

1. Josiah (639-608 B.C.)

Johanan (not a king). Nothing is known of this son except the listing in 1 Chronicles 3:15.	2. Jehoahaz (608) (Shallum)	3. Jehoiakim (608-597) (Eliakim)	5. Zedekiah (597-596) (Mattaniah)
		4. Jehoiachin (597) (Jeconiah or Coniah)	(For some reason, 1 Chronicles 3:15 lists Zedekiah as the third son, but their ages prove otherwise.)

For some reason, the books of Jeremiah and Ezekiel were not compiled in chronological order. We will try to read the messages in connection with the historical events at the time of their writing. This will involve considerable turning back and forth, but the prophecies take on new meaning as we fit them together in the correct sequence.

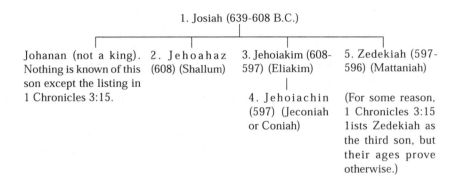

DAY / 208

Today's reading introduces us to Jeremiah, the Lord's prophet before the Babylonian captivity, one of the spiritual giants of Scripture. Notice his reluctance to accept God's call.

Memory gem: "Be not afraid of their faces: for I am with thee to deliver thee, saith the Lord" (Jeremiah 1:8).

Thought for today:

The testimony of millions of people today is that faith in God has been a blessing, and only a blessing to them. This being so, it seems strange that so many people live in a constant state of worry, fear, and uneasiness, when they might be living a wonderful life, having faith in God and believing that He is in charge of His universe. If more people today would just let God be God, let Him run the world, let Him run the universe, let Him guide their lives, quit trying to take His place, we would have a lot more happy people on earth.

One reason why so many people today are worried and full of fear is that they are not willing to put their affairs in God's hands and let Him guide their lives.

There was that young man Jeremiah, evidently quite young when his first vision came to him. I like to read about him whenever things are difficult, when problems and trying situations arise. To anyone who gets to the place where he feels he may not be needed, may not be appreciated, has the least doubt about God's plan for him, read the first chapter of the book of Jeremiah.

When the word of the Lord came to Jeremiah—the very first time, as far as the record goes—he was told that God's plan for him was made before he was born.

Then Jeremiah said, "I am nothing but a child, nothing but a baby; I can't speak; I cannot be a prophet." But the Lord said to him, "Say not, I am a child: for thou shalt go to all that I shall send thee, and whatsoever I command thee thou shalt speak. Be not afraid of their faces: for I am with thee to deliver thee, saith the Lord" (Jeremiah 1:7, 8).

When this young man finally believed that God had a plan for him and that God had put His words in his mouth, he went forward in life and actually shook the nations. He had lots of trouble, lots of conflict, many battles to win. But he always had God's promise to be with him to deliver him.

DAY / 209

Read Jeremiah 4 through 6.

Today's reading: The prophet boldly proclaims the Lord's warnings to a people who refuse to listen; he pleads in vain for repentance, but no one heeds.

Memory gem: "Thus saith the Lord, stand ye in the ways, and see, and ask for the old paths, where is the good way, and walk therein, and ye shall find rest for your souls" (Jeremiah 6:16).

Thought for today:

God's Word is a fire which makes sinners uncomfortable, but warms the heart of the believer. Notice the statement in Jeremiah 5:14: "Wherefore thus saith the Lord God of hosts, Because ye speak this word, behold, I will make my words in thy mouth fire, and this people wood, and it shall devour them."

A true minister of God feels this fire in his heart—this "woe is unto me, if I preach not the gospel" (1 Corinthians 9:16). As Jeremiah said: "His word was in mine heart as a burning fire shut up in my bones, and I was weary with forbearing, and I could not stay" (Jeremiah 20:9).

Oh, that words of burning truth might be proclaimed from every pulpit and in the life of every Christian! What a cleansing it would work in the church, and what a mighty testimony it would be to the world!

For hard hearts God's Word is also a hammer. We read in Jeremiah 23:29: "Is not my word like as a fire? saith the Lord; and like a hammer that breaketh the rock in pieces?"

No heart is too hard for the hammer and the fire—it will either break in conviction and sorrow for the wrong deeds of life and seek God's mercy in Christ, or it will break at last.

Difficult or obscure words:

Jeremiah 4:30. **"Rentest thy face"**—literally, enlargest thine eyes. Ancient Oriental women used a glittering black mineral powder on the edges of their eyelids to make their eyes appear larger and more brilliant.

Jeremiah 5:6. **"Of the evenings"**—better: of the deserts.

Note: Jeremiah's ministry covered more than forty years—from the "thirteenth year" of Josiah (about 626 B.C.) to the end of the eleventh year of Zedekiah (586 B.C.) plus an indefinite period beyond that date (see chapter 44:1).

DAY / 210

Read Jeremiah 14 through 16.

Today's reading: Although good King Josiah made heroic efforts to root out idolatry, he could not change people's hearts. The Lord still sent His pleading call to repentance through Jeremiah.

Memory gem: "Thy words were found and I did eat them; and thy word was unto me the joy and rejoicing of mine heart" (Jeremiah 15:16).

Thought for today:

A young lady was taking a special course in a university and was having a terrible time. One book in particular was especially boring.

After a while this young woman met a young man on the university campus. Somehow he was very attractive, and he felt drawn to her too. It was not long before they were keeping company. He happened to be one of the young teachers there.

One day, after they had been going together for several months, she happened to tell him that she was having a difficult time with her English course and particularly with that book. She said, "That is the driest thing I have ever tried to read. I just can't get interested in it. The print is too fine, the subject is so dull—and the strange thing is," she continued, "the author's name is the same as yours."

"Oh," he replied, "there is nothing strange about it; you see, I wrote that book."

And then she didn't say anything more—in fact, there was nothing more to say.

But when she went home that night, she got that book out, and her mother couldn't get her to bed. "You know, Mother," she said, "it is all in me. I just didn't see through this book before. Why, it's a wonderful book! Somehow I see the whole thing now. This really is *the* book, Mother." And she just stopped everything else and read and devoured and digested that book.

Friends, if you find the Bible dry and difficult, get acquainted with the Author, and you will see His loving face shining out from Genesis to Revelation. From the first verse of the first book to the last verse of the last book, you will find that wonderful One, our Lord Jesus Christ.

DAY / 211

Read Joel; 2 Kings 23:1-20; 2 Chronicles 34:29-33.

Today's reading: The zeal of King Josiah's reformation resulted in the destruction of outward evidences of idolatry even beyond the borders of Judah. Joel prophesied at this time.

Memory gem: "I call heaven and earth to record this day against you, that I have set before you life and death, blessing and cursing: therefore choose life, that both thou and thy seed may live" (Deuteronomy 30:19).

Thought for today:

King Josiah had strong faith in the Word of God; and he realized that because of the idolatry and apostasy and sin of the people, they were now open to all the judgments of God pronounced in this Book. All this came upon him with overwhelming force, for he was a good man—an earnest and devout man. So immediately he sent a delegation to the prophetess who was in Jerusalem, to inquire of the Lord.

As a result of the king's leadership and his earnestness after having heard the message of the Book of God which had been lost in the house of God and was now found, a great revival broke out in the land. King Josiah followed the instruction of the prophetess Huldah, and every word that she sent to the king was later exactly fulfilled.

Should we find this lost Book and read it as did those men of old, it might change our lives as it did theirs. If we would read God's Word, we would find that we needed to change our lives. Like King Josiah, we need to humble ourselves and weep before the Lord and seek His pardon. You see, the king made a thorough work of repentance and reformation, and God accepted his efforts; and all the people made a solemn covenant to keep the commandments of God. Really, friends, isn't this our need today?

Note: Joel gives no clue to the time of his message. We believe that it came during the early part of King Josiah's reign.

DAY / 212

Read Zephaniah; 2 Kings 23:21-25; 2 Chronicles 35:1-19.

Today's reading: Zephaniah was probably a contemporary of Habakkuk, and possibly of Joel, in the early part of King Josiah's reign. He calls for genuine repentance.

Memory gem: "Seek ye the Lord, all ye meek of the earth which have wrought his judgment; seek righteousness, seek meekness: it may be ye shall be hid in the day of the Lord's anger" (Zephaniah 2:3).

Thought for today:

Many things are given to us for a limited time only. Through the prophets, the Lord pleaded with the backslidden kingdom of Judah to return to Him. God's desire was that His name should be exalted among the heathen of the land and that this should be accomplished through the witness of His people.

The call to repentance is still being given, but time is short. Down through the ages God's prophetic timetable has marked the mileposts of human history. We have but a limited time. How are you spending this borrowed time—this extra God-given time? Have you set your house in order?

In one of his great sermons, Dr. Macartney told of an old Saxon king who set out with his army to put down a rebellion in a distant province of his kingdom. When the army of the rebels had been defeated and the insurrection quelled, the king placed a candle in the archway of the castle that served as his headquarters. Then, lighting the candle, he sent his herald to announce to those who had been in rebellion that all who would surrender and take the oath of allegiance while the candle still burned, would be saved. The king offered his clemency and mercy, but the offer was limited to the life of that candle.

We are all living on candle time, so to speak. While the candle still burns, let us accept Christ as our Lord and Saviour. Let us be ready for His coming.

Difficult or obscure words:

Zephaniah 1:4. **"Chemarims"**—idolatrous priests.

Zephaniah 2:3. **"It may be"**—an expression of hope that pleads for the promised protection.

DAY / 213 Read 2 Kings 23:26-37; 2 Chronicles 35:20 through 36:4; Jeremiah 17 and 7.

Today's reading: Good King Josiah, after a valiant attempt to turn his people back to God, dies in disgrace. His sons quickly undo all the results of Josiah's reforms.

Memory gem: "Blessed is the man that trusteth in the Lord, and whose hope the Lord is" (Jeremiah 17:7).

Thought for today:

"By the great mass of the people the call to repentance and reformation was unheeded. Since the death of good King Josiah, those who ruled the nation had been proving untrue to their trust, and had been leading many astray. Jehoahaz, deposed by the interference of the king of Egypt, had been followed by Jehoiakim, an older son of Josiah. From the beginning of Jehoiakim's reign, Jeremiah had little hope of saving his beloved land from destruction and the people from captivity. Yet he was not permitted to remain silent while utter ruin threatened the kingdom. Those who had remained loyal to God must be encouraged to persevere in right doing, and sinners must, if possible, be induced to turn from iniquity.

"The crisis demanded a public and far-reaching effort. Jeremiah was commanded by the Lord to stand in the court of the temple, and speak to all the people of Judah who might pass in and out. From the messages given him, he must diminish not a word, that sinners in Zion might have the fullest possible opportunity to hearken, and to turn from their evil ways."—*Prophets and Kings,* pp. 412, 413.

Note: Jehoahaz (Shallum), not Josiah's oldest son, was made king at his father's death; he reigned three months.

Eliakim, renamed Jehoiakim by Necho, replaced his younger brother; he reigned eleven years.

Nebuchadnezzar's first capture of Jerusalem and taking of captives (including Daniel) occurred in 606/605 B.C.

"Shiloh," mentioned in Jeremiah 7:12, 14, is a reference to the taking of the ark and the destruction of the town by the Philistines in the days of Eli (see Samuel 4:10, 11; 5:1).

Difficult or obscure words:

Jeremiah 7:33. **"Fray"**—an old English word meaning "frighten."

DAY / 214

Today's reading: We continue to read the persistent appeals through Jeremiah for a return to true heart religion. Outward forms alone are not enough.

Memory gem: "They have healed the hurt of the daughter of my people slightly, saying, Peace, peace; when there is no peace" (Jeremiah 8:11).

Thought for today:

In 1823 Victor Hugo wrote in *The Future of Man:* "In the twentieth century war will be dead, the scaffold will be dead, hatred will be dead, frontier boundaries will be dead, dogmas will be dead. Man will live; he will possess something higher than all these—a great country, the whole earth, a great hope, the whole heaven."

Well, the years rolled on, and it was not long before other prophets were predicting still greater and more glorious victories for mankind—world peace, world prosperity, everything but eternal life. They depicted the next stage of history as a paradise where, as one writer put it, "rivers of milk will flow between banks of ice cream, through plains of unlimited abundance."

But what a change has come now—two world wars and all the rest that has followed! The song is different. Yes, we looked for peace, but behold trouble.

What does all this mean to you and to me? Friends, it means that we are seeing the fulfillment of the prophecies of the Holy Bible. We are seeing the words of Christ and the prophets coming true in our day. We are living at five minutes to twelve, four minutes to twelve, three minutes to twelve! The clock is about to strike. We are about to see the most tremendous events in all the history of time. We are about to see the curtain rung down on time and rung up on eternity. Surely we can say, "Now is our salvation nearer than when we believed." Yes much nearer. "The night is far spent, the day is at hand" (Romans 13:11, 12). Shall we not, therefore, do as the apostle urges? "Let us . . . cast off the works of darkness, and let us put on the armour of light" (verse 12).

Let us turn our face toward heaven and be of good courage, for our redemption—yes, our Redeemer—draweth nigh.

DAY / 215

Today's reading: After an introduction to Daniel's remarkable experience, we launch into the first of his prophetic revelations—interpreting the king's dream.

Memory gem: "In the days of these kings shall the God of heaven set up a kingdom, which shall never be destroyed" (Daniel 2:44).

Thought for today:

There it stands in all its terrible beauty—the fifth world kingdom the kingdom without frontiers, the world kingdom of Christ; and it "shall not be left to other people." Why? Because its citizens are immortal. It will not come by the slow absorption of the modern world, but by the sudden interposition of Heaven. And it will be endless, eternal. Those who are its citizens live forever. Their lives measure with the life of God, whom to know is life eternal! (See John 17:3.)

Is it certain? Is it sure? If some weary heart, someone who is filled with doubts and wonderings, asks that question, you can be certain, friend—it is sure! For "the great God," says the prophet, "hath made known . . . what shall come to pass hereafter: and the prophecy is *certain,* and the interpretation thereof sure" (Daniel 2:45, emphasis supplied).

Friend, are you already a citizen of that coming kingdom? If not, will you not give your allegiance to the coming King?

Difficult or obscure words:

Daniel 1:4. **"Children"**—a Hebrew word meaning "youth" or "young men" (see 1 Kings 12:8, where the word is translated "young men)"

Daniel 1:8. **"Meat"**—an old English word meaning food.

Daniel 1:12. **"Pulse"**—an old English word used to translate a Hebrew word meaning "food derived from plants," such as cereals, vegetables, and such fruits as berries and dates.

DAY / 216

Read Jeremiah 26; 35; 25.

Today's reading: Several of Jeremiah's prophecies made use of object lessons. In chapter 35 the Lord used the faithfulness of the Rechabites (a nomad clan) to rebuke Judah's unfaithfulness.

Memory gem: "Thus saith the Lord of hosts, the God of Israel; Jonadab the son of Rechab shall not want a man to stand before me for ever" (Jeremiah 35:19).

Thought for today:

"God sought . . . to bring into sharp contrast the obedience of the Rechabites with the disobedience and rebellion of His people The Rechabites had obeyed the command of their father, and now refused to be enticed into transgression. But the men of Judah had hearkened not to the words of the Lord, and were in consequence about to suffer His severest judgments. . . .

"When men's hearts are softened and subdued by the constraining influence of the Holy Spirit, they will give heed to counsel; but when they turn from admonition until their hearts become hardened, the Lord permits them to be led by other influences. Refusing the truth, they accept falsehood, which becomes a snare to their own destruction. . . .

"The lesson is for us. If the requirements of a good and wise father, who took the best and most effectual means to secure his posterity against the evils of intemperance, were worthy of strict obedience, surely God's authority should be held in as much greater reverence as He is holier than man."—*Prophets and Kings,* pp. 424–426.

Note: Jeremiah 26:2-6 gives a summary of chapter 7:1-15. Then verses 7 and onward tell the reactions of princes and people to Jeremiah's "temple discourse" of chapters 7 through 10.

"Nebuchadrezzar" (Jeremiah 21:2; 25:9; 35:11) is a variant spelling for Nebuchadnezzar, actually closer to the Babylonian.

The "seventy years" of captivity (see Jeremiah 25:11, 12; Daniel 9:2) began with the first taking of Jerusalem by Nebuchadnezzar in 606/605 B.C.

Some of the place names in Jeremiah 25:20-26 cannot be positively identified. Some may be cryptic designations of places known by other names.

DAY / 217

Read Jeremiah 22:1-19 and chapters 18 through 20.

Today's reading: God used all sorts of devices to make His messages to Jehoiakim effective. The acted parable of the potter is one of the most touching.

Memory gem: "Cannot I do with you as this potter? saith the Lord. Behold, as the clay is in the potter's hand, so are ye in mine hand" (Jeremiah 18:6).

Thought for today:

The story in Jeremiah 18:1-6 is God's picture of His dealings with nations and with men. God is the potter, we are the clay—just clay, the dust of the earth. But out of it, under the hand of God, comes the new life of usefulness and beauty. I like that old song:

Have thine own way, Lord! Have Thine own way!
Thou art the Potter; I am the clay.
Mold me and make me after Thy will,
While I am waiting, yielded and still.

Some months ago, a group of us saw a well-known potter at work. We watched as, under his skillful fingers, a ball of clay became a tall and beautiful vase. A little boy in the crowd asked the potter where he got his design. The artist seemed unconcerned, oblivious to everything around him, and went right on working. Then, in answer to the question, he simply paused long enough to touch his head. Yes, he carried his design there. In the mind of the skilled potter there was a design for the vessel, an image of just what it would be when finished. And sure enough, many strange shapes at last evolve into a classic vase, a work of art.

In the mind of God there is a design for each human life. If we yield our lives to Him, He can mold us into the very image of Christ.

Difficult or obscure words:

Jeremiah 20:3. **"Magor-missabib"**—literally, "fear on every side" (see verse 10; Psalm 31:13).

DAY / 218 Read Jeremiah 36:1-4; 45; 36:5-32; 12; 2 Kings 24:1-16; 2 Chronicles 36:5-10.

Today's reading: How stubborn Jehoiakim was in rejecting the Lord's messages! One certainty stands out: God's Word survives all efforts to destroy it.

Memory gem: "Then the word of the Lord came to Jeremiah . . . saying, Take thee again another roll, and write in it all the former words that were in the first roll" (Jeremiah 36:27, 28).

Thought for today:

There are far too many penknife Christians today! Did you ever hear of a penknife Christian? Well, we have the record of God's warning sent through the prophet Jeremiah. The words of Jeremiah were written in a book or scroll and were read to the king as he sat in his winter palace. The message condemned many of the deeds of both the king and the people and called for personal and national repentance. It was, in fact, an unpopular message.

You see, the book began to condemn the king, so he took his spite out on the book itself by cutting out the pages he did not like and throwing them into the fire, until the whole book was gone When he started using his penknife on God's Word, he didn't stop until it was all gone. Some of the princes appealed to him to save it—at least, not to burn it—but he wouldn't listen. It was contrary to his wicked life—it condemned his exactions on the poor, his luxury in the time of trouble, his oath-breaking in public office, his disobedience to God—and he didn't like it. So he used the knife on it.

Now you see what we mean by "penknife Christians"—people who have the name of Christians, who believe in God and the Holy Scriptures, but who at the same time reject any part of the Bible that does not suit them. They simply cut it out—do away with it, as far as they are concerned.

Friends, we need the Bible—God's Book—God's Word—the Holy Scriptures. We need this mighty Book in our homes, in our offices, in our pockets, and, above all, in our minds and hearts. And may God help us to believe it all.

Note: Nebuchadnezzar's second group of exiles (including Ezekiel) was taken from Jerusalem with captive King Jehoiachin in 597 B.C.

DAY /219 Read Jeremiah 22:20-30; chapters 13 and 23; 2 Kings 24:17-20; 2 Chronicles 36:11-16.

Today's reading: In the heart of warnings and reproofs to apostate Judah, we find a question that points to the root of much apostasy—conditions in the home.

Memory gem: "Where is the flock that was given thee, thy beautiful flock?" (Jeremiah 13:20).

Thought for today:

Oh, father, you are the best man that a boy knows—do not blast his faith in you. You owe it to him, to God, to your family, and to your country to keep faith with your boy. When the father leads the way to heaven it means everything in the world. We, as fathers, can never pass the responsibility off on mother, the school, or the church. We must sometime hear the question we will have to answer: "Where is the flock that was given thee, thy beautiful flock?" (Jeremiah 13:20).

This is an hour of decision for us all. Let us make the right decision, with the blessing of Christ, and say, "As for me and my house, we will serve the Lord" (Joshua 24:15). Your family needs Christ.

Mother, are you doing all you can to fight back the waves of paganism and sin that threaten our homes today? The big question of the hour is, What's the matter with our *families?* If the cynical spirit of some circles goes much farther, it will be a sad day for our country. Hundreds of thousands of families broken by divorce each year are but only a symptom of shifting foundations. Of the thousands of babies born each day in our land, how many will be welcomed into a real home?

There are millions of mothers who gladly sacrifice everything for their children; but, mothers, are you neglecting the supreme thing? You go without new clothes so that Mary may have the very latest and keep up with her set in school. You skimp and save so that John may have the chance to go on with his education. And millions of dollars are expended on the very latest ideas in teaching those children of ours the "three R's" of education. But there is one "R" very few have at home, or anywhere now—religion.

And if the foundations of religion are not laid in the home, it is doubtful that they will ever be laid at all.

DAY / 220

Read Jeremiah 24; 29; 30.

Today's reading: The prophecy of the seventy years of captivity is repeated. But in the midst of doom and gloom, a beautiful promise shines out.

Memory gem: "Ye shall seek me, and find me, when ye shall search for me with all your heart" (Jeremiah 29:13).

Thought for today:

In many ways we see that Isaiah 45:15 is true—God is a God that hides Himself. But, notwithstanding all obscurity, it is important for us to remember that God has amply revealed Himself. Though God hides Himself, there comes a voice from heaven, saying, "I have not spoken in secret" (Isaiah 45:19). All that we need to know, we can know if we believe His word. No obscurity hides His divine invitation for us to seek Him, and His revelation in the Bible is plainly His gracious seeking after us. He is no hidden God to those who sincerely desire to know His will.

We must be wholehearted if we expect to find God. It is the great purpose of divine revelation to make us know that God loves us and has given us His Son that in Him we may know God and possess His righteousness. What do we need more than that knowledge and that possession? "And this is life eternal," said our Saviour, "that they might know thee the only true God, and Jesus Christ, whom thou hast sent" (John 17:3). Whatever may be dark in the ways of God to men, this is clear: He has come to us in His Son, our Lord Jesus Christ, for "God was in Christ, reconciling the world unto himself" (2 Corinthians 5:19).

Many things which we should like to know are not written in the book of divine revelation, whether in the volume of nature, of human history, of our own hearts, or even the Bible. But those things that are for our salvation are written that we may believe that Jesus is the Son of God, and, may have life in His name (see John 20:31).

When God seems hidden, we must have faith to remember that what we need to know, we can know; that many things which are dark now will be clear later; that our partial knowledge will be enlightened when we shall know even as we are known (see 1 Corinthians 13:12).

Note: As verse 1 of chapter 24 indicates, we have now come in our reading to the reign of Zedekiah, last king of Judah.

DAY / 221

Read Jeremiah 31; 27; 28.

Today's reading: These chapters reveal a striking contrast—God's forgiving love to those who repent, and the hopeless fate of those who persist in wickedness.

Memory gem: "They shall all know me, from the least of them unto the greatest of them, saith the Lord: for I will forgive their iniquity, and I will remember their sin no more" (Jeremiah 31:34).

Thought for today:

There was a little boy at our house who slipped out one day to watch a heavy scraper at work cutting out a roadway on the side of the mountain. This was contrary to his mother's instruction; but, as she was away for a few hours, the temptation was great. It was so nice to play behind the chugging tractor! But things went wrong, and he got into trouble. While by God's blessing he was not killed, in a moment he was all scratched up and covered with dirt and had lost a shoe. He began to cry and call for his daddy; then he came hobbling into the study where Daddy was at work on a sermon for *The Voice of Prophecy* broadcast.

Did that father forgive him? Ah, yes. And as he stood there in his penitent tears and fright and dirt, with one shoe off and one shoe on, I think his father only loved him the more. Would he turn him away? Never in this world.

It's when we come to our heavenly Father for help—when we run to Him in our danger and loss and need and disobedience— that we find help. It is only when we want to be forgiven that we are forgiven.

Someone reading this story may look into his own heart, and it will look so dark that he will say, "I'm afraid I'm beyond forgiveness." If you are looking at yourself and are utterly discouraged, look in another direction. Friend, you have looked at yourself and you are discouraged. Of course you are when you do that. Look now at Christ, and you will have hope.

Note: Chapter 31 continues the message of chapter 30, which Jeremiah wrote after the interchange of letters with the false prophets.

Jeremiah 27:1 says, "In the beginning of the reign of Jehoiakim." Verse 12 says, "I spake also to Zedekiah." Several Hebrew manuscripts have "Zedekiah" in verse 1, and the whole chapter, with chapter 28, obviously belongs to Zedekiah's time.

DAY / 222

Read Jeremiah 46; 47; 48; Obadiah.

Today's reading: Many of the Lord's warning messages were directed to Judah's neighboring nations. Here Jeremiah speaks against Egypt, the Philistines, and Moab; Obadiah, against Edom. But in these solemn judgments we find words of hope for God's people. The little book of Obadiah is undated, but it seems to belong to the period of Zedekiah's reign.

Memory gem: "Fear thou not, O Jacob my servant, saith the Lord: for I am with thee" (Jeremiah 46:28).

Thought for today:

On August 6, 1916, a tugboat belonging to the Niagara Falls Power Company was working in the Niagara River. A scow attached to the tug broke loose and started a wild race for the falls a little way down the river. There were two men aboard, apparently doomed. It was impossible to land on either shore, and they rushed along at frightful speed, at the mercy of the racing current, while those on shore were powerless to help—when suddenly, with a mighty lunge, the scow leaped up on a great rock hidden just beneath the surface. There it stopped, in the midst of the raging waters, just a few hundred feet above the roaring Niagara Falls.

The people on the Canadian shore (which was the nearer) began making frantic efforts to save the men before the dashing waters should dislodge the scow and force them to the terrible plunge. Finally, a group of lifesavers arrived from Fort Niagara, thirteen miles away. And they threw a rope to the scow, which enabled the men to make a safe landing.

Those who are in the great river of time today know the danger. Like these two men, they feel the pull of the current of sin, but imagine that the place where the plunge to eternal destruction takes place is far, far down the stream. Yet, the rapids of life are short, and the thunder of the mighty falls of eternity can be heard—if we listen.

But God has set a Rock in this river, as He set it in the Niagara. This Rock is the Rock of Ages, and it is the only hope of men and women drifting to eternal ruin. Lifesavers—men and women who have themselves been saved and who are equipped for saving—are ready to help those who cling to the Rock of Ages. Will you lay hold on this mighty Rock today?

DAY / 223

Read Jeremiah 49 and 50.

Today's reading: It may seem somewhat strange that the prophet who urged the Jews to submit to Babylon would predict the downfall of the empire—but he did so in no uncertain terms.

Memory gem: "Come, and let us join ourselves to the Lord in a perpetual covenant that shall not be forgotten" (Jeremiah 50:5).

Thought for today:

I might say a word about the riches of Babylon. In the prophecy of Jeremiah we read: "Chaldea [Babylon] shall be a spoil: all that spoil her shall be satisfied, saith the Lord" (Jeremiah 50:10). "A sword is upon her treasures; and they shall be robbed" (verse 37). "Abundant in treasures, thine end is come" (Jeremiah 51:13).

The little word *all*—"all that spoil her shall be satisfied"—implies that Babylon would be often despoiled. Nothing like this prophecy was predicted concerning other cities mentioned in prophecy. How did the prophets know there would be riches enough to tempt, and even satisfy, spoiler after spoiler? But so it was.

Cyrus, the king of Persia, took much treasure from Babylon when he captured the city in 539 B.C. Xerxes and his army took 150 million dollars in gold alone, we are told. Alexander the Great found vast wealth for himself there and also gave the value of $50 to each soldier in his army. Two hundred years later the Parthians ravaged Babylon, and then came the Romans, according to the prophecy, for the same purpose of seizing treasure. No wonder Babylon has been called by some historians, the "golden city of a golden age."

Note: Compare the striking similarity of wording in the following:
Jeremiah 49:7—Obadiah 8
Jeremiah 49:9, 10a—Obadiah 5; 6
Jeremiah 49:14-16—Obadiah 1-4.

Difficult or obscure words:

Jeremiah 49:31. **"Wealthy"**—better: undisturbed, or carefree.

DAY / 224

Read Jeremiah 51.

Today's reading: We finish the prophecy against Babylon. Some portions of it were fulfilled by the Persian conquest, but other parts remained unfulfilled until centuries later.

Memory gem: "Babylon shall become heaps, a dwelling place for dragons, an astonishment, and an hissing, without an inhabitant" (Jeremiah 51:37).

Thought for today:

Babylon was situated in one of the most fertile valleys in the world, with plenty of water for irrigation. By all human prognostication it should have remained inhabited down through the ages. Great Babylon, the city of Bel, fought against God's city, Jerusalem, taking its people captive. Jerusalem became the slave of Babylon. Yet Babylon and its people have vanished like a dream in the night, while Jerusalem and its people still remain.

"Without an inhabitant," said the prophet. You who have been to Babylon today know that it is still uninhabited—just a few keepers about to take tourists through.

Think of the other cities in existence when Jeremiah predicted Babylon's demise: Damascus, Jerusalem, Athens, Rome, Antioch, Alexandria, Sidon—all have remained continuously cities of consequence to our present day. But it remained for Babylon, the greatest and richest of all the cities of that time, to sink into utter insignificance. How to explain it? God said it would be so.

In Jeremiah 51:58 we are told that "the broad walls of Babylon shall be utterly broken." For centuries after this prediction, the walls of Babylon were the strongest and greatest walls known at that time in the western world. The Great Wall of China had already been built, but it was not so strong or broad as the walls of Babylon, according to the reports. The wall of China is still standing, but the walls of Babylon have disappeared—shapeless mounds of earth.

Difficult or obscure words:

Jeremiah 51:2. **"Fanners"**—winnowers, those who separate the chaff from grain by throwing it into the air so that the wind carries away the chaff.

Jeremiah 51:3. **"Brigadine"**—rather: armor.

Jeremiah 51:36. **"Sea"**—a Hebrew word sometimes used for river.

DAY / 225

Today's reading: Another exiled Hebrew served as God's messenger. Daniel spoke in the royal court; Ezekiel spoke to his fellow exiles as well as to the Jews still in Judah. Psalm 137, of unknown authorship, fittingly expresses the sadness of Israelites in exile.

Memory gem: "By the rivers of Babylon, there we sat down, yea, we wept, when we remembered Zion" (Psalm 137:1).

Thought for today:

"Through Daniel and others of the Hebrew captives, the Babylonian monarch had been made acquainted with the power and supreme authority of the true God; and when Zedekiah once more solemnly promised to remain loyal, Nebuchadnezzar required him to swear to this promise in the name of the Lord God of Israel. Had Zedekiah respected this renewal of his covenant oath, his loyalty would have had a profound influence on the minds of many who were watching the conduct of those who claimed to reverence the name and to cherish the honor of the God of the Hebrews.

"But Judah's king lost sight of his privilege of bringing honor to the name of the living God. . . .

"While Jeremiah continued to bear his testimony in the land of Judah, the prophet Ezekiel was raised up from among the captives in Babylon, to warn and to comfort the exiles, and also to confirm the word of the Lord that was being spoken through Jeremiah. During the years that remained of Zedekiah's reign, Ezekiel made very plain the folly of trusting to the false predictions of those who were causing the captives to hope for an early return to Jerusalem. He was also instructed to foretell, by means of a variety of symbols and solemn messages, the siege and utter destruction of Jerusalem."—*Prophets and Kings,* pp. 447, 448.

Note: "The thirtieth year" of Ezekiel 1:1 is equated with the "fifth year of Jehoachin's captivity" in verse 2. We can only speculate on the event marking the beginning of the period (maybe Ezekiel was thirty years old), but the fifth year of the captivity would be 593/592 B.C. All other events in the book are dated from this point.

DAY / 226

Today's reading: After Ezekiel received his commission as a prophet, the Lord began sending stern rebukes and solemn warnings—often to be acted out in symbolism—to the ease-loving inhabitants still in Jerusalem before its final overthrow.

Memory gem: "Riches profit not in the day of wrath: but righteousness delivereth from death" (Proverbs 11:4).

Thought for today:

With several friends, I was privileged to visit the "throne room" of one of the great banks of the world, but not in my own country. There I saw a blaze of riches in gold and precious stones almost beyond the dreams of avarice—crowns, scepters, and jewelry set with diamonds, rubies, and pearls worth millions and millions of dollars.

Is it safe in that guarded strong room below the surface of the earth? Is anything safe today except a soul that rests itself in God? During the last few years great revolutions have taken place. New hands took over the levers of the world. Possessors of riches became refugees. Wealth gathered through the ages was dissipated, lost, destroyed, or changed hands overnight.

There is a day coming when "they shall cast their silver in the streets, and their gold shall be removed: their silver and their gold shall not be able to deliver them in the day of the wrath of the Lord: they shall not satisfy their souls, . . . it is the stumblingblock of their iniquity" (Ezekiel 7:19).

No man can enter through the gates of the heavenly city burdened with things of this earth. One's love must not be on these things. Money is not a burden if it is dedicated to God to be used as He directs to be a blessing to humanity and to His cause. But if a man worships these things, if his love is upon them, then they are a burden that will destroy him at last.

Will you not today consecrate not only your heart, but all that you have to God? If you do this, you will never have to worry about a bank failure, for your treasure will be in the bank of heaven, which never fails.

Note: The prophetic periods of 390 and 40 days (prophetic years) of Ezekiel 4:5, 6 cannot be determined, because no clue is given as to the beginning point or points.

Today's reading: Temple worship sank to new depths of degradation during the reign of Judah's last king, giving reason for the impending doom. Still God looked for a genuine reformation.

Memory gem: "I will give them one heart, and I will put a new spirit within you; and I will take the stony heart out of their flesh, and I will give them an heart of flesh" (Ezekiel 11:19).

Thought for today:

"In the sixth year of the reign of Zedekiah, the Lord revealed to Ezekiel in vision some of the abominations that were being practiced in Jerusalem, and within the gate of the Lord's house, and even in the inner court. The chambers of images, and the pictured idols, . . . in rapid succession passed before the astonished gaze of the prophet.

"Those who should have been spiritual leaders among the people . . . were seen offering incense before the idolatrous representations that had been introduced into hidden chambers within the sacred precincts of the temple court. . . .

"There were still 'greater abominations' for the prophet to behold. At a gate leading from the outer to the inner court he was shown 'women weeping for Tammuz' and within 'the inner court of the Lord's house, . . . at the door of the temple of the Lord, between the porch and the altar, were about five and twenty men, with their backs toward the temple of the Lord, and their faces toward the east; and they worshiped the sun toward the east.'

"And now the glorious Being who accompanied Ezekiel throughout this astonishing vision of wickedness in high places in the land of Judah, inquired of the prophet: 'Hast thou seen this, O son of man? Is it a light thing to the house of Judah that they commit the abominations which they commit here? for they have filled the land with violence, and have returned to provoke Me to anger.' "—*Prophets and Kings,* pp. 448, 449.

DAY / 228

Read Ezekiel 12 through 14.

Today's reading: Ezekiel goes through some more play-acting to drive home the Lord's warnings against wickedness. In chapter 14, verses 3 and 4, he points out that idolatry is often a matter hidden in the heart.

Memory gem: "The heart is deceitful above all things, and desperately wicked: who can know it?" (Jeremiah 17:9).

Thought for today:

When men decide in their hearts that they will not obey God their prayers are of no avail until they repent and surrender to the Lord. When a man sets up his idols in his heart and then prays to God, God will answer him according to his idols.

If we persistently slight God's truth and God's mercy, His Spirit will finally go from us. There will be no more conviction of sin, no true repentance, no forgiveness.

Suppose that late on some dark night you see my home on fire, and to save my life you try to ring my telephone. But no warning call is possible because I have disconnected the phone that my sleep may not be disturbed. I sleep on—to fiery destruction. So God sends warning and conviction to men by the Holy Spirit.

We may set the alarm clock; but if we pay no attention to it or turn it off a few times, soon we can sleep right through its clatter. We become hardened to its warning.

So in spiritual things, many are "past feeling" (Ephesians 4:19). Their hearts become "fully set in them to do evil" (Ecclesiastes 8:11). In Christ's day the leaders of His nation rejected the Light of the world, and their house, the beautiful temple, was left unto them "desolate" (Luke 13:35). The presence of God had departed. So in the last days, the great world multitude will turn away from the Spirit of God and be carried away with a strong delusion.

Some reading these words may hear God's call to repent. Don't say No. Make it Yes. Don't delay. Saying Yes to God means choosing everlasting life.

Difficult or obscure words:

Ezekiel 13:10. **"Untempered mortar"**—whitewash, which might make a wall look all right without strengthening it.

DAY / 229

Read Ezekiel 15 and 16.

Today's reading: God uses an allegory to illustrate the folly of His people's apostasy. He adopts an infant, gives her security and riches, and brings her fame; then she turns her back on Him. Still God loves her!

Memory gem: "I will establish my covenant with thee; and thou shalt know that I am the Lord" (Ezekiel 16:62).

Thought for today:

An interesting story came out some years ago about an old man who was found half dead in one of the streets of New York City. The authorities picked him up and took him to Bellevue Hospital. During the twenty-six days he was there he wouldn't tell them who he was or anything about his friends or life. He just said he had lost all his money or it had been stolen from him, and that he wanted to go back to Serbia to die.

He died there in the hospital. As they were getting him ready to be buried in a potter' s field, someone suggested that they ought to look in his dirty clothes. They did so and found his pockets full of money, stocks, and bonds. Then, when his clothes were ripped apart, they were found to be filled with money and other valuables.

Why had he lived and died as a pauper? No one knows. He suffered privation and sickness and practically starved himself.

But how many people in this world are like that in spiritual things! They don't live up to their opportunities. They live a pauperized life. To them life doesn't amount to much—just a succession of days. Life is to know and to feel and to do. It is to have the deep love of God in the heart. Life, my friend, is what we make it with God.

DAY / 230

Read Ezekiel 17 through 19.

Today's reading: These chapters contain some unusual parables and prophecies. Chapter 18 gives a clear explanation of God's method of dealing with sin and repentance.

Memory gem: "I have no pleasure in the death of him that dieth saith the Lord God: wherefore turn yourselves, and live ye" (Ezekiel 18:32).

Thought for today:

In Ezekiel 18, verses 2 to 20, we are plainly told that when a son sees all his father's sins, but turns away from them and does right he shall surely live. After telling us that "the soul that sinneth, it shall die" and "the sons shall not bear the iniquity of the father," the Lord says: "Repent, and turn yourselves from all your transgressions; so iniquity shall not be your ruin. Cast away from you all your transgressions, whereby ye have transgressed; and make you a new heart and a new spirit: for why will ye die, O house of Israel?" (verses 30, 31).

Families and nations die out when sin flourishes. In Ezekiel 16:49 we are told that Sodom was filled with pride, fullness of bread, and idleness. You see, sin will destroy itself eventually.

But, is there hope for us and our children? Yes. If God had His way with us, all sin and suffering, even death, would be gone (see Matthew 4:23; 8:16; Luke 4:40; Matthew 10:1).

Let us be thankful for the last part of the second commandment. Not only is the iniquity of the fathers to exert its influence unto the third and fourth generation of them that continue to hate God, but He shows mercy unto thousands of them that love Him and keep His commandments (see Exodus 20:5, 6).

God is able and willing to deliver us from our sins and from the effects of our sins. The only question is, Is it best for Him to do so under all circumstances? We know that God will forgive our sins and give us His justifying grace whenever we turn to Him. There is no doubt about that, and there is no time limit on it. But, as to the effects of sin, we know that they will all be taken away when the earth is made new. Every one of us must give account of himself to God, and every one of us may have a place in the kingdom of Christ. Will you not make your decision for Him today?

DAY / 231

Read Ezekiel 20 and 21.

Today's reading: In chapter 20 the Lord reviews His dealings with Israel through the centuries, showing the efforts He had made to keep the people from evil.

Memory gem: "Moreover also I gave them my sabbaths, to be a sign between me and them, that they might know that I am the Lord that sanctify them" (Ezekiel 20:12).

Thought for today:

Not only is the Sabbath a memorial of Creation, but it is also a sign between God and His people (see Exodus 31:13).

Sanctifying power is in God and not in us. We have it only as a gift from Him. Unfortunately, the ancient church drifted into error on this point. It made the mistake of trusting to power possessed by man for sanctification, a righteousness provided by human works; and this is a common modern error too.

We often hear or read the doctrine that everyone has a power within him with which he can in some way work out his own salvation, that our evolving, inherent abilities are leading us from a lower to a higher state.

These perverted notions lead to the natural conclusion that man does not need a personal Saviour and are just as definitely idolatry and unbelief as any that has ever appeared in the world. In fact, they make man his own savior, his own god.

But the Sabbath was given to deliver from such false philosophy. It is a recurring sign that God possesses sanctifying, redeeming power.

We look to the Maker of man, the Creator of man, as our Redeemer. We can trust in Him who has creative power, possessed by God and God alone, to save us by creating us anew.

Knowing these facts, it seems difficult to imagine any other reasons for a weekly rest day. The Sabbath stands upon an unchanging foundation. It is part of an eternal law, and it is a memorial for all generations. It is an everlasting sign of sanctifying, redeeming power; power that makes man righteous, which comes only from God, and not from man's works at all. It is a perpetual defense against apostasy and atheism. It will be a blessing to every child of God who comes to know its place in the great plan of salvation.

Note: See **Difficult or obscure words** on next page.

DAY / 232

Today's reading: These chapters point out some of the sins that brought disaster on Judah's people. In chapter 22, verses 18 and 22, the evils are represented as dross that must be skimmed off as the pure metal is melted in the furnace.

Memory gem: "The words of the Lord are pure words: as silver tried in a furnace of earth, purified seven times" (Psalm 12:6).

Thought for today:

"In these days of peril shall we show less devotion to the truth of God, and less fervent attachment to His law, than in former years? The very condition of things exists which Christ declared would be, prior to His second coming in power and glory. The prevailing ungodliness tends to paralyze and even to destroy true faith and piety. But this is the very time when the gold of Christian integrity will shine brightest, in contrast to the dross of hypocrisy and corruption. Now is the time for Christ's chosen to show their devotion to His service—the time for all His followers to bear the noblest testimony for their Master by standing firm against the prevailing current of evil.

"As we see the results which have followed a disregard of God's law—dishonesty, theft, licentiousness, drunkenness, and murder—we are prepared to say with the psalmist, 'I love thy commandments above gold; yea, above fine gold'; 'in keeping of them, there is great reward.' When the divine law is set aside, the greatest misery will result, both to families and to society. Our only hope of better things is to be found in a faithful adherence to the precepts of Jehovah." —*Sons and Daughters of God,* p. 54.

Difficult or obscure words for Day/231:

Ezekiel 21:21. **"Made his arrows bright"**—rather: shook arrows together, a common method of divination.

Ezekiel 21:27. **"Overturn"**—the threefold repetition of the word (literally "a ruin, a ruin, a ruin") is a Hebrew device to indicate intensity.

DAY / 233

Read Jeremiah 37:1-15; Chapters 21 and 34; 32:1-25.

Today's reading: People do strange things in a crisis. The king and the nobles of Jerusalem repented and made a covenant to free all their oppressed countrymen. Then, when the crisis passed, they reclaimed all their servants. Still the Lord loved them.

Memory gem: "Unto this people thou shalt say, Thus saith the Lord; Behold, I set before you the way of life, and the way of death" (Jeremiah 21:8).

Thought for today:

The story is told of two farmers who had trouble with each other for years. It all started over some little dispute that did not amount to anything, but it kept growing until they could agree on nothing—except that they were enemies. Here they were, with farms adjoining, where they might have helped each other with good-neighbor enjoyment. But the old grudge dragged on.

Finally, one day a rattlesnake bit one of the men, and his life was despaired of. He was on the very edge of the grave and decided to call in his neighbor enemy and ask his forgiveness.

When the neighbor came into the room, he said, "Jim, I am going to die and I want you to forgive me for all my meanness. I want to make the old thing right."

His neighbor assured him he was glad to do it—to be friends as though there had never been any trouble at all.

And then the sick man said, "But remember, if I get well, the old score still stands!"

Was that real repentance? No, of course not. To repent means to forsake the wrong and to be truly sorry for it.

If all professed Christians should ever really try to make things right with a sincere heart, we would have a revival that would shake the nation.

Note: Zedekiah's perfidy in seeking help from Egypt brought Nebuchadnezzar's armies to Jerusalem again. An Egyptian army actually invaded Judah, forcing the Babylonians to raise the siege and drive off this threat. Having defeated the Egyptians, Nebuchadnezzar returned to the final siege of Jerusalem in January of 588 B.C. It lasted until July of 586 B.C.—thirty months.

DAY / 234

Read Jeremiah 32:26-44; Chapter 33; Ezekiel 24 and 25.

Today's reading: The vacillating king allowed Jeremiah to be imprisoned, but God still sent message after message calling for repentance. Ezekiel in Babylon was also giving the warning.

Memory gem: "Call unto me, and I will answer thee, and shew thee great and mighty things, which thou knowest not" (Jeremiah 33:3).

Thought for today:

The prophet Jeremiah was at one time shut up in prison by the king of Judah, while Jerusalem was being besieged by the armies of Babylon. It was a dark and terrible time. In this discouraging hour, the word of God came to Jeremiah in the prison where he was confined. Here is the message:

"Thus saith the Lord, the maker thereof [that is, the maker of heavens and earth], the Lord that formed it, to establish it; the Lord is his name; call unto me, and I will answer thee, and shew thee great and mighty things, which thou knowest not" (Jeremiah 33:2, 3). The original words for "great and mighty things" mean literally "incomprehensible" or "mysterious" or "hidden" things.

God did show wonderful things, hidden things, which the world did not yet know because these events had not yet happened. But God, who sees the end from the beginning, sees the future as well as He knows the past, better than we know it. The prophecies of Holy Scripture outline many of the events of the future in order to give us faith in the Word of God.

As was said by a wise man centuries ago, "Man proposes, but God disposes." There are many things contained in the Bible which skeptics have denied and held up to ridicule. But later on, after the excavation of some biblical site, the Bible statements have been proved true.

My friend, you can trust the Bible. You can lean hard upon it, and it will not fail you.

Difficult or obscure words:

Ezekiel 24:6. **"Scum"**—better: rust. The words represent Jerusalem as an iron pot corroded with rust.

Ezekiel 24:17. **"Bread of men"**—probably meaning a funeral feast.

DAY / 235

Read Jeremiah 37:16 through chapter 39.

Today's reading: Weak-kneed King Zedekiah knew what he should do, but he feared the wicked nobles—he just couldn't make a stand for the right. But Ebed-melech, an Ethiopian eunuch, acted to rescue Jeremiah.

Memory gem: "But Jeremiah said, . . . Obey, I beseech thee, the voice of the Lord, which I speak unto thee: so it shall be well unto thee, and thy soul shall live" (Jeremiah 38:20).

Thought for today:

"Even to the last hour, God made plain His willingness to show mercy to those who should choose to submit to His just requirements. Had the king chosen to obey, the lives of the people might have been spared, and the city saved from conflagration; but he thought he had gone too far to retrace his steps. He was afraid of the Jews, afraid of ridicule, afraid for his life. After years of rebellion against God, Zedekiah thought it too humiliating to say to his people, I accept the word of the Lord, as spoken through the prophet Jeremiah; I dare not venture to war against the enemy in the face of all these warnings.

"With tears Jeremiah entreated Zedekiah to save himself and his people. With anguish of spirit he assured him that unless he should heed the counsel of God, he could not escape with his life, and all his possessions would fall to the Babylonians. But the king had started on the wrong course, and he would not retrace his steps. He decided to follow the counsel of the false prophets, and of the men whom he really despised, and who ridiculed his weakness in yielding so readily to their wishes. He sacrificed the noble freedom of his manhood, and became a cringing slave to public opinion. With no fixed purpose to do evil, he was also without resolution to stand boldly for the right. Convicted though he was of the value of the counsel given by Jeremiah, he had not the moral stamina to obey; and as a consequence he advanced steadily in the wrong direction."—*Prophets and Kings,* pp. 457, 458.

Difficult or obscure words:

Jeremiah 38:6. " **Dungeon**"—literally "pit" or "cistern."

Jeremiah 38:11. **"Clouts"**—an old English word for "rags."

DAY / 236 Read Ezekiel 29:1-16; 30:1-19; 2 Kings 25; 2 Chronicles 36:17-21; Jeremiah 52.

Today's reading: The persistent sins of God's people, despite repeated appeals for reformation and warnings of disaster, finally brought about their ruin. Beautiful Jerusalem was utterly broken up.

Memory gem: "How doth the city sit solitary, that was full of people! how is she become as a widow!" (Lamentations 1:1).

Thought for today:

Over in England a man owned a great python. He had captured it when it was just a tiny snake in the jungle. And, as the snake grew into a large serpent, twelve to fifteen feet long, with power enough to crush a man in its coils, he demonstrated his power over it in public exhibitions. He had trained it to wrap itself around his body until nothing of the man showed except a part of his face. He would give the command: "Wind!" And the snake would wind itself around and around his body. Then he would give the command: "Unwind!" and the snake would unwind itself from his body. It obeyed him implicitly.

Someone remonstrated with him, "Someday that snake will fail to unwind itself, and will crush you to death."

But he only laughed. "I have had him ever since he was a baby. I can make him mind me. I am the master, and he must obey."

But there came a night when the man commanded the snake to wind about his body. It obeyed. And then he commanded it to unwind. The spectators saw a strange motion like a great wave over the snake—the man's eyes began to bulge—and people heard a dull, snapping sound as of bones breaking.

The snake had turned back to the law of the jungle. He had sensed the good meal that the thing he was wrapped around would make. The snake was still a snake—it had not changed.

And so it is with sin, friends—any sin!

Note: Evil-Merodach (2 Kings 25:27 and elsewhere) is called Amel-Marduk in secular history. He was the son and successor of Nebuchadnezzar.

DAY / 237

Today's reading: Jeremiah, released from prison by the conquering Babylonians, chooses to remain faithfully at his post with the poor people in Judah. He soon sees anarchy at work and more trouble ahead.

Memory gem: "Many are the afflictions of the righteous: but the Lord delivereth him out of them all" (Psalm 34:19).

Thought for today:

It was T. DeWitt Talmage, the great preacher, who told the story of the ship *Arctic* which was struck by another ship in the North Atlantic and was going down. Some of its men got off in lifeboats, some on rafts; but three hundred went to the bottom with the ship.

During all those hours of calamity, Stuart Holland, a young man who belonged to the crew, stood at the signal gun as it sounded out across the sea, boom, boom, boom. There was no radio in those days, no way to seek help at a distance; only the hope that some passing ship might hear the boom of the signal gun. The engineer had forsaken his place; he was gone. The man at the helm had left the ship. Finally all the powder was used up; the signal gun could be fired no more. But young Holland broke into a magazine and brought out more powder, and again the gun boomed its plea over the ocean. He fired until the ship went down. He did his best.

DAY / 238

Read Jeremiah 42 through 44.

Today's reading: The history of Judah's decline ends sadly. We have no record of what happened to Jeremiah and the others after Johanan forced the cowardly flight into Egypt.

Memory gem: "I the Lord thy God will hold thy right hand, saying unto thee, Fear not; I will help thee" (Isaiah 41:13).

Thought for today:

The prophet Jeremiah said to an important leader of his time: "Be not afraid of the king of Babylon, of whom ye are afraid; be not afraid of him, saith the Lord: for I am with you to save you, and to deliver you from his hand" (Jeremiah 42:11).

But the man was afraid, and he stayed afraid. He was more afraid of the king of Babylon than he was of disobeying God, and so he fled into the land of Egypt—exactly what the Lord, through Jeremiah, told him not to do.

I have told the story again and again, and I tell it again here—a story of my youngest son when he was about five years old. One night when it was exceedingly dark, he and I took a walk up into the mountain in back of our home. The trail wound among the live oak trees, and there wasn't a ray of light. As we started out he talked constantly, but as the trail got darker and steeper, he talked less. Finally, taking my hand and walking as close to me as he could get, he said in almost a whisper, "Daddy, we're not afraid, are we?"

No, *we* were not, but *he* was. Yet the touch of my hand gave him courage and faith. He would go anywhere I would go. His fear and his confidence were a sermon to me. They brought back to my mind these words of Scripture: "For I the Lord thy God will hold thy right hand, saying unto thee, Fear not; I will help thee" (Isaiah 41:13).

Read Psalms 74 and 79; Lamentations 1 and 2.

Today's reading: The two psalms may be the product of Jeremiah or some other writer of this period; they vividly reflect the anguish experienced at this time.

Memory gem: "Help us, O God of our salvation, for the glory of thy name: and deliver us, and purge away our sins, for thy name's sake" (Psalm 79:9).

Thought for today:

"The sorrow of the prophet over the utter perversity of those who should have been the spiritual light of the world, his sorrow over the fate of Zion and of the people carried captive to Babylon, is revealed in the lamentations he has left on record as a memorial of the folly of turning from the counsels of Jehovah to human wisdom. Amid the ruin wrought, Jeremiah could still declare, 'It is of the Lord's mercies that we are not consumed' and his constant prayer was, 'Let us search and try our ways, and turn again to the Lord.' Lamentations 3:22, 40.

"While Judah was still a kingdom among the nations, he had inquired of his God, 'Hast Thou utterly rejected Judah? hath Thy soul loathed Zion?' . . . 'Do not abhor us, for Thy name's sake.' Jeremiah 14:19, 21. The prophet's absolute faith in God's eternal purpose to bring order out of confusion, and to demonstrate to the nations of earth and to the entire universe His attributes of justice and love, now led him to plead confidently in behalf of those who might turn from evil to righteousness.

"But now Zion was utterly destroyed; the people of God were in their captivity. Overwhelmed with grief, the prophet exclaimed: 'How doth the city sit solitary that was full of people! how is she become as a widow!' Lamentations 1:1."—*Prophets and Kings,* pp. 461, 462.

Difficult or obscure words:

Psalm 74:13, 14. **"Dragons"** and **"leviathan"**—evidently symbolic references to the destruction of Egypt's armies in the Red Sea at the Exodus.

Lamentations 1:7. **"Sabbaths"**—a Hebrew word found only here in the Scriptures. It is not the word used frequently for "sabbaths" in other places. It more likely means a forced inactivity.

Lamentations 2:20. **"Of a span long"**—another word occurring nowhere else. It may mean something desired or cherished.

DAY / 240

Today's reading: In the very center of this sad book of Jeremiah's weeping (chapter 3, verses 22-41) is found one of the most beautiful expressions of confidence in God's mercy.

Memory gem: "It is of the Lord's mercies that we are not consumed, because his compassions fail not. They are new every morning: great is thy faithfulness" (Lamentations 3:22, 23, see also verses 21 through 33).

Thought for today:

How about it, friend? Do you appreciate the mercy of God? Do you go on and on and on in your life of selfishness? You are still here. Every morning brings you a new day. You have food to eat. You have friends. Your heart keeps beating. Do you appreciate all this? Have you ever said Thank You to God? How merciful He is! Surely "the Lord is merciful and gracious, slow to anger, and plenteous in mercy" (Psalm 103:8).

Did you ever stop to think that "merciful" is one of God's names? Read it for yourself in Exodus 34:6.

The publican in the temple was ashamed even to lift up his eyes to heaven, but smote upon his breast and prayed the sinner's prayer: "God be merciful to me a sinner" (Luke 18:13).

Why shouldn't that be our prayer today, the prayer of our generation?

Difficult or obscure words:

Lamentations 3:49. **"Trickleth down"**—rather: runs, flows, or pours out, to make a vigorous parallel with verse 48.

Lamentations 4:3. **"Sea monsters"**—probably better: jackals.

Lamentations 5:10. **"Black"**—better: hot, descriptive of the fever brought on by famine.

DAY / 241

Read Ezekiel 27; 28; 30:20-26.

Today's reading: Among some remarkable prophecies concerning Tyre and Sidon, we find in chapter 28 one of the descriptions of Satan's fall, in a message to the "king of Tyrus."

Memory gem: "Thou wast perfect in thy ways from the day that thou wast created, till iniquity was found in thee" (Ezekiel 28:15).

Thought for today:

There was another city near Tyre—in fact, a sister city, thirty miles to the north—which had been in competition with Tyre for centuries: the city of Sidon. When the prophet made his prediction about successful Tyre being obliterated and not being rebuilt (see Ezekiel 26), Sidon was declining. Anyone judging by the situation in Ezekiel's time would have said that Sidon was the one to be destroyed, and not Tyre.

Sidon's decline continued for centuries. In 351 B.C. the city was captured and utterly destroyed by Artaxerxes Ochus, king of Persia. But it was immediately rebuilt.

Notice that God's judgment upon Sidon, recorded in Ezekiel 28:21-23, was not to destroy her—no utter extinction here—but blood in her streets, wounded in her midst, the sword on every side, warfare about her. And this has been her history, to the very present minute in which we are speaking. I have visited Sidon a number of times and actually preached there on the waterfront, overlooking the harbor where the fishing boats still come in.

Tyre was to be destroyed; Sidon was to remain. History proves God spoke the truth.

Suppose Ezekiel had said that both Tyre and Sidon would be destroyed, which would certainly seem likely, as they had the same kind of business and were close together. And suppose that he said that neither would be rebuilt. Then the 10,000 inhabitants of Sidon would be a living proof of the falsity of the prophecy. How did it happen the prophet was right in both cases? The answer is that he was inspired by God to write history before it occurred.

Note: Verses 11 through 19 of Ezekiel 28 contain language that could not apply to any human king. It seems logical to consider this passage as a description of the real power behind the wicked Tyrian king—Satan himself. Compare these verses with Isaiah 14:12-14.

DAY / 242

Read Ezekiel 26; 31; and 32.

Today's reading: We take another look at prophecies foretelling the fate of cities and nations. The predictions about Tyre are particularly striking.

Memory gem: "The grass withereth, and the flower thereof falleth away: but the word of the Lord endureth for ever" (1 Peter 1:24, 25).

Thought for today:

In the time of Daniel, Isaiah, Ezekiel, and other prophets of God, Tyre was one of the greatest commercial cities of the world. It was to the Middle East what New York City is to the Western world today. Right at the height of her power and glory, in 590 B.C., when it seemed that she would stand forever, the prophet Ezekiel declared under the inspiration of God that the city would be destroyed, never to be rebuilt.

History comes to the witness stand and tells us that soon after this prophecy was given, Nebuchadnezzar, king of Babylon, after besieging the city for thirteen years, took Tyre and destroyed it and left the buildings in ruins. But the prophecy called for more than this. The very dust of Tyre was to be cast into the sea, leaving a bare rock to be used for spreading fishing nets.

For two and a half centuries the ruins of Tyre stood as a challenge to the truth of prophecy. Then from the west came Alexander the Great to attack the new Tyre, which was built on an island half a mile from the shore. Again the accuracy of prophecy was vindicated. Alexander took the ruins of the old city to build a causeway to the island city. The very dust was scraped from the site and dumped into the sea.

But the prophecy goes farther: it declares that Tyre was never to be rebuilt again. This challenge has faced the world for twenty-five centuries and faces it today. The building of one city would disprove the Bible; but the city of Tyre as a great commercial center has never been rebuilt. Tyre is gone. The Bible still endures.

Difficult or obscure words:

Ezekiel 26:11. **"Garrisons"**—rather: pillars, probably referring to the two famous columns in the temple of Baal.

Ezekiel 31:15-17. **"Grave," "hell"**—the same Hebrew word in all three places—*she 'ol.*

DAY / 243

Today's reading: Chapter 33 is full of instructions for God's people at any time in history—good for Christians today, tomorrow, or any other time.

Memory gem: "I have set thee a watchman unto the house of Israel; therefore shalt thou hear the word at my mouth, and warn them from me" (Ezekiel 33:7).

Thought for today:

It is paramount for each Christian to seek every opportunity to witness for Christ and to warn men of danger. And if we do, many will thank us at last for flagging them down on the road to destruction.

I shall never forget one terrible winter day when my wife and I were driving across the state of Kentucky. All the rivers were over their banks. It was a time of great flood. A storm of sleet was beating down upon us, and suddenly we saw a frantically waving lantern ahead. As we drew nearer, we saw a farmer who had assumed the duty of protecting the motorists on that lonely road. In the emergency, he was the only thing between us and destruction. A few yards ahead the road went down into water over fifteen feet deep.

So, by our lives as well as by our words, we must wave the lantern of warning and give the word of encouragement.

Friend, life's highway may lead you to heaven or to hell; to life or to death. Which shall it be? It is the most important highway that any of us have ever traveled thus far. So today we call upon all men to turn from the way that leads to destruction and take the way—the only way—that leads to life everlasting, to heaven and homeland. And here it is: "Jesus saith unto him, I am the way, the truth, and the life: no man cometh unto the Father, but by me" (John 14:6).

Will you come, my friend, and will you come today?

Difficult or obscure words:

Ezekiel 35:15. **"Idumea"**—Edom. The Greeks and Romans later used the name Idumea, and the translators have used it here (see also Ezekiel 36:5).

DAY / 244

Today's reading: Many of Ezekiel's prophecies foretold what God planned for His people if they would truly repent. Chapter 37 may be considered a parable to show that God would restore Israel even if nothing remained but "dry bones."

Memory gem: "A new heart also will I give you, and a new spirit will I put within you" (Ezekiel 36:26).

Thought for today:

We think of the nation of Israel, God's own people, brought out of the land of Egypt by His mighty power and great miracles, as we read in the first five or six books of the Bible. We see them growing into power under King David and King Solomon; then we see them in apostasy in Babylon; and, even after that lesson, again we see them drifting away from the service of God until Jerusalem was destroyed by Roman armies and this honored people scattered over the earth. Yet here is the promise of God: "I will . . . do better unto you than at your beginnings: ye shall know that I am the Lord" (Ezekiel 36:11).

Reading the rest of the chapter, we find that this prophecy was made nearly 600 years before Christ, during the time of Israel's trouble and sorrow. Ezekiel himself was in the land of captivity.

This prophecy was fulfilled in the return of Israel to the Holy Land. God has a way of changing things, even against the will of mighty nations and kings. Had Israel gone on and on in the service of God, this chapter would have been fulfilled in a far more glorious way than it was, for God's promises are almost always based upon conditions. But the time will come when, in its complete spiritual fulfillment, this prophecy will indeed find God's true Israel enjoying more glorious blessings than at their beginning.

In the twenty-sixth and twenty-seventh verses, we read of the new heart that will be given—in other words, conversion, the new birth. The promise goes on and includes the entire world in the kingdom of glory which is to come, when God's holy flock will walk by the river of life and enjoy the fruit of the tree of life.

DAY / 245

Read Ezekiel 38 and 39.

Today's reading: These two chapters have caused a great deal of speculation, but no clear proof has been established on the meaning of Gog and Magog or the events described. However, you will notice that both chapters close with the promise of an end of conflict as God's glory is revealed.

Memory gem: "Thus will I magnify myself, and sanctify myself; and I will be known in the eyes of many nations, and they shall know that I am the Lord" (Ezekiel 38:23).

Thought for today:

When the Lord gave the land of Canaan to the children of Israel, it was only a temporary possession. It was a type of their final inheritance in the earth made new, renewed as it was in the days of Eden. But through unbelief they lost it. Had they remained faithful, the city of Jerusalem would have stood forever (see Jeremiah 17), and the throne of David would have been occupied by righteous kings until the Saviour Himself came as the Seed of David. His reign then would have been established upon that very throne, and Israel would have been a mighty nation in righteousness encircling the world.

But they lost their opportunity, they turned away from God's plan, they followed the big crowd. So the rest which they might have received when Joshua led them into the Land of Promise, they failed to get.

But man's failure does not mean God's failure. His plans go on for what is best for you and me. He ordains that the rest for which His people earnestly long may be secured through Jesus Christ. Spiritually it may be ours here and now.

Difficult or obscure words:

Ezekiel 39:2. **"Leave but the sixth part of thee"**—probably better: lead thee (as one leads a child). The whole clause comes from one obscure Hebrew word occurring only here in Scripture.

Ezekiel 39:11. **"Passengers"**—rather: those who pass through, or travelers. No particular valley can be identified for this place.

DAY / 246

Read Ezekiel 40 and 41.

Today's reading: Chapters 40 through 48 give a detailed description of the temple that was never built and a plan for the division of the land that was never carried out. Much speculation has been done in attempting to explain these chapters, but we suggest that a careful reading in search of a blessing is all that concerns us here.

Memory gem: "We have thought of thy lovingkindness, O God in the midst of thy temple" (Psalm 48:9).

Thought for today:

The Bible tells us of three places of worship where God met His people Israel: the tabernacle of Moses, Solomon's temple, and the temple built under Zerubbabel, Ezra, and Nehemiah.

A fourth temple is described in great detail in the prophecy of Ezekiel, chapters 40 to 48. The prophet was told to show the plans for it to the Israelites if they would repent and turn to God.

This great temple was never built. Of course it would be out of place now, because in it were to be offered sacrifices pointing forward to the death of Jesus.

We may all learn a lesson from the temples of God. He desires our loving worship. He sent His own Son to die for us, as represented by the sacrifices offered in the temples of old. Jesus spoke of the temple of His body. The church is a temple, and each individual member of the church is a temple of the Holy Spirit.

The Saviour is now finishing His work in the great sanctuary-temple in heaven, and someday God Himself will dwell with us. The Holy City itself will be a temple of refuge, a holy place forever for the people of God. May we all share that land, that day, and that glory.

Note: The words "beginning of the year" (Ezekiel 40:1) come from the Hebrew *ro'sh hashshanah,* meaning "head of the year." This is the only occurrence of this expression in Scripture.

DAY / 247

Read Ezekiel 42 and 43.

Today's reading: Ezekiel in vision saw the glory of God fill the great temple. Now we await, according to Christ's own promise, the coming of Jesus "in his own glory, and in his Father's, and of the holy angels" (Luke 9:26).

Memory gem: "When the Son of man shall come in his glory, and all the holy angels with him, then shall he sit upon the throne of his glory" (Matthew 25:31).

Thought for today:

What a day that will be! What a dawning of the morning! The night of sin will be over at last. The powers of darkness will be vanquished, with the Lord of light triumphant over all.

The coming King is on His way. There can be no doubt about that. The signs of His return are as plain as if they were written in flaming letters in the sky. Soon the glorious pageantry of His advent will burst upon our mortal sight. Streaming past the glowing constellations of the watching universe, the most sublime procession of the ages will move toward this planet for the final scenes of its tragic history. At its head will be Jesus, crowned with many crowns, as King of the ages, King of creation, King of the world, and King of kings.

What will you do then? Many will flee in fear and shame from His presence. Others will look up into His face with gladness, saying, "Lo, this is our God; we have waited for him, and he will save us: this is the Lord: we have waited for him, we will be glad and rejoice in his salvation" (Isaiah 25:9). Which will you do?

God grant that you may crown Him King in that great day—King of your heart forever!

DAY / 248

Read Ezekiel 44 through 46.

Today's reading: After completing the description of the temple, the Lord gave instructions for restoring a righteous nation. It would be well for us to consider the general principles involved.

Memory gem: "They shall teach my people the difference between the holy and profane, and cause them to discern between the unclean and the clean" (Ezekiel 44:23).

Thought for today:

According to a famous story, England awoke one day and found that the Bible was gone; not only the book itself, but every quotation from it and every reference to it. Every bit of its influence was gone; all trace of its power was wiped out. Every echo of its music, every picture in art, every act or production of the mind and heart of man, every influence of the Bible, was gone. Great literature could hardly be understood—Shakespeare was practically unreadable, Ruskin looked like a moth-eaten tapestry, and everyday speech stammered and faltered. A change passed over everything. Life became vulgar and hectic. All restraints were thrown off; instincts ran wild; life became not so much tragic, as tedious, trivial, and frivolous.

"Well," you say, "that's just a terrible dream." True—but something like that has really happened, friends, not only in England, but in America, in Australia, in every part of the world. It is not that the Bible is not in existence, not available. It is that it is unknown. Few people read it, compared with a hundred years ago. They not only do not read it, but they do not often hear it read. Many have no idea of how to read it or of what it means.

So we see today a whole generous, charming, intelligent, troubled generation without the Bible. People are trying everything else. Many ancient philosophies have been resurrected, and people are trying them. They try psychology, psychiatry, and many other things that may contain much good, but not the real answer demanded by the human heart. Many try sedative pills and pick-me-up pills. They try various exercises, diets, hypnosis, and so on and on. Why not try the Bible?

Listen, friend, you might be missing the best thing that could come to you. Don't risk it. Open God's Book and read it for yourself. Read all of it.

DAY / 249

Read Ezekiel 47; 48; 29:17-21.

Today's reading: As we read the end of Ezekiel's prophecies, the vision of the temple and the new nation closes on an assuring note. The last prophecy concerns a somewhat cryptic message to Nebuchadnezzar.

Memory gem: "The name of the city from that day shall be, The Lord is there" (Ezekiel 48:35).

Thought for today:

Several times in the Old Testament the name of God—transliterated as "Jehovah"—is combined with another word to picture some aspect of God's character as meeting human need. One of these appears in the last verse of Ezekiel 48: "The name of the city from that day shall be [Jehovah Shammah], The Lord is there."

Turning to the "shepherd's psalm," we read the words that appear to go with this divine title: "I will fear no evil: for thou art with me."

In the sunshine and in the shadows, in life and in death, the Lord is there; He is with us. We fear no evil when the Lord is there.

Jesus is called "Immanuel," "God with us" (Isaiah 7:14; Matthew 1:23). The apostle Paul says of Christ that "in him all the fulness of God was pleased to dwell" (Colossians 1:19, RSV). Of the true church, it can also be said that the Lord is there (see Ephesians 2:19-22).

But the final and supreme fulfillment of the prophecy will come in the earth restored, when John's vision will at long last be a glorious reality. We read in Revelation 21:2-4:

"And I John saw the holy city, new Jersualem, coming down from God out of heaven. . . . And I heard a great voice out of heaven saying, Behold, the tabernacle of God is with men, and he will dwell with them, and they shall be his people, and God himself shall be with them, and be their God. And God shall wipe away all tears from their eyes: and there shall be no more death, neither sorrow, nor crying, neither shall there be any more pain: for the former things are passed away."

Then we shall fear no evil, for "the Lord is there"—Jehovah Shammah.

DAY / 250

Today's reading: Many years elapsed between the events of Daniel 3 and those of Daniel 4. Then more years later came Belshazzar's ill-fated reign. Daniel was about eighty years old when he read the cryptic writing on the wall.

Memory gem: "Thou art weighed in the balances, and art found wanting" (Daniel 5:27).

Thought for today:

Belshazzar's feast was the drunken debauch par excellence, led by the king and the great men of the government. It revealed the decadence of high society, the failure of the intellectuals, the final end of the civilization. As you read the story, you see three great pictures on the wall—revelry, revelation, and retribution.

Now the whole thing is being reenacted before us among the nations of our own civilization. There was a worldwide depression; then a second world war brought its desolation upon us; and now, what do we have? Repentance, peace, and righteousness? No! We seem to be entering into a modern Belshazzar's feast.

This age of great intellectual and scientific light is a dark night spiritually for the world. The revelry goes on about us today amidst our economic anxieties. Our amusement life is largely non-Christian—in fact, anti-Christian. We may put "In God we trust" on our money, but do we trust Him?

We have had warnings enough. We have seen the handwriting on the wall. God has been writing His message of the approaching judgment day. As Belshazzar in his day had warning of things to come, so with us now.

Can we not in the events of our day and in the words of Holy Scripture and in the movings of the Holy Spirit in our hearts, hear God's bells of grace and mercy pealing out His message of invitation and warning? They have not yet sounded a dirge or a knell. Let us respond to God here and now.

Note: The fall of Babylon occurred in 539 B.C.

"Darius the Median" of Daniel 5:31 and of chapter 6 has not been identified in secular history. Cyrus the Great was the acknowledged first emperor of the new Medo-Persian Empire. After Cyrus completed the conquest of the Babylonian territory, he may have placed the aged Darius (sixty-two years old) in charge of the Babylonian homeland as "king." Darius apparently died after a reign of less than two years.

Today's reading: After the familiar story of Daniel in the lions' den we launch into six chapters of prophecy. Today we find a series of symbols that closely parallel the great image of chapter 2.

Memory gem: "The saints of the most High shall take the kingdom, and possess the kingdom for ever, even for ever and ever" (Daniel 7:18).

Thought for today:

Since the march of history in its broad outline fulfills the divine predictions in the Book of God, we can see that history is, as someone has said, really "His story." In the prophecies of the Bible, especially those of Daniel and the Revelation, we actually have history in advance, and we can read tomorrow's headlines.

No wonder this prophecy is of extreme interest to all of us. God's hand is still upon the nations. He watches them. Remember this: Babylon, the nation that carried Judah captive, is gone. Medo-Persia, which cast its terrible laws of genocide against Israel, is gone. Grecia, whose representatives persecuted the people of God, is gone. Rome, whose armies destroyed Jerusalem in A.D. 70, is gone. All these mighty nations had contact with God's representative people on earth, and these four mighty nations are gone. They have sunk into the deep grave of the past, and only their memory and the artifacts of buried cities remain. These raging beasts from the sea have become the ghosts of nations.

But the church of Christ still lives. The day will come when "the saints of the most High shall take the kingdom, and possess the kingdom for ever, even for ever and ever."

Then we shall have the worldwide peace that all men long for. But we can never have this until we first have the peace of God in our hearts, the peace which passes human understanding or explanation, the peace which comes through surrender and forgiveness.

Even today, while the storms of national strife and hatred are raging in the world, you may have peace in your heart. He said: "Peace I leave with you, my peace I give unto you. . . . Let not your heart be troubled, neither let it be afraid" (John 14:27).

Difficult or obscure words:

Daniel 7:9. **"Cast down"**—better: placed or set up.

Daniel 7:25. **"Laws"**—singular, the law.

DAY / 252

Today's reading: Daniel takes another prophetic look, but it begins with Medo-Persia. One part of the eighth chapter caused Daniel deep anxiety, and his question was not resolved until after the fall of Babylon (in chapter 9). Unfortunately, we cannot here take up a detailed study of these vital prophecies, but in tomorrow's "Thought for today" we will give an explanation somewhat longer than usual.

Memory gem: "And the kingdom and dominion, and the greatness of the kingdom under the whole heaven, shall be given to the people of the saints of the most High" (Daniel 7:27).

Thought for today:

In the book of Daniel we find a remarkable statement that throws a searchlight ray down the dark vistas of the ages and locates world events with surprising accuracy. It is found in Daniel 8:14. "Unto two thousand and three hundred days; then shall the sanctuary be cleansed."

This could not have reference to a mere temple on earth, made with hands. That sanctuary-temple was lying in ruins when Daniel wrote these words. In the New Testament we find indications that the cleansing of the sanctuary foretold by the prophecy must take place in the heavenly sanctuary (see Hebrews 9:24-28).

And we see that the cleansing of the celestial sanctuary must be the final judgment of every human being. In the fourteenth chapter of Revelation we are told that the hour of judgment is come, when God is sending a worldwide message to all the earth.

The holy prophet Daniel had a vision in four parts, and an angel had been commissioned by God to explain its meaning to him. The explanation had reached the fourth part, which pertained to the 2,300 days. At this point Daniel fainted (Daniel 8:27) under the tremendous strain of watching such momentous events in vision. He was sick for some time. Later, as he slowly recovered, he studied diligently the prophecy of Jeremiah to see whether he could find some clue to the meaning of the time prophecy. Jeremiah had foretold the restoration of Jerusalem, the city where the earthly sanctuary had been located before its destruction.

Daniel concluded that the vision referred to the sanctuary to be rebuilt in Jerusalem after the people had gone back from their captivity. So he began to pray for that restoration, as recorded in Daniel 9.

DAY / 253

Read Daniel 9.

Today's reading: As Daniel prayed, the same angel returned to finish the explantion which had been cut off so suddenly by Daniel's sickness. The angel had said, just before the prophet fainted, "The vision of the evening and the morning [that is, the 2,300 days] which was told is true." And now he has come back to give the prophet "skill and understanding" as to its meaning.

Memory gem: "When the fulness of the time was come, God sent forth his Son, made of a woman, made under the law" (Galatians 4:4).

Thought for today:

In order to make things clear to the prophet Daniel, the angel began by giving him a shorter period to deal with—the first part of the long prophetic time prophecy of the 2,300 days.

It is a little like the way a schoolteacher explains how distances are measured on a world map. First, the scale of miles in one corner is explained; then this is placed on the large map to get the distance in miles. The 2,300-day period is a time map of the world's events. The angel first provided a smaller scale of years, so that the longer period might be better understood. Also, if the shorter period fit exactly events in the then-near future, he and we would be sure that the longer one would fit events in the far future.

So let us put ourselves at the time of Daniel as we study. According to the scale of time, 490 days (70 weeks) would extend from the proclamation to restore Jerusalem (the event for which Daniel had been praying) to the complete fulfillment of the prediction in Daniel 9:24-27 concerning Jerusalem, her temple, and her people. And the 483 days (69 weeks) would reach from the issuing of the same decree to the anointing of Christ at His baptism—that is, to the Messiah, which is the Hebrew word for "anointed" (see Acts 10:38; Luke 3:21, 22).

If we make a careful comparison of the secular history of the times with the statements in Ezra 7:11-26, we find that this decree of the great Persian king of the civilized world went forth in the autumn of the year 457 B.C. This was the decree by Artaxerxes to restore and build Jerusalem, which had been desolated many years before by Nebuchadnezzar, king of Babylon.

Looking back at it from our day, we can see that the angel must have been speaking in prophetic time, in which the word *day* is used to represent a year (see Numbers 14:34; Ezekiel 4:6). For there were exactly 483 years between the dates 457 B.C. and A.D 27, the latter year being the one in which Christ appeared at the Jordan River for baptism. It was then that He was anointed by the Holy Ghost which lighted upon Him in the form of a dove.

We read in Mark 1:14, 15: "Now after that John was put in prison, Jesus came into Galilee, preaching the gospel of the kingdom of God, and saying, The time is fulfilled, and the kingdom of God is at hand: repent ye, and believe the gospel."

"The time is fulfilled." "This," in effect says our Lord, "is the reason why you should give attention to what I say. I have fulfilled the great time prophecy, and My appearance at the very time that has been a subject of prophetic forecast for five centuries proves that I am the Messiah, the Christ whom you have been expecting."

Daniel 9:27 says, "And he shall confirm the covenant with many for one week: and in the midst of the week he shall cause the sacrifice and the oblation to cease." In what way did He do this? He did it by dying as the Lamb of God upon the cross. The sacrifice of innocent lambs had for centuries pointed the faith of the people to the death of Christ as an atonement for their sins.

And His crucifixion was to take place "in the midst of the week." At that time, says verse 26, "shall Messiah be cut off." There at the middle point of the last seven-year period of the prophecy, "in the midst of the week," the cross was set up, "towering o'er the wrecks of time."

Christ began His work on time, He completed it on time; and there upon the cross He cried, "It is finished" (John 19:30). The apostle Paul declares in Galatians 4:4 that "when the fulness of the time was come, God sent forth his Son." His coming was timed to the need of men and the fulfillment of divine prophecy. His coming as a babe at Bethlehem, His baptism at the Jordan, His death upon the cross—all fulfilled the most exacting prophecies and prove the Bible to be true.

When Christ died in the midst of that last week of the prophecy, He was "cut off, *but not for himself,*" as we read in Daniel 9:26. That is the eternal beauty and wonder of it all. He was cut off for all men—for us, for you, and for me.

At the end of the seventieth week, the exclusive opportunities of the gospel were taken from the chosen people, and the message of salvation through Christ went to the Gentile world after the stoning of Stephen in A.D. 34. That is the year that ends the 490-year period of 70 weeks of Daniel's prophecy. So we see that the simple scale of years fits exactly with the signal events of early Christianity.

It remains for us to take the scale and apply it to the long 2300-day period. Beginning at the same date—namely, 457 B.C.—we can compute that 2,300 years from 457 brings us to A.D. 1844, about the middle of the nineteenth century.

So the sanctuary leaps the great gulf of historic time starting in the period before Christ, and changes from an ancient shadow to a very modern substance, as we might put it. The figure and the prophecy have served their purpose. We now have the reality.

Difficult or obscure words:

Daniel 8:7. **"Choler"**—an old English word meaning "anger."

Daniel 8:14. **"Days"**—literally, evening mornings, a Hebrew expression meaning whole days.

Daniel 9:24. **"Are determined"**—a Hebrew word occurring only here in Scripture. In other Hebrew sources it is used to mean "are cut off," or "are decreed," as well as "are determined." Here the context favors "are cut off" from the longer period of the 2,300 evening mornings that Gabriel is explaining.

THE 2300-DAY PROPHECY

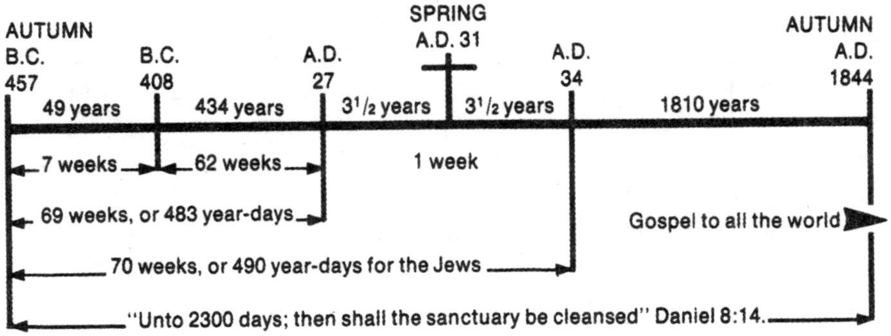

Today's reading: The book of Daniel concludes with two remarkable chapters. Chapter 11 foretells in remarkable detail events in Middle Eastern history down through the centuries. Chapter 12 accurately pinpoints the scientific awakening of modern times—and then seals the prophecy until that time.

Memory gem: "Go thou thy way till the end be: for thou shalt rest, and stand in thy lot at the end of the days" (Daniel 12:13).

Thought for today:

Two thousand five hundred years ago the spokesman from heaven addressed God's prophet Daniel with this announcement "But thou, O Daniel, shut up the words, and seal the book, even to the time of the end: many shall run to and fro, and knowledge shall be increased" (Daniel 12:4).

What an exact and amazing forecast this is of our times! How striking the fulfillment! Every word true to the letter, and fulfilled on time, too, as all God's prophecies are.

These last 150 years have witnessed greater changes than any thousand years of the past. Yes, than all past history! Formerly the masses of mankind led quiet lives about their own homes; but now, by fast train, mighty steamship, automobile, motorbus, and jet plane, the multitudes "run to and fro." Practically the entire world seems to be afflicted, or blessed, with the wanderlust—aggravated by acute speeditis!

Consider this great Bible prophecy and its fulfillment. God declared that in "the time of the end," knowledge would be increased. And now, see the fulfillment of this prophecy in the world today. We witness the worldwide enlightenment of mankind, free education, public school systems, state universities, free libraries, cheap newspapers, radio and television broadcasts, the most colossal pyramiding of human discovery, invention, and knowledge since the creation of the world.

God's divine forecast declared that knowledge would increase and many should "run to and fro." Even the confirmed skeptic and agnostic must admit the fulfillment of this prophecy. Thus the Bible is proved to be an up-to-date guidebook. And in this very century, yes, this very year in which we live, behold the index finger of God pointing to the prophetic time chart. This is "the time of the end," the time when the end is near.

DAY / 255

Read 2 Chronicles 36:22, 23; Ezra 1 through 3; Psalms 85; 126.

Today's reading: The seventy years of captivity ended, and King Cyrus permitted the exiles to return to Jerusalem. For fifty years the city and the beautiful temple had lain in ruins. Now a handful of loyal Israelites (most of them born in exile) would undertake a resotration.

Memory gem: Surely his salvation is nigh them that fear him; that glory may dwell in our land" (Psalm 85:9).

Thought for today:

"Could those who failed to rejoice at the laying of the foundation stone of the temple, have foreseen the results of their lack of faith on that day, they would have been appalled. Little did they realize the weight of their words of disapproval and disappointment; little did they know how much their expressed dissatisfaction would delay the completion of the Lord's house.

"The magnificence of the first temple, and the imposing rites of its religious services, had been a source of pride to Israel before their captivity; but their worship had ofttimes been lacking in those qualities which God regards as most essential. The glory of the first temple, the splendor of its service, could not recommend them to God; for that which is alone of value in His sight, they did not offer. They did not bring Him the sacrifice of a humble and contrite spirit. . . .

"A congregation may be the poorest in the land. It may be without the attractions of any outward show; but if the members possess the principles of the character of Christ, angels will unite with them in their worship. The praise and thanksgiving from grateful hearts will ascend to God as a sweet oblation."—*Prophets and Kings,* pp. 565, 566.

Note: The decree by King Cyrus allowing the Jewish exiles to return to their homeland was issued in 537 B.C.; the first exiles returned in 536 B.C., at the end of the seventy years.

In Scripture the books of Ezra, Nehemiah, and Esther give the only historical record of postexile Israelites. They do not, however, cover the period exhaustively or in unbroken sequence. Large gaps remain unknown.

The first three chapters of Ezra cover the time from the decree of Cyrus to the dedication of the rebuilt altar about two years later.

DAY / 256

Read Ezra 4 through 6.

Today's reading: Years passed. King Cyrus died, enemies stopped the work, and the people's zeal flickered out. Then two prophets aroused the people, and a new king issued a second work permit. The temple was completed and dedicated.

Memory gem: "And with them were the prophets of God helping them" (Ezra 5:2).

Thought for today:

"Under the favor shown them by Cyrus, nearly fifty thousand of the children of the captivity had taken advantage of the decree permitting their return. These, however, in comparison with the hundreds of thousands scattered throughout the provinces of Medo-Persia, were but a mere remnant. The great majority of the Israelites had chosen to remain in the land of their exile, rather than undergo the hardships of the return journey and the reestablishment of their desolated cities and homes.

"A score or more of years passed by, when a second decree quite as favorable as the first, was issued by Darius Hystaspes, the monarch then ruling. Thus did God in mercy provide another opportunity for the Jews in the Medo-Persian realm to return to the land of their fathers. The Lord foresaw the troublous times that were to follow during the reign of Xerxes—the Ahasuerus of the book of Esther—and He not only wrought a change of feeling in the hearts of men in authority, but also inspired Zechariah to plead with the exiles to return. . . .

"It was still the Lord's purpose, as it had been from the beginning, that His people should be a praise in the earth, to the glory of His name. During the long years of their exile He had given them many opportunitites to return to their allegiance to Him. Some had chosen to listen and to learn; some had found salvation in the midst of affliction."—*Prophets and Kings,* pp. 598, 599.

Note: Verses 6 through 23 of Ezra 4 present problems. The kings named here and the events narrated seem not to fit the natural sequence of the story. Space limitations in this book prohibit a discussion of the problems. Just assume that the story interrupted at the end of verse 5 resumes again with verse 24—that verses 6 to 23 describe later events which Ezra included here to round out all opposition encountered by the Jews.

Today's reading: The book of Haggai tells plainly God's message to the discouraged builders in Jerusalem. Zechariah contains more obscure symbolism.

Memory gem: "Be strong, all ye people of the land, saith the Lord, and work: for I am with you, saith the Lord of hosts" (Haggai 2:4).

Thought for today:

What is our main object in life? What is the goal that we are trying to reach? Where does all of our interest lie? The most important thing in this world is not a fat bank account, large real estate holdings, or great material wealth, but being right with God and being prepared for eternity.

The Christian life is one of stewardship and partnership; for, after all, everything belongs to God. We read in Psalm 24:1: "The earth is the Lord's, and the fulness thereof; the world, and they that dwell therein."

But God has entrusted to us that which is His, and He expects us to deal with Him as faithful stewards. He is the One who gives us power to gain wealth, as we read in Deuteronomy 8:11, 17, 18.

Those who realize God's ownership and His divine sovereignty, return to their Maker one tenth of their increase in recognition of His ownership. This unselfish relationship with God reveals the heart of a true partner, one who is really a laborer together with God (see 1 Corinthians 3:9).

Please don't misunderstand me. The possession of goods or of wealth is not in itself a sin. It is "the love of money" which "is the root of all evil" (1 Timothy 6:10). In a fully surrendered life, lucre is no longer king.

In the Gospels of Matthew, Mark, and Luke, one verse in every six deals with the money question, so it must be an important item in a person's life. Sixteen of the twenty-nine parables narrated by Christ had to do with money. He does not ask how much we have, but what we are doing with what we have. He came to lift us out of our selfishness and guide our steps along the path of faith to the mount of blessing and eternal life. So, really, money is not everything. Christ is!

DAY / 258

Today's reading: Some of Zechariah's predictions (like those of other prophets) concerned the judgments of God on other nations. We call attention to one of those predictions in the "Thought for today."

Memory gem: "The Lord their God shall save them in that day as the flock of his people: for they shall be as the stones of a crown, lifted up as an ensign upon his land" (Zechariah 9:16).

Thought for today:

Here is another important city which is mentioned by prophecy. We will notice just two sentences about the city of Ashkelon which was also on the Mediterranean seacoast, in what is now the territory of the modern republic of Israel. Today there is hardly a ruin to be seen. Everything is hidden underground—the city has been so completely destroyed. Let us read what the prophets Zephaniah and Zechariah say. Remember, these prophecies were made centuries before Christ:

"Ashkelon [shall be] a desolation" (Zephaniah 2:4).

"Ashkelon shall not be inhabited" (Zechariah 9:5).

Ashkelon was founded 1800 years before Christ, and it was at the height of its glory while Jesus was here on earth 1800 years later. There was certainly no sign of any impending disaster to the city for nearly 2000 years after the prophets had made their prediction at the inspiration of the Holy Spirit.

This city actually grew in magnificence and power for centuries after the prediction of its destruction was made. In A.D. 636 it passed over to the control of the Arabs. During the Crusades it was the key to southwestern Palestine, and was finally captured by the Crusaders in 1153 after a six-month siege. Thus it was still a powerful city fifteen centuries after the prophet foretold its destruction.

Finally, in 1270, the sultan Beibars I destroyed its fortifications and blocked its harbor with stones. Now it has lain desolate for more than 700 years.

Difficult or obscure words:

Zechariah 5:7. **"Talent"**—literally, a round disk. A heavy leaden lid on the vessel.

Zechariah 5:8. **"It"**—rather: her.

DAY / 259

Read Zechariah 10 through 14.

Today's reading: These chapters begin with a beautiful promise of God's blessing on His people and end with a vision of hope.

Memory gem: "Ask ye of the Lord rain in the time of the latter rain; so the Lord shall make bright clouds, and give them showers of rain, to every one grass in the field" (Zechariah 10:1).

Thought for today:

It is God's promise and design that His Spirit shall be poured out in abundant measure upon the proclamation of this everlasting gospel—poured out as the latter rain. Too often we lack the power of the Holy Spirit in our preaching because we do not ask, we do not pray for it. Listen to the words of the divine promise:

"For I will pour water upon him that is thirsty, and floods upon the dry ground: I will pour my spirit upon thy seed, and my blessing upon thine offspring: and they shall spring up as among the grass, as willows by the water courses" (Isaiah 44:3, 4).

I appeal especially to gospel ministers, church elders and officers of all grades, and to believers everywhere: "Ask, and ye shall receive" (John 16:24). Is it not time to preach the Word, to preach Christ with power—to be loyal to Him, loyal to His Book, loyal to His truth, and loyal to His cross? So may we claim the outpouring of the Holy Spirit in abundance, far exceeding Pentecostal days. Its power is needed to change human hearts, to bring a new life, to bring peace to hearts now at war with themselves. Shall we not seek that power today?

We cannot work for Christ without the Holy Spirit, His promised representative. Christ Himself is gone, but the Holy Spirit is here. Let us pray for the rain—the latter rain—and then go to work, expecting our prayers to be answered and God's promises fulfilled.

DAY / 260

Read Esther 1 through 3.

Today's reading: Many exiled Hebrews chose to remain in foreign lands instead of returning to Judah. Today we find that the enemies of God's people hatch a plot to exterminate them.

Memory gem: "Judge me, O God, and plead my cause against an ungodly nation: O deliver me from the deceitful and unjust man" (Psalm 43:1).

Thought for today:

"Conditions in the Medo-Persian realm were rapidly changing. Darius Hystaspes, under whose reign the Jews had been shown marked favor, was succeeded by Xerxes the Great. It was during his reign that those of the Jews who had failed of heeding the message to flee, were called upon to face a terrible crisis. Having refused to take advantage of the way of escape God had provided, now they were brought face to face with death.

"Through Haman the Agagite, an unscrupulous man high in authority in Medo-Persia, Satan worked at this time to counterwork the purposes of God. Haman cherished bitter malice against Mordecai, a Jew. Mordecai had done Haman no harm, but had simply refused to show him worshipful reverence. Scorning to "lay hands on Mordecai alone," Haman plotted "to destroy all the Jews that were throughout the whole kingdom of Ahasuerus, even the people of Mordecai.

"Misled by the false statements of Haman, Xerxes was induced to issue a decree providing for the massacre of all the Jews 'scattered abroad and dispersed among the people in all the provinces' of the Medo-Persian kingdom. A certain day was appointed on which the Jews were to be destroyed and their property confiscated. Little did the king realize the far-reaching results that would have accompanied the complete carrying out of this decree. Satan himself, the hidden instigator of the scheme, was trying to rid the earth of those who preserved the knowledge of the true God."—*Prophets and Kings,* pp. 600, 601.

Note: The Ahasuerus of Esther has been positively identified as Xerxes (son and successor of Darius I), who reigned from 486 to 465 B.C. (He is not the Median Ahasuerus mentioned in Daniel 9:1.)

DAY / 261

Read Esther 4 through 6.

Today's reading: The plot thickens! The enemies of God's people almost succeeded in exterminating them. But Esther came to the kingdom for such a time of crisis.

Memory gem: "Who knoweth whether thou art come to the kingdom for such a time as this?" (Esther 4:14).

Thought for today:

"The plots of the enemy were defeated by a Power that reigns among the children of men. In the providence of God, Esther, a Jewess who feared the Most High, had been made queen of the Medo-Persian kingdom. Mordecai was a near relative of hers. In their extremity, they decided to appeal to Xerxes in behalf of their people. Esther was to venture into his presence as an intercessor. 'Who knoweth,' said Mordecai, 'whether thou art come to the kingdom for such a time as this?' . . .

"The crisis that Esther faced demanded quick, earnest action; but both she and Mordecai realized that unless God should work mightily in their behalf, their own efforts would be unavailing. So Esther took time for communion with God, the source of her strength. 'Go,' she directed Mordecai, 'gather together all the Jews that are present in Shoshan, and fast ye for me, and neither eat nor drink three days, night or day: I also and my maidens will fast likewise; and so will I go in unto the king, which is not according to the law: and if I perish, I perish."—*Prophets and Kings,* p. 601.

"Through Esther the queen the Lord accomplished a mighty deliverance for His people. At a time when it seemed that no power could save them, Esther and the women associated with her by fasting and prayer and prompt action, met the issue, and brought salvation to their people.

"A study of women's work in connection with the cause of God in Old Testament times will teach us lessons that will enable us to meet emergencies in the work today. We may not be brought into such a critical and prominent place as were the people of God in the time of Esther; but often converted women can act an important part in more humble positions."—Ellen G. White Comments, *Seventh-day Adventist Bible Commentary,* vol. 3, p. 1140.

Today's reading: Esther's courageous actions saved her people. The shadow of doom was transformed into the assurance of life. God's people in all ages have looked forward to final victory over the forces of evil.

Memory gem: "He that dwelleth in the secret place of the most High shall abide under the shadow of the Almighty" (Psalm 91:1).

Thought for today:

"The trying experiences that came to God's people in the days of Esther were not peculiar to that age alone. . . . The same spirit that in ages past led men to persecute the true church, will in the future lead to the pursuance of a similar course toward those who maintain their loyalty to God. Even now preparations are being made for this last great conflict.

"The decree that will finally go forth against the remnant people of God will be very similar to that issued by Ahasuerus against the Jews. . . . The reverence of God's people for His law is a constant rebuke to those who have cast off the fear of the Lord. . . .

"Satan will arouse indignation against the minority who refuse to accept popular customs and traditions. Men of position and reputation will join with the lawless and the vile to take counsel against the people of God. Wealth, genius, education, will combine to cover them with contempt. . . . On this battlefield will be fought the last great conflict in the controversy between truth and error. And we are not left in doubt as to the issue. Today as in the days of Esther and Mordecai, the Lord will vindicate His truth and His people."—*Prophets and Kings,* pp. 605, 606.

Note: It is interesting to note that Esther 8:9 is the longest verse in the Bible, containing 43 Hebrew words in the original, or 192 letters.

Verse 10 mentions the animals used by the messengers. The Hebrew words are of obscure meaning and not the ones usually denoting camels, etc. A more likely translation is that the men were "mounted couriers riding on swift horses that were used in the king's service, bred from the royal stud" (RSV). Verse 14 uses some of the same words.

DAY / 263

Read Ezra 7 through 9.

Today's reading: We now come to the third decree for restoring and rebuilding Jerusalem—seventy-nine years after the first one by Cyrus and twenty-three years after the second. At this point Ezra led a large group of priests and Levites to Jerusalem.

Memory gem: "The hand of our God was upon us, and he delivered us from the hand of the enemy, and of such as lay in wait by the way" (Ezra 8:31).

Thought for today:

The people of God had been in captivity in a foreign land for seventy years. When the time came for them to be restored to their own land, God moved upon the heart of the great king of Persia, Cyrus, to issue a decree stating that all who wanted to return might do so. Years later Darius the Great reaffirmed this permission with a second decree.

Finally, in order to give the returned exiles full status as a Persian province, God caused Artaxerxes I (Longimanus) to issue a third and final decree (see Ezra 6:14), enabling the Jews to complete the restoration. A copy of his decree to this effect is found in Ezra 7:12-26. This royal pronouncement decreed the restoration and rebuilding of Jerusalem as well as restoration of civil government to the land.

According to the seventh chapter of Ezra, this decree was issued in the seventh year of Artaxerxes' reign. Historical records show that this seventh year of Artaxerxes was 457 B.C. So 457 B.C. became the starting point for the seventy weeks (see Daniel 9:24-27) that were cut off for the Jewish people as a nation in Palestine under the rule of God (see Day/253 for a discussion of this prophetic period.)

Friend, you can depend on the Lord Jesus. He is the Messiah.

Note: A few dates from secular history for comparison with Bible events:

490 B.C.—Persian invaders defeated at Marathon.

483 B.C.—Vashti rejected. The feast may well have been a strategy session to plan revenge for Marathon.

480 B.C.—Persian navy demolished at Salamis.

479 B.C.—Probable date for selection of Esther.

457 B.C.—Decree by Artaxerxes restoring civil government to the Jews.

DAY / 264

Today's reading: Ezra succeeded in bringing about some good reforms in Judah, but God saw that a strong political leader was needed. He raised up Nehemiah to meet the challenge.

Memory gem: "The God of heaven, he will prosper us; therefore we his servants will arise and build" (Nehemiah 2:20).

Thought for today:

"Ezra's arrival in Jerusalem was opportune. There was great need of the influence of his presence. His coming brought courage and hope to the hearts of many who had long labored under difficulties. Since the return of the first company of exiles under the leadership of Zerubbabel and Joshua, over seventy years before, much had been accomplished. The temple had been finished, and the walls of the city had been partially repaired. Yet much remained undone.

"Among those who had returned to Jerusalem in former years there were many who had remained true to God as long as they lived; but a considerable number of the children and the children's children lost sight of the sacredness of God's law. Even some of the men entrusted with responsibilities were living in open sin. Their course was largely neutralizing the efforts made by others to advance the cause of God; for so long as flagrant violations of the law were allowed to go unrebuked, the blessing of Heaven could not rest upon the people.

"It was in the providence of God that those who returned with Ezra had had special seasons of seeking the Lord. The experiences through which they had just passed, on their journey from Babylon, unprotected as they had been by any human power, had taught them rich spiritual lessons. Many had grown strong in faith; and as these mingled with the discouraged and the indifferent in Jerusalem, their influence was a powerful factor in the reform soon afterward instituted."—*Prophets and Kings,* pp. 618, 619.

Note: Nehemiah received his commission as governor of Judah in 444 B.C.

DAY / 265

Read Nehemiah 3 through 5.

Today's reading: Nehemiah, a man of action, inspired the dispirited builders with zeal. He met opposition and threats of violence with confident faith in God—and with vigorous action to counter the enemies' moves. But he also took measures to clean out corruption among God's people.

Memory gem: "Also I said, It is not good that ye do: ought ye not to walk in the fear of our God because of the reproach of the heathen our enemies?" (Nehemiah 5:9).

Thought for today:

"The customs of the world are no criterion for the Christian. He is not to imitate its sharp practices, its overreaching, its extortion. Every unjust act toward a fellow being is a violation of the golden rule. Every wrong done to the children of God is done to Christ Himself in the person of His saints. . . .

"The slightest departure from rectitude breaks down the barriers and prepares the heart to do greater injustice. Just to that extent that a man would gain advantage for himself at the disadvantage of another, will his soul become insensible to the influence of the Spirit of God. Gain obtained at such a cost is fearful loss.

"We were all debtors to divine justice; but we had nothing with which to pay the debt. Then the Son of God, who pities us, paid the price of our redemption. He became poor that through His poverty we might be rich. By deeds of liberality toward His poor we may prove the sincerity of our gratitude for the mercy extended to us. 'Let us do good unto all men,' the apostle Paul enjoins, 'especially unto them who are of the household of faith.' Galatians 6:10. And his words accord with those of the Saviour: 'Ye have the poor with you always, and whensoever ye will ye may do them good.' Mark 14:7. 'Whatsosever ye would that men should do to you, do ye even so to them: for this is the law and the prophets.' Matthew 7:12."—*Prophets and Kings,* pp. 651, 652.

Note: To the three enemies listed in chapter 2, another is added in Nehemiah 4:7—the Ashdodites, or Philistines. A look at a map of the period reveals that Nehemiah's little province of Judah was completely encircled by hostile neighbors: Samaria on the north, Ammon across the Jordan on the east, Edom on the south, and Ashdod on the west.

DAY / 266

Read Nehemiah 6 through 8.

Today's reading: In only fifty-two days of concerted effort the walls were finished and the gates were set up. Imagine the joyful celebration that followed as the people observed the Feast of Tabernacles.

Memory gem: "This day is holy unto our Lord: neither be ye sorry; for the joy of the Lord is your strength" (Nehemiah 8:10).

Thought for today:

"In Nehemiah's firm devotion to the work of God, and his equally firm reliance on God, lay the reason of the failure of his enemies to draw him into their power. The soul that is indolent falls an easy prey to temptation; but in the life that has a noble aim, an absorbing purpose, evil finds little foothold. The faith of him who is constantly advancing does not weaken; for above, beneath, beyond, he recognizes Infinite Love, working out all things to accomplish His good purpose. God's true servants work with a determination that will not fail, because the throne of grace is their constant dependence.

"God has provided divine assistance for all the emergencies to which our human resources are unequal. He gives the Holy Spirit to help in every strait, to strengthen our hope and assurance, to illuminate our minds and purify our hearts. He provides opportunities and opens channels of working. If His people are watching the indications of His providence, and are ready to cooperate with Him, they will see mighty results."—*Prophets and Kings,* p. 660.

Note: For some reason, Tobiah is not mentioned in Nehemiah 6:2. He may have been unwilling to attempt personal violence on Nehemiah. Later (see verses 17-19) it is revealed that he was related by marriage to some of the Jewish leaders, apparently trying to accomplish his designs by intrigue.

"Gashmu" (verse 6) is a variant spelling of Geshem (see verse 2).

Nehemiah's "register" of the original returnees under Zerubbabel (see Nehemiah 7:5-73) differs only slightly from Ezra's (see Ezra 2:1-70). It is quite easy to account for the differences.

DAY / 267

Read Nehemiah 9 through 11:14.

Today's reading: After the seven days of the Feast of Tabernacles, the people gathered for a rededication of themselves to God. They formulated and signed a solemn covenant.

Memory gem: "Nevertheless for thy great mercies' sake thou didst not utterly consume them, nor forsake them; for thou art a gracious and merciful God" (Nehemiah 9:31).

Thought for today:

"Nehemiah's efforts to restore the worship of the true God had been crowned with success. As long as the people were true to the oath they had taken, as long as they were obedient to God's word, so long would the Lord fulfill His promise by pouring rich blessings upon them.

"For those who are convicted of sin and weighed down with a sense of their unworthiness, there are lessons of faith and encouragement in this record. The Bible faithfully presents the results of Israel's apostasy; but it portrays also the deep humiliation and repentance, the earnest devotion and generous sacrifice, that marked their seasons of return to the Lord.

"Every true turning to the Lord brings abiding joy into the life. When a sinner yields to the influence of the Holy Spirit, he sees his own guilt and defilement in contrast with the holiness of the great Searcher of hearts. He sees himself condemned as a transgressor. But he is not, because of this, to give way to despair; for his pardon has already been secured. He may rejoice in the sense of sins forgiven, in the love of a pardoning heavenly Father. It is God's glory to encircle sinful, repentant human beings in the arms of His love, to bind up their wounds, to cleanse them from sin, and to clothe them with the garments of salvation."—*Prophets and Kings,* p. 668.

Difficult or obscure words:

Nehemiah 9:4. **"Stairs"**—literally, ascent; probably the high pulpit of Nehemiah 8:4, where the word used means "tower," or high scaffold.

DAY / 268

Read Nehemiah 11:15 through chapter 13.

Today's reading: Chapters 11 and 12 carry through to the final ceremonies dedicating the wall. Then a gap of unknown duration occurs. In verse 6 of chapter 13 we learn that Nehemiah left Jerusalem for "certain days." On his return he found it necessary to take strong measures again in rooting out evil practices.

Memory gem: "Remember me, O my God, concerning this, and wipe not out my good deeds that I have done for the house of my God" (Nehemiah 13:14).

Thought for today:

"In the work of reform to be carried forward today, there is need of men who, like Ezra and Nehemiah, will not palliate or excuse sin, nor shrink from vindicating the honor of God. Those upon whom rests the burden of this work, will not hold their peace when wrong is done, neither will they cover evil with a cloak of false charity. They will remember that God is no respecter of persons, and that severity to a few may prove mercy to many. They will remember also that in the one who rebukes evil, the spirit of Christ should ever be revealed.

"In their work, Ezra and Nehemiah humbled themselves before God, confessing their sins and the sins of their people, and entreating pardon as if they themselves were the offenders. Patiently they toiled and prayed and suffered. That which made their work most difficult was not the open hostility of the heathen, but the secret opposition of pretended friends, who, by lending their influence to the service of evil, increased tenfold the burden of God's servants. These traitors furnished the Lord's enemies with material to use in their warfare upon His people. Their evil passions and rebellious wills were ever at war with the plain requirements of God.

"The success attending Nehemiah's efforts shows what prayer, faith, and wise, energetic action will accomplish."—*Prophets and Kings,* p. 675.

Note: Nehemiah's twelve-year term as governor ended in 432 B.C. He probably returned in about 425 B.C. (The same date is usually assigned to Malachi's prophecy.)

DAY / 269

Read Malachi.

Today's reading: One would suppose that God's people had finally learned to obey and trust the Lord, but the Old Testament's last message calls for repentance. It closes, however, with a prophecy of final victory over evil.

Memory gem: "The Lord, whom ye seek, shall suddenly come to his temple, even the messenger of the covenant, whom ye delight in: behold, he shall come, saith the Lord of hosts" (Malachi 3:1).

Thought for today:

What does God say about those who are unfaithful in tithes and offerings? Listen to these strong words of Malachi 3:8: "Will a man rob God? Yet ye have robbed me. But ye say, Wherein have we robbed thee? In tithes and offerings."

Could it be that many of the physical curses that have come upon the natural world have been due to unfaithfulness on the part of the inhabitants of the world? Why not try Him? Those who have, have found His blessing always with them. They have found that He lives up to His word. They have found that He fulfills His word; and what He promises, He does.

There was A. A. Hyde, the Mentholatum king, who was bankrupt and owed $100,000. Then he pledged God a faithful tithe. Someone brought him a formula and said, "Manufacture it." He did, and you know the rest.

A boy named William was sixteen years old and poor, just starting out to make his way in life. He knelt on a towpath with the captain of a canal boat and listened to the captain's prayer. Then the captain said: "Someday someone will be the leading soapmaker in New York. It might as well be you. You know soap and candlemaking. Make an honest soap and give a full pound. Be a good man, and give the Lord what belongs to Him."

That boy was William Colgate. And he did pay his tithe—first one tenth, then two tenths, later three, four and five tenths. Finally he gave it all.

If all professed believers were faithful in tithes and offerings, churches would be adequately supported everywhere; there would be no temptation to employ unscriptural means to secure money for church expense; and the gospel message would be sent quickly to all the world.

Note: Most Bible scholars date Malachi's prophecy as about 425 B.C.—either shortly before or during Nehemiah's second term as governor. Certain features favor the period before Nehemiah returned; for example, the call for reform in paying tithe (see Nehemiah 13:10-12). Some scholars, however, give a date as late as 415 B.C. In any event more than 400 years elapsed before the birth of Jesus and the opening of the New Testament.

Since the Bible contains no record for events during this long silent period, we must depend on secular history to tell us what happened.

It was a turbulent period for troubled Judah. Waves of conquest swept back and forth over the land, bringing distress and desolation. When Alexander's Grecian Empire split up among rival rulers, Palestine became a battleground between the Seleucid monarchs of Syria and the Ptolemies of Egypt—both Grecian dynasties. One of the Syrians, Antiocus Epiphanes, desecrated the temple by offering swine on the altar in 168 B.C. Smoldering Jewish resentment broke into open revolt, and three years later Judas Maccabaeus restored the temple services. Judas was killed in battle in 161 B. C., and his brother Jonathan carried on the struggle. External attacks and internal factional violence continued until 151, when Jonathan was made governor general in Palestine under Syrian control. Unrest and disorder continued almost constantly.

Finally the Romans, who had been dominating affairs in Egypt and the Near East for a hundred years, stepped in to stablize conditions. Pompey entered Jerusalem in 63 B.C., and from that time onward Judea (the Roman name for Judah) was controlled by rulers loyal to Rome. Herod, a "converted" Idumean (Edomite) who ruled when Jesus was born, gained his throne with the aid of Roman arms and by the slaughter of thousands of Jews.

Into this uneasy peace imposed by Roman power (Pax Romana) the Prince of Peace came to proclaim a kingdom of love.

DAY / 270

Read John 1:1-18; Luke 1:1-4; Matthew 1:1-17; Luke 3:23-28; 1:5-56.

Today's reading: Two of the Gospel writers give us detailed genealogies of Jesus human family.

Memory gem: "The Word was made flesh, and dwelt among us, (and we beheld his glory, the glory as of the only begotten of the Father,) full of grace and truth" (John 1:14).

Thought for today:

The virgin birth of Christ is demanded by at least three things in the Sacred Record. First, the preexistence of Christ is plainly declared in the Bible. Jesus prayed His Father to glorify Him with the glory which He had with the Father before the world was made (see John 17:5). Therefore, the holy Son of God existed before He was born of the virgin Mary in Bethlehem. This fact demands a virgin birth, not a normal human birth.

Second, the Scriptures teach that Jesus was sinless. They declare that He was "holy, harmless, undefiled, separate from sinners" (Hebrews 7:26). In fact the Bible declares Christ's deity. He was "Emmanuel, . . . God with us" (Matthew 1:23). He who was a supernatural being must enter the world as the Son of man in a supernatural way.

Third, for centuries divine prophecy had declared that He—the Messiah, the Christ, the Redeemer of this world—would come and would ultimately sit upon the throne of His father David. To His kingdom there would be no end, and it would be worldwide. Isaiah 9:7. If Jesus had been merely a man, the son of Joseph, His legal father, He could never sit on the throne of David. According to Bible prophecy, no natural descendant of King Jechonias could ever hold that position. Listen to these words: "O earth, earth, earth, hear the word of the Lord. . . . Write ye this man childless, a man that shall not prosper in his days: for no man of his seed [that is, of Jechonias's direct bodily descent] shall prosper, sitting upon the throne of David, and ruling any more in Judah" (Jeremiah 22:29, 30, see also Matthew 1:11). Jesus, not being Joseph's natural son, but only his legal son, could sit there. He had not only a divine right, but a legal right to that place.

DAY / 271 Read Matthew 1:18-25; Luke 1:57 through 2:38; Matthew 2; Luke 2:39-52.

Today's reading: The familiar stories about the angelic choir, the shepherds, and the wise men impress on our minds anew the unique circumstances of the birth of Jesus Christ our Lord.

Memory gem: "Thou shalt call his name JESUS: for he shall save his people from their sins" (Matthew 1:21).

Thought for today:

How simple was the cradle of the Babe of Bethlehem! It was just a crude manger, no doubt filled with hay or straw. And this baby was an unusual one. He had been mentioned by a holy prophet hundreds and hundreds of years before. "Unto us a child is born" (Isaiah 9:6).

This baby was named by an angel months before He was born, and His name was Jesus. The very town in which He was to be born had been pointed out more than six hundred years earlier (see Micah 5:2).

Isn't it strange that God chose the little town of Bethlehem, five miles south of Jerusalem, for the great event of the Saviour's birth? He was not born in Jerusalem, the capital of Judea and the headquarters of God's people. He was not born in Rome, the capital of the world. He was not born in one of the great cities of India, China, or Persia, but in a small village of Judea. The name of the town was significant, too, for Bethlehem means "house of bread." Later on, Jesus called Himself "the bread of life" (John 6:35).

God sent His own Son into this world to be born as a babe, to grow up into manhood, to die on the cross for our sins, and then ascend to His Father in heaven. But that was not the last that this world would see of Him, for the promise is that He will come back again, not as a babe, but as a glorious king.

Jesus was the baby who changed history. He was the Saviour of the world who was crucified on Calvary, but who rose from the dead and ascended to heaven. And He will be the King of kings and Lord of lords when He comes to this earth again—not in a lowly stable, but in clouds of glory; not with a baby's cry to His attentive mother, but with a mighty shout that will awaken the dead.

DAY / 272 Read Matthew 3:1 through 4:11; Mark 1:1-13; Luke 3:1-23; 4:1-13; John 1:19-51.

Today's reading: When Jesus reached the age of "about thirty," he was anointed by the Holy Spirit as the Messiah. We read about the three great temptations and then about the calling of the first disciples.

Memory gem: "And lo a voice from heaven, saying, This is my beloved Son, in whom I am well pleased" (Matthew 3:17).

Thought for today:

Jesus of Nazareth had heard of the work of His cousin, John the Baptist; and knowing that the time had come for His own public ministry to begin, He joined a company journeying to the Jordan River, and there requested baptism of John. John recognized that Jesus was different from the others; he exclaimed, "I have need to be baptized of thee, and comest thou to me?"

Jesus answered, "Suffer it to be so now: for thus it becometh us to fulfil all righteousness" (Matthew 3:14, 15).

That is what Jesus said: "It becometh us"—or it is proper for us, it is our duty—"to fulfill all righteousness." And His baptism was a part of it.

So John led the Saviour down into the Jordan and buried Him beneath the water. But we must always remember that our holy Saviour did not receive baptism as a confession of guilt on His part, but to identify Himself fully with sinners. He took the steps that we must take and did the work that we must do. He was an example to us.

Now, friend, I ask you this question: Have you been baptized? If not, why not? And I will ask just one more qustion, the one asked by the godly Ananias of Saul at the time of his conversion: "And now why tarriest thou? arise, and be baptized, and wash away thy sins, calling on the name of the Lord" (Acts 22:16).

Your baptism will show your faith in the death of Christ, who washes away our sins in His own blood (see Revelation 1:5). Why should you delay?

DAY / 273

Read John 2 through 4.

Today's reading: Of five incidents in Christ's early ministry two involve conversations with one person—one a ruler of the Jews, the other a Samaritan woman. Both discussions reveal important spiritual truths.

Memory gem: "The water that I shall give him shall be in him a well of water springing up into everlasting life" (John 4:14).

Thought for today:

Come with me this clear, beautiful day—join us in the bus. There are over forty of us. We are traveling southward from Samaria. It is a beautiful country, with hills and valleys. Now we see before us two mountains—turn slightly eastward—one on the south, one on the north. Between them nestles a small town called Nablus, which is an abbreviation of Neapolis or "new city."

We ride through the town, and, turning southeast, we see on our left great piles of rock—outlines of walls, towers. The ruins of the city of Shechem are being excavated by archaeologists.

A few hundred yards farther south, on the left side of the road, is a wall surrounding Jacob's well. Most archaeologists have no doubt that it is the actual well of Jacob, mentioned in the fourth chapter of John. I remember the first time I ever sat down at the well where Jesus once sat. Strange to say, there was a woman there who drew water out of the well for me. I was glad to drink. It was clear, cool, and sweet. How refreshing on that warm day of our journey!

Are you thirsty today? Is there something you feel you need and never can find? Are you dissatisfied in some way with your life? If so, remember that the spiritual thirst which God sends to the soul needs the water of life.

Christ invites, "Let him that is athirst come. And whosoever will, let him take the water of life freely" (Revelation 22:17). There is no cost, no charge. Just come and receive it. Come to the well, as did the woman of old, and hear the blessed words of eternal life, and find your life changed, as hers was. Find Jesus—not only a prophet, but the blessed Messiah for whom we have looked so long, the only hope of Jew and Gentile, the Lover of all men and women and young people and boys and girls.

Come and sit down here by the well. Drink of the water of life freely. And may you be blessed, saved, and satisfied.

DAY / 274 Read John 5; Luke 4:14-30; Matthew 4:12-22; Mark 1:14-20; Luke 5:1-11.

Today's reading: Christ's early ministry in Judea ends as He begins a year of work in Galilee. "He came unto his own, and his own [people] received him not" (John 1:11).

Memory gem: "He hath sent me to bind up the brokenhearted, to proclaim liberty to the captives, and the opening of the prison to them that are bound" (Isaiah 61:1).

Thought for today:

On the Sabbath morning in the Nazareth synagogue, our Saviour read from the prophet Isaiah and applied the prophecy to Himself. He was opening the prison to set people free.

Do you believe that? Why shouldn't we believe it? If that scripture is true and Jesus told the truth—and He did, for He is the truth—on that very Sabbath day in old Nazareth the prison doors were flung open, and the spirits in prison came out free men (see 1 Peter 3:18, 20). That's the prison Jesus was talking about—the prison house of sin.

He was opening the doors that Sabbath day, not somewhere inside the earth to disembodied souls or spirits, but to people with the chains of sin clanging about them, people whose lives were fettered with evil, people like us, conscience-smitten, who knew the right but often did not do it. He was talking to spirits in prison, people who had been under the control of the devil for years, people with the chains of habit upon them. Right then and there they were free—"This day is this scripture fulfilled in your ears."

Friend, it can happen to you this day, this moment. You can go free and leave the prison behind you forever. Not only will He raise you from the dead if you fall asleep in Christ, but He will raise you from the death of sin right now. From that prison house you will be delivered. Doors will open. The chains will fall.

Just now, do you desire freedom from this prison house of habit and of evil? Jesus says: "If the Son therefore shall make you free, ye shall be free indeed" (John 8:36).

Nothing is too hard for Him. If you desire it, this freedom is for you now in Christ.

DAY/275 Read Mark 1:21 through 2:14; Luke 4:31-44; 5:12-28; Matthew 8:14-17; 4:23-25; 8:2-4; 9:2-9.

Today's reading: A good share of Christ's ministry consisted of healing sufferers, always in response to their faith and always with the purpose of freeing them from sin.

Memory gem: "When Jesus saw their faith, he said unto the sick of the palsy, Son, thy sins be forgiven thee" (Mark 2:5).

Thought for today:

An unforgettable story about five men is recorded in the second chapter of Mark's Gospel. One of them was hopelessly ill. The other four were his friends. These men had heard of Jesus, and they attempted to bring their friend to Him.

The Saviour was in a house packed with those who had come to hear Him and those who had come for help. There wasn't even standing room outside near the door. What a preacher Jesus was! So different from most of us. Today people seem to like to sit as far away from the preacher as they can, and leave a "great gulf fixed" between the pulpit and the hearer, which nobody could cross over in human friendship or spiritual fellowship. But with Jesus it was different. They tried to get as close to Him as they could, to hear every word from His holy lips.

So these four men came, bringing their sick friend. Yes, they went up on the flat roof of this Palestinian house, pulled off the tiles, and made an opening large enough for their purpose. They must have used ropes, because they let the bed or pallet right down in front of Jesus. There was the sick man, needing His healing power! And notice the significant words of the fifth verse: "When Jesus saw their faith, he said unto the sick of the palsy, Son, thy sins be forgiven thee."

Notice, He saw their faith—not only the faith of the sick man, but the faith of the four men who brought him. Who were these men of faith? Jones, Smith, Johnson, and Hunter? We do not know their names. Christians Anonymous! They were not looking for credit or reputation or personal glory. They were seeking help for their friend. They were coming to Jesus in faith. They were working for God without any thought of human reward.

What God needs in the world today is more Christians Anonymous, more of His servants who seek the glory of Christ more than anything else in the world.

DAY / 276

Read Matthew 12:1-21; Mark 2:23 through 3:19; Luke 6.

Today's reading: The rabbis had imposed so many rules involving Sabbath observance that God's holy day had become burdensome. Jesus tried to show that the Sabbath could be "a delight, the holy of the Lord, honourable" (Isaiah 58:13).

Memory gem: "The sabbath was made for man, and not man for the sabbath: therefore the Son of man is Lord also of the sabbath" (Mark 2:27, 28).

Thought for today:

Since Jesus is Lord of the Sabbath, the Sabbath is the Lord's day. It was made for man, that is, mankind—not merely for Adam alone, but for all of his descendants to the end of time.

These are the very same words that are used in reference to the marriage relationship, when the apostle said that the woman was made for the man (see 1 Corinthians 11:9). This certainly does not mean that only Adam, or some one particular race of people, has a right to marriage. Marriage is for mankind, and so is the Sabbath. It was made for man in the beginning, before sin entered the world. The Sabbath and marriage are the two holy institutions that have come to us from those wonderful Eden days before the dark shadows of sin and death came over the earth.

Notice, Jesus did not say that the Sabbath was made *by* man, but that it was made *for* man. The reason the Lord made the seventh day the Sabbath was that He made the world in six days. Man did not make the world. In fact, man was not created when the world was formed. He did not appear until the sixth day. All the works of God existed before Adam was created, and the holy Sabbath was the first complete day that he enjoyed. Surely, through his lifetime, he never forgot it. And God says to us today, "Remember the Sabbath day, to keep it holy."

Note: The naming of the twelve apostles differs slightly in the four lists (see Matthew 10:2-4; Mark 3:16-19; Luke 6:14-16; Acts 1:13). For the most part the differences are only in the order. One man, however has three different names: Lebbaeus, Thaddaeus, and Judas (not Judas Iscariot). Another one, Bartholomew, is called Nathaniel in John's Gospel.

Today's reading: Christ's well-known Sermon on the Mount presents tremendous spiritual truths.

Memory gem: "Let your light so shine before men, that they may see your good works, and glorify your Father which is in heaven" (Matthew 5:16).

Thought for today:

The world needs light. It has always needed light, but it needs it now more than ever before. The Word of God is light. "Thy word is a lamp unto my feet, and a light unto my path," we read in Psalm 119:105. And so, every Christian should be a lamplighter, a lamp holder. It is the responsibility of all God's people to turn on the light. As the apostle says in Philippians 2:15, 16: "that ye may be blameless and harmless, the sons of God, without rebuke, in the midst of a crooked and perverse nation, among whom ye shine as lights in the world; holding forth the word of life." That's the way to shine—holding forth God's Word—and it is the only way.

As a boy I lived in a city where the lamplighter came around every night. He put his ladder up to each lamppost and lighted the gas lights. One could follow his progress down the streets as the lights came on. The whole aspect of the city was changed in a short time. Light is deadly to ghosts, goblins, germs, burglars, and racketeers. Light in a city is a policeman that never takes a bribe, never gets drunk, never goes to sleep on duty, never takes a vacation. As light is a savior to a city, so Jesus Christ is the Light of the world, and His Word brings salvation.

Let us not forget our duty to turn on the light. Let us tell others about Jesus Christ. Let us go forth with a united, obedient testimony. Let us be faithful and fearless for God.

Difficult or obscure words:

Matthew 5:3. **"Blessed"**—better: happy, or fortunate.

Matthew 5:15. **"Candle"** and **"candlestick"**—rather: lamp, and lampstand. Tallow candles were unknown in New Testament times. Light came from shallow bowls containing oil and a wick.

Matthew 5:15. **"Bushel"**—rather: measuring pot. Most homes had an earthenware vessel of about two gallons (eight liters) capacity for measuring or storing grain or flour.

DAY / 278

Read Luke 7:1-10; Matthew 8:5-13; 9:27-35; Luke 8:1-3; 7:11-17; Matthew 12:22-50; Mark 3:20-35; Luke 11:14-32; 8:19-21.

Today's reading: Among other things, we read Jesus' description of the sin which God cannot forgive—commonly called the "unpardonable sin."

Memory gem: "Whosoever speaketh against the Holy Ghost, it shall not be forgiven him, neither in this world, neither in the world to come" (Matthew 12:32).

Thought for today:

The context of the startling words of Matthew 12:32 shows that our Lord had performed a mighty miracle, and His bitter enemies could not deny the fact. It is also evident that some of them recognized in their hearts that Christ's miracles were performed by the power of God. Yet they publicly attributed Christ's miracle to the power of the devil. They were willing to go to this extreme to destroy His popularity and influence with the people. It was when they made this wicked charge, knowing it to be false, that Jesus spoke about what we call the "unpardonable sin."

Our Lord declares that all manner of sin shall be forgiven unto men. And for this we thank God! There is hope for everyone who repents and forsakes his sin. Let no one say, "I am sorry for my wicked life and want to be saved, but there is no hope for me. Since I did a certain thing, committed a particular sin, I am hopeless." Do not believe it for one minute, for Jesus plainly says, "All manner of sin and blasphemy shall be forgiven unto men," and He means just that. He calls you just as you are.

If all manner of sin . . . shall be forgiven unto men," why does our Lord warn us that the blasphemy "against the Holy Ghost hath never forgiveness" (Mark 3:29)? The reason is clear, when we refer to what the Scriptures say about the Holy Spirit of God.

The Holy Spirit is the only agent God uses to bring repentance to a human soul; and if a man persistently grieves away, or drives way, the Spirit of God, his heart will harden and he will have no more conviction of sin—will not repent—and therefore will not be forgiven. No man who has any concern for his sins has committed the unpardonable sin. There is forgiveness for you, but don't delay.

DAY / 279

Read Matthew 13:1-53; Mark 4:1-34; Luke 8:4-18.

Today's reading: Much of Jesus' teaching was in the form of parables—stories about familiar objects or experiences to dramatize spiritual truth. Today we read several of these.

Memory gem: "He that received seed into the good ground is he that heareth the word, and understandeth it; which also beareth fruit, and bringeth forth, some an hundredfold, some sixty, some thirty" (Matthew 13:23).

Thought for today:

" 'The sower soweth the word.' Christ came to sow the world with truth. . . . He who had stood in the councils of God, who had dwelt in the innermost sanctuary of the Eternal, could bring to men the pure principles of truth. . . . It is to His personal ministry among men, and to the work which He thus established, that the parable of the sower especially applies.

"The word of God is the seed. Every seed has in itself a germinating principle. In it the life of the plant is enfolded. So there is life in God's word. Christ says, 'The words that I speak unto you, they are Spirit, and they are life.' John 6:63. 'He that heareth My word, and believeth on Him that sent Me, hath everlasting life.' John 5:24. In every command and in every promise of the word of God is the power, the very life of God, by which the command may be fulfilled and the promise realized. He who by faith receives the word is receiving the very life and character of God.

"Every seed brings forth fruit after its kind. Sow the seed under right conditions, and it will develop its own life in the plant. Receive into the soul by faith the incorruptible seed of the word, and it will bring forth a character and a life after the similitude of the character and the life of God."—*Christ's Object Lessons,* pp. 37, 38.

Difficult or obscure words:

Matthew 13:21. **"By and by"**—literally: immediately, or at once. Old English usage was the exact opposite of our modern meaning.

DAY / 280

Read Matthew 8:18 through 9:1, 10-26;
Mark 4:35 through chapter 5; 2:15-22.

Today's reading: A storm on the lake accompanied a storm in the minds of men. Jesus exercised His power to bring peace in both areas.

Memory gem: "Go home to thy friends, and tell them how great things the Lord hath done for thee, and hath had compassion on thee" (Mark 5:19).

Thought for today:

The story of Christ's victory over the evil powers in control of men's minds is a very significant account. The unseen demons evidently believed the time would come when they would meet punishment; they apparently recognized Christ. They knew Him to be the Son of God and Judge of the universe, and they were concerned; they were frightened. This was an audible message from the spirit world. The demons used the lips, tongues, and voices of human beings to communicate. The men had become, willingly or unwillingly, mediums through which unseen spirits spoke.

The poor men who were thus freed from the control of demons were not merely suffering from a form of insanity or from a naturally caused disease. From the conversation which Christ carried on with the demons, it is plain that the Lord Jesus understood perfectly the intelligence with which He was dealing. They were not the spirits of dead men. They were mighty intelligences of the unseen world. They were of that host of angels who fell from heaven with Lucifer and since that day have carried on unceasing warfare against God and His work on earth. Jesus plainly recognized the presence and agency of these evil spirits, and He dealt with them as such.

After the departure of the demons, the victims were entirely changed. They were calm, subdued, intelligent, gentle. Speaking of one of the men, the Scripture says he was "clothed and in his right mind."

Note: Matthew says that two demon-possessed men confronted Jesus; Mark and Luke mention only one. We presume that one man was dominant. Matthew, an eyewitness, no doubt saw two men; Mark and Luke, writing what others reported, apparently thought of only the one.

DAY / 281

Read Luke 8:22-56; 5:29-39; Matthew 11:2-30; Luke 7:18-35.

Today's reading: The third account of the storm, the healing of the demoniac, and other events is followed by the sad story of John the Baptist in prison.

Memory gem: "Go your way, and tell John what things ye have seen and heard" (Luke 7:22).

Thought for today:

"John [the Baptist] was troubled to see that through love for him, his own disciples were cherishing unbelief in regard to Jesus. Had his work for them been fruitless? Had he been unfaithful in his mission, that he was now cut off from labor? If the promised Deliverer had appeared, and John had been found true to his calling, would not Jesus now overthrow the oppressor's power, and set free His herald?

"But the Baptist did not surrender his faith in Christ. The memory of the voice from heaven and the descending dove, the spotless purity of Jesus, the power of the Holy Spirit that had rested upon John as he came into the Saviour's presence, and the testimony of the prophetic scriptures—all witnessed that Jesus of Nazareth was the Promised One.

"John would not discuss his doubts and anxieties with his companions. He determined to send a message of inquiry to Jesus. . . . And he longed for some word from Christ spoken directly for himself.

"The disciples came to Jesus with their message, 'Art Thou He that should come, or do we look for another?' . . .

"The Saviour did not at once answer the disciples' question. As they stood wondering at His silence, the sick and afflicted were coming to Him to be healed. The blind were groping their way through the crowd; diseased ones of all classes, some urging their own way, some borne by their friends, were eagerly pressing into the presence of Jesus. . . . While He healed their diseases, He taught the people. . . . He spoke to them the words of eternal life.

"Thus the day wore away, the disciples of John seeing and hearing all. At last Jesus called them to Him and bade them to go and tell John what they had witnessed. . . . The evidence of His divinity was seen in its adaptation to the needs of suffering humanity."—*The Desire of Ages,* pp. 216, 217.

DAY / 282

Read Matthew 9:36 through 11:1; Mark 6:1-29;
Matthew 13:54 through 14:12; Luke 9:1-9.

Today's reading: The ordination of the twelve apostles and the instructions for their first mission precede the account of the shameful execution of John the Baptist.

Memory gem: "He that findeth his life shall lose it: and he that loseth his life for my sake shall find it" (Matthew 10:39).

Thought for today:

The late A. E. Housman, a professor at Cambridge University, was one of the most distinguished scholars of his time. In 1933 he gave an address at that university on "The Name and Nature of Poetry." In it he said that "the most important truth which has ever been uttered, and the greatest moral discovery ever made in the moral world" were these words of Jesus: "He that findeth his life shall lose it: and he that loseth his life . . . shall find it."

Now, of course, we have heard preachers say that since we were children. We have read it ourselves in the New Testament. But who was Professor Housman? He was an atheist, a pessimist. We are told that he even contemplated suicide at one time; yet he declared that the man who thinks only of himself is not living the full life and will not get much out of life. It was clear even to him, as he looked on life through many years of careful study, that adjustment to this world is not always the happiest and best thing. Here we find a man who was himself an unbeliever, or at least thought he was, quoting those paradoxical words of Jesus.

"He that loseth his life for my sake shall find it." Willing to give up anything in this world in order to please Christ; willing to do God's will in spite of everything else! Instead of making our own selfish plans, ideas, and enjoyments the center of living, we are to make the Word and work of Christ central. We are to do everything for His sake. Surely we must agree that this is the greatest truth ever uttered, the most profound moral discovery of all time.

Difficult or obscure words:

Matthew 10:10. **"Shoes"**—literally: sandals. Mark 6:9 says that the apostles were to wear sandals; the context in Matthew indicates that they should not carry an extra pair.

Mark 6:25. **"By and by"**—at once.

DAY / 283

Read Matthew 14:13-36; Mark 6:30-56; Luke 9:10-17; John 6:1 through 7:1.

Today's reading: Typically human, Peter wanted to show off. When he took his eyes off Jesus and realized his peril, his boastful faith failed to support him!

Memory gem: "When he saw the wind boisterous, he was afraid; and beginning to sink, he cried, saying, Lord, save me" (Matthew 14:30).

Thought for today:

The apostle Peter was tested regarding his trust and faith in Christ, and he was in great fear.

No one can doubt Peter's love for his Master. The miracle which Jesus was performing in walking on the water, Peter also performed for a time. But when he transferred his gaze from Jesus to the angry waters, he began to sink because "he was afraid." Then he prayed the shortest prayer recorded in the Bible: "Lord, save me."

"And immediately Jesus stretched forth his hand, and caught him, and said unto him, O thou of little faith, wherefore didst thou doubt?" (Matthew 14:31).

Peter was afraid because he looked upon the stormy billows rather than upon Christ. His faith failed; he was afraid. And this lesson is for us. We are often afraid because we do not look in the right direction. We look at the trouble, we look at the storm, we look at the battle, rather than to Jesus.

How shall we learn to trust when we are in trouble? What is the Christian's secret of a happy life? Here is a text we should never forget, for it tells us to do just what Jesus did: "Faith cometh by hearing, and hearing by the word of God" (Romans 10:17).

If we listen to the Word of God, if we read the Word of God, if we feed upon the Word of God, it will actually become faith in our hearts and drive away all fear.

All the hundreds of promises in His Word are ours when we believe them. This is the secret of a happy life, a life of faith.

DAY / 284

Read Matthew 15:1 through 16:28; Mark 7:1 through 8:26.

Today's reading: Jesus' only recorded miracle outside of Palestine proper was performed for a Phoenician woman. Jesus treated the woman in typical Hebrew fashion at first in order to teach His disciples an important lesson.

Memory gem: "Is he the God of the Jews only? is he not also of the Gentiles? Yes, of the Gentiles also" (Romans 3:29).

Thought for today:

"The Saviour's visit to Phoenicia and the miracle there performed had a yet wider purpose. Not alone for the afflicted woman, nor even for His disciples and those who received their labors, was the work accomplished; but also 'that ye might believe that Jesus is the Christ, the Son of God; and that believing ye might have life through His name.' John 20:31.

"The same agencies that barred men away from Christ eighteen hundred years ago are at work today. The spirit which built up the partition wall between Jew and Gentile is still active. Pride and prejudice have built strong walls of separation between different classes of men. Christ and His mission have been misrepresented, and multitudes feel that they are virtually shut away from the ministry of the gospel. But let them not feel that they are shut away from Christ. There are no barriers which man or Satan can erect but that faith can penetrate.

"In faith the woman of Phoenicia flung herself against the barriers that had been piled up between Jew and Gentile. Against discouragement, regardless of appearances that might have led her to doubt, she trusted the Saviour's love. It is thus that Christ desires us to trust in Him. The blessings of salvation are for every soul. Nothing but his own choice can prevent any man from becoming a partaker of the promise in Christ by the gospel."—*The Desire of Ages,* p. 403.

Note: "Magdala" (Matthew 15:39) and "Dalmanutha" (Mark 8:10) are probably variant names for the same place.

DAY / 285

Read Matthew 18; Mark 8:27 through 9:1 and verses 30-50; Luke 9:18-27, 43-50.

Today's reading: Jesus tried over and over to teach His followers the true nature of His mission and the way to salvation. They had difficulty in learning these lessons.

Memory gem: "He is able also to save them to the uttermost that come unto God by him, seeing he ever liveth to make intercession for them" (Hebrews 7:25).

Thought for today:

A young man had been living a free and easy life, unmindful of any serious claims his God might have upon him. Then the Holy Spirit spoke to his heart, and he came under deep conviction. Realizing his lost condition and his great need, he hurried to his pastor for counsel. He said, "Pastor, I am a lost man."

The minister's startling reply was, "Well, that's fine!"

The young man, desperate and in anguish of soul, said: "But, sir, you don't understand. I tell you that I am a lost man, and you say it's fine. I am lost! lost!"

"Well, that's good," said the minister. "Jesus Christ came to seek and to save that which was lost."

Young people, I want you to know that the Lord is seeking for those who, like this young man, realize that they are lost and in need of a Saviour. Just come to Jesus as you are. Confess your sins to Him; pour out your heart to Him. He is full of compassion, and He understands.

If something has been holding you back from accepting this wonderful Christ, just bow your head now and ask God to forgive your sins. Begin a program of daily Bible study. Get acquainted with the Prince of Peace, the One who can give you peace of mind, the One who has promised to come again. Then, on that glorious day, we shall all be able to say: "Lo, this is our God; we have waited for him, and he will save us: this is the Lord; we have waited for him, we will be glad and rejoice in his salvation" (Isaiah 25:9).

DAY / 286

Read Matthew 17:1-27; Mark 9:2-29; Luke 9:28-42.

Today's reading describes one of the high points of Christ's ministry—the transfiguration.

Memory gem: "There came a voice out of the cloud, saying, This is my beloved Son: hear him" (Luke 9:35).

Thought for today:

Christ on the mount of transfiguration had received the testimony of Moses and Elijah. But there was one more voice needed, the voice of God, and now it spoke. The voice from heaven came not in testimony to any fact, but to a person, for Jesus was God's beloved Son.

Hear Him! His words will be in harmony with the law and the prophets. The sacrifices and offerings of the law pointed forward to Him. The predictions of the prophets of the Old Testament, like searchlights, penetrated the gloom of the future, revealing the cross and the crown—our Saviour's first advent to die for a lost world, and His second coming in glory which is still future in our day. The voice from the cloud commanded: "Hear Him! Hear Him reverently. Hear Him implicitly. Hear Him alone."

Friend, are we in sympathy with heaven about Christ? Do we hear Him? Is His Word law to us? Do we like it when He speaks sharp things as well as smooth things? Does His Word prevail with us against everything else? Surely it would help us if we would stop and think that whenever Christ speaks to us the Father is standing by, saying in our ears as it were, "Hear that!"

The transfiguration of our Saviour is of great interest and importance to us, not only because it actually occurred in the past and encourages us now in the present, but for what it teaches us of the future. For all ages, it is like the vision of the burning bush in which was the presence of God. The transfiguration promised Christ's disciples then, and His followers now, that there is a glory yet to come. The glory kindled on the mount of transfiguration shines through the darkness of this world and points to the resurrection day when Christ will come in glory and gather His people—not three only, but all His people of all ages—and they will be with Him forevermore.

DAY / 287

Read John 7:2 through chapter 8.

Today's reading: Throughout His ministry, Jesus had frequent clashes with religious leaders. Some of His most important teachings came from His remarks on these occasions.

Memory gem: "Jesus stood and cried, saying, If any man thirst, let him come unto me, and drink" (John 7:37).

Thought for today:

Every Christian ought to search his own life, dig deep in the Word of God, and find new strength in prayer. Jesus said that every true believer in Him was to be like a living well, an artesian well, overflowing with spiritual help to other people.

If we profess to believe in Him but do not help others, it is because our lives are spiritually dry and desolate. It is because we do not really have the love of God in our hearts and are destitute of the Holy Spirit. What terrible harm a professing Christian can do when in such a condition! He is like a dry well in the desert.

About thirty miles south of Tacna, Arizona, almost on the Mexican border, there is a place called Tinajas Altas, which means "High Tanks." It is a series of basins on the desert hillside which catch and hold rainwater. Sometimes they are full; often they are entirely dry. In the early days this was a favorite watering place for the pioneers.

On the slopes above Tinajas Altas are many graves. Most of them are hard to identify now, but about thirty years ago Ike Proebstal, well-known desert man, counted 160 graves, and every one was the grave of a man who had died of thirst. Men had staggered across the hot desert with one last hope, of finding water in the "High Tanks." They had hoped, but hope failed them. They found no water, and they died.

But what about the man who is hoping against hope that he will find faith in your life? purity in your heart? He is famished for the water of life, and he finds the well dry, the waters drained away in the desert of selfishness!

Friend, in this crisis hour of this world a solemn call from God comes to each of us. Will you give your heart to Christ today and take the steps you know you ought to take to keep your spiritual life charged with the water of life?

May God give us grace to live right and be ready to help those who look to us as examples of living faith.

DAY / 288

Read John 9:1 through 10:31; Matthew 19: 1, 2; Mark 10:1; Luke 9:51 through 10:24.

Today's reading: After Jesus healed the blind man on the Sabbath, He again encountered the bitter prejudice of the religious bigots. Again He defended Himself with deeply spiritual teaching.

Memory gem: "I am the good shepherd, and know my sheep, and am known of mine" (John 10:14).

Thought for today:

"In a beautiful pastoral picture He [Jesus] represents His relation to those that believe on Him. No picture was more familiar to His hearers than this, and Christ's words linked it forever with Himself. Never could the disciples look on the shepherds tending their flocks without recalling the Saviour's lesson. They would see Christ in each faithful shepherd. They would see themselves in each helpless and dependent flock.

"This figure the prophet Isaiah had applied to the Messiah's mission in the comforting words, 'O Zion, that bringest good tidings, get thee up into the high mountain; O Jerusalem, that bringest good tidings, lift up thy voice with strength; lift it up, be not afraid; say unto the cities of Judah, Behold your God! . . . He shall feed His flock like a shepherd: He shall gather the lambs with His arm, and carry them in His bosom.' Isaiah 40:9-11. . . .

"Christ applied these prophecies to Himself, and He showed the contrast between His own character and that of the leaders in Israel. The Pharisees had just driven one from the fold, because he dared to bear witness to the power of Christ. They had cut off a soul whom the True Shepherd was drawing to Himself. In this they had shown themselves ignorant of the work committed to them, and unworthy of their trust as shepherds of the flock. Jesus now set before them the contrast between them and the Good Shepherd, and He pointed to Himself as the real keeper of the Lord's flock. . . .

"Every soul is as fully known to Jesus as if he were the only one for whom the Saviour died. The distress of every one touches His heart. The cry for aid reaches His ear. He also knows who gladly hear His call, and are ready to come under His pastoral care. He says, 'My sheep hear My voice, and I know them, and they follow Me.' He cares for each one as if there were not another on the face of the earth."—*The Desire of Ages,* pp. 476–480.

DAY / 289

Read Luke 10:25-42; John 10:32-42; Luke 11:1-13, 33-54; 12:1-34.

Today's reading: Among Jesus' teachings, warnings, and parables, the lesson of the rich fool stands out as particularly applicable to modern materialists.

Memory gem: "Riches profit not in the day of wrath: but righteousness delivereth from death" (Proverbs 11:4).

Thought for today:

"God said unto him, Thou fool, this night thy soul shall be required of thee: then whose shall those things be, which thou hast provided?" (Luke 12:20).

That's the big question, isn't it? Whose will they be? This man was wise in the ways of business. There's nothing wrong about that. Not one word is said against him as a businessman. There is no suggestion that he was dishonest. The trouble was, he was covetous. He worshiped his possessions. He worshiped things. There are millions today who worship things. They want more things—better automobiles, finer houses. But Jesus says, "A man's life consisteth not in the abundance of the things which he possesseth."

So it was with this rich man. He was getting ready to enlarge things. He had big visions, big ideas. He was successful, but he craved greater success. But God said to him, "Thou fool, this night thy soul shall be required of thee."

You see, he valued things above his soul. Instead of regarding this life as offering him the opportunity to prepare for the next, as a kindergarten to the great university of the beyond, as the day of salvation to get ready for the day of glory, as the time for doing good and finding true goodness, he focused his interest on things. He put his money in the wrong bank.

Note: The "feast of the dedication" (John 10:22), also known as the "festival of lights," is called "Hanukkah" by devout Jews. It occurs in our November or December.

DAY / 290

Read Luke 12:35 through chapter 14.

Today's reading: Excuses, excuses! People invited to a "great supper" offered lame excuses for not attending. Another of our Lord's parables examines our attitudes toward spiritual values.

Memory gem: "[He] sent his servant at supper time to say to them that were bidden, Come; for all things are now ready" (Luke 14:17).

Thought for today:

These men spoken of in Luke were not invited to a funeral or even to hear a lecture. They were not asked to visit a hospital or a prison. They were to go to a feast. The holy gospel of Jesus Christ is represented as a feast. It was to take place in the evening. The Bible speaks of the "marriage supper" of God's Son: "Blessed are they which are called unto the marriage supper of the Lamb" (Revelation 19:9).

Oh, my friends, we don't want to miss that feast, that appointment with God; and yet, according to this story Jesus told, these people wanted to be excused.

More than nineteen hundred years have rolled away since Jesus told this story. Some tell us that the world has grown wiser, though we do not often hear them say it has grown better. Wiser, they say. But tell me this, Have men any better excuses today than they had in Christ's time?

Suppose you take your pen and write out your excuse:

"Just now (or yesterday, or last week, or whenever it was) I received an earnest invitation from one of Your servants to be present at the marriage supper of Your only-begotten Son, Jesus Christ. Please have me excused because ________" and sign your name to it. How would it sound to the King of heaven?

Let us write out another answer:

"While reading these words (or listening to a gospel sermon, or whenever it was) I received an invitation from one of Your messengers to be present at the marriage supper of Your only-begotten Son, Jesus Christ; and I hasten to reply. By the grace of God I will be present."

Will you sign that? May the Lord help you to make that decision today. You must accept it or reject it. To make no decision is itself a decision not to accept the loving request of the heavenly Father and remember—God does not accept excuses.

DAY / 291

Read Luke 15 and 16.

Today's reading: Three parables represent three kinds of lost sinners: the lost sheep—knowing it is lost but not knowing how to return; the lost coin—totally unaware of its situation; the lost son—fully conscious of his condition and painfully aware of his own responsibility.

Memory gem: "When he came to himself, he said, . . . I will arise and go to my father" (Luke 15:17, 18).

Thought for today:

The universal struggle in which people in all walks of life find themselves involved is the struggle to be somebody, to achieve a sense of personal significance.

One of the interesting Bible narratives tells about a young man in an Eastern country who was dissatisfied with his lot in life. He wanted to leave home and become somebody.

Here was a young man who had the means with which to enjoy the good things of life. He was all by himself now, with no one to curtail his movements or actions. But the influence of godless companions soon deprived him of his substance, and he found himself without either friends or money.

Friend, if you want to be a "somebody," you must first realize that without God you are a "nobody," for whoever attempts to live apart from Him is a nobody. If you have chosen such a life, you are spending money for that which is not bread, and labor for that which satisfieth not (see Isaiah 55:2).

The story of the prodigal son is a story of you, a story of me. As we have strayed away from the Father, we have wanted to live life on our own terms. We have wanted to make our own goals. We have wanted to leave God out of our reckoning. Then finally, in desperation, we have turned to Him. There the Lord is waiting for us, just as the father was waiting for his prodigal son to return.

Are you willing to return to the Lord Jesus? It means complete surrender. That's the price of the Christian life. It may not always be the easiest life, but it will always be the happiest one. Life will take on a new meaning. My prayer is that you will open your heart's door to the loving Saviour, realizing your great need of forgiveness, your great need of a new life, a new goal, a new outlook. You may have all this today. Yes, you can be changed from a nobody to a somebody.

DAY / 292

Read Luke 17:1-10; John 11; Luke 17:11-37.

Today's reading: Without doubt the greatest single miracle performed by Jesus was that of restoring to life a man who had been dead four days. The story gives us confidence in His promise to raise all who die with their hope anchored in Him.

Memory gem: "If we believe that Jesus died and rose again, even so them also which sleep in Jesus will God bring with him" (1 Thessalonians 4:14).

Thought for today:

Jesus Christ called death a sleep, but His disciples could not understand this. They believed that there was no hope once a person had died, but they were to learn that in Jesus Christ there is hope beyond the tomb.

Previous to this raising of Lazarus from the dead, it was hard for the followers of Jesus to realize what He meant when He said, "I am the resurrection, and the life." Death is a cessation of life. Humanly speaking, there is no hope after death. But the great hope of the Christian is the resurrection. Jesus Christ is the resurrection and the life.

This change will take place at the second coming of Christ. Those who have faith in Him; those who believe in His death, burial, and resurrection; those who receive His power in their life day by day will be a part of that resurrection.

It is with this hope that we can face with confidence and courage the few years of life here on this earth. This is really the only hope that you or I have—hope in Christ, hope in His second coming, hope in the resurrection.

You can have the assurance of life beyond the grave. You can have the assurance of meeting your loved ones again. What a privilege, what a joy, to be sons of God and children of the resurrection!

Difficult or obscure words:

Luke 17:6. **"Sycamine"**—the black mulberry.

Luke 17 7. **"By and by"**—at once.

Luke 17:37. **"Eagles"**—rather: vultures. Jesus here quoted a Jewish proverb common at that time.

DAY / 293

Read Matthew 19:3-30; Mark 10:2-31; Luke 18:1-30.

Today's reading: For the last time Jesus leaves His beloved Galilee and sets out for Jerusalem, knowing full well the fate that awaits Him there. Tucked in among other teachings, we find a story about two men and their prayers.

Memory gem: "The publican, standing afar off, would not lift up so much as his eyes unto heaven, but smote upon his breast saying, God be merciful to me a sinner" (Luke 18:13).

Thought for today:

Do you find that your prayers fall far short of what you really want to say? Do you ever feel a deep heart longing to speak to God, but just can't find the words? It has always comforted me to know that God has made provision for us even in this. Sometimes we do not know what to pray for as we ought to, and we may say things that God knows are not the things we meant to say. And here is His good Word: "Likewise the Spirit also helpeth our infirmities: for we know not what we should pray for as we ought: but the Spirit itself maketh intercession for us with groanings which cannot be uttered. And he that searcheth the hearts knoweth what is the mind of the Spirit, because he maketh intercession for the saints according to the will of God" (Romans 8:26, 27).

Think of it! Our poor, stammering, human prayers are translated by the Spirit into the very language of heaven and presented according to the will of God! Prayers are heard that come up before the Lord according to His will. Oh, how we need the wonderful ministry of the Holy Spirit in our lives every day! We all should feel as earnest about our need as did Isaac Watts when he wrote his great hymn:

Come, Holy Spirit, heavenly Dove
With all Thy quickening powers;
Kindle a flame of sacred love
In these cold hearts of ours.

God loves us. John 3:16 proves it. Christ loves us. The Holy Spirit loves us (see Romans 15:30). Why should we not respond to this triple love and give our hearts to the Lord?

Difficult or obscure words:

Luke 18:3. **"Avenge me"**—better: Do me justice.

DAY / 294

Read Matthew 20; Mark 10:32-52; Luke 18:31 through 19:28.

Today's reading: Tremendous truths shine out from these pages, each one of great value to us. In His commendation of Zacchaeus, Jesus stated the purpose of His mission—the words of our memory gem.

Memory gem: "The Son of man is come to seek and to save that which was lost" (Luke 19:10).

Thought for today:

A picture program was being held in a little church in central England several years ago. All the children in the neighborhood were there on the front seats, listening to the speaker who was showing the Bible pictures. Someone came to the door and passed a note up to the minister, who stopped to read it and then said, "A report has just come to us that Mary Jones is lost. Her parents don't know where she is, and her father and the policemen are out hunting for her all over town." Well, no Mary Jones responded, and they went on with the service.

After it was over and they turned on the lights, there was Mary Jones on the front seat. A lady said, "Why, Mary, didn't you hear the announcement that you were lost and that your parents were looking for you? Why didn't you speak up?"

Mary answered, "I wasn't lost. I knew where I was all the time. I was right here in church."

You know, friend, there are many people today who don't know that they are lost. There are thousands of people lost right in church, sometimes on the front seat. Sometimes some of us preachers get lost—in the winding paths of modern speculation. We get lost in the philosophic subtleties of our supposed modern superiority. Some of us are just plain lost in sin.

We need to be found by somebody, somebody who is out seeking the lost for Jesus. Oh, my friend, you may not know that you are lost; but if you do come to the realization that you are lost from the fold of Christ, I pray that something in this book may help you back to the fold of the true Shepherd, the only place where you will find peace and confidence and hope and rest.

DAY / 295

Read Matthew 26:1-16; Mark 14:1-11; Luke 7:36-50; 22:1-6; John 12:1-11.

Today's reading: These two events occurred before the beginning of the Passion Week—probably on the night after the Sabbath. It was the reaction of Judas to Christ's rebuke at Simon's feast that precipitated the betrayal.

Memory gem: "Verily I say unto you, Wheresoever this gospel shall be preached in the whole world, there shall also this, that this woman hath done, be told for a memorial of her" (Matthew 26:13).

Thought for today:

Someone has said that the very name "Judas Iscariot" seems to have a hiss in it. We may have thought of him as a gnarled, twisted character from boyhood on, sulking through life with a malevolent gleam of hate in his eye. But that is certainly the wrong idea. Judas had many attractive virtues. He was a man of real promise, faithful in many of the tasks assigned to him in Christ's earlier ministry. The name Judas means "praise." His second name, Iscariot, may sound harsh and bitter, but some think it simply means "man of Kerioth," identifying the town from which he came. True, he became a thief; he became bitter and critical.

At the feast where a penitent woman anointed the feet of Jesus with costly spikenard perfume, Judas found fault. He said, "This should have been sold and given to the poor." He had come to the place where any special honor shown Jesus irked him. One might say that he lived in the negative.

This reminds me of a minister who, while riding on a tramcar in New York City, passed a beautiful church. A fellow passenger turned to him and said, "If those Christians would stop building fine churches and give their money to the poor, it would be much more to their credit."

"I have heard a similar remark before," said the minister.

"Indeed, and by whom, may I ask?"

"Judas Iscariot," was the reply.

Difficult or obscure words:

Matthew 26:7. **"Alabaster box"**—better jar, or flask. These ancient flasks carved from soft stone often had the contents sealed in, so that the flask had to be broken open (see Mark 14:3).

DAY / 296

Read Matthew 21:1-11, 18-22; Mark 11:1-14, 20-26; Luke 19:29-44; John 12:12-19; Matthew 21:12-17; Mark 11:15-19; Luke 19:45-48.

Today's reading: Three episodes are narrated: (1) The triumphal entry into Jerusalem—popularly called Palm Sunday. (2) The cursing of the barren fig tree. The curse was pronounced on Monday morning; the withered condition was observed Tuesday morning. (3) The cleansing of the temple. This occurred on Monday.

Memory gem: "Hosanna to the Son of David: Blessed is he that cometh in the name of the Lord; Hosanna in the highest" (Matthew 21:9).

Thought for today:

"Christ was following the Jewish custom for a royal entry. The animal on which He rode was that ridden by the kings of Israel, and prophecy had foretold that thus the Messiah should come to His kingdom [see Zechariah 9:9.] No sooner was He seated upon the colt than a loud shout of triumph rent the air. The multitude hailed Him as Messiah, their King. . . . The disciples received this as proof that their glad hopes were to be realized by seeing Him established on the throne. . . .

"Never before had the world seen such a triumphal procession. It was not like that of the earth's famous conquerors. No train of mourning captives, as trophies of kingly valor, made a feature of that scene. But about the Saviour were the glorious trophies of His labors of love for sinful man. There were the captives whom He had rescued from Satan's power, praising God for their deliverance. The blind whom He had restored to sight were leading the way. The dumb whose tongues He had loosed shouted the loudest hosannas. The cripples whom He had healed bounded with joy, and were the most active in breaking the palm branches and waving them before the Saviour. Widows and orphans were exalting the name of Jesus for His works of mercy to them. The lepers whom He had cleansed spread their untainted garments in His path, and hailed Him as the King of glory. Those whom His voice had awakened from the sleep of death were in that throng."—*The Desire of Ages,* pp. 570–572.

DAY / 297

Read Matthew 21:23 through 22:22; Mark 11:27 through 12:17; Luke 20:1-26.

Today's reading: Tuesday of that eventful week was a busy day. When Jesus arrived in Jerusalem that morning, a delegation of religious leaders challenged His authority and tried to trap Him into saying something they could condemn.

Memory gem: "Render therefore unto Caesar the things which are Caesar's; and unto God the things that are God's" (Matthew 22:21).

Thought for today:

In the United States we are blessed with a government which derives its just powers from the consent of the governed; a land where everyone has the right to worship God according to the dictates of his own conscience; a land where the highest law states that "Congress shall make no law respecting an establishment of religion, or prohibiting the free exercise thereof."

Think what this means to us all—Jew and Gentile, Protestant or Catholic, or in whatever other circle of connection we find ourselves. We are free to serve God without molestation. This is the principle that Christ taught; we are to render to Caesar—civil government—that which is Caesar's, and to God that which is God's.

We must never forget this last part of it—the things of God are to be rendered to God:

1. Our *faith:* "Without faith it is impossible to please him: for he that cometh to God must believe that he is, and that he is a rewarder of them that diligently seek him" (Hebrews 11:6).

2. Our *love:* "And he answering said, Thou shalt love the Lord thy God with all thy heart, and with all thy soul, and with all thy strength, and with all thy mind; and thy neighbour as thyself" (Luke 10:27).

3. Our *obedience* to God's commandments: "Whosoever therefore shall break one of these least commandments, and shall teach men so, he shall be called the least in the kingdom of heaven: but whosoever shall do and teach them, the same shall be called great in the kingdom of heaven" (Matthew 5:19).

To serve our country best, we must serve God best—with better homes, better churches, better schools, but above all with better hearts. Back to God! Back to the Bible! Back to prayer! Back to faith! Back to obedience!

DAY / 298

Read Matthew 22:23 through 23:39; Mark 12:18-44; Luke 20:27 through 21:4.

Today's reading: The confrontation between Jesus and the religious authorities continues. When the challengers finally retreat in confusion, Jesus sits and watches people give their offerings.

Memory gem: "Thou shalt love the Lord thy God with all thy heart, and with all thy soul, and with all thy mind. . . . Thou shalt love thy neighbour as thyself" (Matthew 22:37-39).

Thought for today:

The first four of the Ten Commmandments concern our relationship to God, and the last six, our conduct toward men. We may refrain from the worship of other gods, the making of idols, and profane swearing; we may remember the Sabbath day to keep it holy, but if we are hateful and mean and bitter and petty and dishonest and hardhearted toward our fellowmen, our religion is vain.

Love is the fulfilling, not the abolishing, of the law. "Love thy neighbour," and so love God (see Romans 13:8-10).

When "the love of God is shed abroad in our hearts by the Holy Spirit" (Romans 5:5), we shall indeed love our neighbor.

Not only are we to show love to our neighbor in kindness and courtesy and aid to those in physical need about us, but we are also to help those who are suffering from the deeper and more terrible spiritual hunger in the world.

"Love thy neighbour," and the church will never lack support; it will not be driven to seek the revenue of oyster suppers, grabbag socials, and games of chance. Your tithes and offerings will support the ministry of Christ's church with liberality and dignity.

"Love thy neighbour," and the work of God will go forward because you may be the only Christian somebody knows; people who never read a printed Bible are always reading living ones.

If we love our neighbor, our service to others is looked upon in heaven as if it were done for Christ Himself.

Difficult or obscure words:

John 12:36. **"Did hide himself"**—meaning that Jesus went away into seclusion. This was the end of His public ministry.

Matthew 24:28. **"Carcass . . . eagles"**—better: dead body, vultures. This was probably a popular proverb of that time. The intended application cannot be determined with certainty. The proverb was used in a similar way in Luke 17:37.

DAY / 299

Read John 12:20-50; Matthew 24; Mark 13.

Today's reading: We are still on Tuesday of the Passion Week. After the Greek seekers found Jesus, He went with His disciples out of the city and gave the remarkable prophecy about signs of His second coming.

Memory gem: "This gospel of the kingdom shall be preached in all the world for a witness unto all nations; and then shall the end come" (Matthew 24:14).

Thought for today:

Now comes the question, Will the world in general be prepared to meet Jesus? The answer is found in Matthew 24:30:

"And then shall appear the sign of the Son of man in heaven: and then shall all the tribes of the earth mourn, and they shall see the Son of man coming in the clouds of heaven with power and great glory."

Why will a great many people not be prepared for this wonderful event? It is because they say that the Lord delays His coming (see verse 48). They do not expect Him to come soon.

What will the world in general be doing when the Lord comes? Verses 37 to 39 say that affairs will be going on as usual—social life, business life, "eating and drinking, marrying and giving in marriage, until . . . the flood came, and took them all away; so shall also the coming of the Son of man be." It will be an unexpected event to most of the people of the earth. The whole human race will be face-to-face with the ultimate, with finality, with the end.

Remember this, Christ appears the second time "without sin"—that is, not dealing with sin on the cross as He did before— but "unto salvation" (Hebrews 9:28). This blessed hope will change a human life (see 1 John 3:3).

We do not know the day or the hour of Christ's return. Not even the angels know this (see Matthew 24:36). But we are to know when it is near.

"Watch therefore: for ye know not what hour your Lord doth come" (Matthew 24:42).

"The proper attitude for a Christian is to be always looking for his Lord's return," said D. L. Moody.

The best days, the days of heaven on earth, are still ahead. Jesus is coming!

DAY / 300

Read Luke 21:5-38; Matthew 25.

Today's reading: We have another account of our Lord's great prohecy. We assume that, while He is speaking, darkness falls, and He tells a story based on a wedding procession that could be seen in a village below the mountain.

Memory gem: "When these things begin to come to pass, then look up, and lift up your heads; for your redemption draweth nigh" (Luke 21:28).

Thought for today:

We are looking out on a human civilization that, in the view of many people, is in danger of collapse. Human civilization is not able to save itself; that is clear. After thousands of years, war is still with us; crime is here and climbing fast; fear, heartache, death have not been conquered yet. The return of Jesus is God's answer to earth's great problems. "The kingdoms of this world" must become "the kingdoms of our Lord, and of his Christ" (Revelation 11:15). That is the only hope, the gloriously certain hope, called in the Bible the "blessed hope."

Christ has given signs of His coming. He says that we may know when He is "near, even at the doors" (Matthew 24:33). These signs have appeared. Now we know of a surety that the Lord's coming is at hand. "Heaven and earth shall pass away," He said, "but my words shall not pass away" (Mark 13:31).

A little longer, and we shall see the King in His beauty. A little longer, and He will wipe all tears from our eyes. A little longer, and He will present us "faultless before the presence of his glory with exceeding joy" (Jude 24).

DAY / 301

Read Matthew 26:17-35; Mark 14:12-31; Luke 22:7-39; John 13.

Today's reading: Apparently Jesus spent Wednesday and most of Thursday in quiet retirement somewhere outside the city. The record picks up the narrative on Thursday afternoon with preparation for the supper in the upper room.

Memory gem: "As often as ye eat this bread, and drink this cup ye do shew the Lord's death till he come" (1 Corinthians 11:26).

Thought for today:

Jesus is sitting at a table, a table in an upper room. Around this table with Him are gathered twelve men, young and old. The work of our Saviour is nearly finished. The next few hours will witness His betrayal, His condemnation, His crucifixion, His burial and resurrection. It is one of the greatest crisis hours of all the ages.

Look at that interesting mix, those disciples at the table. There is one class not represented among the twelve; as Alexander McGuire reminds us, no perfect people were among the apostles. Those pioneers of Christianity were not more wise, true, or noble, nor more worldly, false, or cowardly than are Christians generally today. They were like us. They were relatively obscure men and, as a lot, apparently not greatly gifted. They were mostly unlearned and weak in themselves; yet they could do all things through Christ who would strengthen them.

Someone has said that charcoal needs only a rearrangement of its atoms to become a diamond. So it was with those men as they sat there around the table. Among them was the betrayer, the one with dark thoughts. He was present at this sacramental service. He partook of the bread and wine. He heard the words, "This do in remembrance of me" (Luke 22:19). Sitting there in the very presence of the Saviour, the betrayer considered his own dark purpose.

Jesus had made every effort to save Judas. He had washed his feet in the ordinance of humility. He had broken bread with him and shared with him the wine, the symbols of His own broken body and shed blood. What an appeal the Saviour had made to him! Until Judas closed the door and went out into the darkness, he had not passed beyond the possibility of repentance. Now he had made the final decision. He had crossed the boundary line. He went out, "and it was night."

DAY / 302

Read John 14 through 16.

Today's reading: After the group in the upper room had sung a hymn, they went out into the moonlit night. Along the way to Gethsemane, Jesus talked to them about serious and wonderful truths.

Memory gem: "If I go and prepare a place for you, I will come again, and receive you unto myself; that where I am, there ye may be also" (John 14:3).

Thought for today:

I remember a little boy I knew, about five years old, whose grandfather loved him greatly. He took the boy with him everywhere he went, and sometimes he would take him on trips up into the Rocky Mountains, where he used to go trapping. When the little fellow's legs would wear out, the grandfather, a strong man, would put him on his back and carry him for miles.

One evening they were in the mountains miles away from home; and, although it was after sunset, the grandfather had to go farther up the canyon to look after some traps.

He found a large rock with a hole in it about five feet from the ground, just about the size of the little boy. So he put him in it and said, "Now, don't be afraid; nothing can get you up here. You can go to sleep if you want to; nothing will harm you. And I will come back in an hour and take you home."

The little boy lay there. The night closed in, dark, the wind moaned around that big rock, and the coyotes began to howl. And if there is anything on earth that is mournful, it is that. And the boy had an imagination which had often gotten him into trouble; but his grandfather had said, "I will come back," and on that promise he fell asleep.

Grandfather did come back, and he carried the boy home.

I know how the little boy felt; I know how scared he was, because I was that boy. But Grandfather said he would come back and he had never told me a lie. Neither my grandfather nor my father ever told me anything that was not true, so I believed every word they said. I always found it to be true.

Jesus has told us, "I am coming back." He didn't do it to fool us; He didn't do it to calm us and then leave us alone forever—for eternity. Oh, no, He is coming back. "Even so, come, Lord Jesus!"

Today's reading: We have the privilege of "listening" as our wonderful Saviour prays for us. We also read a few of the psalms that Jesus may have sung with His disciples—some containing Messianic prophecies.

Memory gem: "Sanctify them through thy truth: thy word is truth" (John 17:17).

Thought for today:

The seventeenth chapter of John contains Jesus' great prayer, His prayer as High Priest. Here we find some wonderful, wonderful things. Jesus was praying just before He died. When a person is praying his last prayer on earth, and he knows it, it is a very solemn thing. I have heard people pray their last prayer when they knew they were dying. This is Jesus' last prayer for His people, this great prayer in the seventeenth chapter of John.

Here we have this incomparable high-priestly prayer of Jesus in which He asks for many things for His people. He asks that we might be one. You know, it is a shame to find Christian people broken up into cliques—warring, antagonistic groups. It is a terrible thing for a church to have divisions in it because somebody wasn't elected to be deacon, because somebody said something about somebody else. Those things are always going to happen, and if we do not have enough Christianity to have love for God and for unlovely people and to get along smoothly in those experiences, we are in great spiritual need. We need to pray more for each other.

Jesus prayed for His people, that they might be kept faithful, kept from evil. That was a wonderful prayer, and it included us today. It was a prayer to keep His people from getting into wrong things, to keep us from getting so involved in business that we lose our hope and faith. Jesus prayed for all that. And He prayed that His people might live for God, carry out their mission, and go into all the world and give the gospel. He prayed that they might eventually be with Him where He is going to be.

DAY / 304

Read Matthew 26:36-75; Mark 14:32-72; Luke 22:40-65; John 18:1-27.

Today's reading: We are taken through the agony in Gethsemane, past the shameful betrayal, and into the courtyard at the home of Annas for an illegal night trial—and Peter's denial.

Memory gem: "Watch and pray, that ye enter not into temptation: the spirit indeed is willing, but the flesh is weak" (Matthew 26:41).

Thought for today:

The tragic experience of Judas is a sermon that eloquently sounds a warning to everyone. It is a supreme example of wasted *opportunity.* Think of it: Judas was with Jesus three and a half years; he was given all the opportunities the other apostles had; yet in the end, that wonderful education, with Jesus as the teacher, brought him no good. He died a lost man, as Jesus indicates in His great high-priestly prayer (see John 17:12).

Judas is also a disastrous example of wasted *influence.* He could have been another Simon Peter; he could have written one of the books of the New Testament; we might today have had the "Gospel according to Judas Iscariot." It could have been a blessing to the world. He might have written some epistles. Instead of this, his last contact with Jesus was that lying kiss which had its part in breaking the heart of the Saviour.

There are thousands like Judas today, wasting their influence. You who are reading this now—if you have had a Christian father, a Christian mother, if you have had church privileges, if you have known what it was to serve God and now you are wasting your life—remember you are drawing nearer and nearer to that dark night on which Judas crossed over the line, never to return.

In the third place, Judas wasted his *eternity.* Our life here on earth is brief, but we have time enough to prepare for the great eternity to come. Someday the twelve apostles will sit on twelve thrones judging the twelve tribes of Israel; but Judas will not be one of them. Another will have taken his place. We cannot imagine those eternal vistas of glory, of joy, of learning, endless ages of service for Jesus, for it is written that the redeemed will "follow the Lamb whithersoever he goeth" (Revelation 14:4).

DAY / 305

Read Luke 22:66-71; Matthew 27:1, 3-10, 2, 11-14; Mark; 15:1-5; Luke 23:1-5; John 18:28-38; Luke 23:6-12; Mark 15:6-47.

Today's reading: From the "kangaroo court" before Annas, Jesus went before the official assembly of the elders, hastily called. Then, condemned by His own people, He appeared before the Roman governor—vacillating and weak-willed Pilate—and the pompous Herod Antipas.

Memory gem: "Who shall ascend into the hill of the Lord? or who shall stand in his holy place? He that hath clean hands, and a pure heart; who hath not lifted up his soul unto vanity, nor sworn deceitfully" (Psalm 24:3, 4).

Thought for today:

What a scene to hand down through the pages of history! Before a fallible human judge stood the One who is the Judge of all the earth! He who has the greater light has the greater sin. Pilate and the Roman soldiers were comparatively ignorant of Christ. In rejecting Christ, those who know the most are the most guilty. What about you and me? We are responsible for the light that we have.

But what about Pilate's hands? All the waters of the seven seas could never cleanse them. Like Pilate we may deny responsibility, but our denial only adds to our sin and declares that we recognized the sin when we committed it.

Let us not pour condemnation upon Pilate or upon those other men of his time who condemned Jesus and chose to free Barabbas. What would you have done in Pilate's place if your job were at stake, your very life at stake? What you would have done then is revealed by what you are doing now. Are you serving Christ now? Are you confessing Him every day?

The apostle Paul says that Jesus Christ "witnessed a good confession" before Pontius Pilate (1 Timothy 6:13). What is our witness today? Do we confess our faith in our homes, in the office, in the shop, at work or at play, wherever we are? Do we witness a good confession? That is the question that comes to us today from Pilate's judgment hall.

DAY / 306

Read Luke 23:13-56; John 18:39 through 19:42; Matthew 27:15-66.

Today's reading: These chapters are about the "old rugged cross, the emblem of suffering and shame," and about the One who hung on that cross for you and for me.

Memory gem: "He was wounded for our transgressions, he was bruised for our iniquities: the chastisement of our peace was upon him; and with his stripes we are healed" (Isaiah 53:5).

Thought for today:

Jesus died for the salvation of all men. He sacrificed Himself to save His enemies. The Bible says in Romans 5:8, "that, while we were yet sinners [enemies], Christ died for us."

So, if He died for us, our sins really killed Him. When Jesus died, His Father was not receiving a gift from Him; He was making a gift to us. "God was in Christ, reconciling the world unto himself" (2 Corinthians 5:19). Jesus' death provided the atonement. As our High Priest He ministers that atonement to us.

The intelligent follower of Jesus Christ will never shift the blame to the shoulders of the Jewish people or to the Roman government, but will assume equal responsibility with every other man in this world for the tragedy that took place there on old Golgatha's hill. Dr. Loraine Boettner quotes a Christian litany which runs: "Who was the guilty? Who brought this upon Thee? Alas, my treason, Jesus, hath undone Thee. 'Twas I, Lord Jesus, I it was denied Thee: I crucified Thee."

Should we not all say this? The Jewish people, the Gentile world, all the nations of yesterday and today, the generals, the politicians, the diplomats, the scientists in their laboratories, the Protestants, and the Catholics, people of no religion—all of us should beat our breasts and cry for the forgiveness of God.

Not until we realize that we crucified Jesus can we really understand God's love and saving mercy. When we hear that moving spiritual, "Were you there when they crucified my Lord?" we must answer, "Yes, Lord, I was there." You and I were there. We were all there. Our sins put Him on the cross. His love, not Roman nails, held Him there. So let us live for Him and show by our lives of humble obedience that we do love Him who first loved us. (See note under Day/307.)

DAY / 307

Read Matthew 28:1-15; Mark 16:1-11; Luke 24:1-12; John 20:1-18; Luke 24:13-49; Mark 16:12, 13; John 20:19-23.

Today's reading: The resurrection is the highpoint of Christianity. Death could not hold the Lord of life in captivity. We serve a risen Saviour, who promises everlasting life to all who believe.

Memory gem: "Why seek ye the living among the dead? He is not here, but is risen" (Luke 24:5, 6).

Thought for today:

With the flashing glory of heaven, the mighty angel descended. The Bible says there was an earthquake caused by this event. The soldiers who were guarding the tomb fell, stunned, before the glory. The angel broke the seal and rolled back the great stone—yes, rolled it back and sat upon it. Death was conquered; Christ had risen. The dark night which had enshrouded the hearts of men for thousands of years was broken; the morning had come.

From this great stone, as from a pulpit, the angel preached the first sermon after the resurrection of Christ. The congregation were the holy women, who trembled with fear as the glorious being, with a countenance like lightning and in raiment white as snow, declared his brief message, his everlasting sermon of hope:

"Fear not ye: for I know that ye seek Jesus, which was crucified. He is not here: for he is risen, as he said. Come see the place where the Lord lay. And go quickly, and tell his disciples that he is risen from the dead" (Matthew 28:5-7).

That is the greatest news the world ever had. Christ was crucified, He died, and He arose from the dead. That is the gospel; that's hope, that's glory, that's life, that's immortality. Come and see; go and tell. That is the message of the angel to the world.

Note: (For Day/306 and Day/307.) The "seven words" of Jesus on the cross do not appear in all the Gospels; no one writer mentions more than three. Arranged in order they appear as follows:

1. "Father, forgive them" (Luke 23:34).
2. "You will be with me in paradise" (Luke 23:43, NIV).
3. "Woman, behold thy son" (John 19:26, 27).
4. "Why hast thou forsaken me?" (Matthew 27:46; Mark 15:34).
5. "I thirst" (John 19:28).
6. "It is finished" (John 19:30).
7. "I commend my spirit" (Luke 23:46).

DAY / 308

Read John 20:24 through chapter 21; Matthew 28:16-20; Mark 16:14-20; Luke 24:50-53; Acts 1:1-11.

Today's reading: Christ's earthly mission culminated in His ascension. During His last few days on earth, Jesus gave His followers their commission and the promise of power to accomplish the work.

Memory gem: "Ye shall receive power, after that the Holy Ghost is come upon you; and ye shall be witnesses unto me . . . unto the uttermost part of the earth" (Acts 1:8).

Thought for today:

Some people say. "If I get a call, I'll witness for Jesus. If I am employed by the church or some religious organization, then I will witness for Him." We are not to wait for that. We do not need a special call. We already have Christ's call, "Ye shall be witnesses unto me." There is no *if, but,* or *when* about it. The question is, Are you a witness?

Joseph Tyega, a national pastor in the Cameroons, West Africa, came to America for study at Princeton Seminary. During the winter vacation he underwent an operation at the Presbyterian Hospital in New York City. While in bed recuperating, he found himself with an absolute unbeliever on one side and a cynical graduate student of philosophy, the son of a foreign diplomat, on the other.

As Mr. Tyega was reading his Bible one day, the graduate student remarked: "Do you believe that stuff? It's foolish."

Whereupon Mr. Tyega replied, "It says right here that philosophers would call it foolish."

Through the witness of this African student, both the graduate student from Europe and the American skeptic accepted Christ as their Saviour.

And that is the way it goes around the world. Call the witnesses! "Ye are my witness," said Jesus.

Friend, what is your testimony? Are you a witness to the converting, saving, upholding power of Christ?

DAY / 309

Read Acts 1:12 through chapter 3.

Today's reading: The 120 disciples waited and prayed. The power came. Men and women, transformed by the Holy Spirit, launched the movement that swept the gospel of Jesus Christ to the ends of the earth.

Memory gem: "Peter said unto them, Repent, and be baptized every one of you in the name of Jesus Christ for the remission of sins, and ye shall receive the gift of the Holy Ghost" (Acts 2:38).

Thought for today:

By the wonderful manifestation of power on the Day of Pentecost, the timid disciples were fitted for a special work and transformed into fearless witnesses for Christ. They were enabled to preach the gospel in various foreign languages to the multitudes from all the civilized world who were gathered at Jerusalem for the Feast of Pentecost.

But more than this, they preached with power. Men were convicted of sin and cried out, "Men and brethren, what shall we do?" (Acts 2:37).

The apostles' sermons were not moral lectures, ethical discussions, or ingenious philosophical essays. Far from it. Their lanugage was simple, but their words came "in demonstration of the Spirit and of power" (1 Corinthians 2:4). Their subject was the resurrection of Christ as a fulfillment of prophecy. Even Peter, who had denied His Lord in fear, now became the mighty apostle whose sermons led to the conversion of three thousand people in one day.

O for that flame of living fire
Which shone so bright in saints of old;
Which bade their souls to heaven aspire,
Calm in distress, in danger bold!

Remember, Lord, the ancient days;
Renew Thy work, Thy grace restore;
And while to Thee our hearts we raise,
On us Thy Holy Spirit pour.
—William H. Bathurst

DAY / 310

Read Acts 4 and 5.

Today's reading: The embryo church ran into trouble almost immediately. Opposition and persecution from the religious establishment could be expected; but corruption among the believers?

Memory gem: "Why hath Satan filled thine heart to lie to the Holy Ghost? . . . Thou hast not lied unto men, but unto God" (Acts 5:3, 4).

Thought for today:

I never hear of many boys being named Ananias, do you? The people were bringing in money to forward the great gospel message, as people do today. God didn't tell them that they had to give it, but out of willing hearts they wanted to give. Of course, Ananias and Sapphira wanted to give something too, and they thought, "Here, we will sell our property. We will give part of it, because that will give us a high standing among the believers; and we will keep part of it, because that will give us a good bank account, something to fall back upon." And so this husband and wife agreed together to do this thing.

Ananias came in and laid the money down, and somehow he evidently directed the attention of the people and the apostles to it as though he and his wife had given all. The apostles asked, "Is this all?" He said, "Yes, it is."

Then the Holy Spirit revealed the whole thing to the apostles. You know the sad story. The man fell over dead. The Scripture says they "wound him up, and carried him out, and buried him." I like that expression "wound him up"—the burial cloth, I suppose—and that was the end of it. Then the wife came in later and told the same story, and the same thing happened to her.

As they breathed their last sighs, those around might have heard that whisper: "God means what He says. 'The way of transgressors is hard!'"

My friend, don't delay doing what God wants you to do.

Difficult or obscure words:

Acts 5:5. **"Gave up the ghost"**—literally: expired.

Acts 5:24. **"Doubted"**—rather: were perplexed.

DAY / 311

Read Acts 6 and 7.

Today's reading: A powerful sermon in defense of the gospel arouses such bitter animosity that the speaker becomes the first Christian martyr.

Memory gem: "He kneeled down, and cried with a loud voice, Lord, lay not this sin to their charge. And when he had said this he fell asleep" (Acts 7:60).

Thought for today:

Just before Stephen was put to death as a martyr, he gave a ringing testimony in which he mentioned two men especially—Joseph and Moses—both of whom are types of Christ. Both were used by God to save the people of Israel in times of trouble, but in each case the people had to accept them as lord as well as deliverer.

Those who heard Stephen that day recognized the lesson that he was trying to teach them. The very Christ who had died on the cross and had been rejected by them was to be their Saviour and Lord. Stephen told them plainly, as the apostle Peter had said on the Day of Pentecost, that this same Jesus whom they had crucified, God had made both Lord and Christ.

And this is the need of the Christian church today. Christ must be enthroned in the hearts of all believers, that they may be true disciples and witnesses, that they may be the real servants of God in this troubled world. Jesus as Master must have personal, direct, and absolute control of the one who accepts Him as Saviour.

If you have accepted Christ's death for you, then you no longer live for yourself, but unto Him. It is only when you make this full surrender daily that you begin to "grow in grace, and in the knowledge of our Lord and Saviour" (2 Peter 3:18). This is the work of sanctification, into which we must all enter.

Difficult or obscure words:

Acts 6:1. **"Grecians"**—literally: Hellenists; that is, Greek-speaking Jews. We have no indication that large numbers of Gentiles had become Christians at this early time.

Acts 6:3. **"Seven men"**—popularly called deacons, but this title is not applied to them in the Scriptures. Later, in Paul's epistles, men appointed to this kind of work were called deacons. Some commentators think that these seven men may be the "elders" of Acts 11:30 and onward.

DAY / 312

Read Acts 8 and 9.

Today's reading: We are introduced to the man who became perhaps the greatest Christian missionary—Saul of Tarsus, later known as Paul, Christ's apostle to the Gentiles.

Memory gem: "He is a chosen vessel unto me, to bear my name before the Gentiles, and kings, and the children of Israel" (Acts 9:15).

Thought for today:

Before Paul was converted he was armed with letters of arrest and went from city to city to seize and punish all who called Jesus "Lord." You remember the story of the Damascus road. Christ appeared to Paul in glory. Paul saw the shining face of Christ, the marks of the thorns, the nail-pierced hands, the wound in His side.

Paul *saw* the Lord, and his eyes were dim to this world ever after. A voice from heaven said, "Saul, Saul, why persecutest thou me?" Saul said, "Who art thou, Lord?" The answer came back, "I am Jesus whom thou persecutest" (Acts 9:4, 5).

How was Saul persecuting Jesus? He was persecuting Jesus in the person of His followers. "As ye have done it unto one of the least of these my brethren," Jesus declared, "ye have done it unto me" (Matthew 25:40).

When the first Christian martyr, Stephen, was stoned to death, Saul held the coats of the men who did the cruel work. He was with them in it. He was guilty of persecuting Jesus in the person of Stephen. But Paul never forgot something about that terrible experience: Stephen's face looked like the "face of an angel" (Acts 6:15).

The servants of Christ put to death by persecution were maligned as the offscouring of the earth, when they actually were the saints of the Lord. Think of the wonderful meeting someday in the better land when Paul meets those whom he persecuted! Someone has put these words into his mouth just before he himself died as a martyr for Jesus:

Saints, did you say!
Ah, those remembered faces!
Dear men and women that I sought and slew!
How when we met within the heavenly places
Will not I weep to Stephen and to you!

DAY / 313

Read Acts 10 and 11.

Today's reading: A series of providential events and a peculiar vision convinced Peter that God loves Gentiles. Believers in Antioch of Syria first acquired the title of Christians.

Memory gem: "The Lord knoweth them that are his. And, Let every one that nameth the name of Christ depart from iniquity" (2 Timothy 2:19).

Thought for today:

Living a Christian life is more than merely becoming a Christian, joining the church, making a profession of faith. It is the daily surrendering of our life to Christ and allowing Him to help us meet the daily grind—the problems, joys, sorrows, and sufferings of life.

My good friend, Pastor Jesse C. Stevens, now asleep in Christ, once preached a sermon on this subject of "How to Live a Christian Life," and it impressed me deeply. He said that first of all we must decide what a Christian is. There would be little use discussing how to live a Christian life, if we did not know what a Christian truly is. It is not merely church membership that makes a Christian, though that is important. One might join every church in the world, if that were possible, but that would not make him a Christian.

To be a Christian is to live the life of Christ, to obey Him as far as we know His will, to follow His example and teaching as it is recorded in the Holy Scriptures. It means to follow Him—in other words, to be a disciple, for that is what a disciple is, a follower. We read in Acts 11:26: "The disciples were called Christians first in Antioch."

The followers of Christ were called Christians because Christ was the main theme of their preaching, their teaching, their conversation, and their living.

We can live this Christian life only as there is a vital spiritual connection between us and Christ; and this is the work of the Holy Spirit. Our part of the Christian life is to read, study, digest, assimilate the Word of God under the guidance of the Holy Spirit.

Where is the best place to live the Christian life? Right where we are. When? Today, now. This is not only for our own good and blessing, but that we may help reveal Christ's love and saving power to all the world.

DAY / 314

Read Acts 12 and 13.

Today's reading: A puppet monarch, in order to gain popularity, executes one apostle and plans a repeat. A miracle thwarts his scheme. With chapter 13 we begin a new section concentrating on Paul's missionary adventures.

Memory gem: "We wrestle not against flesh and blood, but against principalities, against powers, against the rulers of the darkness of this world, against spiritual wickedness in high places" (Ephesians 6:12).

Thought for today:

In New Testament times, Elymas the sorcerer withstood Paul and Barnabas at Paphos on the island of Cyprus. The same heathen principles, the same claims, the same actions, the same powers, the same supposed dealing with the dead, the same communion with demons are in the world today.

We are not speaking of mere legendary tales about ghosts and goblins, black cats, or old women riding on broomsticks through the air. We are speaking of unseen powers which control the minds and bodies of people today and have done so since ancient times.

There is nothing actually new in the great occult explosion of today except that it is modernized, streamlined, and brought up to date in a hundred forms so as to be palatable to all classes of our society.

There is a danger that many may be drawn into the terrible delusion which is about to sweep the world. It is time for us to study God's Word as we have never studied it before. The Scriptures command us to "resist the devil," and the promise is that he will flee from us.

Surely Christians who have apostolic warning of such things (see Galatians 5:19-21) will have nothing to do with the delusive practices of ancient or modern times.

Difficult or obscure words:

Acts 12:4. **"Easter"**—literally: Passover. This is the only place in the Bible where the translators used this Anglo-Saxon name of a pagan festival instead of the correct name for the Hebrew Passover.

Ephesians 6:12. **"Spiritual wickedness"**—rather: spiritual hosts of wickedness.

DAY / 315

Read Acts 14 and 15.

Today's reading: The report of great numbers of Gentiles being converted brought to the surface an unanswered question in the early church: Should these new Christians observe Mosaic ceremonies? Notice the words of Peter in our memory gem.

Memory gem: "We believe that through the grace of our Lord Jesus Christ we shall be saved, even as they" (Acts 15:11).

Thought for today:

"There is no such contrast as is often claimed to exist between the Old and the New Testament, the law of God and the gospel of Christ, the requirements of the Jewish and those of the Christian dispensation. Every soul saved in the former dispensation was saved by Christ as verily as we are saved by Him today. Patriarchs and prophets were Christians. The gospel promise was given to the first pair in Eden, when they had by transgression separated themselves from God. The gospel was preached to Abraham. The Hebrews all drank of that spiritual Rock, which was Christ."—*Signs of the Times,* September 14, 1882.

"Shrouded in the pillar of cloud, the world's Redeemer held communion with Israel. Let us not say, then, that they had not Christ. When the people thirsted in the wilderness, and gave themselves up to murmuring and complaint, Christ was to them what He is to us—a Saviour full of tender compassion, the Mediator between them and God. After we have done our part to cleanse the soul temple from the defilement of sin, Christ's blood avails for us, as it did for ancient Israel."—*Youth's Instructor,* July 18, 1901.

Difficult or obscure words:

Acts 14:12. **"Jupiter . . . Mercurius"**—the Greek Zeus, chief of the gods and his son Hermes.

DAY / 316

Read Acts 16 and 17.

Today's reading: Paul, on his second missionary journey, first revisited some of the cities he had evangelized before. Then, by divine direction, he entered the European continent.

Memory gem: "Study to shew thyself approved unto God, a workman that needeth not to be ashamed, rightly dividing the word of truth" (2 Timothy 2:15).

Thought for today:

While it may be interesting to know what position a minister holds, it is more important to know what he preaches. Is it the truth? Is it in harmony with the Word of God? These are the questions we need to settle, as did the ancient Bereans who, according to Acts 17:11, "received the word with all readiness of mind, and searched the scriptures daily, whether those things were so."

That is what many need today—the appeal to the Scriptures rather than to denominational prejudice. It would be as unreasonable for a judge, before he heard the evidence, to pass sentence in a court case on the grounds that he did not like the defendant's name, as it is to condemn a preacher, a sermon, or a radiobroadcast which we have not heard, merely on the ground that he or it is not within our own denominational circle.

It is good to remember that millions are where they are, as to religious denomination, through the accident of birth or association rather than through study or conviction. We need to recognize that others are as honest as we—and as anxious for the light. But opportunities differ, and environments are often not the same. Let us not attempt to judge human hearts. God alone can do this.

While one says, "This is the way!" and another says, "No, this is the way!" Jesus holds out His nail-pierced hands to us and says, "I am the Way!" The world has drifted a long, long journey from that Way and needs to turn back. The church needs to turn back. We all need to turn back to the Way revealed in God's Word. The religious thinkers of today need to forget their divergent philosophies and come back to 1 John 1:7 and obey it in simple faith. It reads: "But if we walk in the light, as he is in the light, we have fellowship one with another, and the blood of Jesus Christ his Son cleanseth us from all sin."

DAY / 317

Read James.

Today's reading: Many Bible students believe that this is the first of the general epistles to be written. The author was probably the James who presided at the Jerusalem council (Acts 15), one of Christ's stepbrothers.

Memory gem: "To him that knoweth to do good, and doeth it not, to him it is sin" (James 4:17).

Thought for today:

The greatest sinner in town may be a preacher; he may be a Sunday School teacher or the leading businessman. He may or may not be a professed Christian. This greatest sinner may be an old man or an old woman, a young man or a young woman. Oh, friend, the solemn truth is that the greatest sinner in this town is the person who has had the greatest light but fails to walk in it. And our memory gem for today proves that statement.

You say, "I know those things are true. I know I should walk in the light I have heard—in church, in reading my Bible, over the radio—and I plan to do it; but it is not convenient now. Don't push me, preacher! I will do it when I get ready. I really will."

But, friend, don't you know that every day, every hour, every second, that you fail to walk in that recognized light, you are piling up a load of sin on your record? You believe that message you have heard, yet you are holding back. You still cherish that secret sin, that unfaithfulness, that dishonesty. You are still clinging to that liquor bottle. You are a slave to that pipe, that cigar, that cut of tobacco, that pinch of snuff, that cigarette. You still hold onto that practice, that sin. God knows all about it—and probably more people know than you think.

Every man and woman who knows to do good and does it not, "to him it is sin." The Bible says so. There is no middle ground. Jesus said, "He that is not with me is against me; and he that gathereth not with me scattereth abroad" (Matthew 12:30).

There is only one way to be ready to face God in the judgment, and that is to fall on your knees and say right now, "God, forgive me! In Christ's name give me a new life and help me to live right before my children. Help me to be true and to follow the light I know." God will forgive you, and you will be surprised to find that your friends will forgive you too!

DAY / 318

Today's reading: While Paul worked in Corinth, he learned of certain errors that had already crept into the church at Thessalonica. He wrote a letter to set matters straight.

Memory gem: "We which are alive and remain shall be caught up together with them in the clouds, to meet the Lord in the air: and so shall we ever be with the Lord. Wherefore comfort one another with these words" (1 Thessalonians 4:17, 18). (Read carefully verses 13 to 18.)

Thought for today:

Christian believers everywhere have a right to hear these words read to them in times of sorrow by their pastors and ministers. Notice: "Wherefore comfort one another with these words." This is apostolic authority for words of comfort when our hearts are broken.

Personally, I know how comforting these words are. Some time ago we lost one of the brightest jewels in our family. She was beautiful, sweet of character, loving, and a great lover of the Lord Jesus Christ, and suddenly she was taken from us. In two terrible hours she was gone from us. Then how wonderful were these words, how blessed was the hope, the hope of "the glorious appearing of the great God and our Saviour Jesus Christ" and "our gathering together unto him" (Titus 2:13; 2 Thessalonians 2:1).

The believer is not immortal now, but he has eternal life, which is promised to him in Jesus Christ (see 1 John 5:11, 12). Immortality will be given him at the second coming of the Lord, "in a moment in the twinkling of an eye, at the last trump" (1 Corinthians 15:52).

The only way to become immortal and to live for all eternity with Christ is to accept God's plan by accepting God's Man, His only Son, our Lord Jesus Christ. How do we do this? By receiving Him as Saviour and Lord.

Can we imagine what our sensations will be on that resurrection morning? We cannot, of course. Glorious coming day! Let us lift up our heads and rejoice, for our redemption draweth nigh. Jesus is coming! When we hear the words of Christ, "Surely I come quickly," may our response and prayer be, "Even so, come, Lord Jesus" (Revelation 22:20).

DAY / 319

Read 2 Thessalonians; Acts 18:18 through 19:22; and 1 Corinthians 1.

Today's reading: Some believers in Thessalonica got the idea that Jesus would return right away; therefore, they reasoned, they should do nothing but wait. Paul had to correct that notion by a second letter from Corinth. He left Corinth, reported in Jerusalem, returned to Antioch, and then started a third journey. Arriving at Ephesus, he ran into several problems, including disturbed reports of conditions in Corinth.

Memory gem: "With thee is the fountain of life: in thy light shall we see light" (Psalm 36:9).

Thought for today:

Notice with me 2 Thessalonians 2:10, 11: "They received not the love of the truth, that they might be saved. And for this cause God shall send them strong delusion, that they should believe a lie."

It is a terrible thing to believe a lie, isn't it? But those people are really going to believe it.

Nearly the whole world refuses truth, rejects truth, neglects truth, puts off, hesitates, waits, stops, doesn't obey, doesn't do, doesn't follow. Finally the Holy Spirit leaves them, and they believe a lie. This is the great delusion, the strong delusion.

Friend, I want to be delivered from strong delusions, and I believe the only way is to do as Cornelius did. If you will read the whole chapter of Acts 10, you will find that Cornelius was a man who already prayed to God. He was a praying man; he gave money to God; he loved the people of God; he even had services in his own home. He had gone a long way in the service of the Lord, and God had blessed him. He might have said, "Well, now I am a servant of God; the Lord helps me; He accepts my prayers; why should I accept this advanced light? I am receiving the blessing of God already." But when Cornelius heard about a man who might bring him more light, what did he do? Friend, he made a great effort to get that man to his house so that he might receive that advanced truth. Had Corenlius not done that, he would have drifted away into darkness.

Oh, friend, be like Cornelius. Look for the light in order to walk in it, not merely for curiosity. "If any man will do his will, he shall know of the doctrine" (John 7:17).

Today's reading: As Paul begins to deal with the problems in the Corinthian church, he first exalts Jesus Christ as the only hope of salvation; then he plunges into a treatment of the epidemic of sin.

Memory gem: "I determined not to know anything among you, save Jesus Christ, and him crucified" (1 Corinthians 2:2).

Thought for today:

A few persons were watching a blind man who had taken his stand on a bridge in a certain great city where he was reading from his Braille Bible. A man on his way home paused a moment out of curiosity—he wondered what was going on.

Just then the blind man was reading Acts 4:12: "For there is none other name under heaven given among men, whereby we must be saved." And as the man looked on, the blind man lost his place. While trying to find it with his fingers he kept repeating the last words he had read: "None other name, none other name!"

Some laughed at his embarrassment, but this man on the edge of the group walked away deeply impressed, for he had been under conviction of sin for some time. He had altered his habits, he had made good resolutions, he had performed religious exercises, but still he hadn't found peace.

Ringing in his ears were those words: "None other name, none other name!"—the words the blind man had been repeating. When he retired at night, those words kept chiming in his soul: "None other name, none other name!"

At last he found the victory. "I see it now," he said. "I have been trying to find peace through my works, my resolutions, my reformation, my prayers. It is Jesus alone who can save me. Lord, I receive You as my Saviour." From that moment the joy of salvation was his.

Oh, friend, there is no other name in earth or heaven, no other name but His. In no other name may we be forgiven. Will you not accept Him here and now?

DAY / 321

Today's reading: Paul gets down to specifics on the subject of sins plaguing even God's people. The apostle offers positive suggestions for curing the plague.

Memory gem: "What? know ye not that your body is the temple of the Holy Ghost which is in you, which ye have of God, and ye are not your own? For ye are bought with a price; therefore glorify God in your body, and in your spirit, which are God's" (1 Corinthians 6:19, 20).

Thought for today:

If each of us is a living temple for the indwelling of God and for His glory, it is supremely important how we live. How do we treat God's temple? Is it ever defiled by our way of living, thinking, eating, drinking, or whatever we may name?

We should ask ourselves this question, "Does our living temple need cleansing?" When we give ourselves to Christ as His servants, we are dedicated to Him. In 1 Corinthians 6:11, it is written: "But ye are washed, but ye are sanctified, but ye are justified in the name of the Lord Jesus, and by the Spirit of our God."

In the literal temple on earth, which was a figure of the heavenly temple above, the Father and the Son had their dwelling place. Strange and wonderful is the promise of Jesus concerning the living temple, man himself. Listen to the words of our Saviour as recorded in John 14:23: "If a man love me, he will keep my words and my Father will love him, and we will come unto him, and make our abode with him."

Christians are the temples of the Holy Ghost. God's Spirit lives in every Christian, unless He has been grieved away by an evil life. This is why Christians should put away every wrong habit. We should constantly remember that we are living temples and that God, by His Spirit, dwells within us. This will make life different, wonderful, glorious, happy, and successful.

Note: 1 Corinthians 6:12 is evidently a Greek proverb current in Paul's day. As is often the case, a translation loses the sense of the original saying, in this case a play on words. A paraphrase that suggests the meaning of the proverb is this: "All things are in my power, but I shall not be brought under the power of any." Paul certainly did not mean to teach that "all things" mentioned in verses 9 and 10 "are lawful"!

DAY / 322

Today's reading: Again and again the apostle points to control of the physical body as an important part of maintaining spiritual health.

Memory gem: "Whether therefore ye eat, or drink, or whatsoever ye do, do all to the glory of God" (1 Corinthians 10:31).

Thought for today:

Real temperance is absolute abstinence from all that is evil, and the moderate and proper use of that which is good. Self-discipline is essential to temporal achievement in this world.

"Every man that striveth for the mastery is temperate in all things" (1 Corinthians 9:25). Those who succeeded in winning the laurel crown of victory at the Olympic games were temperate in their eating and drinking. They took the right kind of exercise. They did this to obtain an earthly crown which would soon fade away. But how much more necessary it is for us in our spiritual quest, as the apostle reminds us in verse 25: "Now they do it to obtain a corruptible crown; but we an incorruptible."

Let me say this: We are not going to have perfect temperance by merely shutting off intoxicating drinks, bad as they are. We must start by civilizing the kitchen. As Henry Ward Beecher said, "We must apply scientific wisdom and knowledge to the department of cookery. Bad cooking is a perpetual temptation to drink." We are not to be indifferent to the health of the body. We are not to deceive ourselves into thinking that intemperance is no sin and will not affect our spirituality. Yes, eating wisely is a part of temperate living. And after all is said and done, temperance must begin in our thinking. States of mind and prevailing habits of thought register themselves in bodily, as well as moral, conditions. Right thinking leads to health. Right thinking leads to happiness. Right thinking leads to God, "for as [a man] thinketh in his heart, so is he," declares the Holy Word in Proverbs 23:7. Therefore, we appeal to you, friend, in the words of Holy Writ: "Gird up the loins of your mind, be sober" (1 Peter 1:13).

Then the fruits of true temperance will be in your life, will be seen in you wholly—spirit, soul, and body.

Difficult or obscure words:

1 Corinthians 10:25. **"Shambles"**—the public market.

DAY / 323

Read 1 Corinthians 12 through 14.

Today's reading: In the middle of a study on the "gifts of the Spirit" lies the "love chapter," which, the apostle says, shows "a more excellent way."

Memory gem: "[Love] doth not behave itself unseemly, seeketh not her own, is not easily provoked, thinketh no evil" (1 Corinthians 13:5).

Thought for today:

The real secret of the successful Christian life, the obedient life, the life in harmony with the commandments of God, is the love of Christ in the heart. Love does no harm to others. Love does not hate, love does not rejoice in the troubles of other people. Love forgives, love is patient. It has no envy. It is not full of spiritual pride. It is not selfish, is not easily provoked, does not always see something wrong in the acts of others.

That's what often happens in families: the first love cools off, and the husband and wife do not treat each other as they did at the beginning of their marriage. If this is the condition in your family, then repent and do the first works. Do you remember how you used to treat the girl you married? Do you remember how careful you were of your personal appearance? Yes, you were well groomed. You had a smiling face. You performed little acts of courtesy. You brought her gifts and flowers. You expressed your love. Well, do those things again and see what happens.

And you, too, wife. Do you remember when you first fell in love? Act in the same way now. Ask God to help you, and He will.

It is the same in the Christian life. If we perform our religious duties merely as duties, our spiritual experience will be a drudgery. There are too many long-faced Christians today, Christians who have lost the joy of their salvation. This is because their love is cold and their service is based on a bleak duty rather than upon the outworking of the love of God in the heart. God's love is the same in all kinds of weather. No matter what happens, God still loves us, and it is our privilege to love Him.

DAY / 324

Read 1 Corinthians 15 and 16; Acts 19:23 through 20:1.

Today's reading: Among other errors the apostle sought to correct was a denial of the resurrection. After finishing the Corinthian letter, we turn back to Paul's experiences in Ephesus.

Memory gem: "If in this life only we have hope in Christ, we are of all men most miserable. But now is Christ risen from the dead, and become the firstfruits of them that slept" (1 Corinthians 15:19, 20).

Thought for today:

Rich and poor, believer and unbeliever, saint and sinner, the brave man and the coward—we must all face the great enemy, death. Here we need one of the greatest of all chapters in the Bible, the fifteenth chapter of 1 Corinthians. Through our tears we can repeat its promises by the graveside of those we love.

The dead shall live again. Death is a temporary separation. We may die, but we shall live again if we are the children of God.

As far as a sinful man is concerned, death is the end. Science has done great things, but it cannot raise the dead. The greatest scientist on earth cannot bring life to the nonliving. Life comes only from antecedent life. Men can take life, but they cannot give life.

When you are near the valley of the shadow, think of these words: "We shall all be changed. . . . This mortal must put on immortality."

Pointing to the Congo River, David Livingstone asked the tribesmen of interior Africa, "Where does your great river go?" They always answered, "It is lost in the sands." They did not know that beyond the sands the mighty Congo flowed into a limitless ocean.

God's child is not lost in the sands of time, nor forever imprisoned in the narrow tomb, but he will find his way at last to the measureless ocean of God's immortality.

Difficult or obscure words:

1 Corinthians 16:23. **"Maranatha"**—an Aramaic expression meaning "our Lord comes" or "our Lord, come."

Acts 19:24. **"Diana"**—the Greek goddess Artemis. The Roman Diana was not the same deity.

DAY / 325

Read 2 Corinthians 1 through 3.

Today's reading: After Paul sent his rather stern letter (1 Corinthians) to the troubled church, he worried that he might have been too severe. He dispatched a second one from Macedonia before going on to Corinth in person.

Memory gem: "Ye are manifestly declared to be the epistle of Christ ministered by us, written not with ink, but with the Spirit of the living God; not in tables of stone, but in fleshy tables of the heart" (2 Corinthians 3:3).

Thought for today:

If one is to be a letter from Christ, he must seek to obey the teachings of Christ and follow the example of Christ—all by the grace of Christ. Remember, my friend, you are a letter from Christ to those where you work in the shop, in the office, the home, on the farm, on shipboard, at the airport. They may never hear a chapter of Scripture read or a sermon. Therefore, they must hear of Jesus from you.

One big question that faces us is this: Does the world see Jesus in me, in you? What do they see when they look at us? Remember, you are the best Christian that somebody will ever know. In the Bible we have the gospel according to Matthew, according to Mark, according to Luke, according to John; but what is the gospel according to you, according to me?

An anonymous poet wrote:

You are writing a gospel,
A chapter each day.
By deeds that you do,
By words that you say.
Men read what you write,
Whether faithless or true;
Say, what is the gospel
According to you?

Millions of the busy, friendly people around us do not know where they are spiritually. The experience of too many in our generation is like the last message of Amelia Earhart, flying over the South Pacific with her navigator. From somewhere off New Guinea, in the gathering tropical storm, her failing radio spelled out the words: "Fuel almost gone. Position doubtful."

Are you a letter from Christ, or is your position doubtful?

DAY / 326

Today's reading: In these chapters the great apostle gives instruction on various aspects of practical godliness, drawing often on his own experience for examples.

Memory gem: "Behold, now is the accepted time; behold, now is the day of salvation" (2 Corinthians 6:2).

Thought for today:

When Dwight L. Moody was holding meetings in Farwell Hall, Chicago, he spoke on the life of Christ every Sunday night. Listen to his words:

"When Mr. Sankey and I were in Chicago preaching, we had been five Sunday nights on the life of Christ. We had taken Him from the cradle, and on the fifth night we had just gotten Him into the hands of Pilate, and Pilate didn't know what to do with Him.

"I made one of the greatest mistakes that night that I have ever made. When I had nearly finished my sermon, I said, 'I want you to take this home with you, and next Sunday night we will see what you will do with Him.'

"I started home. They were ringing the fire alarm, and it proved to be the death knell of the city, the great Chicago fire. People rushed through the streets, crazed with fear, and some of those who were at the meeting were burned to death. Oh, what a mistake to put off the answer! May God forgive me. Today the Saviour calls; for refuge fly!"

So I am not going to put off until next week my appeal to anyone to take a stand for Christ. Do it now! Tomorrow may not be yours. "Now is the time of salvation." Now! Now! Now!

Are you putting off, delaying, neglecting the great decision? Won't you make it now? Simply bow your head with me and say: "O God, I come to Thee in the name of Christ. Forgive my sins. Guide me. Lead me into the truth of Thy Word. By Thy grace, I will follow Thee to the end. In Christ's name. Amen."

Difficult or obscure words:

2 Corinthians 5:11. **"Terror"**—an unfortunate translation of a word elsewhere always translated "fear." The "fear of the Lord" always means a feeling of profound reverence for the Lord.

2 Corinthians 6:12. **"Straitened"**—restricted, or restrained.

2 Corinthians 6:12. **"Bowels"**—a term used by the ancients to mean the center of emotional feeling.

DAY / 327

Read 2 Corinthians 7:2 through chapter 10.

Today's reading: In chapter 7 Paul expresses his joy in knowing that his first letter accomplished its purpose; it brought "godly sorrow" that worked "repentance to salvation not be repented of."

Memory gem: "A new heart also will I give you, and a new spirit will I put within you: and I will take away the stony heart out of your flesh, and I will give you an heart of flesh" (Ezekiel 36:26).

Thought for today:

What we need today is the new man! Culture, education, science—these are good, but not good enough. The president of a great university looks at the world about us and says that education is not a sure hope, but it is our only hope. But, friend, it will require more than education. The selfish hearts of men must be changed. They need a new nature, a regeneration, and this can come only from God.

A man moved onto an old farm and went to the pump for a bucket of water. But the next-door neighbor was there and said "Look here, my friend; that water is not safe. The family who lived here before used it, and it poisoned all of them."

"Is that so?" replied the man. "I'm glad you told me. I'll soon make it safe. I have a remedy." So he went out to his truck and got a big bucket of white paint and a can of putty. He puttied up all the cracks and painted the pump. He stepped back to look at his fine-looking job. Then he said, "Now I'm sure it is all right—it looks good."

What a fool to think he could change the water by painting the pump! So it is with every single one of us; we must be changed inside, regenerated, born again spiritually, before the part of the world which we can influence can be as it ought to be. Make the fountain good, and the stream will be good. When God makes us new men and women, everything will be new, for we will be "created in righteousness and true holiness" (Ephesians 4:24).

Difficult or obscure words:

2 Corinthians 7:11; 10:6. **"Revenge"**—rather: punishment of the immoral offender. Verb: to punish.

2 Corinthians 8:1. **"We do you to wit"**—old English for "we wish to make known to you."

DAY / 328

Read 2 Corinthians 11 through 13; Acts 20:2, 3.

Today's reading: In these closing chapters of the letter, Paul mentions the experiences he has endured in Christ's service—several of them not detailed in the book of Acts.

Memory gem: "He said unto me, My grace is sufficient for thee: for my strength is made perfect in weakness" (2 Corinthians 12:9).

Thought for today:

"The apostle Paul was highly honored of God, being taken in holy vision to the third heaven, where he looked upon scenes whose glories might not be revealed to mortals. Yet all this did not lead him to boastfulness or self-confidence. He realized the importance of constant watchfulness and self-denial. . . .

"Paul had a very humble opinion of his own advancement in the Christian life. He says, 'Not as though I had already attained, either were already perfect.' Philippians 3:12. He speaks of himself as the chief of sinners. Yet Paul had been highly honored of the Lord. He had been taken, in holy vision, to the third heaven, and had there received revelations of divine glory which he could not be permitted to make known. . . .

"Paul had a view of heaven, and in discoursing on the glories there, the best thing he could do was to not try to describe them. He tells us that eye had not seen nor ear heard, neither had entered into the heart of man the things which God hath prepared for those that love Him. So you may put your imagination to the stretch, you may try to the very best of your abilities to take in and consider the eternal weight of glory; and yet your finite senses, faint and weary with the effort, cannot grasp it, for there is an infinity beyond." Ellen G. White Comments, *SDA Bible Commentary,* vol. 6, p. 1107.

Difficult or obscure words:

2 Corinthians 11:6. **"Rude"**—literally: unskilled.

DAY / 329

Read Galatians 1 through 3.

Today's reading: During the three months Paul spent in Corinth (see Acts 20:3), he learned of the demoralizing work by "Judaizers"—converted Jews who insisted that Christians must observe all the Jewish ceremonies. Keep in mind Paul's purpose in writing as you read this letter.

Memory gem: "I am crucified with Christ: nevertheless I live; yet not I, but Christ liveth in me; and the life which I now live in the flesh I live by the faith of the Son of God, who loved me, and gave himself for me" (Galatians 2:20).

Thought for today:

This is regeneration—being born again. Now the Holy Spirit's mighty power has brought about the miracle of spiritual creation. We are new creatures (a new creation) in Christ Jesus.

When a man has a new heart or mind, his life will be changed. If he claims to be born again and beats his wife, cheats in business, and forgets to pray, you may be pretty sure that his claims are greatly exaggerated, for a new heart makes a new life. This is the only way we can live a happy Christian life.

We may not understand how God changes a man's heart, but we can see the effect of the change. We cannot see the wind, but we can see the evidence of it—the drifting clouds, the waving trees, the nodding flowers, the tossing waves. "So," says Jesus, "is every one that is born of the Spirit" (John 3:8).

We have seen men and women, time after time, have this wonderful experience; and you can have it too, friend, if you surrender yourself to Jesus. He can help you. He is anxious to help you and to deliver you from all your sins and bad habits.

Difficult or obscure words:

Galatians 1:13. **"Conversation"**—rather: conduct.

Note: In all of Paul's letters except this one he found something to say in commendation. Nothing of that nature appears here. Rather, he says, "I marvel" (Galatians 1:6). He is amazed at the believers' departure from the true faith so soon.

DAY / 330

Read Galatians 4 through 6.

Today's reading: Precious gems of truth sparkle all through Paul's argument in defense of righteousness by faith. Our memory gem picks out one of them.

Memory gem: "Because ye are sons, God hath sent forth the Spirit of his Son into your hearts, crying, Abba, Father" (Galatians 4:6).

Thought for today:

This Spirit, which is the Holy Spirit, is the Comforter whom Jesus promised. We know that the witness of this Spirit, this Comforter, who is to comfort and confirm us in the faith, is true; for He is called "the Spirit of truth" (John 14:17).

But how does the Holy Spirit bear witness? The answer is, by bringing to our remembrance the Word which has been recorded, the Word which He inspired holy men to write. When this Word is brought to our remembrance, it is as if the Holy Spirit were speaking directly to us in an audible voice. So we can by faith accept the fact that we are the children of God. Then we can cry, "Father, Father," as the apostle says.

What a glorious truth then breaks upon our soul! We realize that we are truly the children of God. He is our Father. We are not alone in this world. We are not alone in this universe. We are not alone at any hour of the day or night. We now know that we have the witness in ourselves. It is not merely an impression, an emotion that may pass away, but the actual word and promise of God Himself. God does not ask us to base our faith upon any thing unsubstantial as an impression or an emotion. He gives us something more reliable than that. Anyone who trusts in the feelings of his own heart is a fool, for the Scripture says so (see Proverbs 28:26). The witness that we are to trust is the unchangeable, unfailing, eternal Word of God. And we may have this witness through the Spirit in our own hearts. Then we can say, "Thanks be unto God for his unspeakable gift" (2 Corinthians 9:15).

Difficult or obscure words:

Galatians 4:6. **"Abba, Father"**—two words meaning "father," the first Aramaic (the common speech of Palestine) and the second Greek (see also Mark 14:36 and Romans 8:15).

DAY / 331

Today's reading: Apparently shortly after completing the letter to the Galatians, Paul wrote to the Romans. In this epistle he covers the same subject—righteousness by faith in Jesus.

Memory gem: "I am not ashamed of the gospel of Christ: for it is the power of God unto salvation to every one that believeth" (Romans 1:16).

Thought for today:

The apostle Paul was not ashamed of the gospel because the gospel actually did the things he claimed for it. It actually changed men's lives. When the apostle Paul preached the gospel, people were converted. Thieves became honest. The impure became pure. The faithless became true. I'll tell you something, friend: the gospel does the very same thing today. It changes men. It changes them from inside out. It is more than just a coating or veneer of civilization and culture on the outside. The gospel changes the heart by the miracle-working power of God. It brings conversion, justification, sanctification, and finally, when Jesus comes, glorification.

I have seen lives changed by this miracle power of God revealed in the gospel. The mail coming in to the Voice of Prophecy tells us of hundreds, thousands, who have been gloriously changed by the presence of the gospel.

We do not need to be ashamed of the gospel today, for it is still power—"the power of God unto salvation to every one that believeth." Will you believe? Will you give your heart to Christ? If you want to break the chains of habit, give your heart to Jesus. If you want to overcome in the battle of life, give your heart to Him. If you want to change your thinking, give your heart to Christ. If you want to change your ways of living, give your heart to Christ. If you want to be happy in this world, give your heart to Him.

Just now say, "I will, Lord—God helping me, I will accept Christ as my personal Saviour. Fill my heart with Thy Spirit. Point out to me my sins and give me grace to overcome. Send the Holy Spirit into my life to cleanse me and to lead me. This I ask in Jesus' name. Amen."

And, friends, He will do it, and you will find as the apostle did that the gospel of Christ is "the power of God unto salvation to every one that believeth."

DAY / 332

Read Romans 3 and 4.

Today's reading: In the first two chapters Paul bore down hard on those who prided themselves on their ancestry. Now he places their Jewish ancestry in proper perspective, though making plain that ritual works of the law cannot earn salvation.

Memory gem: "Do we then make void the law through faith? God forbid: we establish the law" (Romans 3:31).

Thought for today:

What does the phrase mean, the "righteousness of God without the law" (Romans 3:21)? Is this in harmony with the statement that all God's commandments are righteousness? Yes. There is no contradiction. God's law is not ignored in the process of righteousness by faith. Notice carefully now. Who gave the law? Christ gave it. How did He speak it? As one having authority, even as God. The law came from Christ as well as from the Father, because They are one. It is simply a declaration of the righteousness of His character. Therefore the righteousness that comes by the faith of Jesus Christ is the same righteousness that is revealed in the law.

On one side stands the law, a swift witness against every sinner. It cannot change, and it cannot and will not call a sinner a righteous man. It cannot be bribed by any amount of penance or good deeds or works. On the other side stands Christ, full of grace as well as truth. He calls the sinner to Him and offers to forgive him. At last, weary and in despair of his struggle to get righteousness from the law, the sinner listens to the voice of Jesus and flees to Him. Hiding in Christ, he is covered by His righteousness.

And now look at the change. The sinner receives by faith from Christ what he could never have obtained by struggling. He receives it as a gift. He has not earned it. He has believed, and it was counted to him for righteousness. He now has all the righteousness that the law requires, and it is the genuine article. The law, which formerly condemned him, now witnesses to the genuineness of his righteousness. Before God he is a righteous man, with the righteousness "which is through the faith of Christ, the righteousness which is of God by faith" (Philippians 3:9).

That is the only way to be safe, my friend. And you can be certainly sure this very day if you believe on the Lord Jesus Christ as your complete and perfect righteousness.

DAY / 333

Read Romans 5 through 7.

Today's reading: We penetrate to the heart of Paul's theology. It will help us to keep in mind that Paul's purpose is to overthrow confidence in works, not to destroy the moral law.

Memory gem: "Know ye not, that to whom ye yield yourselves servants to obey, his servants ye are to whom ye obey; whether of sin unto death, or of obedience unto righteousness?" (Romans 6:16).

Thought for today:

If faith establishes the law, it does not abolish it. The law of God points out sin. "I had not known sin, but by the law" (Romans 7:7). In fact, if there were no law there would be no sin. "Where no law is, there is no transgression" (Romans 4:15).

Numerous cults now deny the reality of sin. They claim we have but to free our minds from the idea of sin. One writer expresses a popular idea that "there is no law save that which he himself imposes."

When we look at the terrible increase of crime and violence today, we are convinced that many have accepted this theory. They have rejected the law of God and are depending upon mere unsanctified human will to impose a check upon the downward rush to destruction.

The Bible tells us that sin is the transgression of God's law. The wages of sin is death (see Romans 6:23), and all have sinned (see Romans 3:23). Man cannot be justified by his own works, because the penalty of sin is not works but death. Christ died for our sins (see 1 Corinthians 15:3). He paid the penalty demanded by the law. Christ took the sinner's place—our place. He died for us. We accept, by faith, His vicarious death for our sins. God has already accepted it. God's holy law is satisfied. We stand justified before it—not by our works nor our righteousness, but by Christ's righteousness imputed to us. Thus Christ's death upon the cross, to meet the death penalty for transgression of the law, forever vindicates the law as the righteousness of God.

Jesus paid it all,
All to Him I owe;
Sin had left a crimson stain:
He washed it white as snow.
—Mrs. E. M. Hall

DAY / 334

Read Romans 8 and 9.

Today's reading: Paul now turns from the painful struggle with sin to a view of the peace and freedom offered in Christ. Then in chapter 9 he takes up the problem of why God's chosen people refuse to accept the salvation of the gospel.

Memory gem: "He that spared not his own Son, but delivered him up for us all, how shall he not with him also freely give us all things?" (Romans 8:32).

Thought for today:

Not only did Jesus reveal God to men, He also demonstrated the possibility of a life of victory over sin. He was "in all points tempted like as we are, yet without sin" (Hebrews 4:15). And by this sinless life He condemned all sin in human life, as we read in Romans 8:3: "What the law could not do, in that it was weak through the flesh, God sending his own Son in the likeness of sinful flesh, and for sin [that is, as the sacrifice for our sins], condemned sin in the flesh."

That is one reason why some men hated Christ when He was here. The very purity and holiness of His life condemned them. That is why some hate Him now—hate His doctrines, hate His teaching, hate His gospel. They resent it.

Christ has not only given us the perfect example of God among men, but He has made it possible for us to live a holy and righteous life here on earth. He has revealed the power of God, which is ours as a gift from heaven, all based upon the supreme gift of His own life on Calvary's cross.

Our situation is like that of a man in prison, condemned to die. Someone brings him a key. He may unlock the prison door and go free. If he does not, it is his own fault if he dies in the dungeon. So the key that God has given us through Christ is His grace, His divine gift. Oh, friend, use that key; unlock the door.

Difficult or obscure words:

Romans 8:19, 20, 39. **"Creature"**—rather: creation, as the same word is translated in verse 22. The word in this sense means "the thing (or things) created."

Romans 9:13. **"Hated"**—a common biblical expression meaning "regarded with less favor," or "loved less" (for similar usage see Genesis 29:30, 31; Luke 14:26; John 12:25).

DAY / 335

Today's reading: Paul continues his appeal to Israelites of the flesh, wishing that all of them would believe the good news about Jesus Christ.

Memory gem: "If thou shalt confess with thy mouth the Lord Jesus, and shalt believe in thine heart that God hath raised him from the dead, thou shalt be saved" (Romans 10:9).

Thought for today:

Believe in Jesus Christ. Believe the gospel, the good news about Him—that He took our place on the cross and died for our sins, that He was buried in Joseph's new tomb, that He rose again from the dead, that He ascended to heaven. We must believe that He is our Saviour from sin, and that through faith in Him we have eternal life.

And before we can believe that He saved us from our sins, we must believe that there is such a thing as sin, and we must believe that we are sinners.

If we truly believe, we will repent before we are baptized. We must be able to say from a true heart, "I believe that Jesus Christ is the Son of God." A person must be able to understand what he is doing before he is ready for baptism. He must be a candidate for eternal life. He must believe the gospel. He must repent. He must pray.

No one can believe for you. No one can ask for baptism in your place, repent in your place, or pray in your place. No, you must do it yourself. You must believe, pray, confess, be baptized.

If there is a soul reading these words who is not baptized, do not put it off. Start to prepare for it. Such is the command of our Lord Jesus Christ. Such is His example for us.

DAY / 336

Read Romans 12 through 14.

Today's reading: In these chapters Paul gives practical advice on the Christian's relationship with other people in daily life, including our duties as citizens.

Memory gem: "Render to Caesar the things that are Caesar's, and to God the things that are God's" (Mark 12:17).

Thought for today:

A true Christian will be the best citizen of his country. He will be faithful and peace-loving. He will not cheat on his taxes, for he is commanded by the Lord to "render therefore to all their dues; tribute to whom tribute is due; custom to whom custom; fear to whom fear; honour to whom honour" (Romans 13:7).

He is commanded to "be subject to principalities and powers, to obey magistrates, to be ready to every good work" (Titus 3:1).

A true Christian is to submit himself "to every ordinance of man for the Lord's sake" (1 Peter 2:13). He is to pray for the rulers of the land and for the peace of the realm (see 1 Timothy 2:1, 2).

As a citizen he should enjoy freedom of speech and of action. He should enjoy the right of appeal against accusation. There should be no condemnation without fair trial. He should have freedom to worship God according to the dictates of his conscience so long as he does not interfere with the rights of others.

Do we have real conviction? Do we know why we believe? Do we have a real trust in God? As Dr. William Temple, archbishop of Canterbury (1942-1944), said: "Freedom of conscience, that is the sacred thing. Not freedom to do what I choose or to fulfill my own purpose, but freedom to do what I ought, and to fulfill God's purpose for me."

Would it not be well for each of us to open up the great Book of God and study again the principles of religious freedom, religious liberty? Should these principles not be taught to our children? Should they not be preached in every pulpit? In this way, and this way alone, we may have a new birth of freedom.

DAY / 337

Read Romans 15 and 16.

Today's reading concludes the book of Romans. Paul closes his argument on a triumphant note of joy in the Lord. Then he adds a chapter of greetings and blessings.

Memory gem: "Now the God of hope fill you with all joy and peace in believing, that ye may abound in hope, through the power of the Holy Ghost" (Romans 15:13).

Thought for today:

Are you enjoying your Christian life? If you are not, friend, you need to seek the Lord for a new birth.

Don't be like the man who sailed from New Orleans to New York. He had come down from Kansas or Nebraska; and, as he had never been on the water before, he was looking forward to this boat trip. After he had bought his ticket, he had only $1.75 to last him until he got to New York where some friends were going to give him a job. He knew the trip would take four or five days, so he said to himself, "I'll just get a bag, and fill it full of crackers and cheese and will eat that until I get to New York."

On the ocean you often develop an appetite. At noon he heard the luncheon bell ring, and everybody went down to the dining room. He could smell the cooking food, and it made him hungry, so he went behind the smokestack, got out the sack, and began to eat crackers and cheese. By the evening of the second day, the man found his cheese was moldy and the crackers were all soaked up with sea air. He got the steward to one side and said, "I am a poor man and I am about starved. What would one meal cost?"

The steward said, "What is the matter with you? Are you crazy?"

"No, but I am hungry. I think I could afford one meal."

"Well, why don't you go down and eat? Don't you know that when you bought your ticket, you paid for your meals all the way to New York? Go down to the dining room and eat."

Many a Christian today is doing that very thing spiritually. He is living spiritually on crackers and cheese while God wants us there at the supper table to enjoy the good things of His kingdom.

Friend, every day we can be happy, no matter what comes. That is what is in store when we are children of God, when we have been born again. Oh, my brother, sister, friend, live up to your opportunities and your privileges.

DAY / 338

Read Acts 20:3 through chapter 21.

Today's reading: Paul and his company leave Corinth for the trip to Jerusalem. At a weekend stopover in Troas, Paul holds a farewell meeting with believers. Then he goes on toward Jerusalem, despite repeated warnings.

Memory gem: "As ye have therefore received Christ Jesus the Lord, so walk ye in him" (Colossians 2:6).

Thought for today:

In the New Testament, the first day of the week is mentioned eight times (see Matthew 28:1; Mark 16:2, 9; Luke 24:1; John 20:1, 19; Acts 20:7; 1 Corinthians 16:2). Six of these texts refer to the same day, on which the resurrection of our Lord occurred. In 1 Corinthians 16:2 the apostle Paul directed the saints to look after their secular affairs on the first day of the week.

In all the New Testament there is a record of only one religious meeting held upon that day, and even that was a night meeting after midnight (see Acts 20:7-12). There is no intimation that those early believers ever held a meeting on the first day of the week, either before or after that one time, or that it was their custom to meet on that day.

There is no scriptural record of any requirement to "break bread" upon the first day of the week. Jesus celebrated the Lord's Supper on Thursday evening, as is clear from Luke 22, and the disciples broke bread every day, according to Acts 2:42-46.

Nowhere in the Scriptures does it say that the first day of the week commemorates the resurrection of Christ. This concept is a tradition of man which makes void the law of God (see Matthew 15:19). We are plainly told in Romans 6:3-5 that Christian baptism commemorates the burial and resurrection of our Lord.

Finally, the New Testament is totally silent with regard to any change of the Sabbath day or to any sacredness of the first day. It is true that, several centuries after Christ, Christians began gradually to apply the fourth commandment to the first day.

We must remember that true righteousness, which is true commandment keeping, comes not by our own efforts to keep any law, even God's holy law. It comes only by faith in Christ, whose holy righteousness, through the grace of God, is counted to us when we believe. As converted, regenerated Christians, it is our duty to walk in all the light that comes to us.

DAY / 339

Read Acts 22 through 24.

Today's reading: Paul, having been arrested as a disturber of the peace, tries to quiet the disturbance by speaking to the angry mob. The Roman commander decides that the only safe course is to send Paul to the Roman governor.

Memory gem: "As he reasoned of righteousness, temperance, and judgment to come, Felix trembled, and answered, Go thy way for this time; when I have a convenient season, I will call for thee" (Acts 24:25).

Thought for today:

Many a sermon has been preached about Paul before Felix; but should it not rather be called "Felix before Paul"? Before the interview was ended, Paul was the judge, and Felix, the governor, was condemned. Felix and his brother Pallas were servants of the emperor of Rome and had won great favor at court. For several years Felix had been the procurator of the Roman province of Judea, and the Roman historian Tacitus tells us in one of his bitterest sentences that "he wielded his kingly authority with the spirit of a slave, with all cruelty and lust."

Drusilla knew of the true God, though she had drifted away from obedience to His law of purity and righteousness. It was before this notorious couple—Felix and Drusilla—that the apostle Paul, by special appointment, spoke concerning the faith in Christ. "And as he reasoned of righteousness, temperance, and judgment to come, Felix trembled" (Acts 24:25).

The apostle might have spoken of something else before these two notorious sinners. He might have spoken as a Greek philosopher, anxious to please his hearers. But no, he spoke of "righteousness" before an unjust judge; of temperance and self-control before this sinful, self-indulgent pair; of "judgment to come" before these two who thought they could do anything without any moral obligation. Felix did not wish to be inconvenienced, to be troubled, to be distracted from his joys and sins. This man of perpetual compromise, this man with the habit of adjournment, adjourned Paul's case. He deferred it. But here before Paul he had adjourned his own case.

Let us leave Felix with the silence of ages, and look into our own hearts. What do we say? Are we still waiting for a convenient season? It will never be more convenient than right now.

DAY / 340

Read Acts 25 through 27.

Today's reading: Unable to receive a fair trial before the vacillating provincial governors, Paul exercises his right as a Roman citizen by appealing to the emperor. His trip to Rome turns out to be a thrilling adventure.

Memory gem: "There stood by me this night the angel of God, whose I am, and whom I serve, saying, Fear not, Paul; thou must be brought before Caesar: and lo, God hath given thee all them that sail with thee" (Acts 27:23, 24).

Thought for today:

The twenty-seventh chapter of Acts is the greatest shipwreck story of all time, and there was a real reporter right there to write it down. When you read that chapter, you are right in the storm with the apostle and the doctor-reporter. You hear the wind whistle through the rigging, the boom of the waves, the crashing of the mast, the snapping of ropes. You see the anchor dragging behind, the sailors trying to get out of the ship. Through the night you hear the thunder of the breakers on an unseen shore. The ship caught between the rocks, is being smashed to pieces. See those bobbing heads through the waves—some passengers escaping on pieces of the ship—all getting to land safely.

Then you know what happened—a big bonfire was built. Everyone huddled around it, shivering with the cold, trying to dry out, the apostle Paul with them. He gathered a large bundle of sticks; and as he threw them on the fire, a venomous viper fastened itself on his hand. The crowd stood looking at him. In their superstition they assumed that he was some murderer, who, while he had escaped the vengeance of the sea, was now by divine justice about to die. When the apostle shook off the viper into the fire and no harm came to him, they changed their minds and thought he was a god. After that they had every confidence in him.

Friend, from this experience we should learn to shake off the vipers of unbelief, sin, evil tempers, bad language, doubt, idolatry, prejudice—all things that ruin our influence in the community, in the church, and our standing with God. Their poison enfeebles us and repels others. Let's shake them off! Then we will find a new endowment of spiritual power, joy, and peace in living, and at last a home in the heavenly land and a life that measures with the life of God.

DAY / 341

Today's reading: The book of Acts ends with Paul under house arrest in Rome. The rest of his story we have to piece out from his own writings and from tradition. We are reasonably certain that the Epistle to the Ephesians was written during these two years in Rome.

Memory gem: "By grace are ye saved through faith; and that not of yourselves: it is the gift of God: not of works, lest any man should boast" (Ephesians 2:8, 9).

Thought for today:

When sin first entered the world, God's grace was already there. It declared that if the sinner would accept the death of Christ instead of his own death—to which he had been condemned by his transgression of God's law—then the sinner might go free. Christ's life was guaranteed to the sinner in Eden, and men were saved on that guarantee, even though Christ did not die upon the cross for four thousand years. They looked forward by faith to the Redeemer who was to come. We look back to the cross for salvation and celebrate the Lord's Supper to show our faith in the Redeemer who did come.

We know that the grace of God was extended to men before the cross, because we read in Genesis 6:8 that "Noah found grace in the eyes of the Lord." And Titus 2:11 says, "The grace of God that bringeth salvation hath appeared to all men." So God's grace is worldwide and extends to all the ages of time.

Not one person will enter heaven who has not been saved by grace. Salvation cannot be earned. It comes only as the gift of God through faith. People were not saved in the old dispensation by keeping the law and in the new dispensation by grace. In every dispensation and at all times, people have been saved by grace—and grace alone.

If men before the cross could have been saved by their own efforts, then they could do something that no one can do now. In that case, in heaven they could be telling of their own power to earn salvation, while all the redeemed since the cross would be praising Christ as the one who had given them eternal life. In such a situation heaven would be divided. But, thank God, it will not be so. There will be no divided heaven. Everyone who gets there will be ascribing praise to Christ for His gift of eternal life.

DAY / 342

Read Ephesians 4 through 6.

Today's reading: Paul had good practical advice for the Christians in Ephesus—good for us too. To illustrate our battle with the powers of evil, he uses the armor worn by Roman soldiers.

Memory gem: "Take unto you the whole armour of God, that ye may be able to withstand in the evil day, and having done all, to stand" (Ephesians 6:13).

Thought for today:

Today, every Christian needs a sword. The Christian's life is not a joke, not a vacation. It is a battle and a march, and in this battle we need the whole armor of God; especially do we need the sword.

What is this sword that we need? It is "the sword of the Spirit." Do you have this weapon? The Word of God, the Holy Scriptures, is the invincible sword. Its edge is never turned, its strength is never broken, it defeats every enemy. There is nothing like it to pierce the heart of men.

There is nothing like it to turn aside the attacks of Satan. That's how Jesus used it. He met the most specious arguments of His enemies with quotations from the Holy Scriptures. He faced the greatest theologians of His day with plain, unvarnished declarations of Scripture. And when He met the great tempter face-to-face, He defeated him with mighty sword thrusts—"It is written," "It is written," "It is written" (Matthew 4:4, 7, 10).

DAY / 343

Read Colossians.

Today's reading: Colossians is another letter written from Rome during Paul's first imprisonment. Like Galatians, it was written specifically to combat false doctrines threatening the believers.

Memory gem: "As ye have therefore received Christ Jesus the Lord, so walk ye in him: rooted and built up in him, and stablished in the faith, as ye have been taught, abounding therein with thanksgiving" (Colossians 2:6, 7).

Thought for today:

While the law of God is eternal in character, it would not be true to say that the rites and ceremonies which God gave to Israel as a nation are eternal. This ceremonial system consisted mainly of types and shadows. All the offerings, feast days, even the priesthood itself, were typical of the sacrifice and ministry of Christ our Lord; and they all met their glorious fulfillment in the offering of our Saviour on Calvary's cross. This, we believe, is what was meant by the apostle Paul when he wrote that Christ "abolished in his flesh the enmity, even the law of commandments contained in ordinances" (Ephesians 2:15).

What did Jesus do with this law of ordinances? We read in Colossians 2:14: "Blotting out the handwriting of ordinances that was against us, which was contrary to us, and took it out of the way, nailing it to his cross." These things were, as the apostle said, "a shadow of things to come" (verse 17).

Every sacrifice of bleeding lambs pointed forward to Jesus. He was the reality that cast the shadow. Today we have the Lord's Supper, which is a form or ordinance that points back to Jesus. If we were to sacrifice lambs on the altar today, we would be denying that Christ had yet appeared.

The Old Testament promised a Saviour, in prophecy and ceremony, in feast and sacrifice. The New Testament reveals a Saviour who came and fulfilled the promises. He was the true "Lamb of God, which taketh away the sin of the world" (John 1:29). He will come again to receive unto Himself all those who are His. To each one of us comes His gracious invitation: "Come unto me, all ye that labour and are heavy laden, and I will give you rest" (Matthew 11:28).

Are you weary of the burden of sin? Then accept His invitation, "Come." Come to Christ now!

DAY / 344

Read Philippians.

Today's reading: Paul—still a prisoner in Rome—wrote to the believers in Philippi as a friend to friends. He gave good spiritual counsel. A recurring theme in this letter is the advice to rejoice.

Memory gem: "Rejoice in the Lord alway: and again I say, Rejoice" (Philippians 4:4).

Thought for today:

Every true Christian has a right to be happy, and ought to be happy. Faith in God should bring joy. The psalmist says, "My soul shall be joyful in the Lord: it shall rejoice in his salvation" (Psalm 35:9).

Why shouldn't we be glad? Jesus says we should be happy. Our sins have been forgiven. Jesus is alive and, through His Holy Spirit, is with us now.

By faith, Christians can keep themselves in the atmosphere of Christ's love. We should not spend our time going over all our sorrows, disappointments, and troubles; but we should think of the happy times we have had, of the interesting things, the beautiful things. God's mercy has been over us; Christ's presence has been with us. Let us put our confidence in Him and look for joy.

We may be called upon to suffer for Christ's sake. If so, think of these words in 1 Peter 4:14: "If ye be reproached for the name of Christ, happy are ye." Why? "For he hath clothed me with the garments of salvation" (Isaiah 61:10).

Difficult or obscure words:

Philippians 1:1. **"Bishops"**—from a Greek word meaning "overseers," "superintendent," or "guardian" over the church. Not a high ranked clergyman with authority over many pastors and churches as bishops of a later era.

Philippians 1:1. **"Deacons"**—from a Greek word meaning "servants" or "helpers."

DAY / 345

Read 1 Peter.

Today's reading: No positive date can be established for Peter's epistle to Christians scattered throughout what is now Turkey. Internal evidence suggests the time during or just preceding Nero's persecution of Christians about A.D. 64 or 65.

Memory gem: "Christ also hath once suffered for sins, the just for the unjust, that he might bring us to God, being put to death in the flesh, but quickened by the Spirit" (1 Peter 3:18).

Thought for today:

Peter writes that Christ "went and preached unto the spirits in prison" (1 Peter 3:19).

We ask, When did this preaching take place? The answer is in the passage of Scripture itself. Notice the words: "when once the longsuffering of God waited in the days of Noah."

That clause settles it. Christ preached to those "spirits in prison" when God's mercy was pleading with souls just before the Flood came in the days of Noah.

Now we read in the verse 19, "By which also he [that is, Christ] went and preached unto the spirits in prison." "By which" refers back to the preceding verse—to the "Spirit," the Holy Spirit of God, through whom Christ spoke. Our Saviour's preaching back in the days of Noah was "by the Spirit," and we have the words of Scripture to that effect (see Genesis 6:3). The Holy Spirit was the agency of that preaching. The Holy Spirit, the Spirit of Christ, through Noah, gave a message of warning to that pre-Flood generation, just as Christ preached through His apostles by the Holy Spirit and as today He preaches through earnest men in the same way. The gospel is not preached on earth by Christ Himself in the flesh, but by His servants; yet it is counted just the same as if it were done by Him. It is called the "gospel of Christ," but it is preached by Christ's representatives, His true ministers.

But someone asks: "What about the phrase 'spirits in prison'? How can 'spirits' mean living people?" Is it possible for a man to be in spiritual bondage while alive in this world? The Bible says so. In Hebrews 2:14, 15, we read that Jesus purposed "through death" to "deliver them who through fear of death were all their lifetime subject to bondage."

In fact, there are thousands of "spirits in prison" right now. There is deliverance for you right now.

DAY / 346

Read 2 Peter and Jude.

Today's reading: The second letter by Peter was probably written soon after the first, and shortly before his martyrdrom, about A.D. 67 in Rome. Jude, probably a brother of the James who presided at the Jerusalem Council, seems to have written his letter about the same time as Peter wrote his second.

Memory gem: "We have also a more sure word of prophecy; whereunto ye do well that ye take heed, as unto a light that shineth in a dark place, until the day dawn, and the day star arise in your hearts" (2 Peter 1:19).

Thought for today:

The word of prophecy is more sure—stronger evidence—than actually hearing the voice of God. Think of it. Why is this?

One reason is that, with every year that goes by, the miracle of a fulfilled prophecy becomes greater. Here stands the Word of God written down by the prophet. The years go by, and it may seem that the events predicted by prophecy are the ones most unlikely to take place. Then suddenly they happen—perhaps after decades, centuries, or even millenniums. But the prophecy always comes true. And the reason is that these prophecies were not made by man, but "holy men of God spoke as they were moved by the Holy Ghost." God spoke through them.

How can we neglect such a book as the Bible, sustained by such unimpeachable sources as history and human experience? Surely, my friend, if we can trust the Bible because of all its great prophecies fulfilled, history proving that God spoke the truth, then just as truly we can believe what it says about salvation, and we can have faith in the words of Christ, the very Son of God Himself.

Do you want peace in your heart? Do you want the burden of condemnation and sin to leave your soul? Do you want to be free? Then listen to what the Bible says. Each word is important.

Are you willing to listen to God's Word and to believe it when you hear it? Will you trust God? In other words, will you have faith in Him? Surely we can depend upon the word of the great Creator, the One who has guided human history to fulfill the prophecies of His servants, the One who loves you so that He was willing to send His own Son to die for you. Surely you can rest upon His word, believe it, and find eternal life and peace right here in this world.

DAY / 347

Today's reading: Paul's Epistle to Philemon, written toward the end of the first imprisonment in Rome, is a letter to a friend about a runaway slave, Onesimus. The letter to Titus was apparently written about the same time as the first one to Timothy. Paul had left Titus in charge of the work on Crete.

Memory gem: "I thank my God, making mention of thee always in my prayers, hearing of thy love and faith, which thou hast toward the Lord Jesus, and toward all saints" (Philemon 4 and 5).

Thought for today:

Philemon's slave, Onesimus, had run away to the city of Rome where the apostle was a prisoner. In some way Paul met Onesimus there, and under his patient and loving ministry Onesimus was converted.

And now the great servant of God is sending Onesimus back to his master, Philemon, who also is a Christian, with this beautiful letter. The apostle suggests that he really needs the services of Onesimus and that he actually belongs to him because he has brought him to Christ. Yet he says that Philemon, himself being a convert, should be willing to receive the apostle's word as a command to take his servant back with Christian kindness.

How could Philemon resist such an appeal as this? "I do not command you," Paul said in effect, "though I might do so; but I beseech you, for love's sake, forgive Onesimus; receive him again, not merely as a servant, but as a beloved brother."

The apostle offers to stand good for any damages or to pay any debt that Philemon may consider Onesimus owes him.

I should like to have been present when Philemon opened this letter and read it, after taking it from the hand of Onesimus. What mixed feelings must have overwhelmed him! And then those words, "for love's sake." A letter from "Paul the aged," aged in the service of God, bearing the marks and scars of his sufferings for Jesus. Tears must have trickled down Philemon's face. Yes, I think he embraced Onesimus and received him back as a member of his household, as "a brother beloved," and all "for love's sake."

Difficult or obscure words:

Titus 1:12. **"Slow bellies"**—lazy gluttons.

DAY / 348

Read I Timothy.

Today's reading: It seems quite clear that Paul wrote this letter during a period of travel after his release from prison in Rome and before his second arrest. Timothy was pastor of the church in Ephesus at the time.

Memory gem: "Godliness with contentment is great gain" (1 Timothy 6:6).

Thought for today:

How often I have heard people say that money is the root of all evil. The Bible does not say that. Rather, it says, "The love of money is the root of all evil: which while some coveted after, they have erred from the faith, and pierced themselves through with many sorrows" (1 Timothy 6:10).

Money is to be used in the right way. It is to bring health and blessing, not only to ourselves but to others. It gives us the opportunity to be liberal, to be self-sacrificing.

God reserves a part of our money as His own. In ancient times it was called the tithe—one tenth. Many Christians today lay aside one tenth of the increase, or profit, for God's work. Then, in addition to this, from their own nine tenths, they make freewill offerings to the work and cause of God. Is not this a good way continually to remind ourselves that it is God who gives us the power to get everything that we have in this world, and that we are workers together with Him, sharers with Him in what He is doing for men?

The love of money is the root of all kinds of evil. Think of the crimes committed to obtain it—wars innumerable, raids, murders, robbery, thievery.

At the Devil's booth are all things sold,
Each ounce of dross costs its ounce of gold;
For a cap and bells our lives we pay,
Bubbles we buy with a whole soul's tasking:
'Tis heaven alone that is given away,
'Tis only God may be had for the asking.

—James Russell Lowell.

Will you not today consecrate not only your heart, but all that you have to God? If you do this, He will guide you and keep you and all yours. He will be your banker, and you will never have to worry about a bank failure, for your treasure will be in the bank of heaven, which never fails.

DAY / 349

Read 2 Timothy.

Today's reading: This letter has been called Paul's last will and testament. It was written by the great apostle during his second imprisonment and shortly before his execution.

Memory gem: "I am now ready to be offered, and the time of my departure is at hand. I have fought a good fight, I have finished my course, I have kept the faith" (2 Timothy 4:6, 7).

Thought for today:

Your Christian life and mine is not to be a matter of here and there, a little now and then; in the church and out, and back again; up today and down tomorrow. It must be from henceforth, every day, always, until "the roll is called up yonder."

None of us has had any more tests of perseverance and patience than did the apostle Paul. For years he went without a home, without regular pay. He had to make tents to earn his living in some places. In other places he was supported by some of his friends. He was shipwrecked. He was whipped more than once, mobbed, beaten, left for dead, wounded, rejected, imprisoned; and finally received the death sentence as a martyr for Christ (see 2 Corinthians 11:23-28).

In the old days of trouble, when William, Prince of Orange, received a letter from mighty King Philip of Spain threatening him with the confiscation of all his goods and the loss of his life, he did not surrender his faith or his country. The courage which came from his Christian faith inspired Prince William to fling back this challenge in the face of the tyrant: "I am in the hands of God. My worldly goods and my life have long since been dedicated to His service. He will dispose of them as seems best to His glory and my salvation."

These were the words of a man who knew his Lord and believed that He was able to save to the uttermost. It was the speech of a man not only self-reliant but God-reliant, who believed and rested on the promises of God. He could face conflict, he could suffer the woundings of the foe, for his heart was unafraid. Like the apostle, he could say: "Henceforth there is laid up for me a crown of righteousness, which the Lord, the righteous judge, shall give me at that day: and not to me only, but unto all them also that love his appearing" (2 Timothy 4:8).

DAY / 350

Read Hebrews 1 through 3.

Today's reading: We begin a survey of the important Epistle to the Hebrews—full of inspirational value and gems of truth.

Memory gem: "God . . . hath in these last days spoken unto us by his Son, whom he hath appointed heir of all things, by whom also he made the worlds" (Hebrews 1:1, 2).

Thought for today:

The earth itself, with all its scientific mysteries, is a memorial to the wisdom and power of the Son of God; and the glittering dome of night above us shows the works of His hands. This mighty Son, whose workmanship we see about us and above us, is none other than Jesus of Nazareth, the Christ of our salvation. He made the worlds.

The hand of Christ, the Master Workman, had been seen in the vast dome of stars long ages before Leeuwenhoek ground his first lenses or Galileo put them in the first telescope. As men began to peer out into the boundless void with stronger and stronger eyes—the mighty glasses of great astronomical observatories—they were struck with silent wonder at the awesome vastness of the universe. The human mind can have no conception of the endless and gigantic creation about us.

The creation testifies of its Creator as the eternal infinite God. "All thy works shall praise thee, O Lord," said David with the tongue of inspiration (Psalm 145:10). He must have been gazing out into the blue-black sky as there on the verdant meadows of heaven began to blossom, one by one, the lovely stars, "the forget-me-nots of the angels."

We rejoice in the human Christ, a humble Galilean carpenter; but we must know too that He was, and is, the Son of God Most High—that the very heavens are the work of His hands. His works praise Him when His worshipers are silent.

And the Son, by whose hand the heavens were created, emptied Himself of His infinite glory and veiled His divinity in a human form. He took our nature; He became a man and died for our sins on the cross that cruel men had made for Him at old Jerusalem. Christ's love and infinite humiliation in our redemption is as incomprehensible to us as is His work of creation. We cannot understand it all with our finite minds, but we can thank our heavenly Father for the gift of His Son, our Lord Jesus Christ.

DAY / 351

Read Hebrews 4 through 6.

Today's reading continues the appeal of chapter 3 for accepting Christ. Then it gives a short discussion of God's "rest" before launching the detailed study of Christ's priesthood.

Memory gem: "There remaineth therefore a rest to the people of God. For he that is entered into his rest, he also hath ceased from his own works, as God did from his" (Hebrews 4:9, 10).

Thought for today:

Millions of people are nervous, run-down, dissatisfied, and ill today because they do not follow God's plan of rest. It is held by many authorities that man himself is built on the principle of the seventh portion of time being dedicated to the enjoyment of repose. Both body and mind need relaxation from the pressure of worldly pursuits and cares. Even from a medical point of view, it seems that the Sabbath forms part of the remedial system of nature. The God who created man knows what is good for him, but so many men do not realize what is good for themselves.

But the Sabbath was not to be a period of physical rest alone. Notice the command of God: "Remember the sabbath day, to keep it holy" (Exodus 20:8). There is the matter of holiness involved in it, a matter of religious and spiritual worship. D. L. Moody saw this and said that this Sabbath question is a vital one for the whole country. If we give up Sabbath, soon the church goes; and if we give up the church, the home goes; and as the home goes, the nation goes. Sad to say, that is the direction in which millions of people are traveling today.

Let us remember this: Only those who believe have entered into God's rest. Hebrews 4:3. Only those who keep themselves holy can keep the Sabbath holy. True Sabbath keeping is a spiritual service to be rendered by a Spirit-filled person. The Sabbath should be a bit of heaven transferred to earth.

Note: The word translated "rest" in Hebrews 4:9 is a totally different word from the nouns and verbs for "rest" in other verses of chapters 3 and 4. The word occurs nowhere else in the Bible or in classical Greek literature. A careful study of the context makes it clear that this word *(sabbatismos)* means more than the Sabbath rest; it covers the spiritual rest, and particularly the Christian's rest. However, from numerous other texts it can be shown that keeping God's Sabbath is a definite part of the spiritual rest God wishes His people to enter.

DAY / 352

Today's reading: The epistle discusses at length the differences between the Aaronic and the Melchizedek priesthoods, showing that Christ surpasses earthly priests in every way.

Memory gem: "By his own blood he [Christ] entered in once into the holy place, having obtained eternal redemption for us" (Hebrews 9:12).

Thought for today:

There are many today who feel that by organization, effort, money, plans, councils, they can elevate, refine, and regenerate humanity without blood atonement. But this is nothing more or less than a modern following of the example of Cain, and the history of Cain shows what must be the result. Humanity has no power to regenerate itself.

Christ alone is our Sin Bearer, and He died to atone for the sins of the world. The central theme of the sanctuary service of old, the central doctrine of the Christian faith, is the atoning blood. There is no other way to be saved than by the blood of Christ. All need to be saved, all need to be saved from sin, and all may be saved through the blood of the cross.

The French Protestant scholar Muretus was an exile from his own country. He fell seriously ill while in Lombardy and was taken to a hospital for outcasts. He overheard the doctors consulting about him in Latin, not thinking that a poor pauper could understand the language of the learned. They said, "Let us make an experiment upon this worthless body." And from his sickbed, the scholar startled them by rising on his elbow and replying in Latin, "Yet for this worthless body, Jesus Christ has died."

For our redemption, we look only to the blood of the cross.

Speaking of the Royal Air Force that mounted up with wings as eagles to protect their motherland, Winston Churchill said, "Never in the history of mankind have so many owed so much to so few." But when we think of the atoning blood of the cross and of Jesus who died on Calvary for us, we say, "Never in the history of the universe has mankind owed so much to One."

DAY / 353

Today's reading: We conclude the study of the ancient sanctuary service as a type of Christ's ministry. Then follows the well-known "faith chapter."

Memory gem: "Having a high priest over the house of God; let us draw near with a true heart in full assurance of faith" (Hebrews 10:21, 22).

Thought for today:

In the earthly sanctuary the offerings were the bodies and blood of animals. Our High Priest offers His own life, His own blood, His own body, crucified for us. The shadows of the earthly sanctuary pointed to the reality of the new, even to Christ, our Lamb as well as our High Priest. The writer tells us that those sacrifices of lambs and calves could not actually take away sins or make the one who did the service perfect (see Hebrews 9:9). But our High Priest offers His own sacrifice for us. This offering does take away sins. Our High Priest appears now in heaven for us.

Christ came, we are told, to do the will of God (see Hebrews 10:5-9). Thus He was not merely to be obedient to God in His life here on earth, though He was obedient; but the will of God which He obeyed was the divine will which declared "the offering of the body of Jesus Christ" (Hebrews 10:10) as necessary for our salvation. Christ lived obediently, died obediently, and offered Himself upon the cross. His act was the perfect sacrifice by the perfect Priest, for Himself both priest and offering. So, by God's grace and eternal love, He "obtained eternal redemption for us" (Hebrews 9:12). That redemption cannot be improved upon; it is the final redemption, because it is "eternal." It is "one sacrifice for sins for ever" (Hebrews 10:12).

This wonderful epistle opens with the statement that the Son, Jesus Christ, "himself purged our sins" (Hebrews 1:3). The last chapter brings in the same tremendous salvation truth (see Hebrews 13:20, 21). Here we have again the blood of the eternal offering, the blood of Christ, with the result that salvation is offered freely to us all.

Difficult or obscure words:

Hebrews 11:17. **"Only begotten"**—literally, unique. Isaac was the only son qualified for the birthright blessing.

DAY / 354

Read Hebrews 12 and 13.

Today's reading: The epistle closes with earnest appeals for the believing Christian to live a life that demonstrates true Christianity.

Memory gem: "Let us run with patience the race that is set before us, looking unto Jesus the author and finisher of our faith" (Hebrews 12:1, 2).

Thought for today:

We live in an eye-minded age. The art of reading—at least, of reading anything very instructive or heavy—is unknown to millions and is being lost by other millions. This is the age of the picture book, the picture magazine, the moving picture, and television.

What are we looking at? What do we see? Much that we cannot escape seeing is not good. But what do we look upon with pleasure? What do we study? By beholding, we become changed (see 2 Corinthians 3:18).

What do we look at? What do we delight in? Isn't it about time for us to dedicate our eyes to Jesus Christ? Remember, only Christ is the perfect example. Even those who follow Him the nearest are not perfect.

Friends traveling through Italy were one day examining Guido's famous fresco, the *Aurora,* in a great palace of that country. Many artists were there busily copying the great painting, and the tourists noticed that each artist differed from the others in his portrayal of this immortal work. After a while the attention of the guide was called to the fact that one artist had painted the horses a different color and that another had differed in some other detail, and so on. With an expressive gesture, the guide replied, "Don't look at them; look only at the original."

Let us look at Christ for guidance and consecrate our eyes to the holy and the true and the beautiful and the right.

Difficult or obscure words:

Hebrews 12:2. **"Author"**—literally: leader, originator, founder. The word is translated as "Prince" in Acts 3:15 and 5:31 and as "captain" in Hebrews 2:10. In classical Greek the word is used for the progenitor of a clan or in speaking of the mythical heroes. Here the meaning obviously should cast Jesus as the heroic Leader or Prince.

DAY / 355

Read 1 John 1 through 4.

Today's reading: It is believed that John wrote his three epistles in his old age, probably about A.D. 90 to 95. Although no destination is named, the letters may have been sent to Ephesus, where John labored for many years before his arrest and exile.

Memory gem: "Ye know that he was manifested to take away our sins; and in him is no sin" (1 John 3:5).

Thought for today:

Today we hear few sermons about the perfection of Christ. Christ could not be perfect, holy, and sinless unless He were divine. All men are by nature imperfect; in fact, the Scripture declares plainly that all men have sinned.

Jesus is a man, but not a mere man. He is a true man, but not only a man.

Walter B. Knight reports the experience of Lakhan Singh, the street preacher in India. Before his conversion from Hinduism, he went on innumerable pilgrimages to the so-called holy shrines seeking peace of heart. He was asked by a missionary, "But how were you first drawn to Christ?"

He replied, "One day I stopped to listen to a street preacher in Shahjahanpur who declared that the Lord Jesus Christ was a sinless incarnation. There are many incarnations in the Hindu religion. Some of them are cruel, capricious, and murderous; but none of them are sinless. I was deeply impressed with this. I continued to think about it. But I had no peace of mind until I accepted the sinless Son of God as my Saviour. For forty years I have been joyously preaching Him!"

So it is indeed true. Among all the people born on earth, only of Christ can it be said, "In him is no sin."

Difficult or obscure words:

1 John 3:9. **"His seed"**—The antecedent of "his" is obviously "God." God's "seed," or regenerating power, abides in the born-again Christian so that he no longer goes on sinning.

DAY / 356

Read 1 John 5 and 2 and 3 John.

Today's reading: The aged apostle said a great deal about love and about sinless living. He expressed a concern about physical well-being also.

Memory gem: "Beloved, I wish above all things that thou mayest prosper and be in health, even as thy soul prospereth" (3 John 2).

Thought for today:

Dr. Adam Clarke, the great Methodist commentator, reminds us that three things are pointed out in this inspired passage—three things of great importance: (1) health of body; (2) health of soul; (3) prosperity in secular affairs.

If you want these three things, seek for them in prayer and sensible living. Health is an extremely important asset; next to our soul's salvation, the most important thing in life is health. No one can enjoy life without a certain amount of health.

Millions of people who are not in the so-called poverty class are not properly nourished and as a result do not have good health. One reason for this is plain ignorance. They do not know what the body needs, they do not know the first principles of nutrition, they do not eat and drink properly.

Anyone who continually breaks the laws of physical living will suffer the penalty. Millions do not drink enough good, pure water. They forget that the body is largely made of water. A human body is something like an electrolytic battery. Another neglect is exercise. People ride where they ought to walk. If they need to get a spool of thread or a quart of milk at the corner store, they'll drive two or three blocks to get it instead of walking.

Another significant lack in the lives of millions is trust in God. As a result they do not have peace of mind and are under continual tension and worry. Minds are seething with dissatisfaction and fear of tomorrow. No wonder we see so much ill health.

It is well for us to remember that God loves mankind. He desires the optimum well-being of the human race. God is the Creator of the world and of all things. He is the Creator and Redeemer of mankind. He loved the world so much that He gave His own Son to redeem sinful men. This proves His concern for us. His concern includes physical things too.

DAY / 357

Read Revelation 1 through 3.

Today's reading: The generally accepted view dates the Revelation at about A.D. 96. John, exiled to Patmos by the persecution of Emperor Domitian, received a vision of glorious assurance that his Lord was far greater than any earthly ruler.

Memory gem: "Blessed is he that readeth, and they that hear the words of this prophecy, and keep those things which are written therein: for the time is at hand" (Revelation 1:3).

Thought for today:

The book of Revelation, the last book of the Holy Bible, is especially important to the people living in the last age of the world. But many Christians have neglected this wonderful book of prophecy, and some even have the idea that it was sealed; but its very name, Revelation, means just the opposite. And in its first chapter we find a blessing for those who read and hear the words of this book—our memory gem for today.

Notice, this book of New Testament prophecy is not the revelation of John. Rather, it is "the Revelation of Jesus Christ, which God gave unto him, to shew unto his servants things which must shortly come to pass; and he sent and signified it by his angel unto his servant John" (Revelation 1:1).

Everything in this great book of prophetic symbols has been revealed by Christ, and because of that it ought to be of the deepest interest to all Christians. Not only so, but it reveals Christ's plans for His people and for the world.

The apostle John was an old man, exiled from other Christians on the lonely island of Patmos, when the vision of Revelation came to him. His enemies could shut him away from friends and fellow believers, but they could not keep the gates of heaven closed or hide him from the face of his Saviour.

In the midst of his exile the apostle John was permitted to see a vision of tomorrow. On the Lord's day, when the Lord's people were meeting for divine worship and Christian fellowship, which John on his lonely island prison could not share, suddenly the heavens were opened, and he saw visions of God.

Note: "Revelation" (Greek *apokalupsis*) means "an unveiling."

"Asia" was the Roman name for a province in the western part of Asia Minor, now part of modern Turkey.

DAY / 358

Read Revelation 4 through 7.

Today's reading: As John views the glories around the throne of God, his attention is called to a book "sealed with seven seals." The opening of each seal produces an impressive scene.

Memory gem: "It shall be said in that day, Lo, this is our God; we have waited for him, and he will save us: this is the Lord; we have waited for him, we will be glad and rejoice in his salvation" (Isaiah 25:9).

Thought for today:

We are living down in the latter days of the sixth seal. Soon will come the trump of God, the shout of our Redeemer, the voice of the archangel which awakens the dead. Those of us who are asleep in death will be raised to glorious immortality, and those who are living will "be changed, in a moment, in the twinkling of an eye" (1 Corinthians 15:51, 52). Then we shall all go home, "and so shall we ever be with the Lord" (1 Thessalonians 4:17).

Remember, we are now living just before the mountains begin to tremble, the islands to move; just before the heavens depart as a scroll when it is rolled together; just before the great prayer meeting when unbelievers pray to rocks and mountains to hide them. Now, in this wonderful hour, it is our privilege to give our hearts to Christ, to give Him our lives, and to serve Him faithfully. Now is the time to walk with Him every day. Now is the time to pray that God will make preachers out of some of the young men who are studying His Word today—great preachers, greater than the world has ever yet heard. If we are but willing, He will take men from the bench, from the office, from the trucks, from the fields, from everywhere—and women too. He will make us all into workers for Him and use us where we are in the worldwide preaching of the gospel such as the world has never seen.

Will you not let God have your heart now? Will you not let Him use you in some way to spread the gospel message of hope and blessing to earth's remotest bounds, thereby hastening the glorious coming of Christ to take us home? May God help us all to be ready for the wonderful days just ahead.

DAY / 359

Read Revelation 8 through 11.

Today's reading: After chapter 7 makes a pause in the opening of the seals, chapter 8 returns to the process. Then it immediately introduces a new sequence—the seven trumpets. Then chapters 10:1 through 11:14 break the discussion of the trumpets with another parenthetical element.

Memory gem: "When the Son of man shall come in his glory, and all the holy angels with him, then shall he sit upon the throne of his glory" (Matthew 25:31).

Thought for today:

Silence in heaven? Yes, silence in heaven!

This is the end of the sevenfold history of redemption, the completion of God's plan for men in the Christian dispensation. It is the end of the story, when God puts a period to history. It is the "divine event, to which the whole creation moves." It is the return of Jesus in power and great glory.

Heaven is emptied of its angel throng. The songs of many angels round about the throne are stilled, because the singers are not there. They are with Jesus on the gladdest mission of all their blessed ministry for the heirs of salvation.

When our Lord returns in His glory, He will have "all the holy angels with him" (Matthew 24:31). Not one will be left behind. Heaven will be emptied of its angel throng as they accompany Him to earth to gather together His elect. Earth's sky will be all aglow with radiant forms. Think of the music here—songs such as human ears have never heard since shepherds watched their flocks on the starlit hills of Judea! Heaven is silent, but earth is not. When the righteous return with Christ and the holy angels to the Father's home above, heaven will be no longer silent. At the coronation of the King the whole universe will rejoice in glorious song!

Friend, you and I may have a part in that song—the song of the redeemed as they praise the Lamb for His victory.

Difficult or obscure words:

Revelation 9:11. **"Abaddon"**—a Hebrew word meaning "destruction."

Revelation 9:11. **"Apollyon"**—from a Greek word meaning "a destroyer."

Revelation 11:7. **"Beast"**—a different word from the "beasts" of Revelation 4:6. This wild beast symbolizes an anti-God power.

DAY / 360

Read Revelation 12 through 15.

Today's reading: What tremendous visions! The woman clothed with the sun, strange beasts, angel voices sounding from the sky, Christ descending on a cloud, angels holding vessels full of a potent mixture—powerful symbols indeed!

Memory gem: "Fear God, and give glory to him; for the hour of his judgment is come: and worship him that made heaven, and earth, and the sea, and the fountains of waters" (Revelation 14:7).

Thought for today:

The more we study nature, the more we see the evidence and marks of a Master Workman. No mere apprentice started the constellations in their majestic march across the midnight sky or kindled the myriad blazing suns in the Milky Way! No novice planned the atomic arrangement in the molecule, the whirl of electrons, or the laws of chemical reaction.

The indelible signature of the Master Workman is everywhere: in the vibrations of light and sound, in the eye of an insect, in the ear of man, in the color of a sunset, in the bright shimmer of stars. He made them; He sustains them.

The power and divinity of Jesus Christ need to be proclaimed today. The so-called modernism in the church today and the evolutionary doubt expressed in many a pulpit have sadly reduced some preachers to mere animated question marks.

In this age of evolutionary skepticism, the world and the church need a strong message as an antidote to the anti-scriptural naturalism which dominates modern thinking. In the fourteenth chapter of Revelation we have just such a worldwide message described. In fact, we read there the main parts of the message itself and find that it announces God's call back to creationism and away from evolution.

This mighty message declares that this is a moral universe because men must face the judgment hour; and it calls upon all men to worship the living God, whose creative power is proclaimed by every part of the universe. These words in Revelation 14:7 are quoted almost verbatim from the fourth commandment, where the Sabbath which Christ made at creation and honored in His flesh, is described. Surely, such a prophetic forecast of a world message which exalts Christ as Creator and Redeemer should claim our earnest attention.

DAY / 361

Read Revelation 16 through 18.

Today's reading: The seven angels, one at a time, pour out the mixture they have been holding; fearful results follow. Then John sees the final end of mystical Babylon.

Memory gem: "He that dwelleth in the secret place of the most High shall abide under the shadow of the Almighty" (Psalm 91:1).

Thought for today:

The word "Armageddon" appears only once in the Bible, and that is in the sixteenth chapter of Revelation. It occurs in the story of the seven last plagues which are to fall upon the earth just before the coming of the Lord in glory and power. Armageddon is evidently a picture of what happens under the sixth of these seven plagues.

According to this prophecy, at Armageddon the kings of the earth will be gathered for the battle of that great day of God Almighty. What is the outcome of this battle? The answer is in verse 17: "And the seventh angel poured out his vial into the air; and there came a great voice out of the temple of heaven, from the throne, saying, It is done."

In other words, "It is finished." This is the end of the age, the close of the human history of the world. God's voice proclaims, "It is done." So it is clear that the battle of Armageddon is at the very end of time, as pictured in Scripture prophecy. It will bring the final great division of mankind. It will make manifest the destiny of every human soul. It brings the end of the great controversy between good and evil that began when sin entered the mind of Lucifer in heaven. Before this mighty battle and its immediate effects are over, the earth will be cleansed of all its sin and prepared to be the glorious home of God's redeemed.

This conflict has its spiritual and literal phases. It is a battle, a war, named after a location or a place. But it is also in its spiritual aspect the devil's final struggle against God's kingdom.

The signboards along the highway of time say to us: "Jesus is coming. Get ready. Prepare to meet thy God!"

Whatever you do, do not say, "I will wait until I see those armies gathering to Armageddon; then I will give my heart to God." No man knows beforehand the exact order of events or how they will occur. The climax will come suddenly. Now is your day. Now is your hour and mine. Is your decision made?

DAY / 362

Read Revelation 19 and 20.

Today's reading: First we hear all heaven astir in preparation for the marriage supper of the Lamb. Then we view the fearful events at the beginning and at the end of what we call the millennium.

Memory gem: "Blessed are they which are called unto the marriage supper of the Lamb" (Revelation 19:9).

Thought for today:

If we think of the Holy City as the bride, then we know that the city is ready. But it remains for the inhabitants of the glorious city—for you and me as Christians—to be ready, for soon the Bridegroom will ride forth in all His glory and authority as a conqueror to claim His own.

He comes forth as King of kings and Lord of lords. No wonder the unprepared inhabitants of earth flee to the rocks and the mountains, begging to be hidden, buried, "from the face of him that sitteth on the throne, and from the wrath of the Lamb" (Revelation 6:16).

In contrast to this are the wedding guests—the waiting church. The promise is: "Blessed are they which are called unto the marriage supper of the Lamb" (Revelation 19:9).

When the Bridegroom comes, He leads His people back to the kingdom of His Father, to partake of the marriage supper. Jesus spoke of this coming event when He told His disciples that they would "eat and drink at my table in my kingdom" (Luke 22:30).

The waiting ones are the bride for whom He comes. The kingdom and subjects of the kingdom are all one. As guests they go into the wedding feast; as the bride they share the wedding gift bestowed by the Father as a token of His affection when "the kingdom and dominion, and the greatness of the kingdom under the whole heaven" are given to the saints. "The time came that the saints possessed the kingdom" (Daniel 7:22, 27). Beautiful day, wonderful possession, glorious kingdom, heavenly marriage!

Let me ask you the question, Are you preparing for a place in the marriage supper of the Lamb? "Blessed and holy" are such as do it. Through God's grace, and in His due time, may that blessedness and holiness be yours and mine.

DAY / 363

Read Revelation 21 and 22.

Today's reading: "The great controversy is ended. Sin and sinners are no more. The entire universe is clean. One pulse of harmony and gladness beats through the vast creation. . . . All things . . . declare that God is love."—*The Great Controversy,* p. 678.

Memory gem: "Behold, the tabernacle of God is with men, and he will dwell with them, and they shall be his people, and God himself shall be with them, and be their God" (Revelation 21:3).

Thought for today:

This earth will be renewed. It will be an eternal witness to the love of God. God's people will not be pilgrims wandering about a sin-cursed world which Satan claims as his own. They will be coming back home again, back to the garden from which they were driven. Eden lost will be Eden restored. The tree of life, which was here on earth once before, will be brought back from the heavenly land.

This is man's long-lost home. It was lost through sin; it is regained through grace. It is the "first dominion" (Micah 4:8), restored to the human family when God makes all things new. It is the "restitution of all things" (Acts 3:21). The New Jerusalem will descend "from God out of heaven" and be the capital of the restored kingdom (see Revelation 21:2).

Look at the measurements of the city: 1,500 miles—some say on each side, some say the distance around. In either case, it is the greatest city the world has ever known. There will be room in it for everybody. Should it have been possible for all the people who have ever lived in the earth to be saved, there would still be room for them. There is always room for you, for anyone. "Whosoever will" may "take the water of life freely," we read right here in the same chapter where it speaks of the wonder world of tomorrow.

DAY / 364

Read Psalms 65 through 68; 135 and 136.

Today's reading: Whether you read these last two assignments at Thanksgiving time (as suggested in the introduction) or as the final readings in the series, the theme is the same—praise to God for His goodness and mercy.

Memory gem: "O give thanks unto the Lord; for he is good: for his mercy endureth for ever" (Psalm 136:1).

Thought for today:

The fourth Thursday in November is Thanksgiving Day, and I am in favor of it. It began with the very beginning of the settlement of our country by the Pilgrim Fathers, who came to this land seeking a refuge from religious intolerance and persecution.

What sought they thus afar?
Bright jewels of the mine?
The wealth of the seas? the spoils of war?
They sought a faith's pure shrine!
Aye, call it holy ground,
The soil where first they trod:
They have left unstained what there they found—
Freedom to worship God!
—Felicia Hemans.

Our first national Thanksgiving proclamation was issued by George Washington in 1789. He recommended to the people of the United States, on the request of both houses of Congress, that they set aside a day of public thanksgiving and prayer on Thursday, the twenty-sixth of November, "to be devoted by the people of these States to the service of that great and glorious Being who is the beneficient Author of all the good that was, that is, or that will be."

He also suggested that humble prayer be offered to God, not only thanking Him for the great blessings that the nation was enjoying, but seeking God's help that our national government might be a blessing to all the people by constantly being a government of wise, just, and constitutional laws, discreetly and faithfully executed and obeyed. What better wish could we have for our nation and our people today?

DAY / 365

Read Psalms 145 through 150.

Today's reading: This group of six psalms brings the collection to a triumphant end in a burst of praise to God.

Memory gem: "While I live will I praise the Lord: I will sing praises unto my God while I have any being" (Psalm 146:2).

Thought for today:

Thankfulness is the very heart of the gospel. It is the heart of the Bible. It is the heart of Christian life.

Jeremy Taylor, of the Church of England, once said, "Every furrow in the book of Psalms is sown with the seed of thanksgiving."

Thanksgiving is a universal solvent for the troubles and worries of the heart. Thanksgiving is the divine catalyst that makes the miracle of a Christian life a reality.

Even though you may be suffering, even though you may have disappointments and sorrows, you can still thank God for the blessings you enjoy. You can even thank God for the things that have troubled you, for they have helped to develop your character, helped to prepare you for a place in God's service here and for a place in His kingdom of glory to come.

George Matheson, one of Scotland's preachers, finally came to the place where he could even thank God for his blindness. He said: "My God, I have never thanked Thee for my thorn. I have thanked Thee a thousand times for my roses, but never once for my thorn. I have been looking forward to a world where I shall get compensation for my cross, as itself, a present glory. Teach me the glory of my cross. Teach me the value of my thorn. Show me that I have climbed to Thee by the path of pain. Show me that my tears have made my rainbow."

And we can never forget the words of his song:

O joy that seekest me through pain,
I cannot close my heart to Thee;
I trace the rainbow through the rain,
And feel the promise is not vain
That morn shall tearless be!

So let us say with the great apostle, "In every thing give thanks" (1 Thessalonians 5:18). And above all, and through it all, and forever, let us be thankful for God's greatest gift, the Lord Jesus Christ, the assurance of God's love for us.